The
HOUSE
& GARDEN®
book of essential
ADDRESSES

Published 1997 by Design Line,
PO Box 300, London W11 3WE. Tel/Fax: 0171-221 6600.
Copyright © 1997 Interior Design Line Ltd

Compiled by: Nicolette Le Pelley and Cheryl Knorr
Designed by: Michael Tighe and David Vallade
Illustrations by: Joan Hecktermann

British Library Cataloguing in Publication Data.
A catalogue record for this book is available from the British Library.

ISBN   0 9530079 0 1

Printed in Great Britain by Butler & Tanner

INTRODUCTION

Finding the right product or specialist is like looking for a needle in a haystack. Even those who (like ourselves) have spent many years in the field of interior decoration, find the detective work tedious and time consuming. For those who only make occasional forays into this bewildering world, the challenge is even more daunting. Suddenly, that useful scrap culled from a home interest magazine or a weekend supplement is nowhere to be found.

So where to turn? Running Design Line's telephone information service brought home to us the scale of the problem. We were surprised to discover that the need for a helping hand proved as great amongst the specialist trade as it did amongst the general public.

Who called us? Everyone, literally. The decorator looking for an eiderdown maker. The caller looking for enamelled French house numbers. The architect wanting to verdigris his chairs. The butler who despaired of ever finding replacement blue glass linings for his salt cellars. There was even the gentleman in Vienna who needed twenty velvet and brocade curtains cleaned by a London specialist.

Hence this directory. We have tried to make it as user-friendly as possible by grouping entries under 235 precise headings easily located via the table of contents. In addition, there is an index by company name at the back of the book.

The companies listed are our selections and ours alone - we have not accepted any payment for inclusion in this directory. We have not included everyone, nor can we vouch for the quality of every product or every service listed. Our aim has been to answer Design Line's most frequently asked questions in a handy format, whilst also covering more off-beat categories and items.

We discover interesting companies all the time. We would very much welcome readers' suggestions for our next edition.

Nicolette Le Pelley

Cheryl Knorr

CONTENTS

1 KITCHENS & TABLEWARE

TRADITIONAL/PLAIN FITTED KITCHENS	11
MODERN FITTED KITCHENS	13
MODERN KITCHEN ACCESSORIES	14
MINI-KITCHENS	14
FREE-STANDING KITCHEN FURNITURE	14
SINKS & TAPS	15
KITCHEN WORKTOPS & SURFACES	16
INDUSTRIAL AND DOMESTIC APPLIANCES	18
OTHER KITCHEN APPLIANCE MANUFACTURERS	20
ONE-STOP KITCHEN/ TABLEWARE SHOPS	21
CATERING SUPPLIERS	22
CHINA & GLASSWARE	23
KITCHEN ANTIQUES	25
CUTLERY	25
TABLE LINEN & TEA TOWELS	25
OTHER SPECIALIST SERVICES & SUPPLIERS	26

2 BATHROOMS

BATHROOM SHOWROOMS	29
MANUFACTURERS & DISTRIBUTORS OF FITTINGS AND TAPS	31
PLUMBING SUPPLIERS	34
STEEL/GLASS/ WOOD FITTINGS	34
RECLAIMED FITTINGS & TAPS	35
FITTED BATHROOM CABINETS	36
BATHROOM CUPBOARDS	36
BATHROOM SURFACES	37
HEATED TOWEL RAILS	37
BATHROOM ACCESSORIES	38
SPECIALIST SERVICES AND SUPPLIERS	41

3 FURNITURE

TRADITIONAL UPHOLSTERED FURNITURE	43
REPRODUCTION FURNITURE	45
CHAIR & STOOL SPECIALISTS	48
PINE FURNITURE	49
PAINTED / DECORATIVE FURNITURE	49
UNPAINTED / UNCOVERED FURNITURE	51
CONTEMPORARY FURNITURE & UPHOLSTERY	51
FURNITURE MAKERS	54
METAL FURNITURE	55
DESKS	57
LEATHER FURNITURE	57
PERSPEX FURNITURE & ACCESSORIES	58
ETHNIC FURNITURE & ACCESSORIES	58
SCREENS	60
SHELVING	61
OFFICE FURNITURE	61
CONTRACT FURNITURE	62
OTHER SUPPLIERS & SERVICES	63

4 BEDS & BEDDING

NEW BEDS	65
ANTIQUE BEDS	67
OTHER BEDS	68
MATTRESSES & DIVANS	68
HEADBOARDS	70
BEDLINEN & TOWELS	70
THROWS / BLANKETS / BEDSPREADS	73
SPECIALIST SERVICES & PRODUCTS	74

5 FABRICS

WHERE TO SEE A LARGE SELECTION	77
MAJOR FABRIC COMPANIES	78
UTILITY FABRICS / TICKINGS / FELTS	81
SHEERS / VOILES / LACE	82
CREWEL	83
SILK	84
TARTANS & PLAIDS	85
VELVET / CORDUROY / CHENILLE	86
REAL & FAKE LEATHER / SUEDE	87
ANIMAL PRINTS & IMITATION FUR	88
TRIMMINGS	88
OTHER SPECIALIST SUPPLIERS & SERVICES	90

6 WALLPAPER

WHERE TO SEE A LARGE SELECTION	93
ARCHIVE / HANDPRINTED WALLPAPER	94
TEXTURED WALLPAPER (FLOCK, HESSIAN, ANAGLYPTA)	95
FAUX-WOOD, FAUX-STONE, FAUX-BOOK WALLPAPER	96
TARTANS / PLAID WALLPAPER	97
METALLIC PAPERS	97
PRINT ROOM PAPERS	97
OTHER SUPPLIERS & SPECIALIST SERVICES	97

7 FLOORING

NATURAL MATTING	101
CARPETS & STAIR-RODS	102
NEEDLEPOINT RUGS	104
AUBUSSONS / ORIENTAL RUGS	104
KELIMS / DHURRIES	105
CONTEMPORARY RUGS	105
OTHER RUGS	106
WOOD FLOORING	106
RECLAIMED WOOD FLOORING	107
LINO / VINYL / RUBBER / CORK FLOORING	107
TILE SHOPS WITH A LARGE SELECTION	110
CERAMIC TILES	111
MARBLE / TERRAZZO TILES	112
STONE TILES	112
TERRACOTTA TILES	114
MOSAIC	114
ENTRANCE MATS	115
OTHER SPECIALIST SUPPLIERS & SERVICES	115

8 LIGHTING

TRADITIONAL	117
CHANDELIERS	120
LAMPSHADES	121
CANDLES, CANDLESTICKS & STORM LANTERNS	122
WROUGHT-IRON CANDLESTICKS & CANDELABRA	122
UNUSUAL	123
CONTEMPORARY / LOW VOLTAGE	124
OFF-BEAT	127
OUTSIDE LIGHTING	127
SPECIALIST FITTINGS	128
LIGHTING CONSULTANTS	129

CONTENTS

9. DOORS & WINDOWS

OLD DOORS	131
NEW & REPRODUCTION DOORS	132
TRADITIONAL DOOR & CABINET FITTINGS	133
MODERN DOOR & CABINET FITTINGS	134
CERAMIC & GLASS FITTINGS	135
WINDOWS / ROOFLIGHTS / FANLIGHTS	136
SHUTTERS	137
GLASS MANUFACTURERS & SUPPLIERS	138
STAINED GLASS SUPPLIERS & ARTISTS	140
OTHER SPECIALIST SERVICES & SUPPLIERS	140

10 CURTAINS & BLINDS & SOFT FURNISHINGS

CURTAIN MAKERS	143
CURTAIN POLES	145
SECONDHAND CURTAINS	147
BLINDS & AWNINGS	147
RE-UPHOLSTERY	149
FABRIC WALLING	150
OTHER SPECIALIST SERVICES	151

11 HEATING & COOLING

ANTIQUE & NEW FIREPLACES	153
GAS FIRES	156
CLUB FENDERS	157
STOVES	157
RADIATORS	159
UNDERFLOOR HEATING	160
FANS & AIR CONDITIONING	161
OTHER SPECIALIST SERVICES & SUPPLIERS	161

12 RESTORERS & CRAFTSMEN

BUILDING RESTORERS	163
STONE / MARBLE	164
POTTERY & PORCELAIN	164
LIGHTING	165
METAL / SILVER	165
TEXTILES / CARPETS	166
LEATHER	167
FURNITURE	167
GLASS	169
PAINTINGS	170
OTHER SPECIALISTS	170

13 ANTIQUES

LONDON ANTIQUES ARCADES	173
LONDON ANTIQUES MARKETS	174
THE 'BIG FOUR' LONDON AUCTION HOUSES	174
ENGLISH & CONTINENTAL EARLY COUNTRY FURNITURE	175
ENGLISH & CONTINENTAL FURNITURE & DECORATIVE ITEMS	176
FRENCH DECORATIVE FURNITURE & ACCESSORIES	178
SWEDISH / NEO-CLASSICAL / BIEDERMEIER	178
ARTS & CRAFTS / 20TH CENTURY DESIGN	178
ANTIQUE TEXTILES	179
ANTIQUE CARPETS & RUGS	180
ANTIQUE LIGHTING	182
PAINTINGS	183
ANTIQUE PRINTS & MAPS	183
ANTIQUE ORIENTAL CERAMICS & WORKS OF ART	184
ANTIQUE POTTERY & PORCELAIN	185
ANTIQUE GLASS	186
ANTIQUE SILVER	186
ANTIQUE CLOCKS & BAROMETERS	187
OTHER ANTIQUE DEALERS	187

14 SPECIALIST SUPPLIERS & SERVICES

PAINT	191
WOOD FINISHES	193
STENCILS / PIGMENTS & SPECIALIST SUPPLIERS	194
DECORATIVE PAINTERS	195
RESTORATION MATERIALS	196
SPECIALIST CLEANERS	197
DYERS	198
PAINT STRIPPING	198
METALWORK / IRONWORK	199
METAL SHEETING / CHICKEN WIRE / RADIATOR GRILLES	200
PLASTERWORK	201
FRAMERS	202
JOINERS	204
WOOD CARVING	204
WALL PANELLING	205
STAIRCASES & PARTS	206
ARCHITECTURAL FEATURES	207
BUILDERS' MERCHANTS & TIMBER YARDS	208
GYM & GAME ROOM EQUIPMENT	209
SECURITY	209
AUDIO-SYSTEMS	210
OTHER SPECIALISTS	210

15 CHILDREN

CHILDREN'S FABRICS & WALLPAPERS	213
CHILDREN'S FURNITURE	214
PLAY HOUSES & EQUIPMENT	216
CHILDREN'S ACCESSORIES	216

16 ARCHITECTURAL SALVAGE

LONDON	219
SOUTHERN ENGLAND	220
CENTRAL ENGLAND	221
NORTHERN ENGLAND	222
WALES	222
SCOTLAND	223
NORTHERN IRELAND	223
REPUBLIC OF IRELAND	223

17 ACCESSORIES

ONE-STOP	225
PRINTS / PAINTINGS / FRAMES	226
CERAMICS	228
GLASS	229
MIRRORS	230
WOODEN ACCESSORIES	232
SILVER	232
TÔLEWARE	233
BASKETS	233
CUSHIONS	233
PLASTER & RESIN CASTS	234
FAKE BOOKS	235
STORAGE	236
FLORISTS & ARTIFICIAL FLOWERS	237
OTHER SUPPLIERS	238

CONTENTS

18 GARDENS

ONE-STOP	241
ANTIQUE GARDEN FURNITURE & ORNAMENT	242
NEW & REPRODUCTION STATUARY & ORNAMENT	242
WOODEN FURNITURE	244
METAL GARDEN FURNITURE	245
WICKER/RATTAN/ LLOYD LOOM FURNITURE	246
WIREWORK FURNITURE	247
CONSERVATORIES	247
GARDEN HOUSES/ GAZEBOS / PAVILIONS	248
GREENHOUSES / SHEDS	250
FENCING & WOODEN GATES	250
METAL GATES & RAILINGS	251
CANOPIES & PARASOLS	251
WOODEN TRELLIS & OBELISKS / WILLOW SUPPORTS	252
IRON & WIRE PLANT SUPPORTS	253
FOUNTAINS / WATER PUMPS / TAPS	253
OUTDOOR PAVING & SURFACES	255
SWIMMING POOLS	256
POTS / PLANTERS / WINDOW BOXES	256
ACCESSORIES / TOOLS	257
SPECIALIST NURSERIES	258
MISCELLANEOUS	259

19 COURSES & INFORMATION

HISTORY OF ART COURSES	261
INTERIOR DESIGN COURSES	261
PAINT FINISHES & STENCILLING COURSES	262
GARDEN DESIGN COURSES	263
OTHER COURSES	264
UK DESIGN & GARDEN EXHIBITIONS 1997/1998	265
MAJOR ANTIQUES FAIRS 1997/1998	266
ORGANISATIONS & SOURCES OF INFORMATION	267

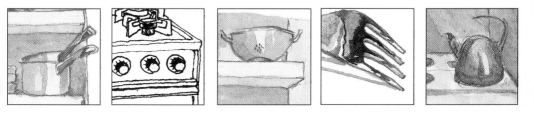

KITCHENS & TABLEWARE

TRADITIONAL/PLAIN FITTED KITCHENS

Crabtree Kitchens
The Twickenham Centre, Norcutt Road,
Twickenham, Middx TW2 6SR.
T:0181-755 1121. F:0181-755 4133.
'Mackintosh' kitchen in hand painted wood
with stained glass details and specially
designed handles. Shaker kitchens and
hand painted armoires in a selection of
finishes (verdigris, buttermilk, dark green
glaze).Top quality, tailored service.

Hayloft Woodwork
3 Bond St, London W4 1QZ.
T: 0181-747 3510. F:0181-742 1860.
Custom-built kitchens, individually designed
in pine, hardwoods or painted finishes. Any
style can be made to commission, either
fitted or freestanding.

Heart Of The Home
Unit 2 Brookway, Kingston Road,
Leatherhead, Surrey KT22 7NA.
T:01372-360502. F:01372-361147.

MDF and timber fitted kitchens along with
replacement cupboard doors.

Charles Hurst
Unit 21, Bow Triangle Business Centre,
Eleanor St, Bow, London E3 4NP.
T:0181-981 8562.
Simple, well proportioned
handmade kitchens.

Harvey Jones
57 New Kings Rd, London SW6 4SE.
T:0171-731 3302. F:0171-371 0535.
'Simple Painted Furniture' range of plain
panelled kitchen units supplied unpainted in
simple Victorian or Shaker styles. The frames
are hardwood with MDF centre panels.

Andrew Macintosh Furniture
462 & 464 Chiswick High Rd,
London W4 5TT.
T:0181-995 8333. F:0181-995 8999.
Hand-painted Shaker style kitchens.

Newcastle Furniture Company
128 Walham Green Court, Moore Park Rd,
London SW6 4DG.
T:0171-386 9203. F:0171-385 1447.

Hand painted or plain wood free-standing or fitted kitchens. Simple, unfussy look drawing on English country and Shaker designs.

Original Door Specialists
298 Brockley Rd, London SE4 2RA. T:0181-691 7162. Reclaimed kitchen cupboards, particularly in pine.

Plain English
The Tannery, Combs, Stowmarket, Suffolk IP14 2EN. T:01449-774028. F:01449-613519. Very simple range of 18th century inspired handmade kitchen cupboards with five different door styles. Usually painted in National Trust colours. Freestanding dressers, larders, farmhouse tables, country chairs. There is also a bespoke service.

Rhode Design Furniture
65 Cross Street, London N1 2BB. T:0171-354 9933. F:0171-354 1006. Handmade painted wooden units with an American colonial/Shaker feel. Also free-standing cupboards. Unpainted MDF or pine cupboards and dressers can also be supplied.

Robinson and Cornish
Southay House, Oakwood Close, Roundswell, Barnstaple, N Devon EX31 3NJ. T:01271-329300. F: 01271-328277. Top quality, bespoke cabinetry including the Biedermeier kitchen in tinted maple and black lacquer. Classic country painted kitchens; maple or wild ash cabinets, cupboards and other free-standing furniture.

Smallbone of Devizes
105-109 Fulham Rd, London SW3 6RL. T:0171-589 5998. F:0171-581 9415. Bespoke kitchens, from the traditional hand painted to the contemporary 'Metropolitan' look. Inspirational showroom.

Templederry Design
Hornacott, South Petherwin, Launceston, Cornwall PL15 7LH. T/F:01566-782461. Bespoke kitchens and interior woodwork at competitive prices. Comprehensive range of factory-produced wooden and laminate kitchen units. Nationwide service.

Trevor Toms Cabinetmakers
Fisherton Mill, 108 Fisherton St, Salisbury SP2 7QY. T:01722-331139. Hand crafted kitchens incorporating details like staggered shelving and walk-in larders. Stockist of Lacanche cookers.

Mark Wilkinson
Overton House, High Street, Bromham Nr Chippenham, Wilts SN15 2HA. T:01380-850004. F: 01380-850184. Antony Worrall Thompson's choice for his own country cottage is a Mark Wilkinson cream tulipwood design. His bespoke collection includes Provencal, Santa Fe and Etruscan styles.

Tim Wood
93 Mallinson Rd, London SW11 1BL. T:0171-924 1511. F:0171-924 1522. A John Makepeace trained craftsman, Tim Wood will undertake commissions ranging from very small kitchens (he made seven kitchens for the prestige development in Observatory Gardens, Kensington W8, including some 'mini-kitchens') to large, stately home interiors (a kitchen in Bath boasts mahogany, satinwood, ebony, bubinga and maple).

Woodstock Furniture
4 William St, London SW1X 9HL. T:0171-245 9989. F:0171-245 9981. Specialists in hardwood kitchens: maple, cherry, oak or ash. Bespoke fitted and free-standing furniture.

MODERN FITTED KITCHENS

*Allmilmö
80 Mersey Way, Thatcham,
Berks RG18 3DL.
T:01635-868181. F:01635-860064.
Innovative, functional top quality German design. 150 front finishes, predominantly lacquer. 500 different cabinets to choose from.

Arc Linea
164 Brompton Rd, London SW3 1HW.
T:0171-581 2271. F:0171-581 7912.
Top end of the market Italian design incorporating bright colours, stainless steel, granite and glass.

Bulthaup
37 Wigmore St, London W1H 9LD.
T:0171-495 3663. F:0171-495 0139.
Streamlined modern kitchens which mix wood, stainless steel and glass. Task lighting is usually incorporated. Excellent storage systems.

Grey & Company
Syning Copse, Rogate, Petersfield,
Hants GU31 5JD.
T:01730-821424. F:01730-821717.
Leading innovator of kitchen design, Johnny Grey creates highly original kitchens in unusual woods with particular attention to design dilemmas.

Humpherson's
2nd floor, Heal's Building,
196 Tottenham Court Rd, London W1P 9LD.
T:0171-636 1666. F:0171-436 4738.
Contemporary, some very modern designs all custom-made with mainly a lacquer and granite high-tech look.

IKEA
2 Drury Way, North Circular Rd,
London NW10 0TH.
T:0181-208 5600.
Call for branches. Modern and inexpensive flat-packed units to build yourself. Computer design service available. 16 different doors, 60 knobs and handles.

Just Kitchens
242-244 Fulham Rd, London SW10 9NA.
T:0171- 351 1616. F:0171-352 1699.
Call for branches. Showroom for a selection of modern German manufacturers and also bespoke, traditional English style kitchens. Good range of worktops.

Guy Mallinson Furniture
7 The Coachworks, 80 Parson's Green Lane,
London SW6 4HU.
T:0171-371 9190. F:0171-371 5099.
Freestanding kitchen furniture handmade to order. A basic frame is customised with various shelves, tops, feet and 'bridges' (butchers' blocks, central islands, slate tops for pastry making). They also offer a customised service for replacement doors. The client can choose from a range of unusual woods and doors are made as grain-matched sets.

*Poggenpohl
Skane-Gripen Kitchens (UK),
Silbury Court, 368 Silbury Blvd, Central Milton Keynes MK9 2AF.
T:01908-606886. F:01908-606958.
The oldest kitchen company in the world (they have been going 105 years).Top of the range high-tech, high-fashion kitchens in all sorts of materials - from solid timber to lacquers, laminates and glass. Ergonomics are a key selling point, like dual height working levels.

*SieMatic
Mobelwerke, GMBH Osprey House,
Rookery Court, Primett Rd,
Stevenage, Herts SG1 3EE.
T:01438-369251. F:01438-368920.
German manufacturer of smart mainly laminated kitchens. Good selection of trendy handles, opaque glass fronted doors, and well engineered corner units.

Viaduct
1-10 Summer's St, London EC1R 5BD.
T:0171-278 8456. F:0171-278 2844.
Agents for Driade's streamlined Italian range combining lacquer, steel and wood with elegant, elongated chrome handles.

* denotes trade supplier. Please phone for retail outlets.

MODERN KITCHEN ACCESSORIES

Aero
96 Westbourne Grove, London W2 5RT.
T:0171-221 1950. F:0171-221 2555.
Mail Order catalogue orderline:
T:0181-871 4030 F:0181-870 8227
Galvanized metal kitchen bins on wheels,
storage tins, dish racks, shelves, cutlery
holders, wall grid panels in smart modern
designs. Selection of chairs and tables too.

Aria
133 and 295 Upper St, London N1 1QP.
T:0171-226 1021. F:0171-704 6333.
Alessi chromeware, unusual dinner
services. Also bed and bathware.

*Authentics
20 High St, Weybridge, Surrey KT13 8AB.
T:01932-859800. F:01932-856493.
Authentics supply the original USA metal
push cans in a selection of colours and
finishes, pedal bins, fire bins, and aluminium
waste bins.

Muji
26 Great Marlborough St, London W1V 1HL.
T:0171-494 1197. F:0171-494 1193.
Call for branches. Minimalist Japanese
range of kitchenware, storage and other
items for the home in neutral colours.

Oggetti
143 Fulham Rd, London SW3 6SD.
T:0171-584 9808. F:0171-581 9652.
Ultra modern accessories. The only company
in England who can provide Alessi's full
range. Also Arzburg chinaware and Iitala
glass from Finland.

MINI-KITCHENS

Bulthaup
See entry under **MODERN FITTED
KITCHENS.**The Bulthaup Workbench is
a freestanding stainless steel unit which
incorporates a hob, a preparation surface
with a shallow sink, hose taps, drawer
and wastebin.

**See also One Stop
Kitchen/Tableware
Shops.**

*Franke
Manchester International Office Centre,
Styal Rd, Manchester M22 5WB.
T:0161-436 6280. F:0161-436 2180.
Mainly known for their range of stainless
steel sinks, their mini kitchenette has a
sink, hob and sits on a base storage unit.

*Hafele
Swift Valley Ind. Estate,
Rugby, Warwicks CV21 1RD.
T:01788-542020. F:01788-544440.
Ingenious pull-out breakfast tables, built-in
ironing boards, folding steps, foldaway
fittings for heavy appliances and pull-out
larders and laundry baskets.

C P Hart
See entry under **SINKS & TAPS.**
The 'Kitcase' portable kitchen on wheels is
a stainless steel sink with a drainer and
mixer tap, two electric hotplates, an electric
water heater, refrigerator, automatic coffee
machine and vacuum jug.

*Northmace
Northmace House,
Taffs Well, Cardiff CF4 8XF.
T:01222-810741. F:01222-813275.
Hotel bedroom equipment supplier whose
range includes a wall-mounted ironing board
with integral wired-in dry iron.

John Strand
34/40 Brunel Road,
Westway Estate, London W3 7XR.
T/F:0181-749 3915.
The 'Hideaway' incorporates a sink,
drainer, two hotplates, a monobloc tap
and a wall mounted grill/oven.
The 'Bauknecht' mini kitchen also has
a refrigerator and storage cupboard.

FREE-STANDING KITCHEN FURNITURE

After Noah
121 Upper St, London N1 1QP.
T/F:0171-359 4281.
And at: 261 King's Road, London SW3 5EL.
T/F:0171-351 2610.

Ever changing selection of old and new scales, accessories, 1940s kitchen tables and meat and cheese safes.

Chalon
The Plaza, 535 King's Road,
London SW10 0SZ.
T:0171-351 0008. F:0171-351 0003.
Painted formal country range including chopping tables with double-ended drawers and optional loose willow baskets.

Country Cookers
See entry under INDUSTRIAL
AND DOMESTIC APPLIANCES.

Deacon & Sandys
Hillcrest Farm Oast, Hawkhurst Rd,
Cranbrook, Kent TN17 3QD.
T:01580-713775. F:01580-714056.
Reproductions of 16th and 17th century Jacobean oak refectory tables. Anything in oak, including custom-made designs: chairs, dressers etc.

Habitat
196 Tottenham Court Rd, London W1P 9LD.
T:0171-631 3880.
For other branches call 0645-334433.
Kitchen department includes excellent selection of tables and chairs in natural and painted wood, metal and rattan. Also a range of eight freestanding units in three colours with solid beech worktops.

Cath Kidston
8 Clarendon Cross, London W11 4AP.
T:0171-221 4000. F:0171-229 1992.
Repainted cupboards and tables, reasonably priced. Selection of café style zinc-topped tables.

Guy Mallinson Furniture
See entry under
MODERN FITTED KITCHENS.

Millenium Design International
1B-D Barnes High St, London SW13 9LB.
T:0181-876 1112. F:0181-876 2105.
Good selection of painted tables, chairs and dressers along with iron kitchen accessories.

The Repro Shop
108 Walcot St, Bath BA1 5BG.
T:01225-444404. F:01225-448163.

Original refectory tables and reproductions made to order in any size.

*Row & Sons
5 Stepfield Ind. Area East,
Witham, Essex CM8 3BW.
T:01376-511101. F:01376-500859.
Manufacturers of butcher's blocks and aluminium tables for professional food preparation.

Shaker
25 Harcourt St, London W1H 1DT.
T:0171-724-7672. F:0171-724 6640.
Also at:
322 King's Rd, London SW3 5UH. T:0171-352 3918. F:0171-376 3494. Selection of Shaker reproduction maple tables, chairs and rockers with woven tape seats.

SINKS & TAPS

GEC Anderson
89 Herkomer Rd, Bushey, Herts WD2 3LS.
T:0181-950 1826. F:0181-950 3626.
Stainless steel sinks and worktops made to measure in any size or shape.

*Armitage Shanks
Old Road, Armitage,
Nr Rugeley, Staffs WS15 4BT.
T:01543-490253. F:01543-491677.
Traditional white Belfast sinks.

Aston Matthews
141-147a Essex Rd, London N1 2SN.
T: 0171-226 3657. F:0171-354 5951.
Ceramic butlers' sinks, including waste disposal models. Also stainless steel and enamelled cast iron sinks.

*Barber Wilsons & Co
Crawley Rd, Westbury Ave, London N22 6AH.
T:0181-888 3461. F:0181-888 2041.
Manufacturer of top quality bath and kitchen taps and accessories.

*Blanco
Oxgate Lane, London NW2 7JN.
T:0181-450 9100. F:0800-282846.
Distributors of inset and underbuilt stainless steel sinks, and silicon sinks in granite and smooth marble effects.

* denotes trade supplier. Please phone for retail outlets.

Brass & Traditional Sinks

Devauden Green, Nr. Chepstow,
Monmouthshire NP6 6PL.
T:01291-650743. F:01291-650827.
Belfast sinks, old fashioned and
contemporary fireclay sinks, solid brass
sinks, complementary taps and free-
standing wooden draining boards.

*Carron Phoenix

Carron Works, Stenhouse Rd, Falkirk,
Scotland FK2 8DW.
T:01324-638321. F:01324-620978.
Range of sinks in plastic, resin-bonded
ceramic and stainless steel.

*Crangrove

Crangrove House, Coronation Rd,
Park Royal, London NW10 7QH.
T:0181-453 0212. F:0181-961 7357.
Wholesalers of stainless steel and Asterite
sinks and coloured and chrome taps.

*Franke

See entry under MINI KITCHENS.
Selection of plastic, pressed steel and
stainless steel sinks.

CP Hart

Newnham Terrace, Hercules Rd,
London SE1 7DR.
T:0171-902 1000. F:0171-902 1001.
Also at:
103-105 Regents Park Rd,
London NW1 8UR.
T:0171-586 9856. F: 0171-722 4437.
Agents for SieMatic kitchens and Blanco,
Franke, Villeroy & Boch and Jacob Delafon
sinks. They also stock their own range of
taps and others by Vola and Hans Grohe.

*Leisure

Meadow Lane, Long Eaton, Notts NG10 2AT.
T:0115-9464000. F:0115-9736602. Large
range of round and square sinks in resin or
stainless steel.

*B & P Wynn & Co

60 Queenstown Rd, London SW8 3RY.
T:0171-498 4345. F:0171-498 4346.
Importers of the French Herbeau range of
copper, brass, nickel and hand-painted
porcelain sinks.

KITCHEN WORKTOPS & SURFACES

TERRAZZO

Pallam Precast

187 West End Lane, London NW6 2LJ.
T:0171-328 6512. F:0171-328 3547.
Infinitely adaptable in shape and colour; can
be cast to fit your kitchen exactly. You can
choose a design from stock or create your
own. Also flooring.

STONE

Delabole Slate

Pengelly Rd, Delabole, Cornwall PL33 9AZ.
T:01840-212242. F:01840-212948.

Kirkstone Quarries

Skelwith Bridge, Ambleside,
Cumbria LA22 9NN.
T:015394-33296. F:015394-34006.
Volcanic stone traditionally known as
Westmoreland green slate.

Lloyd of Bedwyn

91 Church St, Great Bedwyn,
Marlborough, Wilts SN8 3PF.
T:01672-870234. F:01672-871211.
Manufacture and cut to order granite, slate,
marble - any type of stone.

Naturestone

Crossway Silwood Rd. Sunninghill,
Ascot, Berks SL5 0PZ.
T:01344-27617. F:01344-873185.
Slates and quartzite for worktops/flooring.

*Solnhofen Natural Stone

8 The Courtyard, 69 Gowan Ave,
London SW6 6RH.
T:0171-610 6440. F:0171-610 6431.
Importers of German fossilised limestone.

Vitruvius

Unit 20, Ransome's Dock,
35 Parkgate Rd, London SW11 4NP.
T:0171-223 8209. F:0171-924 3045.
Marble and slate.

Zarka Marble

41A Belsize Lane, London NW3 5AU.
T:0171-431 3042. F:0171-431 3879.
All marble supplied.

WOOD

Finewood Floors

Unit 5, Gibson Business Centre, rear of 800 High Rd, London N17 0DH.
T:0181-365 0222. F:0181-885 3860.
Oak, maple, ash, cherry, beech and elm solid hardwoods in 25mm to 40mm thicknesses.

The Hardwood Flooring Co

146-152 West End Lane, London NW6 1SD.
T:0171-328 8481. F:0171-625 5951.
Supply Junckers and own range of worksurfaces.

*Junckers

Wheaton Court Commercial Centre, Wheaton Rd, Witham, Essex CM8 3UJ.
T:01376-517512. F:01376-514401.

FORMICA & LAMINATES

*Baldwin Plastic Laminates

57 Tallon Rd, Hutton Ind Estate, Brentwood, Essex CM13 1TG.
T:01277-225235. F:01277-222586.
Will bond Formica and other laminates to chipboard, MDF and plywood.

*Formica

Coast Rd, North Shields, Tyne & Wear NE29 8RE.
T:0191-259 3000. F:0191-258 2719.
Formica comes in over 550 colours and can be bonded to a variety of surfaces.

Wey Plastics

Canal Bridge, Byfleet Rd, Newhaw, Weybridge, Surrey KT15 3JE.
T:01932-848131. F:01932-848447.
Will bond laminates (Formica, Perspex, Polyrey, Perstorp and Wareite) to MDF and chipboard.

STAINLESS STEEL

Anchor Food Service Equipment

205 Manor Rd, Erith, Kent DA8 2AD.
T:01322-335544. F:01322-350211.
Can provide the indestructible kitchen - from counters to worktops.

GEC Anderson

See entry under **SINKS & TAPS.**

Bragman Flett

30 Gwynne Rd, London SW11 3UW.
T:0171-228 8855. F:0171-228 2312.
Not only stainless steel, but perforated sheet metal, galvanised metal, copper, brass, aluminium - any metal fabrication.

ZINC

Builders Iron and Zincwork

Millmarsh Lane, Brimsdown, Enfield, Middx EN3 7QA.
T:0181-443 3300. F:0181-804 6672.

Metra Non-Ferrous Metals

Pindar Rd, Hoddesdon, Herts EN11 0DE.
T:01992-460455. F:01992-451207.
Suppliers of zinc sheeting.

CORIAN®

DuPont Corian ®

McD Marketing, Maylands Ave, Hemel Hempstead, Herts HP2 7DP.
T:01442-346776. F:01442-346755.
A durable, hygienic mineral based material made only by DuPont. It has a smooth, renewable surface and is available in over 40 colours including plain, veined and granular effects.

MILLENIUM

Hannings Furniture Company

Unit 5/1, The Mews, Brook St, Mitcheldean, Gloucs GL17 0SL.
T:01594-544196. T:01594-544378.
'Millenium' solid cast polyester worksurface. It comes in 24 colours which are speckled like terrazzo. Other colours made to order.

RECYCLED PLASTIC BOARD

Made of Waste

244 Grays Inn Road, London WC1X 8JR.
T:0171-278 6971. F:0171-833 0018.
By appointment. Cheap, eco-friendly and very colourful board made from recycled plastic bottles. It comes in thicknesses from 5mm (for panelling) to 25mm (for worksurfaces and table tops). From £27.70 for 2m by 1m sheets. Minimum order £10

* denotes trade supplier. Please phone for retail outlets.

17

RESIN

Maaz
29 Camden Square, London NW1 9XA.
T/F: 0171-482 2443.
Resin worktops made to order, either
in colour or embedded with objects
of your choice.

FABLON

*Forbo CP
Station Rd, Cramlington,
Northumberland NE23 8AQ.
T:01670-718300. F:01670-718220.
Sticky-backed plastic to use on kitchen
cupboard doors for a quick uplift. Nine
solid colours, 50 different designs.

PYROLAVE

Whitehall Worksurfaces
Exhibition House,
Grape St, Leeds LS10 1BX.
T:0113-2444892. F:0113-2426849.
Made from solidified lava, available in 30
colours with a slight crackle-glaze effect; it's
durable, heat-resistant, but quite pricey.

REINFORCED CAST CONCRETE

Totem Design
14 Arundel Gardens, London W11 2LA.
T:0171-727 3280. F:0171-460 1126.
No size limitations and endless scope for
colouring, inlays and curves.

INDUSTRIAL AND DOMESTIC APPLIANCES

*Aga/Rayburn
P O Box 30, Ketley,
Telford, Shropshire TF1 4DD.
T:01952-642000. F:01952-243138.
Aga, Rayburn and Coalbrookdale stoves.
Available in two and four oven models and
in ten vitreous enamel colours.

*American Appliance Centre
52 Larkshall Rd, Chingford, London E4 6PD.
T:0181-529 9665. F: 0181-529 9666.
Importers of large American fridges,
including Westinghouse and Frigidaire. Sole
UK distributor for Traulsen stainless steel
refrigerators available with or without glass
doors. Also distribute Admiral, Amana, Sub-
Zero, Viking and Jenn-Air.

Barrett Gray
Unit 6, Lancaster Park Ind Estate,
Bowerhill, Melksham, Wilts SN12 6TT.
T:01225-704470. F:01225-705927.
Importer of equipment for the catering
industry including the Riberwerke fridge
freezer - the minimalist's favourite.

Bulthaup
See entry under
MODERN FITTED KITCHENS.
Agents for La Cornue French cookers.

Buyers & Sellers
120-122 Ladbroke Grove, London W10 5NE.
T:0171-229 8468. F:0171-221 4113.
Reductions on well known brands and next
day delivery.

The Chester Cooker Co
18 Elms Lane, Sudbury,
Wembley, Middx HA0 2NN.
T/F:0181-904 4477.
Manufacturers of the heavy duty Chester
industrial cookers. They also do a smaller
four burner version for domestic use.

The Classic American Fridge Company
2 Gate Cottage, Chorleywood Common,
Common Rd, Chorleywood, Herts WD3 5LN.
T/F:01494-792998. By appointment.
Original renovated English and American
40s, 50s, and 60s fridges. There are 30-
50 in stock at any time.

Country Cookers
Bruffworks, Bush Bank,
Suckley, Worcs WR6 5DR.
T:01886-884262. F:01886-884461.
Rebuilt Agas and Rayburns, Nobel cookers,
and reclaimed pine kitchen furniture.

Davis Electrics
19 Mill Lane, Woodford Green,
Essex IG8 0UN.
T:0181-506 2039.
F:0181-505 8700.
Suppliers of the Viking cooker.

EFR
697 High Rd, Seven Kings,
Ilford, Essex IG3 8RH.
T:0181-590 0022. F:0181-599 2870.
Catering supplier with a range which
includes cookers, stainless steel fridges,
dishwashers and ice making machines.
Their 'Morice' domestic cooker is based
on an industrial design.

G D Evans
331-333 High Street,
Slough, Berks SO1 1TX.
T:01753-524188. F:01753-572029.
Discounted ex-display Neff appliances.

*Falcon Catering Equipment
PO Box 37, Lambert,
Falkirk, Scotland FK5 4PL.
T:01324-554221. F:01324-552211.
Quality catering cooking equipment - from
ranges and grills to dish and glass washers.

Flying Duck
320-322 Creek Rd, London SE10 9SW.
T:0181-858 1964. F:0181-852 3215.
Specialists in 50s to 70s design; they
usually have a stock of old fridges and
kitchen equipment.

*Fourneaux de France
30 Albion Close, Newtown Business Park,
Poole, Dorset BH12 3LL.
T: 01202-733011. F:01202-733499.
Importers of the chunky French Lacanche
and Rosières cookers. The Lacanche
refrigerator is in brushed stainless steel
with brass trim and fitted with sturdy
metal baskets.

Garland Catering
Swallowfield Way, Hayes, Middx UB3 1DQ.
T: 0181-561 0433. F:0181-848 0041.
Heavy duty cooking equipment including
the Garland range.

Hansen's Kitchen & Bakery Equipment
306 Fulham Rd, London SW10 9ER.
T:0171-351 6933. F:0171-351 5319.
Supply of kitchens for the catering industry -
everything from cookers to cups;
professional equipment for the serious chef.
Leading supplier of Lacanche cookers.

Hot & Cold
13 Golborne Rd, London W10 5NY.
T:0181-960 1300. F:0181-960 4163.
Whether you are after a ceramic hob,
a wall oven or an entire kitchen, this is a
good source for major brand appliances
and difficult to find options.

Hymas Refrigeration
178 Grove Green Rd, London E11 4EL.
T:0181-539 4222. F: 0181-518 7287.
The catering industry's main source
for supply and service of refrigeration
equipment.

JCA (UK)
Unit 10-20, Chorley Rd,
Blackpool, Lancs FY3 7XQ.
T:01253-300663. F:01253-391011.
Supply Britannia cookers.

Maurice Lay Distribution
Fourth Way, Avonmouth, Bristol BS11 8DW.
T:0117-9823721. F:0117-9826878.
Supply Rosières cookers.

Molesey Refrigeration
51-53 Walton Rd,
East Molesey, Surrey KT8 0DP.
T:0181-979 4619. F:0181-941 7306.
American fridges and supply of all major
brand appliances at competitive prices.

*NCR
Vaux Rd, Sinedon Road Ind Estate,
Wellingborough, Northants NN8 4TG.
T:01933-272222. F:01933-279638.
Agents for the Amana fridge freezer.

Nelson Catering Equipment
Nelson House, 9 Roslin Square,
Roslin Rd, London W3 8DH.
T:0181-993 6198/9. F:0181-993 8979.
Agents for the Falcon Sovereign range. All
sorts of catering equipment supplied. They
also manufacture their own range of dish
and glass washers.

Sanitary Appliances
3 Sandford Rd, Kempton Road Ind Estate,
Sutton, Surrey SM3 9RN.
T:0181-641 0310. F:0181-641 6426.
Suppliers of a large range of sanitary
appliances, including stainless steel sinks.

*** denotes
trade supplier.
Please phone
for retail outlets.**

19

Smeg (UK)
Corinthian Court, 80 Milton Park,
Abingdon, Oxon OX14 4RY.
T:01235-861090. F:01235-861120.
Chunky frost-free refrigerators with convex
doors available in stainless steel or in one of
six colours: blue, red, green, yellow,
burgundy or cream.

OTHER KITCHEN APPLIANCE MANUFACTURERS

AEG (UK)
217 Bath Rd, Slough Berks SL1 4AW.
T:01753-872101. F:01753-872176.

Amana
See NCR under INDUSTRIAL AND
DOMESTIC KITCHEN APPLIANCES.

GEC Anderson
See entry under SINKS & TAPS.

Arc Linea
See entry under MODERN
FITTED KITCHENS. Hobs and sinks.

Ariston
Cowley Business Park, Cowley,
Uxbridge, Middx. UB8 2AD.
T:01895-858200. F:01895-858270.

Atag (UK)
19-20 Hither Green,
Clevedon, Somerset BS21 6XU.
T:01275-877301. F:01275-871371.

Bauknecht
209 Purley Way, Croydon, Surrey CR9 4RY.
T:0181-649 5000. F:0181-649 5060.

Baumatic
Baumatic Buildings, 3 Elgar Ind Estate,
Preston Rd, Reading, Berks RG2 0BE.
T:01734-310055. F:01734-310035.

Belling Appliances
Talbot Rd, Mexborough, S. Yorks S64 8AJ.
T:01709-579900. F:01709-579904.

Blanco
See entry under SINKS & TAPS. Range of
built-in appliances.

Bosch Domestic Appliances
The Quadrangle, Westmount Centre,
Uxbridge Rd, Hayes, Middx UB4 0HD.
T:0181-573 1199. F:0181-756 0140.
Also manufacture a retro-look fridge.

Calor Gas
Appleton Park, Slough, Berks SL3 9JG.
T:0800-626626. F:01753-548121.

Candy
New Chester Rd, Bromborough,
Wirral, Merseyside L62 0PE.
T:0151-334 2781. F:0151-334 9056.

Crangrove
See entry under SINKS & TAPS.

Creda
PO Box 5 Creda Works, Blythe Bridge,
Stoke-on-Trent, Staffs ST11 9LJ.
T:01782-388388. F:01782-392599.

De Dietrich
Intec Four, Wade Rd,
Basingstoke, Hants RG24 8NE.
T:01256-843485. F:01256-843024.

Electrolux
See Tricity Bendix.

Gaggenau (UK)
The Quadrangle, Westmount Centre,
Uxbridge Rd, Hayes, Middx UB4 0HD.
T:0181-561 8811. F:0181-561 8899.

Hoover
Pentrebach, Abercanaid, Merthyr,
Tydfil, Mid Glamorgan CF48 4TU.
T:01685-721222. F:01685-382946.

Hotpoint
Morley Way, Peterborough, Cambs PE2 9JB.
T:01733-68989. F:01733-341783.
Wide range of appliances, including a flat
back fridge which fits neatly against the wall.

Indesit
Cowley Business Park, Cowley, Uxbridge,
Middx UB8 2AD. T:01895-858200.
F:01895-858270.

LEC Refrigeration
Shripney Rd, Bognor Regis,
W Sussex PO22 9NQ. T:01243-863161.
Their range includes a compact fridge.

Liebherr
Liebherr House, 1 Brunswick Court,
Bridge St, Leeds, W.Yorks LS2 7QU.
T:0113-245 9493. F:0113-245 8426.

These are head office addresses. Please phone for local retail stockists and service.

Miele
Fairacres, Marcham Rd,
Abingdon, Oxon OX14 1TW.
T:01235-554455. F:01235-554477.

Moffat
Parkinson Cowan and Tricity Bendix Co,
Cornwall House, 55-77 High St, Slough,
Berks SL1 1DZ.
T:0990-805805. F:01753-872499.

Neff (UK)
The Quadrangle, Westmount Centre,
Uxbridge Rd, Hayes, Middx UB4 0HD.
T:0181-848 3711. F:0181-848 1408.

New World Domestic Appliances
New World House, Thelwell Lane,
Warrington, Cheshire WA4 1NL.
T:01925-627627. F:01925-627623.

Scholtes
Cowley Business Park, Cowley,
Uxbridge, Middx UB8 2AD.
T:01895-858200. F:01895-858270.

Siemens Domestic Appliances
The Quadrangle, Westmount Centre,
Uxbridge Rd, Hayes, Middx UB4 0HD.
T:0181-848 3777. F:0181-569 2771.

Stoves
Stoney Lane, Prescot, Merseyside L35 2XW.
T:0151-426 6551. F:0151-426 3261.

Tricity Bendix
Parkinson Cowan and Tricity Bendix Co,
Cornwall House, 55-77 High St, Slough,
Berks SL1 1DZ. T:0990-805805.
Also sales offices for AEG, Electrolux
and Zanussi.

Viking
Bradshaw Appliances, Kenn Rd,
Clevedon, Bristol BS21 6LH.
T:01275-343000. F:01275-343454.
Professional-type cookers.

Whirlpool
209 Purley Way, Croydon, Surrey CR9 4RY.
T:0181-649 5000. F:0181-649 5060.
Whirlpool and Ignis appliances.

Zanussi
Zanussi House, Hambridge Rd,
Newbury, Berks RG14 5EP.
T:01635-521313. F:01635-523297.

ONE-STOP KITCHEN/ TABLEWARE SHOPS

Carpenters
166-168 Queensway, London W2 4LY.
T/F:0171-229 3664. For other branches
call: 0990-134950. Kitchen equipment
including traditional copper preserving pans,
cast-iron scales, weights, marble pestle and
mortar sets and every day necessities.

The Conran Shop
Michelin House, 81 Fulham Rd,
London SW3 6RD.
T:0171-589 7401. F:0171-823 7015.
Classical plain white porcelain, some with
platinum rims, David Mellor stainless steel
cutlery, simple stemware, handmade
glasses (either frosted or in various colours),
handmade terracotta platters, ergonomic
kitchen utensils, stainless steel dish racks,
cobalt steel pedal bins, boxwood handled
knives - anything for the elegant kitchen
and dining room.

La Cuisinière
81/83 Northcote Rd, London SW11 6PJ.
T/F:0171-223-4487.
All sorts of useful and unusual kitchen
gadgets, from mezzalunas to oyster knives.
They also hire out unusual cake tins (for a
special birthday cake), fish kettles and
jam pans.

* denotes
trade supplier.
Please phone
for retail outlets. 21

Elizabeth David Cookshop
3A North Row, The Market,
Covent Garden, London WC2E 8RA.
T:0171-836 9167. F:0171-240 5279.
Retail outlet for Le Creuset, Mayer and
Fissler, Poole pottery, Poterie Francaise,
Screwpull drinks accessories, Sabatier
knives, baking accessories and a selection
of cookery books.

Divertimenti
139-141 Fulham Rd, London SW3 6SD.
T:0171-581 8065. F:0171-823 9429.
Huge range of brightly coloured tableware,
wicker and wooden accessories, stainless
steel equipment, small electrical appliances
(from blenders to toasters), utensils and
books. Mail order catalogue.

Habitat
See entry under **FREE-STANDING
KITCHEN FURNITURE.** Simple
accessories including white china, vinegar
and oil bottles and jugs, salad spinners,
wooden dish racks, souffle dishes - the
Conran look at a lower price.

Heal's
196 Tottenham Court Rd, London W1P 9LD.
T:0171-636 1666. F:0171-436 5129.
Selection of handmade crockery, ironstone
and formal china; large selection of chrome
accessories and the 'Authentics' range -
from plastic mugs to bins.

Hogarth & Dwyer
240 High St, Guildford, Surrey GU1 3JF.
T:01483-456250. F:01483-456252.
A classic cookware shop for serious cooks -
Delia Smith is a client. Equipment for
anything from paella to pasta.

IKEA
See entry under **MODERN FITTED
KITCHENS.** Selection of utensils, but
especially good value glassware and plain
white china starter sets.

Jerry's Home Store
163-167 Fulham Rd, London SW3 6SN.
T:0171-581 0909. F:0171-584 3749.
American-inspired homewares store with
good value china, glass, table-linen, clocks.

Chrome 'Pushboy' bullet bins and fifties-
style kitchen tables and chairs.

Peter Jones
Sloane Sq, London SW1W 8EL.
T:0171-730 3434. First port of call for any
kitchen item one can think of from packets
of pegs to Alessi. Excellent for small
electrical appliances, china and cutlery.

Liberty
214-220 Regent St, London W1R 6AH.
T:0171-734 1234. F:0171-573 9876.
An eclectic mix of traditional and modern
tableware mainly from Italy, France and the
UK. Everything from a wooden spoon to a
complete set of porcelain dinnerware in their
greatly expanded basement kitchen shop.

David Mellor
4 Sloane Square, London SW1W 8EE.
T:0171-730 4259. F:0171-730 7240.
One of London's oldest 'designer' kitchen
shops. They do their own cutlery, a big
selection of baskets and an extensive range
of fine craft pottery.

The Source
26-40 Kensington High St, London W8 4PF.
T:0171-820 2865. F:0171-820 2762.
And branches in Essex and Southampton
New megastore stacked high with classic
household utensils.

Summerill & Bishop
100 Portland Rd, London W11 4LN.
T:0171-221 4566. F:0171-727 1322.
An inspirational kitchen shop; unusual
tableware, utensils and accessories from
around the world. 80% of their stock is new,
20% antique.

CATERING SUPPLIERS

GEC Anderson
See entry under **SINKS & TAPS.** Stainless
steel worktops, cabinets drawers and
shelves made to order in any size.

Britannia Catering
10 Brunswick Shopping Centre,
Bernard St, London WC1N 1AF.
T:0171-278 3137. F:0171-278 4578.

Catering equipment, especially furniture - trolleys, tables, chairs, dumbwaiters.

Hansen's Kitchen & Bakery Equipment
See entry under **INDUSTRIAL AND DOMESTIC APPLIANCES.**

Leon Jaeggi & Sons
77 Shaftesbury Ave, London W1V 7AD.
T:0171-434 4545. F:0171-494 3591.
Around 6000 lines in kitchen and catering equipment for professional cooks. Re-tinning and repair service for pans.

Pages
121 Shaftesbury Ave, London WC2H 8AD.
T:0171-379 6334. F:0171-240 9467.
8,000 square feet of cookware (200 saucepans), Dualit toasters and all restaurantware.

Staines Catering Equipment
15-19 Brewer St, London W1R 3FL.
T:0171-437 8424. F:0171-287 9463.
Authentic catering supplier - everything from white china to classic pans, from cookers to disposables. Stainless steel shelving and work surfaces to order.

Walley
728 London Rd, West Thurrock, Grays, Essex RM30 3LU.
T:01708-862862. F:01708-860217.
All tableware and catering equipment - down to the uniforms.

CHINA & GLASSWARE

Anta Scotland
Fearn, Tain, Ross-Shire IV20 1XW.
T:01862-832477. F:01862-832616.
Tartan tableware, traditional Scottish thistle and harebell motifs, and a children's range of hand sponged ceramics.

Asprey
165-169 New Bond St, London W1Y 0AR.
T:0171-493 6767. F:0171-491 0384.
Asprey's has three royal warrants: from the Queen, the Queen Mother and the Prince of Wales. They work mainly with five manufacturers - Bernardaud, Haviland and Herend for porcelain and Royal Worcester and Spode for fine bone china. Other manufacturers are also represented (Lalique, Baccarat, Peter Crisp). Exclusive Asprey designs can be personalized with gilded monograms or crests. Popular choice for wedding lists.

Maryse Boxer at Chez Joseph
26 Sloane St, London SW1X 7LQ.
T/F:0171-245 9493. Ceramic oven-to-table spongeware. Crackle-glaze gold and platinum trim porcelain, glasses, cutlery and tablecloths.

Emma Bridgewater
739 Fulham Rd, London SW6 5UL.
T:0171-371 9033. F:0171-584 2457.
Hand decorated spongeware pottery, quirky table-linen and some glassware.

Carden Cunietti
83 Westbourne Park Rd, London W2 5QH.
T:0171-229 8559. F:0171-229 8799.
American 'Brettware' stoneware, German and Belgian glassware, bamboo-handled cutlery from France.

Christofle
10 Hanover St, London W1R 9HF.
T:0171-491 4004. F:0171-491 3003.
Porcelain, silver and crystal tableware.

Designers Guild
267-271 King's Rd, London SW3 5EN.
T:0171-243 7300. F:0171-243 7710.
Wide selection of decorative china and glassware including a hand painted, Italian designed range produced in their own studio and another made by Rosenthal. There's a collection of wine glasses and goblets in bright colours, some imported from Mexico.

The Dining Room Shop
64 White Hart Lane, London SW13 0PZ.
T:0181-878 1020. F:0181-876 2367. New and period china and cutlery. Also antique tableware finding service.

Stephanie Fernald Ceramic Designs
10 Longley Rd, Rochester, Kent ME1 2HD.
T/F:01634-401427. Bone china tableware hand decorated with bugs, fossils, cats, dogs and fishing tackle.

*** denotes
trade supplier.
Please phone
for retail outlets.** 23

General Trading Company

144 Sloane St, London SW1X 9BL.
T:0171-730 0411. F:0171-823 4624.
Everything from Herend hand painted porcelain, Raynaud (from the Limoges region of France), Wedgwood, Spode, Royal Worcester to Emma Bridgewater and Holdenby Design earthenware. Also crystal by Baccarat, Waterford, Dartington and a large range of imported glass. Wedding lists.

Thomas Goode

19 South Audley St, London W1Y 6BN.
T:0171-499 2823. F:0171-629 4230.
Not just for wedding lists - a good place to see a vast selection of smart dinner services, tea and coffee cups, glassware and silverware.

Graham & Greene

7 Elgin Crescent London W11 2JA.
T:0171-727 4594. F:0171-229 9717.
Emma Bridgewater's breakfast range, Arthur Wood's brightly coloured pottery, gingham china, blue and white spongeware, Duralex tumblers, wine, shot and martini glasses - good selection of informal tableware.

Harrods

Knightsbridge SW1X 7XL
T:0171-730 1234. F:0171-581 0470.
Room after room with all major brands of china, porcelain, glassware and silver.

Isis Ceramics

The Old Toffee Factory,
120a Marlborough Rd, Oxford OX1 4LS.
T:01865-722729. F:01865-727521.
Blue and white hand-painted dinnerware, lamps and decorative pieces inspired by 17th and 18th century English delftware.

Geneviève Lethu

132 Brompton Rd, London SW3 1HY.
T/F:0171-581 9939. French tableware, cooking utensils and accessories.

Alison Moore Ceramics

Vyner Cottage, 3 Strensall Rd, Huntington, Yorks YO3 9RF.
T:01904-750236. F:01904-750443.
Bone china tableware with black and white designs from 18th century sources.

Pot Luck

84 Columbia Rd, London E2 7QB.
T:0171-722 6892. (Open only on Sun or by appointment). Oversized, cheap bone china plates and vitreous china hotelware. Huge pasta plates, jumbo cups and saucers; bone china cups and saucers for £2.50. Also undecorated oven to tableware.

Reject China Shop

183 Brompton Rd, London SW3 1NW.
T:0171-581 0739. F:0171-225 2283.
And 30 branches nationwide. All major brands of china (Royal Doulton, Royal Albert, Wedgwood, Haviland, Ginori etc) and glassware (Waterford, Stewart, Lalique, Baccarat).

Reject Pot Shop

56 Chalk Farm Rd, London NW1 8AN.
T/F:0171-485 2326. Seconds of major brands of undecorated bone china and earthenware.

Renwick & Clarke

190 Ebury Street, London SW1W 8UP.
T:0171-730 8913. F:0171-730 4508.
Decorative dinner services, English lead crystal, silver and cutlery.

Villeroy & Boch Factory Shop

267 Merton Rd, London SW18 5JS.
T:0181-870 4168. F:0181-871 1062.
Mainly seconds and discontinued lines, heavily discounted.

*Waterford Wedgwood

Josiah Wedgwood & Co, Barlaston, Stoke-On-Trent ST12 9ES.
T:01782-282293. F:01782-204141.
Call for outlets nationwide. Traditional patterned and white bone china.

William Yeoward

336 King's Rd, London SW3 5UR.
T:0171-351 5454. F:0171- 351 9469.
For other stockists call:

John Jenkins & Sons,

T:01730-821811. F:01730-821698.
Reproductions of Georgian and Regency glassware from some of the great houses of England and Ireland. There are 180 pieces in the range.

See also: One Stop Kitchen/Tableware Shops.

*Young & D
Beckhaven House, 9 Gilbert Rd,
London SE11 5AA.
T:0171-820 3796. F:0171-793 0537.
Retail shop: *Belle du Jour*
13 Flask Walk, London NW3 1HJ.
T:0171-431 4006.Manufacturer/wholesaler
of chunky, rustic, brightly coloured and hand
painted ceramic tableware, tinware,
glassware, galvanised items and furniture.

KITCHEN ANTIQUES

Below Stairs
103 High Street,
Hungerford, Berks RG17 0NB.
T:01488-682317. Specialists in 19th
century kitchen antiques like Victorian herb
cutters, breadcrocks and big tin flour bins.

Ann Lingard
Rope Walk Antiques, 18-20 Rope Walk,
Rye, E.Sussex TN31 7NA.
T:01797-223486. F:01797-224700.
19th and 20th century antique pine
furniture, china, glass, copper, brass
boxes and wooden objects.

Magpie's
152 Wandsworth Bridge Rd,
London SW6 2UH.
T:0171-736 3738. Selection of old kitchen
utensils and accessories: cutlery,
Cornishware, breadboards and bread bins.

Tobias And The Angel
66-68 White Hart Lane, London SW13 0PZ.
T:0181-878 8902. F:0181-878 8902.
Country style kitchen china and utensils,
table linen and decorative accessories.

Wenderton Antiques
T:01227-720295. By appointment.
Specialist in 18th, 19th and early 20th
century kitchen, laundry and dairy items.

CUTLERY

Garrard & Co
112 Regent's Street, London W1A 2JJ.
T:0171-734-7020. F:0171-734 0711.

Extensive range of cutlery, modern
and antique clocks,
novelty items, tea
sets and full dinner
services in sterling
silver and silver
plate. Special items
to commission.

Glazebrook & Co
PO Box 1563, London SW6 3XD.
T:0171-731 7135. F:0171-371 5434.
Stainless steel classics at affordable prices -
20 patterns to choose from.

Kings of Sheffield
319 Regent's St,London W1R7PF.
T:0171-637 9888. F:0171-255 687.
Classic designs in silver, silver plate and
stainless steel. Also
'Holloware' silver plate.

Langfords
Vault 8/10 London Silver Vaults,
Chancery Lane, London WC2A 1QS.
T:0171-242 5506. F:0171-405 0431.
Langfords will custom make silverware,
match family heirlooms and manufacture
trophies and presentation pieces. Large
stock of antique silver and Sheffield plate,
from cutlery to centrepieces.

United Cutlers of Sheffield
4 Grosvenor St, London W1X 9FB.
T/F:0171-493 1471. Fifteen patterns
available in stainless steel, silver plate and
sterling. There are main set sizes, ancillary
items and one-off pieces, direct from
the manufacturer.

TABLELINEN
& TEA TOWELS

The Blue Door
77 Church Rd, London SW13 9HH.
T:0181-748 9785. F:0181-563 1043.
Old and new table linen; tablecloths
made to order.

Bourne Street Linen
T/F:0171-376 1113. (By appointment)
Tea towels inspired by traditional linen glass

**See also: One Stop
Kitchen/Tableware
Shops and China &
Glassware.**

* denotes
trade supplier.
Please phone
for retail outlets. 25

cloths- a cut above the ordinary.
Mail order catalogue.

Maryse Boxer at Chez Joseph
See entry under CHINA & GLASSWARE.
Designer nappery.

Descamps
197 Sloane St, London SW1X 9QX.
T:0171-235 6957. F:0171-235 3903.
French designer table linen.

The Dining Room Shop
See entry under CHINA & GLASSWARE.
Both old and new table linen.

Thomas Ferguson & Co
Scarva Rd, Banbridge,
Co Down, Northern Ireland BT32 3AU.
T:018206-23491. F:018206-22453.
Irish tablelinen.

The Final Curtain Company
T:0181-699 3626.
Tablecloths made to order.

General Trading Company
See entry under CHINA & GLASSWARE.
Le Jacquard Francais collection.

Thomas Goode
See entry under CHINA & GLASSWARE.
Quality table linen.

Genevieve Lethu
See entry under CHINA & GLASSWARE.
French tablecloths and nappery.

The Linen Cupboard
21 Great Castle St, London W1N 7AA
T:0171-629 4062. All the best brands of
table linen at discounted prices.

Nordic Style at Moussie
109 Walton St, London, SW3 2HP.
T:0171-581 8674. Scandinavian range.

Tobias And The Angel
See entry under KITCHEN ANTIQUES
Old fashioned household linen: linen union
tea towels, linen scrim squares, woven
cotton floor cloths and coloured dusters.
Mail order catalogue.

*Turquaz
The Coach House, Bakery Place,
119 Altenburg Gardens, London SW11 1JQ.
T:0171-924 6894. F:0171-924 6868.
Indian cotton table linen. Mail order service.

*Walton & Company
Castle Mills, Trafalgar Rd,
Harrogate, N Yorks HG1 1HW.
T:01423-521964. F:10423-527910.
Household textile importer and distributor:
tablecloths, tablemats, tea towels, dish
cloths and scrim for windows.

White House
51-52 Bond St, London W1Y 0BY.
T:0171-629 3521. F:0171-629 8269.
Traditional top quality table linen.

OTHER SPECIALIST SERVICES & SUPPLIERS

Asprey
See entry under CHINA & GLASSWARE.
The Top Table department offers a
replacement handle service. Old bone
handles that have cracked or become loose
are replaced with new ones made from
a synthetic compound (it can be shaped
to match the original design).
Also customised china.

Berkshire China Co
298 King Street, Fenton,
Stoke-On-Trent, Staffs ST4 3EN.
T:01782-311447. F:01782-599386.
Good value bone china dinner plates, cups,
mugs, printed in-house with monograms,
logos and gilded edges.

Brass & Traditional Sinks
See entry under SINKS & TAPS.
Free-standing maple draining boards.

China Matching Service
Fern Lea, Frogmore,
Kingsbridge, Devon TQ7 2NZ.
T:01548-531372. Will buy and sell
complete or partial services and single
items of discontinued china by many
manufacturers (e.g. Royal Doulton,
Wedgwood, Denby).

Chinasearch
The Old Forge, Tainters Hill,
Kenilworth, Warwicks CV8 2GL.
T/F:01926-512402. By appointment.
Buy and sell recently discontinued dinner

tableware and pottery (Royal Worcester, Royal Doulton, Wedgwood, Hornsey, Poole and Denby) - from one item to a whole service. There's no charge for registration and one's request is kept on file if it can't be fulfilled immediately. They will post world-wide.

Richard Cook
Unit B16, 31 Clerkenwell Close, London EC1R 0AT.
T/F:0171-608 1587. Can refurbish sheer-steel knife blades.

Countrywide Workshops
47 Fisherton St, Salisbury, Wilts SP2 7SU. T:01722-326886. F:01722-411092. Representing 90 workshops, the catalogue provides by mail order hundreds of items from beds to brushes made by disabled ex-servicemen. Re-bristling service also available.

The Dining Room Shop
See entry under CHINA & GLASSWARE. Antique china finding service.

The Domestic Paraphernalia Company
Unit 15, Marine Business Centre, Dock Rd, Lytham, Lancs FY8 5AJ. T:01253-736334. F:01253-795191. The "Sheila Maid" cast iron and pine clothes airer is featured in their mail order catalogue.

Mark Fox
Unit 305, 31 Clerkenwell Close, London EC1R 0AT. T/F:0171-253 6200. Standard replating and repair of damaged cutlery - knives re-bladed, dents removed, spoons and forks straightened or repronged.

Garrard & Co.
See entry under CUTLERY. Silver replating and gilding service. Full silver-smithing in their own workshops.

*Garrods of Barking
Abbey Works, Linton Rd, Barking, Essex IG11 8HU. T:0181-594 0224. F:0181-594 0225. A family owned business which has produced traditional galvanised dustbins for over a century.

Glazebrook & Co
See entry under CUTLERY. Re-plating

service. Damaged pieces can be replaced to make up a complete set.

Thomas Goode
See entry under CHINA & GLASSWARE. Mini-museum for designs created for ruling houses the world over including Sèvres plates designed for Catherine the Great in 1776 (copied in bone china by Goode in the 19th century). Contemporary commissions to order including personalising an existing design with a monogram, coat of arms or family crest.

Lakeland Plastics
Alexandra Buildings, Windermere, Cumbria LA23 1BQ. T:015394-88100. F:015394-88300. Mail order company with all sorts of kitchen gadgets and practical ovenware and storage items - everything from sugar mice moulds to lattice pastry cutters.

Richard Lawton
32-34 Greville St, London EC1N 8TB. T:0171-404 0487. All sorts of repairs to silver and plate, including fitting new handles, replacing blue glass liners, rebristling of brushes, repairing frame backs.

The Royal Doulton Company
Minton House, London Rd, Stoke-on-Trent, Staffs ST4 7QP. T:01782-292292.F:01782-292099. This manufacturer will handle private commissions for one-off, hand-painted designs on any of their existing shapes.

Tablewhere ?
9 Church St, London NW8 8EE. T:0171-706 4586. F:0171-706 2948. Computerised database of old dinner and tea services. Their affiliate, The Collector, specialises in collectables.

The Tenterden Collection
Tenterden House Interiors, 4 West Cross, Tenterden, Kent TN30 6JL. T:01580-764481. F:01580-765531. Over 700 items of pewter based on old designs - everything from underdishes to bowls, wine coolers, cutlery and candlesticks.

* denotes trade supplier. Please phone for retail outlets.

2

BATHROOMS

SHOWROOMS

Abacus
681-689 Holloway Rd, London N19 5SE.
T:0171-281 4136. F:0171-272 5081.
Traditional bathroom showroom (Heritage, Ideal Standard and others). Also kitchens and a builders' merchant.

Alternative Plans
9 Hester Rd, London SW11 4AN.
T:0171-228 6460. F:0171-924 1164.
Very contemporary, mainly Italian, sanitaryware - limestone basins and stainless steel fittings. Plus individually designed continental kitchens.

Aston Matthews
141-147a Essex Rd, London N1 2SN.
T:0171-226 3657. F:0171-354 5951.
Established in 1823, this is the largest stockist of cast-iron baths in England, with 26 models in 16 sizes. Good selection of all other bathroom equipment too: basins, shower heads, ceramic shower trays, stainless steel basins and toilets.They have a range of very small handbasins in both china and steel.

Aylsham Bath & Door
Burgh Rd, Aylsham, Norfolk NR11 6AR.
T:01263-735396. F:01263-734800.
Trade and retail prices for bathroom suites and cast iron baths. Shower specialist. Bespoke kitchens and bedrooms.

Bathroom City
Amington Rd, Tyseley, Birmingham B25 8ET.
T:0121-708 0111. F:0121-706 6561.
Bathroom suites (including whirlpools and steam cabinets); Italian tiles; joinery service.

Bathroom Discount Centre
297 Munster Rd, London SW6 6BW.
T:0171-381 4222. F:0171-381 6792.
Open seven days a week. Bathroom suites and central heating systems. Good selection of whirlpool baths, uncommon sanitaryware, steam showers, pumps, tiles. One can also test showers.

The Bathroom Store
75 Upper Richmond Rd, London SW15 2SZ.
T:0181-870 8888. F:0181-875 9588.

Branches in Fulham and Barnet. Period style sanitaryware at discount prices.

The Bathroom Studio
14 Church Rd, Sidcup, Kent DA14 6BX.
T:0181-302 4023. F:0181-300 3212.
They represent major brands like Ideal Standard, Armitage Shanks, Twyfords and Balterley - plus exclusive ranges such as Villeroy & Boch and Jacob Delafon.

The Bathroom Warehouse Group
Unit 3, Wykeham Est, Moorside Rd, Winnall, Winchester, Hants SO23 7RX.
T:01962-862554. F:01962-840927.
Showroom for bathroom suites, showers, jacuzzis, steam and sauna rooms, with a full design and installation service.

Burge & Gunson
13-23 High St, Colliers Wood,
London SW19 2JE.
T:0181-543 5166. F:0181-543 6610.
Bathroom showroom where you can try out showers, whirlpools and jacuzzis. All sorts of heating and plumbing products - from economy to luxury.

Colourwash Bathrooms
63-65 Fulham High St, London SW6 3JJ.
T:0171-371 0911.
And at:
165 Chamberlayne Rd, London NW10 3NU.
T:0181-459 8918. F:0181-459 4280.
And at:
1 Broom Hall Buildings, London Rd,
Sunningdale, Berks SL5 0DH.
T:01344-872096. F:01344-872257.
Traditional and modern bathroom fittings. Full sourcing service for all UK products. Will always endeavour to match other companies' prices. Design service and recommended installers.

The Complete Bathroom
61-63 Ber St, Norwich, Norfolk NR1 3AD.
T:01603-662716. F:01603-761529.
Domestic or commercial, traditional or modern, bathrooms and kitchens - complete installations including appliances and flooring.

Czech & Speake
39C Jermyn St, London SW1Y 6DN.
T:0171-439 0216. F:0171-734 8587.
High quality reproduction Edwardian range which extends to toiletries in smart packaging.

Designer Bathrooms
The Studio, Cartland Rd, Kings Heath, Birmingham, W.Midlands B14 7NS.
T:0121-444 0102. F:0121-441 1020.
Different special offers every month on towel rails and bathroom suites; they specialise in Villeroy & Boch, Jacuzzi, Teuco.

Richard Doughty Bathrooms
166-172 Little Glen Rd,
Glen Parva, Leics LE2 9TT.
T/F:0116-277 3561. Showroom for bathroom suites, fittings and tiles from Victorian to modern. Design and installation service.

Elon Tiles
66 Fulham Rd, London SW3 6HH.
T:0171-460 4600. F:0171-460 4601.
Contemporary bathroom fittings.

CP Hart
Newnham Terrace, Hercules Rd,
London SE1 7DR.
T:0171-902 1000. F:0171-902 1001.
From reproduction period fixtures and fittings, including roll top cast iron baths on brass feet to Philippe Starck's ultra-modern, ultra-expensive range - a showroom with an extensive selection of products on display (including a Duravit mini-basin, ARC taps etc). Also Siematic kitchens.

Just Bathrooms
Pembroke Ave, Denny End,
Waterbeach, Cambs CB5 9PB.
T:01223-863631. F:01223-576863.

Over 35 suites on display in room settings. Working 'airbaths', jacuzzis, whirlpools, and showers. Also tiles, lighting and accessories.

Lumley's
123-129 Portland Rd, Hove,
Sussex BN3 5QW.
T:01273-746161. F:01273-746116.
Traditional bathroom showroom for brands like Armitage Shanks, Heritage and Twyfords. Free design service - installation can be arranged and all styles sourced.

Miscellanea of Churt
Crossways, Churt, Farnham,
Surrey GU10 2JA.
T:01428-714014. F:01428-712946.
And branches in Bournemouth, Risca and Tring. Claim to have the largest selection of bathroomware in Britain including old stock of 'obsolete' colours. They have their own workshops for the manufacture of bespoke furniture, kitchens and bedrooms.

Original Bathrooms
143-145 Kew Rd, Richmond,
Surrey TW9 2PN.
T:0181-940 7554. F:0181-948 8200.
From Victorian to modern designs, mainly Italian, including coloured basins (terracotta, navy blue) combined with stainless steel and glass. Vast range of showers, saunas and steam cubicles including custom built body sprays and jets.

Max Pike Bathrooms
4 Eccleston St, London SW1W 9LN.
T:0171-730 7216. F:0171-730 3789.
Design and supply standard and unusual bathrooms - from the traditional English bath to high tech designs. Manufacture their own range of baths in 'Vitrite' composite.

Pipe Dreams
72 Gloucester Rd, London SW7 4QT.
T:0171-225-3978. F:0171-589 8841.
Bespoke bathrooms with full installation service. Specialist in steam showers, whirlpools, jacuzzis. They also manufacture their own furniture. Export worldwide.

Ripples
Chelsea House, London Rd,
Bath, Somerset BA1 6DB.

T:01225-447971. F:01225-483725.
And branch in Bristol. Large bathroom showroom for domestic and contract installations. All major brands represented.

Simply Bathrooms
410-414 Upper Richmond Rd West,
London SW14 7SX.
T:0181-878 2727. F:0181-878 2225.
Aqualisa, Salamander, Vitra, Heritage, Kaldewei, Kermi, Hansgrohe and others. Bedroom furniture and a design and installation service.

Sitting Pretty
122 Dawes Rd, London SW6 7EG.
T:0171-381 0049. F:0171-385 9621.
Specialists in Victorian, Art Nouveau and Art Deco style sanitaryware.

West One Bathrooms
46 South Audley St, London W1Y 5DG.
T:0171-499 1845. F:0171-629 9311.
Sourcing service and custom designed bathrooms. Specialise in unusual accessories and continental brassware. Excellent selection of showers.

B & P Wynn & Co
60 Queenstown Rd, London SW8 3RY.
T:0171-498 4345. F:0171-498 4346.
Original collection of taps in nickel, brass, chrome, old copper. French 'Maurice Herbeau' range includes decorated tubs, sinks and wooden throne-like loos; modern Viala suites and fittings.

MANUFACTURERS & DISTRIBUTORS OF FITTINGS & TAPS

Aqualisa Products
The Flyers Way, Westerham, Kent TN16 1DE.
T:01959-560000. F:01959-560030.
High quality showers.

Armitage Shanks
Old Rd, Armitage, Nr Rugeley,
Staffs WS15 4BT.
T:01543-490253. F:01543-491677. Large selection of ceramic and acrylic baths, taps, fittings, showers, vanity units, cubicles and accessories. Domestic and commercial.

All these manufacturers and distributors are trade only. Please phone for local retail stockists.

Barber Wilsons & Co
Crawley Rd, Westbury Ave, London N22 6AH.
T:0181-888 3461. F:0181-888 2041.
Traditional tap manufacturers since 1905:
pillar, china lever, bib taps and manual and
concealed shower and bath fittings.

Bathrooms International
54 The Burroughs, London NW4 4AN.
T:0181-202 1002. F:0181-202 6439.
Distributors for French companies JCD and
THG . There are over 100 items: taps,
sanitaryware, accessories. The taps come in
crystal, gold, brass, copper, nickel and any
other finish.

Bedfordshire Bathroom Distributors
Unit 10/5A, Elston Storage
Depot, Kempston,
Hardwick, Bedford MK45
3NS. T:01234-741441.
F:01234-741278.
Distributors for Qualitas,
Aqualux, Just Tray, Trojan,
Watermill, Allied and
Mayfair Britannia.

Caradon Bathrooms
Lawton Rd, Alsager,
Stoke-on-Trent,
Staffs ST7 2DF.
T:01270-879777. F:01270-873864.
Manufacturer of Doulton acrylic baths and
suites and Twyfords fittings for kitchens and
bathrooms. There are acrylic and steel
baths, fireclay sinks and fittings for hospitals
(baths for the elderly and disabled), offices,
even prisons. Twyfords also has at least
five very small handbasins in seven colours.

Crangrove
Crangrove House, Coronation Rd,
Park Royal, London NW10 7QH.
T:0181-453 0212. F:0181-961 7357.
Manufacturers of bathroom suites, kitchens
and heating and plumbing products.

Danico Brass
31-35 Winchester Rd, London NW3 3NR.
T:0171-483 4477. F:0171-722 7992.
Taps and accessories in many finishes -

All these manufacturers and distributors are trade only. Please phone for local retail stockists.

chrome, chrome/gold, nickel, nickel/gold,
chrome/brass and others.

Daryl Industries
Alfred Rd, Wallasey Wirral,
Merseyside L44 7HY.
T:0151-638 8211. F:0151-638 0303.
Specialists in bespoke and standard
shower enclosures and bath screens.

Jacob Delafon
Unit 1 Churchward, Southmead Park,
Didcot, Oxon OX11 7HB.
T:01235-510511. F:01235-510481.
Largest French manufacturer of ceramic
basins, bidets and acrylic, steel and cast
iron baths.

Dornbracht
UK Agent, Locky's Orchard, Broadmead
Lane, Norton sub Hamdon,
Somerset TA14 6SS.
T:01935-881418. F:01935-881404.
From traditional Victorian cross to modern
single lever taps for the basin, bidet, bath
and shower; thermostatic and mixer taps in
either chrome, gold, platinum or polished
brass. Their newest range has a translucent
coloured jacket which fits over the chrome
taps. Matching range of towel bars, rings,
holders, grab bars, crystal soap dishes,
shelves and tumblers.

Grohe
1 River Rd, Barking, Essex IG11 0HD.
T:0181-594 7292. F:0181-594 8898.
Europe's largest manufacturer of taps
and showers.

A & J Gummers
Unit H, Redfern Park Way, Tyseley,
Birmingham B11 2DN.
T:0121-706 2241. F:0121-706 2960.
Manufacture thermostatic and manual
showers for both commercial and domestic
installations.

Hansgrohe
Unit D1& D2, Sandown Park Trading Estate,
Royal Mills, Esher, Surrey KT10 8BL.
T:01372-465655. F:01372-470670.
Modern shower heads, taps, fittings
and accessories.

Heritage Bathrooms
Unit 1A, Princess St,
Bedminster, Bristol BS3 4AG.
T:0117-963 9762. F:0117-923 1078.
Edwardian and Victorian designs.

Ideal Standard
The Bathroom Works, National Ave,
Kingston-Upon-Hull, E. Yorks HU5 4HS.
T:01482-346461. F:01482-445886.
Manufacturer of contemporary bathroom
suites - 15 in their range.

The Imperial Bathroom Company
Imperial Buildings, Northgate Way, Aldridge,
Walsall, W. Midlands WS9 8SR.
T:01922-743536. F:01922-743180.
Victorian and Edwardian sanitaryware, taps,
accessories and bathroom furniture.

Jacuzzi
17 Mount St, London W1Y 5RA.
T:0171-409 1776. F:0171-495 2353.
Manufacturer of whirlpool baths and
hydrotherapy showers.

Koralle
Coventry Point, Market Way,
Coventry, W Midlands CV1 1EB.
T:01203-257212. F:01203-525321.
Contemporary bathrooms by Royal Dutch
Sphinx and shower enclosures by the
German company Koralle.

Laufen/Bellgrove
Salisbury Rd, Watling St,
Dartford, Kent DA2 6EL.
T:01322-277877. F:01322-225282.
Laufen's modern selection includes a bath
suite by the industrial designer FA Porsche.
Bellgrove distribute sanitaryware and tiles.

Lefroy Brooks
Marston Rd, Wolverhampton WV2 4LX.
T:01902-21922. F:01902-27109.
Traditional Edwardian style taps and shower
fittings, lavatory chinaware and shower
curtain rails including the 'Edwardian hoop'.

The Majestic Shower Company
1 North Place, Edinburgh Way,
Harlow, Essex CM20 2SL.
T:01279-443644. F:01279-635074.
Range of frameless glass shower
screens.Specials made to order.

Matki
Churchward Rd, Yate, Bristol BS17 5PL.
T:01454-322888. F:01454-315284.
Shower screens, trays and surrounds.

Mira Showers
Caradon Mira, Cromwell Rd,
Cheltenham, Gloucs GL52 5EP.
T:01242-221221. F:01242-224721.
Good range of electric power mixer
showers and accessories.

Pegler
St Catherine's Ave, Doncaster,
S.Yorks DN4 8DF.
T:01302-368581. F:01302-367661.
Showers, bathroom fittings and heating
supplies.

Qualitas Bathrooms
Hartshorne Rd, Woodville, Swadlincote,
Derbys DE11 7JD.
T:01283-550550. F:01283-550314.
Six suites in their range.

Roca
Samson Rd, Hermitage Ind Estate,
Coalville, Leics LE67 3FP.
T:01530-830080. F:01530-830010.
Large selection of baths in all shapes and
sizes in cast iron, steel and acrylic.

B C Sanitan
Silverdale Rd,
Newcastle Under Lyme, Staffs ST5 6EL.
T:01782-717175. F:01782-717166.
Period style fittings and accessories.

Shires Bathrooms
Beckside Rd, Bradford, W.Yorks BD7 2JE.
T:01274-521199. F:01274-521583.
Baths, showertrays, WCs, basins, bidets,
taps and mixers.

Showeristic
Unit 10, Manor Ind Estate,
Flintshire CH6 5UY.
T:01352-735381. F:01352-763388.
Standard and made to order range of
shower enclosures.

Sottini
The Bathroom Works, National Ave,
Kingston-Upon-Hull, E.Yorks HU5 4HS.
T:01482-449513. F:01482-445886. Luxury
bathroom suites, furniture and accessories.

**The British Bathroom Council also has a list of members.
T:01782-747074.
F:01782-747161.**

**The National Association of Plumbing, Heating & Mechanical Services Contractors,
14-15 Ensign Business Centre,
Westwood Way Business Park,
Coventry
T:01203-470626.
F:01203-470942
has a list of members all over the country.**

Tantofex
Birches Ind Estate, Imberhorne Lane,
East Grinstead, W. Sussex RH19 1XG.
T:01342-328166. F:01342-410353.
Manufacturer of taps and shower kits
with handles in chrome, gold plate,
brass, acrylic, ceramic and colours.

Technical Exponents
Denham Green Lane,
Denham, Middx UB9 5LA.
T:01753-644004. F:01753-644179.
Manufacturer of two double baths
available in any colour.

Trevi Showers
The Bathroom Works, National Ave,
Kingston-Upon-Hull, E. Yorks HU5 4HS.
T:01482-470788. F:01482-445886.
Ideal Standard's specialist shower division.
They can custom design any shower.

Triton
Triton House, Newdegate St, Nuneaton,
Warwicks CV11 4EU. T:01203-344441.
F:01203-349828. Britain's largest
manufacturer of electric mixer and
power showers.

Twyfords
See Caradon Bathrooms.

Vernon Tutbury
Silverdale Rd,
Newcastle-Under-Lyme, Staffs ST5 6EL.
T:01782-717175. F:01782-717166.
Victorian style bathroom sanitaryware.

Villeroy & Boch UK
267 Merton Rd, London SW18 5JS.
T:0181-871 4028. F:0181-8703720.
Administration only. Continental-look
sanitary ware from this German company,
including Art Deco and modern ranges in
13 colours and 4 different whites.

Vola
Unit 12, Ampthill Business Park, Station Rd,
Ampthill, Bedford MK45 2QW.
T:01525-841155. F:01525-841177.
Arne Jacobsen's elegant range of taps - the
ultimate modern mixer and bib taps for bath,
shower and basin. Also stylish three-hole
combinations and pull out showers.
Minimalist accessories.

PLUMBING SUPPLIERS

Chelsea Plumbing & Heating Centre Suppliers & Installers
425 Kings Rd, London SW10 0LR.
T:0171-352 8757. F:0171-352 2670.
Full range of bathroom suites by Daryl,
Aqualisa and Grohe.

Edwins Plumbing & Heating Supplies
17 All Saints Rd, London W11 1HA.
T:0171-221 3550. F:0171-243 0206.
Good selection of power showers, steam
enclosures, roll top baths, ranging from
budget to top end of the market.
Manufacturers include Philippe Starck,
Vola, Jacuzzi, Imperial and Majestic.

General Plumbing Supplies
66 York Way, London N1 9AG.
T:0171-837 2424. F:0171-833 0058.
Basically a trade counter, but the public is
also welcome. Armitage Shanks, Grohe,
Aqualisa, Triton, Mira, Ideal Standard and
others.

Plumbcraft
Unit 2, Ellerslie Square, off Lyham Rd,
London SW2 5DZ.
T:0171-274 0174. F:0171-737 1435.
Chrome pillar basin taps at £35.23; steel
bathtubs at £64.62. Central heating,
bathroom and kitchen appliances.

Sanitary Appliances
3 Sandford Rd, Kimpton Rd Ind Estate,
Sutton, Surrey SM3 9RN.
T:0181-641 0310. F:0181-641 6426.
Suppliers of taps, chinaware and stainless
steel appliances. They manufacture their
own range of brass taps.

STEEL/GLASS/WOOD FITTINGS

GEC Anderson
89 Herkomer Rd, Bushey, Herts WD2 3LS
T:0181-950 1826. F:0181-950 3626.
Manufacturer of stainless steel sinks, bowls,
baths, mirrors, WCs and worktops for
domestic or commercial use and made to
measure in any shape or size.

Jeff Bell
299 Haggerston Rd, London E8 4EN.
T:0171-275 8481. Can make a glass bath, hand-basin or shower screen to commission.

William Garvey
Leyhill, Upton, Payhembury,
Honiton, Devon EX14 0JG.
T:01404-841430. F:01404-841626.
Iroko wood sinks designed and made to order.

*Santric
Hawksworth, Swindon, Wilts SN2 1DZ.
T:01793-536756. F:01793-512857.
Stainless steel industrial sinks, taps, loos, showers and shower cubicles. Free-standing drench showers.

*W & G Sissons
Carrwood Rd, Sheepbridge,
Chesterfield S41 9QB.
T:01246-450255. F:01246-451276.
Suppliers of hospital and commercial sinks and taps in stainless steel.

RECLAIMED FITTINGS & TAPS

Alscot Bathrooms
The Stable Yard, Alscot Park,
Stratford-On-Avon, Warwicks CV37 8BL.
T/F:01789-450861 (Open Fri, Sat and Sun).
Largest stock of original Art Deco sanitaryware in the country. Also Victorian and Edwardian baths, taps and china fully restored to comply with modern standards.

The Antique Bath and Tap Studio
Chapel Court, Hospital St, Nantwich,
Cheshire CW5 5RP.
T:01270-628108. F:01270-627632.
Supplies restored stove-enamelled period baths and will re-enamel customers' own baths. Refurbished French baths are a speciality. Models with tap in the middle, others with seats. Plus reproduction 1930s handbasins and taps.

Antique Baths of Ivybridge
Erme Bridge Works, Ermington Rd,
Ivybridge, Devon PL21 9DE.
T:01752-698250. F:01752-698266.
And at:

14 Blackboy Rd, Exeter, Devon EX4 6SW.
T:01392-425544. F:01392-425572.
Large stock of roll top baths, shower drench heads, Belfast sinks and taps.

Au Temps Perdu
Architectural Salvage & Antiques,
5 Stapleton Rd, Bristol BS5 0QR.
T:0117-9555223.
French and English bidets, roll top baths, Belfast sinks and renovated taps with guaranteed plating in nickel, chrome or brass.

Baileys
The Engine Shed, Ashburton Ind. Estate,
Ross-On-Wye, Herefordshire HR9 7BW.
T:01989-563015. F:01989-768172.
Original and reproduction fixtures and fittings; cast iron roll top baths. Reconditioned taps, reproduction bath sets, small round (15" across) porcelain sinks - all reasonably priced.

The Bath Doctor
See entry under SPECIALIST SERVICES & SUPPLIERS. Antique French sanitaryware. Normally has 50 to 70 restored baths in stock.

Bathshield
See entry under SPECIALIST SERVICES& SUPPLIERS.
Large stock of Victorian roll-top baths, reconditioned taps, reclaimed basins,
WC's, cisterns and Belfast sinks.

Drummond's of Bramley
Birtley Farm, Horsham Rd,
Bramley, Surrey GU5 0LA.
T:01483-898766. F:01483-894393. Canopy, roll top and plunger baths, marble and pedestal basins, lavatories, wooden loo seats and thunderboxes, Butler and Belfast sinks. They have a specialist vitreous re-enamelling service for customers' baths which they are confident will last for 50 years.

The House Hospital
68 Battersea High St, London SW11 3HX.
T:0171-223 3179.
Salvaged bathroom fittings from schools and houses.

See also chapter on ARCHITECTURAL SALVAGE.

*denotes trade supplier. Please phone for retail outlets

Old Fashioned Bathrooms
Village End, Little London Hill, Debenham, Stowmarket, Suffolk IP14 6PW.
T:01728-860926. F:01728-860446. Original roll top baths, traditional Victorian and Edwardian fixtures including brackets, brass taps and bath racks.

Posh Tubs
Moriarti's Workshop, High Halden, Ashford, Kent TN26 3LZ.
T/F:01233-850155. Specialists in fully restored antique sanitaryware including canopy and plunger baths, towel rails, basins, high and low level cisterns and cast iron radiators. They also offer a restoration service either on or off site for clients' own fittings and a specialist engineering service for taps.

Stiffkey Bathrooms
See entry under **SPECIALIST SERVICES & SUPPLIERS.** Restored English and French baths, basins, taps and mixer taps.

Water Monopoly
16-18 Lonsdale Rd, London NW6 6RD.
T:0171-624 2636. F:0171-624 2631.
Suppliers of top of the range original French and English bath fittings dating from 1880 to 1920. Their unusual selection includes pedestal basins, extra-large baths and accessories. Restoration service.

FITTED BATHROOM CABINETS

Hayloft Woodwork
3 Bond Street, London W4 1QZ.
T:0181-747 3510. F:0181-742 1860.

Plain English
The Tannery, Combs, Stowmarket, Suffolk IP14 2EN.
T:01449-774028. F:01449-613519.

All these companies will make fitted bathroom cabinetry to specific designs, but for many more see also: SPECIALIST SUPPLIERS & SERVICES - Joiners.

36

Robinson and Cornish
Southay House, Oakwood Close, Roundswell, Barnstable, North Devon EX31 3NJ.
T:01271-329300. F:01271-328277.

Smallbone of Devizes
105-109 Fulham Rd, London SW3 6RL.
T:0171-589 5998. F:0171-581 9415.

Tim Wood
93 Mallinson Rd, London SW11 1BL.
T:0171-924 1511. F:0171-924 1522.

BATHROOM CUPBOARDS

*Allibert Bathrooms
Berry Hill Ind Estate, Droitwich, Worcs WR9 9AB.
T:01905-795796. F:01905-794454.
Large selection of mirrored bathroom cabinets.

Aria
133 & 295 Upper St, London N1 1QP.
T:0171-704 1999. F:0171-704 6333.
Simple cabinets to blend with modern designs. 'Visnu' has a chrome interior and a mirrored front with or without inset lights. The 'Porthole' mirrored cabinet comes in four primary colours and 'Tincan' is in blue and white distressed wood.

*Authentics
20 High St, Weybridge, Surrey KT13 8AB.
T:01932-859800. F:01932-856493.
Stainless steel bathroom cabinets with mirrored doors and integrated lighting.

CP Hart
See entry under **SHOWROOMS.**
Good range of bathroom cabinets.

SCP
135-139 Curtain Rd, London EC2A 3BX.
T:0171-739 1869. F:0171-729 4224.
Thomas Erikssons's lacquer medical cross cabinet.

*W Schneider & Co (UK)
Ten Acres, Chobham Rd, Ottershaw, Surrey KT16 0QB.
T:01932-872137. F:01932-875366.
Illuminated mirror cabinets and mirrors for domestic and commercial installations.

BATHROOM SURFACES

Amari Plastics
Unit 2, Cumberland Ave, London NW10 7RL.
T:0181-961 1961. F:0181-961 9194.
Coloured perspex in sheet form.

*GEC Anderson
See entry under **STEEL/GLASS/WOOD FITTINGS.** Stainless steel surfaces manufactured to order.

DuPont Corian®
McD Marketing, Maylands Ave, Hemel Hempstead, Herts HP2 7DP.
T:01442-346776. F:01442-346755.
Corian® is a durable, hygienic solid material made only by DuPont. It comes in 40 colours including plain, veined and granular. Useful for vanity tops, shower trays, wall cladding.

R Denny
Unit 1, Fortune Way, Triangle Business Centre, London NW10 6UF.
T:0181-964 9368. F:0181-964 9369.
Acrylic fabrication - they can apply perspex to many surfaces or manufacture furniture.

Euromarble
155 Bowes Rd, London N11 2JA.
T:0181-888 2304. F:0181-888 9006.
Source for all natural stone - marble, granite, limestone. They will supply or supply and install for both domestic and contract refurbishments.

Charles Hurst
Unit 21, Bow Triangle Business Centre, Eleanor St, London E3 4NP.
T:0181-981 8562.
Kiln dried tongue-and-groove panelling in pine, to four designs (£2.85m plus VAT). Plus high quality bespoke joinery.

*ICI Acrylics
P O Box 34, Darwin, Lancs BB3 1QB.
T:01254-874444. F:01254-873300.
Huge range of perspex.

Kirkstone Quarries
Skelwith Bridge, Ambleside, Cumbria PA22 9NN.
T:015394-33296. F:015394-34006.
Volcanic stone traditionally known as Westmoreland green slate.

Marble Arch
431 & 432 Gordon Business Centre, Gordon Grove, London SE5 9DU.
T:0171-738 7212. F:0171-738 7613.
Marble, granite and limestone for cladding, floors and vanity units.

WH Newson & Sons
61 Pimlico Rd, London SW1W 8NF.
T:0171-978 5000. F:0171-924 1682.
Call for other branches. Timber merchant who stocks tongue-and-groove panelling at 74p per metre for strips 94mm wide.

*Sylmar Technology
Jenna House, Jenna Way, Newport, Pagnell, Bucks MK16 9QA.
T:01908-210505. F:01908-210101.
Distributors of Avonite and Swanstone (solid surface materials similar to Corian) used for pre-moulded sinks, vanity bowls, bathroom surfaces, wall cladding, shower trays and cubicle panels. They can recommend fabricators to make up any of these.

Vitruvius
Unit 20, Ransome's Dock, 35 Parkgate Rd, London SW11 4NP.
T:0171-223 8209. F:0171-924 3045.
Marble for vanity units.

GR Wiltshire
Main Rd, Claybrooke, Magna, Leics LE17 5AQ.
T:01455-202666. F:01455-209041.
Suppliers of all sorts of marine-standard hardwoods, including 'Ekki' wood - a tropical hardwood that is as water resistant as teak.

Zarka Marble
41A Belsize Lane, London NW3 5AU.
T:0171-431 3042. F:0171-431 3879.
All marbles and granites supplied for cladding and bathroom surfaces.

HEATED TOWELS RAILS

*Acova Radiators (UK)
30 Roland Way, Hoo Farm Ind Estate, Kidderminster, Worcs DY11 7RA.
T:01562-753001. F:01562-69413.
Manufacturers of designer and towel drying radiators. There are contemporary designs,

*denotes
trade supplier.
Please phone
for retail outlets

a vertical radiator with a full-height mirror and traditional ball jointed towel rails.

Black Country Heritage
See entry under
BATHROOM ACCESSORIES.

*Dimplex (UK)
Millbrook, Southampton SO15 0AW.
T:01703-785133. F:01703-704892.
Oil filled and dry electric towel radiators and rails in many designs and finishes - chrome, stove enamelled and brass.

*Heating World Group
Excelsior Works, Eyre St, Birmingham, Manchester B18 7AD.
T:0121-454 2244. F:0121-454 4488.
Towel rails in chrome, any enamel finish, even gold plated. They run off central heating, electricity, or either. Special orders.

*Imperial Towel Rails
Unit C, Orbital 5, Orbital Way, Cannock, Staffs WS11 3XW. T:01543-571615.
F:01543-571616. Electric and dual fuel towel rails; tubular bath and shower rails and period style column radiators. They also manufacture an ingenious heated bench which is popular for conservatories.

MHS Radiators
35 Nobel Square, Burnt Mills Ind. Estate, Basildon, Essex SS13 1LT.
T:01268-591010. F:01268-728202.
Range of six contemporary tubular towel rails, including the 'Monobad S' radiator/towel rail.

*Myson
Victoria Works, Nelson St,
Bolton, Lancs BL3 2DW.
T:01204-382017. F:01204-398920.
400 towel warmers in chrome, polished brass, 22 ct gold or colour-matched to order.

*PMP
Stanton Square, Stanton Way,
London SE26 5AB.
T:0181-676 0911. F:0181-659 1017.
70 models of towel radiators in brass, gold or chromium plate.

Radiating Style
Unit 15 Derby Rd, Derby Rd Ind Estate, Hounslow, Middx TW3 3UQ.
T:0181-577 9111. F:0181-577 9222.
Distributors of the 'Ecoterm' heated towel rails in five styles, enamel and metallic finishes, either dual fuel or electric only.

*Vogue
Units 9 & 10 Strawberry Lane Ind Estate, Strawberry Lane, Willenhall,
W. Midlands WV13 3RS.
T:01902-637330. F:01902-604532.
Heated towel rails in traditional and modern designs in a variety of finishes. Bespoke basin stands and shower curtain rails.

*Zehnder
Unit 6, Invincible Rd, Farnborough, Hants GU14 7QU. T:01252-515151. F:01252-522528. Contemporary towel radiators stocked in standard white and to order in over 100 colours.

BATHROOM ACCESSORIES

Aero
96 Westbourne Grove, London W2 5RT.
T:0171-221 1950. F:0171-221 2555.
Selection of magnifying mirrors, modern wood and chrome bath shelves, bath tidy, toilet roll holders and towel rails.
Mail order catalogue orderline T:0181-871 4030. F:0181-870 8227

Architectural Components
4-8 Exhibition Road, London SW7 7HF.
T:0171-581 2401. F:0171-589 4928.
'Demista' bathroom mirrors, medicine cabinets, wooden loo seats, toilet brushes, magnifying mirrors and traditional bathroom accessories.

Aria
See entry under
BATHROOM CUPBOARDS.
Wide range of bathroom accessories from chrome shelves to wicker baskets. Mirrors, wooden bath mats, towels and toiletries.

Bisca Design
Shaw Moor Farm, Harome, Yorks YO6 5HZ.
T:01439-771702. F:01439-771002.
Original range of stainless steel bathtrays, rails, soap, toothbrush, loo roll holders and mirrors, all with a distinctive curl.

Black Country Heritage
Britannia House, Mill St,
Brierley Hill, Worcs DY5 2TH.
T:01384-480810. F:01384-482866.
Accessories for home and top class hotel
bathrooms including towel warmers, tilting,
magnifying or make-up mirrors, shelves,
bathracks, soap and sponge carriers and
washstand supports.

Maryse Boxer at Chez Joseph
26 Sloane St, London SW1X 7LQ.
T/F:0171-245 9493.
Luxurious towels and ceramic accessories
with gold and platinum trim; a complete
storage range of containers, trays and
boxes in black and white.

Julian Chichester Designs
Unit 12, 33 Parsons Green Lane,
London SW6 4HH.
T:0171-371 9055. F:0171-371 9066.
Teak bath mats and racks.

Charles Collinge Architectural Ironmongery
44 Loman St, London SE1 0EH.
T:0171-928 3541. F:0171-620 1326.
Traditional chrome swivel arm towel rails,
wall mounted or extending mirrors and soap
racks; polished brass or chrome towel rails,
tumbler holders and glass shelf supports;
modern polished aluminium range.

The Conran Shop
Michelin House, 81 Fulham Rd,
London SW3 6RD.
T:0171-589 7401. F:0171-823 7015.
Contemporary and unusual accessories
including washstands, cabinets, towels ,
kimonos, washbags, soaps and toiletries.
Good range of shower curtains.

Cubbins & Co
Unit 1, Rampisham Manor,
Dorchester, Dorset DT2 0PT.
T:01935-83060. F:01935-83257.
Wastepaper baskets, tissue box covers,
cotton wool boxes, linen bins, luggage racks,
cotton-reel stools custom made in
customers' own fabric. There is a hand-
painted range of the same items (apart from
the luggage rack and the stool) for which
there is a minimum order of five pieces.

Czech & Speake
See entry under **SHOWROOMS.** Elegant
cistern levers, robe hooks, paper-roll
holders, soap dishes, bath-racks and mirrors
to complement their Edwardian range of
bathroom fittings.

*Dornbracht
See entry under
**MANUFACTURERS & DISTRIBUTORS
OF FITTINGS AND TAPS.**

Graham & Greene
7 Elgin Crescent, London W11 2JA.
T:0171-727 4594. F:0171-229 9717.
Bathroom accessories from Wireworks and
Samuel Heath. Plus a starfish-shaped
collection; wooden bath mats and Emma
Bernhardt's 'Plastics' range.

Habitat
196 Tottenham Court Rd, London W1P 9LD.
T:0171-631 3880.
For other branches call 0645-334433.
Well priced elegant, modern chrome
accessories: towel rails, double hooks, glass
shelves, cabinets fronted with frosted glass,
free-standing and fixed mirrors, laundry
baskets, towels, bathmats and toiletries.

The Heated Mirror Company
Sherston, Wilts SN16 0LW.
T:01666-840003. F:01666-840856.
Selection of framed or plain heated
bathroom mirrors in any size to order.

*Samuel Heath & Sons
Cobden Works, Leopold St,
Birmingham B12 0UJ.
T:0121-772 2303. F:0121-722 3334.

***denotes
trade supplier.
Please phone
for retail outlets**

Traditional, quality accessories: bath racks, rings, towel rails, sponge and toothbrush holders in brass, chrome, antiqued gold or nickel plate.

*Hewi (UK)
Scimitar Close, Gillingham Business Park, Gillingham, Kent ME8 ORN.
T:01634-377688. F:01634-370612.
Large range of solid nylon bathroom accessories in strong colours imported from Germany. Also door furniture.

*Jendico
1 Cork Lane, Glen Parva, Leics LE2 9JR.
T:0116-277 0474. F:0116-277 2941.
Manufacturers of acrylic corner baths, whirlpools and spas; they also have a 'Harmony' range of shower panels, shower canopies and shower curtains and a 'Contourail' aluminium rail which can be shaped to any size.

Jerry's Home Store
163-167 Fulham Rd, London SW3 6SN.
T:0171-581 0909. F:0171-584 3749.
This American-inspired homewares store has a bathroom accessory section which includes chrome stands in various sizes, chrome or porcelain soap dishes, chrome towel hooks, toothbrush holders, hot water bottles and towels in earthy colours.

Cath Kidston
8 Clarendon Cross, London W11 4AP.
T:0171-221 4000. F:0171-229 1992.
'Bathtime' print fabric, wallpaper, towels, mats, bags and a painted white wooden bath rack - all available by mail order.

*NT Laidlaw
Carrs Rd, Cheadle, Cheshire SK8 2BW.
T:0161-491 4343. F:0161-491 4355.
Phone for branches nationwide. Large range of nylon, brass, aluminium and stainless steel bathroom accessories, including equipment for the disabled and shower rails.

Liberty
210-220 Regent Street, London W1R 6AH.
T:0171-734 1234. F:0171-573 9876.
From the traditional Samuel Heath range in chrome and antique gold to the modern Wireworks range of soap dishes, toothbrush holders etc. Toilet seats and matching bath mats in cow and zebra prints, bathroom ceramics and wrought iron shelving. Everything from sponge bags, shower caps and curtains to wooden bath mats and a good range of toiletries.

Maison d'Art International
Acorn House, 21 Effie Rd, London SW6 1EN.
T:0171-371 5017. F:0171-371 5331.
High quality bathroom fittings for the domestic and contract market. Their accessories are in the QE2 and in top London hotels like Grosvenor House and the Savoy.

The Painted Loo Seat Company
Monksheath Hall Workshops,
Chelford Rd, Nether Alderley,
Macclesfield, Cheshire SK10 4SY.
T/F:01625-890048.
Hand-painted MDF seats painted to look like granite, marble, wood or anything else to order.

The Pier
91-95 King's Rd, London SW3 4PA.
T:0171-351 5454. F:0171-351 7710.
Call for branches. Glass, ceramic, wood and metal accessories.

SKK
34 Lexington St, London W1R 3HR.
T:0171-434 4095. F:0171-287 0168.
Illuminated bathroom mirrors.

Satana (UK)
Unit E, Wyndford Ind Estate, Higher Halstock, Leigh, Yeovil, Somerset BA22 9QX.
T:01935-891888. F:01935-891819.
Electrically heated (and condensation free) bathroom mirrors.

The Source
26-40 Kensington High Street,
London W8 4PF.
T:0171-820 2865. F:0171-820 2762.
Branches in West Thurrock and Southampton. Chrome, china and plastic bathroom accessories. Plus brushes, sponges and towels.

Gabriela Trzebinski
Studio 7, Great Western Studios, Great Western Rd, London W9 3NY.
T/F: 0171-266 2175.

Designer loo seats in cow, zebra, leopard, wood, bright colours and others including specials to order. She also has matching fake fur bath mats backed with PVC.

Turnstyle Designs
Village St, Bishop's Tawton,
Barnstaple, Devon EX32 0DG.
T:01271-25325. F:01271-328248.
Unusual reconstituted stone loo roll holders, towel rails and shelving brackets in frog, ammonite, fish and hand print designs.

Water Front
New Inn Farm, Beckley, Oxon OX3 9TY.
T:01865-351133. F:01865-351100.
Traditional, classical styling: bath and sponge racks, robe hooks, shelves, mirrors, towel rails in either chrome, gold, nickel or satin nickel.

B & P Wynn & Co
See entry under SHOWROOMS. 'Jado' range of brassware and accessories; hand decorated sanitaryware and accessories by the French company Maurice Herbeau.

*Zodiac International Company
363 Kenton Road, Harrow, Middx HA3 0XS.
T:0181-909 2203. F:0181-909 1429.
Importers of Spanish chrome and gilt bathroom accessories.

SPECIALIST SERVICES AND SUPPLIERS

The Antique Bath & Tap Studio
See entry under RECLAIMED FITTINGS & TAPS. They guarantee their in situ re-spraying service for one year, their stove re-enamelling for five years.

Antique Baths of Ivybridge
See entry under RECLAIMED FITTINGS & TAPS. Polyurethane enamel finish for baths guaranteed for a year. Tap holes filled or moved. Nationwide service.

The Bath Doctor
Prospect House, Canterbury Rd, Challock,
Ashford, Kent TN25 4BB.
T/F:01233-740532. Open Thurs, Fri and Sat or by appt. Restoration of all sanitaryware and fittings on site or in their workshops.

Bathshield
Blenheim Studio, London Rd,
Forest Row, E.Sussex RH18 5EZ.
T:01342-823243. F:01342-823097.
Quality re-enamelling of baths and basins and restoration of taps. They cover the S.E. of England for work on site. Their workshop restores baths from all over the world.

Drummond's of Bramley
See entry under RECLAIMED FITTINGS & TAPS. Sends baths to Eastern Europe for vitreous re-enamelling in open furnaces. Baths are glass-powder coated, and passed through the furnace six times producing a finish Drummonds are confident will last for 50 years.

Sidney Hardwick
Stream Rd, Upton, Didcot, Oxon OX11 9JG.
T:01235-850263. Handmade stoneware wash basins with matching accessories.

The Lab
16 Lonsdale Rd, London NW6 6RD.
T:0171-372 2973. F:0171-624 2631.
Restoration of baths, basins and tiles. They can resurface cast iron, porcelain, china, ceramic, fibreglass and acrylic. Sanitaryware can be recoloured. Work is done on site. National service.

Posh Tubs
See entry under
RECLAIMED FITTINGS & TAPS.

Renubath
248 Lillie Rd, London SW6 7QA.
T:0171-381 8337. F:0171-381 8907.
Bath polishing, cleaning, chip repairs on sanitaryware; taps overhauled on site. Full resurfacing, sealants and bath strips provided.

Stiffkey Bathrooms
The Chapel, Stiffkey, Norfolk NR23 1AJ.
T:01328-830099. F:01328-830005.
Restorers of antique sanitaryware. Can re-plate in brass, nickel and chrome.

The Water Monopoly
See entry under
RECLAIMED FITTINGS & TAPS.
Restoration (in their own workshops) of any special antique bath.

The Bathroom Restoration Council (T/F:01233-740532) provides a fact sheet and has nine members nationwide.

*denotes trade supplier. Please phone for retail outlets 41

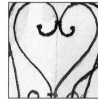

3

FURNITURE

TRADITIONAL UPHOLSTERED FURNITURE

A Barn Full of Sofas & Chairs
Furnace Mill, Lamberhurst, Kent TN3 8LH.
T:01892-890285. F:01892-890988.
In this old mill, the bottom floor has old sofas and chairs; the middle floor holds their traditionally made upholstered furniture, and the top floor is filled with designer fabrics for their re-upholstery service, which is limited to pre-1950s furniture.

Beaumont & Fletcher
261 Fulham Road, London SW3 6HY
T:0171-352 5553. F:0171-352 3545.
Traditional upholstered furniture inspired by Georgian, Empire, Regency and Victorian designs including a Regency day bed and a Pompadour sofa.

*Brunschwig & Fils
10 The Chambers, Chelsea Harbour Drive, London SW10 0XF.
T:0171-351 5797. F:0171-351 2280.

Small collection of upholstered furniture including a curved arm bedroom chair, buttoned ottoman, sofas and traditional armchairs.

Peter Dudgeon
Brompton Place, London SW3 1QE.
T:0171-589 0322. F:0171-589 1910.
Quality collection of sofas, armchairs, dining chairs, ottomans, French chairs and custom made pieces. Re-upholstery service and replicas of old pieces.

*Duresta Upholstery
Fields Farm Rd, Long Eaton,
Nottingham NG10 3FZ.
T:0115-973 2246. F:0115-946 1028.
Over 50 years of experience in manufacturing 'country house' sofas and chairs. There is a selection which is reproduced under licence from the National Trust. Also stools including hide-aways.

Essential Items
Church House, Plungar,
Nottingham NG13 0JA.
T:01949-861172. F:01949-861320.

*denotes
trade suppliers.
Please phone
for retail outlets.

43

Manufacturers of a large range of stools, window seats, bed end stools and ottomans available in calico or in the customer's own fabric. Sizes can also be made up to order.

The Furniture Union
46 Beak St, London W1R 3DA.
T:0171-287 3424. F:0171-498 1012.
Their 'Seventeen Hundreds' range of 18th century upholstered furniture includes Queen Anne and Chippendale armchairs, sofas and stools as well as French carved frame bergères.

Highly Sprung
310 Battersea Park Rd, London SW11 3BU. T:0171-924 1124. F:0171-228 5476.
Call for branches. Sofas, sofabeds and chairs - all made in their own factory. Over 20 sofas and 13 occasional chairs - contemporary look.

Hodsoll McKenzie
See entry under REPRODUCTION FURNITURE.

Howard Chairs
30-31 Lyme St, London NW1 0EE.
T:0171-482 2156. F:0171-482 0068.
Classic collection of fine, hand-sprung upholstered furniture. Elegant reproductions such as Chippendale and classic Chesterfield designs. Banquettes, chaises longues, stools and upholstered headboards.

Kingcome
302-304 Fulham Rd, London SW10 9EP.
T:0171-351 3998. F:0171-351 1444.
Forty different styles, both traditional and contemporary, made to specific size if necessary. Feather and down filled cushions. Selection includes sofas, chaises longues, chairs, and stools.

Lawson Wood
Unit 4 Heliport Est, 40 Lombard, Rd, London SW11 3RE.
T:0171-228 9812. F:0171-738 2499.
Hand made upholstered furniture based on traditional designs but with a contemporary feel. All items can be made in any dimension; cushions are feather and down filled and frames are hardwood with hand tied springs in seats and backs.

Andrew Martin
See entry under REPRODUCTION FURNITURE.

*Parker & Farr Furniture
75 Derby Rd, Bramcote, Nottingham NG9 3GY.
T:0115-925 2131. F:0115-925 9749.
Country house look as well as contemporary designs. Bespoke sizes.

Penrose & Rietberg
Broomes Barns, Pilsley Village, Nr Bakewell, Derbys DE45 1PF.
T:01246-583444. F:01246-583360.
And London showroom. Finely manufactured contemporary sofas, chairs, dining chairs, stools and ottomans for domestic and contract use. Specials can be made to order.

Recline & Sprawl
604 Kings Rd, London SW6 2DX.
T:0171-371 8982. F:0171-371 8984.
There are about 15 designs of sofas and occasional chairs. Everything is made up to order so it can be adapted to a particular length and depth.This is the more traditional arm of Highly Sprung.

David Seyfried
1/5 Chelsea Harbour Design Centre, Chelsea Harbour, London SW10 0XE.
T:0171-823 3848. F:0171-823 3221.
Top quality sofas (including a two and a half sized model), chairs, stools and ottomans inspired by early designs.

George Sherlock
588 King's Rd, London SW6 2DX.
T:0171-736 3955. F:0171-371 5179.
Traditional range of extra large upholstered furniture based on antiques: beech frames, coil springs and duck-feather fillings.

Sinclair Melson

Crane House, Gould Rd,
Twickenham, Middx TW2 6RS.
T:0181-894 1041. F:0181-755 2757.
Large range of upholstered sofas, chairs,
ottomans and stools in all shapes and sizes:
31 sofas, 9 different chairs, headboards
and upholstered screens. Each piece is
manufactured to order and hand sprung with
your choice of filling.

George Smith

587-589 King's Rd, London SW6 2EH.
T:0171-384 1004. F:0171-731 4451.
Classic sofas and chairs. Good source of
kilim-covered furniture as well. Special
orders including sofa beds. Also leather-
covered pieces.

Succession

179 Westbourne Grove, London W11 2SB.
T/F:0171-727 0580.
Some 30 traditionally-made upholstered
styles with the emphasis on plump,
comfortable designs, often covered in
animal prints or suede.

John Tanous

115 Harwood Road, London SW6 4QL.
T:0171-736 7999. F:0171-371 5237.
Established for over 70 years, and
specialising in hand crafted replica mirrors,
they also design and manufacture their own
top quality upholstered chairs (including
leather button-backed dining models and a
studded frame tub chair), sofas made in any
width, sofabeds, stools and love seats.

Wesley-Barrell

Park St. Charlbury, Oxford OX7 3PT.
T:01608-810481. F:01608-811319.
Branches nationwide. Makers of traditional
upholstered furniture since 1895. Also
cherry, oak and ash dining and bedroom
ranges including sofabeds.

William Yeoward

336 Kings Rd, London SW3 5UR.
T:0171-351 5454. F:0171-351 9469.
Sleek, classic, original designs - with a
particularly good number of chairs including
the Howe button-backed model, an elegant
library chair and a 'Smokers Sofa'.

REPRODUCTION FURNITURE

*Altfield

2/22 Chelsea Harbour Design Centre,
Chelsea Harbour, London SW10 0XE.
T:0171-376 5667. F:0171-351 5893.
French reproductions in an antiqued finish
including television cabinets; Ming style
Chinese rosewood furniture.

Arthur Brett & Sons

Hellesdon Park Rd, Drayton High Rd,
Norwich NR6 5DR.
T:01603-486633. F:01603-788984.
Showroom at:
103 Pimlico Rd, London SW1W 8PH.
T:0171-730 7304. Around 300 high quality
reproductions of 18th and 19th century
pieces available with different degrees of
'distressing' or with an 'aged' painted finish.
Special commissions also undertaken.

Brights of Nettlebed

Kingston House, High St, Nettlebed,
Nr Henley-on-Thames, Oxon RG9 5DD.
T:01491-641115. F:01491-641804.
Call for branches in Bristol, Wimborne,
Topsham. Extensive range of 16th-19th
century English reproduction furniture
for the home, office or boardroom. They
produce handmade copies of period
originals (including Art Deco pieces) as well
as machine made reproductions for contract
work.

Bylaw (Ross)

The Old Mill, Brookend Street,
Ross-on-Wye, Hereford HR9 7EG.
T:01989-562356. F:01989-768145.
Also in Norwich. Traditional Tudor four
poster beds, dressers, refectory tables,
pedestal and gateleg tables, TV cabinets
and bookcases all in an English country style
and mainly in carved oak and fruitwood.

*Chanteau

36 Cathcart Rd, London SW10 9NN.
T/F:0171-352 0447. Distributors for many
French furniture companies which specialise
in period style (17th century to Art Deco)
furniture, mirrors and lighting.

*denotes
trade suppliers.
Please phone
for retail outlets. 45

Julian Chichester Designs
Unit 12, 33 Parsons Green Lane,
London SW6 4HH.
T:0171-371 9055. F:0171-371 9066.
Regency reproduction lacquer and gilt tables
and chairs. Unusual coffee tables with velvet
under gilded glass. Seventeenth century
Dutch style table.

*The Classic Chair Company
Studio R, The Old Imperial Laundry,
71 Warriner Gardens, London SW11 4XW.
T:0171-622 4274. F:0171-622 4275.
Painted console tables in Louis XVI,
Georgian, Regency and French Empire
styles; carved, gilded and upholstered
pieces; chairs, bedside and
occasional tables.

R & D Davidson
Romsey House, 51 Maltravers St,
Arundel, W.Sussex BN18 9BQ.
T:01903-883141. F:01903-883914.
Designers and makers of high quality
reproduction period pieces, from a 'Greek
Revival' X-frame stool to a Biedermeier
masur birch sofa table. Also individual
pieces to commission. Four poster beds,
mirrors, bookcases, even some
Art Deco designs.

Deacon & Sandys
Hillcrest Farm Oast, Hawkhurst Rd,
Cranbrook, Kent TN17 3QD.
T:01580-713775. F:01580-714056.
Traditional 17th and 18th century style
English oak furniture: panel backed chairs,
chests, coffers, clothes' presses, dressers,
tables and four poster beds. Plus panelling,
staircases, floors, doors and individual
commissions.Specialist architectural design
service for restoration projects.

Dickson of Ipswich
Baird Close, Hadleigh Road Ind. Estate,
Ipswich, Suffolk IP2 0HB.
T:01473-252121. F:01473-212941.
Finest quality veneered furniture. Selection
includes executive desks, display cabinets,
dining tables,occasional tables and some
Arts and Crafts reproductions. Custom
designed and contract work undertaken.

The Dining Room Shop
62-64 White Hart Lane, London SW13 0PZ.
T:0181-878 1020. F:0181-876 2367.
And at:
Stephanie Hoppen,
17 Walton St, London SW3 2HX.
T:0171-823 9455. Mainly antiques but a
small selection of reproduction dining
furniture and related accessories.

Martin J Dodge
Southgate, Wincanton, Somerset BA9 9EB.
T:01963-32388. F:01963-31063.
Over 100 fine quality reproductions of
English 18th century furniture including
Regency rosewood and Chippendale
lacquered styles.

Elizabeth Eaton
85 Bourne Street, London SW1W 8HF.
T:0171-730 2262. F:0171-730 7294.
Upholstered range, some with beech
frames; chairs which can be painted to
order and simulated bamboo headboards,
tables and dressing table mirrors.

Freud
198 Shaftesbury Avenue, London WC2 3HB.
T:0171-831 1071. F:0171-831 3062.
Suppliers of Charles Rennie Mackintosh
reproduction furniture.

*GLPC International
58 Rowfant Rd, London SW17 7AS.
T:0181-675 7578/6304.
F:0181-675 2470. Distributors of a huge
range representing many French companies
and all periods, styles and price ranges.

*Grange
4 St Paul's St, Stamford, Lincs PE9 2FY.
T:01780-54721. F:01780-54718. Vast
collection including Shaker, Louis XVI,
Louis Philippe and Directoire reproductions.
Charming copies of Marie-Antoinette's
dressing table and Louis Pasteur's writing
table.

Hodsoll McKenzie
52 Pimlico St, London SW1W 8LP.
T:0171-730 2877. F:0171-823 4939.
Six models including the Soane bench, a
bedside cabinet, a button-backed sofa and
chair, and a scroll-leg dining chair.

Howe's Designs

See entry under **LEATHER FURNITURE**.
Handmade furniture and lighting. From
copies of antiques (an Irish pawfoot bench
or a 19th century folding coaching table) to
new designs like a glass-topped table on
a steel base.

*REH Kennedy

White House Rd, Ipswich, Suffolk IP1 5LT.
T:01473-240044. F:01473-240098.
Handmade and hand polished traditional
furniture including campaign chests, brass-
bound sea chests and Wellington chests in
their military style collection. Also traditional
dark oak and fine mahogany reproductions.

Andrew Martin

200 Walton Street, London SW3 2JL.
T:0171-584 4290. F:0171-581 8014.
Large selection of reproduction French sofas
and bergères; elegant stools, tables (dining,
console and coffee), desks in at least 24
finishes - more to order.

Parsons Table Company

362 Fulham Rd, London SW10 9UU.
T:0171-352 7444. F:0171-376 4677.
Fine copies of English and French furniture:
beds, chests of drawers, occasional tables
and a good collection of chairs. They will also
copy antiques for the trade.

Quebec St George

169B High St,
Hampton Hill, Middx TW12 1NL.
T:0181-941 4320. F:0181-979 6626.
Good range of Louis XV and XVI bergères
and dining furniture.

The Repro Shop

108 Walcot St, Bath BA1 5BG.
T:01225-444404. F:01225-448163.
Reproduction oak or fruitwood refectory
tables made to measure with dressers,
racks and chairs to match.

Restall Brown & Clennell

120 Queensbridge Rd, London E2 8PD.
T:0171-739 6626. F:0171-739 6123.
Manufacturers of fine traditional furniture
including an Art Deco range inspired by E.J.
Rhulman. They also represent Leone Cei &
Sons' carved wood and gilt collection.

Adam Richwood

5 Garden Walk, London EC2A 3EQ.
T:0171-729 0976.
F:0171-729 7296.
Fine period reproductions
manufactured by this family
firm which sells to
department stores and the
general public. Mainly
mahogany, yew and
walnut desks, bureaus
and bookcases.

David Salmon

555 King's Rd,
London SW6 2EB.
T:0171-384 2223. F:0171-371 0532.
Museum quality copies of period furniture.
Fully upholstered antique reproductions,
fabrics and wallcoverings. Some of his
traditional pieces hide TV screens and
computer equipment.

Shaker

25 Harcourt St, London W1H 1DT.
T:0171-724 7672. F:0171-724 6640.
And at: 322 Kings Rd, London SW3 5UH.
T:0171-352 3918. F:0171-376 3494.
Unadorned furniture in natural cherrywood
or maple.

DC Stuart

34-40 Poole Hill,
Bournemouth, Dorset BH2 5PS.
T:01202-555544. F:01202-295333.
Hand carved replica furniture. Specialist in
wooden chair frames which can be supplied
'in the raw' or polished, gilded, stained and
upholstered to order. Traditional kitchen and
dining chairs, Chippendale designs. Plus
sofas, stools, tables, bureaus, bookcases
and carved headboards.

Stuart Interiors

Barrington Court, Barrington,
Ilminster, Somerset TA19 0NQ.
T:01460-240349. F:01460-242069.
Reproduction solid oak Elizabethan and
Jacobean furniture as well as a constantly
changing selection of pre-1720 antique
pieces. Plus iron lighting, panelled rooms
and restoration projects.

***denotes
trade suppliers.
Please phone
for retail outlets.**

John Tanous
See entry under **TRADITIONAL UPHOLSTERED FURNITURE.**
Handmade gilt or wood furniture, including bookcases, breakfast, console and dining tables, bedside chests, wardrobes, headboards, pelmets and mirrors. Custom pieces to order.

Tindle
162/168 Wandsworth Bridge Rd, London SW6 2UQ.
T:0171-384 1485. F:0171-736 5630.
Range of stools and ottomans covered in needlepoint. Tôle Regency style trays on stands and two-tier tables. Reproduction Chinoiserie tables and painted occasional furniture.

Titchmarsh and Goodwin
Trinity Works, Back Hamlet, Ipswich, Suffolk IP3 8AL.
T:01473-252158. F:01473-210948. Approximately 30,000 designs in their library - their cabinet makers can hand make furniture to specific requirements.

Villa Garnelo
26 Pimlico Rd, London SW1W 8LJ.
T:0171-730 0110. F:0171-730 0220.
Biedermeier, Empire and Neo-Classical style reproductions.

*Wood & Mott
29 Morses Lane, Brightlingsea, Colchester, Essex CO7 0SD.
T:01206-303929. F:01206-304925.
Manufacturers of traditional reproduction furniture for the trade.

CHAIR & STOOL SPECIALISTS

Beechams Furniture
Unit 2, Romside Commercial Centre, 149 North St, Romford, Essex RM1 1ED.
T:01708-745778. F:01708-764328.
Handmade traditional chair specialist, but can also manufacture desks, tables, bookcases and wooden backed sofas to individuals' requirements. Plus restoration and French polishing.

Caddum Designs
13-14 Peter Rd, Commerce Way Ind Estate, Lancing, W.Sussex BN15 8TH.
T:01903-755606. F:01903-751361.
Huge range of traditional hardwood chair frames which are supplied to upholsterers nationwide.

Chairs
George House, 10B George Rd, Guildford, Surrey GU1 4NP.
T:01483-304648. F:01483-440019.
Limited edition chairs with a theatrical feel.

The Classic Chair Company
See entry under **REPRODUCTION FURNITURE.** Excellent selection of chairs including Irish Chippendale, Regency, rope-back, ladder-back, Gustavian designs and French bergères.

Clock House Furniture
The Old Stables, Overhailes, Haddington, East Lothian EH41 3SB.
T:01620-860968. F:01620-860984.
Widest range of upholstered stools in all shapes and sizes. There are turned, straight, fluted and cabriole legs, or bun feet; some are kelim covered. Fabric supplied or customer's own.

The Dining Chair Company
43 Vincent Square, London SW1P 2NP.
T:0171-630 8595. F:0171-976 6189.
By appointment. Range of dining chairs in Georgian, Gothic, Adam, Spoonback, Stuart

and other styles which can be covered in almost any fabric; wood can be stained or polished; carvers available.

Prue Lane

6 Formosa Street, London W9 1EE.
T/F:0171-266 2629. Small collection of handmade designs including a beech-framed Louis XV armchair and a Louis XV open armchair in fruitwood.

Guy Lewis

Lonsdale, Glue Hill,
Sturminster-Newton, Dorset DT10 2DJ.
T/F:01258-471642. Range of painted and custom designed pieces. He is a specialist in Windsor chairs and settles. The settles come in two or three seat versions; there's an elbow chair and side tables to match. They're made of native hardwoods and the price range is from £450 to £800.

PINE FURNITURE

At the Sign of the Chest of Drawers

281 Upper St, London N1 2TZ.
T/F:0171-359 5909. Old and new pine furniture, and not only chests of drawers. Wooden filing cabinets and anything else made to order.

Eighty-Eight Antiques

88 Golborne Rd, London W10 5NL.
T:0181-960 0827. Pine mine of old tables, dressers, chests of drawers, chairs, shelving, plate racks, trunks; large selection always available.

Fens Restoration & Sales

46 Lots Rd, London SW10 0QF.
T:0171-352 9883.
Restored old pine tables and chairs as well as items made to order from old wood - beds, plate racks, dresser tops. Restoration of all furniture.

Joyce Hardy Pine and Country Furniture

The Street, Hacheston, Suffolk IP13 0DS.
T:01728-746485.
Antique pine dressers, butchers' blocks and kitchen tables, small pieces of furniture and accessories and a range made from old timber. She also does bed and breakfast!

Ann May

80 Wandsworth Bridge Rd,
London SW6 2TF.
T:0171-731 0862. Treasure trove of furniture from old pine to French painted to old upholstered pieces. Small collection of reproduction bookshelves.

DJ Oakes

Hales View Farm, Oakamoor Rd, Cheadle, Stoke-on-Trent, Staffs ST10 4QR.
T:01538-751069. F:01538-750889.
Manufacture English pine furniture, antiques and accessories. Plus furniture made to order from reclaimed timber.

Pine Warehouse

86 Wandsworth Bridge Rd,
London SW6 2TF.
T:0171-371 8476. F:0171-371 0229.
And at:
Pine Grove, 186 Wandsworth Bridge Rd,
London SW6 2UF.
T:0171-731 7673. F:0171-736 3847.
Reproduction pine furniture as well as pieces made from recycled wood.

White Dog Reproductions

20 Half Moon Lane, London SE24 9HU.
T/F:0171-924 9874. Made to measure furniture built from old pine.

PAINTED/DECORATIVE FURNITURE

Jonathan Avery

T/F:01750-22377. By appointment.
Dressers, bookshelves, library bookcases, small cupboards, side tables and mirrors in a Gothic or country style supplied painted to order or unfinished. Mail order.

The Blue Door

77 Church Rd, London SW13 9HH.
T:0181-748 9785. F:0181-563 1043.
Furniture in the Gustavian style, painted in traditional colours or left unfinished. Also antique pieces, tableware, textiles, gifts and accessories in recognisably Swedish style.

*Brunschwig & Fils

See entry under TRADITIONAL UPHOLSTERED FURNITURE.

*denotes trade suppliers. Please phone for retail outlets. 49

Lacquered tray tables, painted tea tables and coffee tables.

David Carter
109 Mile End Rd, London E1 4UJ.
T/F:0171-790 0259.
David Carter is an interior designer who has designed pieces inspired by antiques. There's an '18th century' French mirror stand, a '19th century' French clothes' rail, a trompe l'oeil chair and even a trompe l'oeil fireplace painted on canvas (in any size or shape) which comes in a tube, ready to stick on your wall !

Chalon
The Plaza, 535 King's Rd,
London SW10 0SZ.
T:0171-351 0008. F:0171-351 0003.
Handmade country style painted furniture; especially free-standing kitchen units, tables and cupboards.

Cover Up Designs
9 Kingsclere Park, Kingsclere,
Nr Newbury, Berks RG20 4SW.
T:01635-297981. F:01635-298363.
Painted collection including twelve designs of dressing tables, six designs of TV tables made to fit specific sets, ten designs of ottomans and stools dressed to clients' specifications. Chipboard tables or unpainted tables with MDF tops and pine legs.

Anne Fowler
35 Long Street, Tetbury, Gloucs GL8 8AA.
T:01666-504043. Collection of bedside and writing tables, bookcases, hanging shelves with elegant proportions.

Gentle & Boon
6 St. Gluvias St, Penryn, Cornwall TR10 8BL.
T:01326-377325. F:01326-378317.
By appointment. Pine country style furniture (dressers, armoires, chests of drawers) painted in distressed or colourwashed finishes. Bespoke service as well.

Nicholas Haslam
12-14 Holbein Place, London SW1W 8NL.
T:0171-730 8623. F:0171-730 6679.
Custom made collection of smart and understated painted furniture in any finish -

from subtle distressing to antique patinas. Chests of drawers, faux bamboo consoles, bureaus, an X-frame stool and centre tables. There's also a stool that converts to library steps and a fireside seat/dog kennel based on an 18th design.

*Thomas Messel
Bradley Court, Wotton-Under-Edge,
Gloucs GL12 7PP.
T:01453-843220. F:01453-843719.
High quality painted and decorated furniture. 'Pietra Dura' and 'Marble' painted table tops with neo-classical bases. Hand painted lacquer sabre-leg chairs, tables, and bookcase. Smart black and white lacquer 'Penwork Collection', with the Chinoiserie and neo-classical themes popular in Regency times.

Nordic Style at Moussie
109 Walton St, London SW3 2HP.
T:0171-581 8674. Swedish-style painted furniture and accessories including bedlinen, runners and textiles.

Out Of The Wood
Rowan Cottage, Gascoigne Lane,
Ropley, Hants SO24 0BT.
T:01962-773353. Painted wood furniture: a simple country style bookcase with an integrated settle, sideboards/display cabinets, TV and video corner units, tables and chairs. Anything can be made to commission.

*Porta Romana
Lower Froyle, Nr Alton, Hampshire GU34 4LS. T:01420-23005. F:01420-23008.
Pretty hand painted console tables with Greek key, chequered, Chinoiserie and 'pietra dura' decoration. Plus occasional tables, a Chinese lacquer side table and a glass coffee table. Good lighting collection.

Renwick & Clarke
190 Ebury St, London SW1W 8UP. T:0171-730 8913. F:0171-730 4508.
Distributors of console and side tables by Niermann Weeks and 18th and 19th century style furniture by Elmbourne Fine Reproductions. Also Lutson's embossed, gilded and hand painted leather panels

upholstered on chairs and stools
by Philip Boorman.

Somerset House of Iron
779 Fulham Rd, London SW6 5HA.
T:0171-371 0436. F:0171-371 0068.
Bespoke furniture. They also have a
standard range of antiqued or distressed
country-style painted designs.

Sasha Waddell at Kingshill Designs
Kitchener Works, Kitchener Rd, High
Wycombe, Bucks HP11 2SJ.
T:01494-463910. F:01494-451555.
Simple painted furniture inspired by 18th
century Swedish country houses. Her new
'Ekeby Collection' is the perfect answer for
home offices - the smart painted cupboard
houses computer, keyboard, noticeboard
and lots of filing cabinets.

Winston Yeatts of Warwickshire
14 Emscote Rd, Warwick,
Warwicks CV34 5QN.
T:01926-496761. F:01926-496720.
Decorative hand painted furniture and
accessories including dummy
boards/fireboards, small bookcases, tables
and folding screens. Also mirrors, candle
sconces, boxes and toleware.

William Yeoward
See entry under TRADITIONAL
UPHOLSTERED FURNITURE.
Good range of unusual designs, inspired
by antique originals but with a modern,
masculine look. Examples include a steam-
bent 20s style oak chair and a Gothic four
poster bed. There are occasional tables,
sideboards and bookcases available in
wood or one of many painted finishes.

UNPAINTED/UNCOVERED FURNITURE

Jonathan Avery
See entry under
PAINTED/DECORATIVE FURNITURE.
Can supply his furniture unfinished.

Cover Up Designs
See entry under
PAINTED/DECORATIVE FURNITURE.

The Dormy House
Sterling Park, East Portway Ind Estate,
Andover, Hampshire SP10 3TZ.
T:01264-365808. F:01264-366359.
Range of MDF or chipboard furniture
designed to be covered with fabric. 'Instant
tables' for dining, dressing and TVs,
screens, blanket boxes, bedroom and dining
chairs, footstools, bedheads. They can
provide a complete soft furnishing service in
customer's own fabric or can source fabrics
if required.

Maison
Grand Illusions, 2-4 Crown Rd, St.
Margarets, Twickenham, Middx TW1 3EE.
Orderline:
0181-892 2151. F:0181-744 2017.
Mail order company with over forty pieces of
French country-style furniture which can be
supplied in natural wood to paint oneself, or
in a wide choice of colours with different
degrees of 'ageing'.

Moriarti's
High Halden, Nr Ashford, Kent TN26 3LY.
T:01233-850214. F:01233-850524.
Large range of furniture ready for painting.

Scumble Goosie
Lewiston Mill, Toadsmoor Rd, Brimscombe,
Stroud, Gloucs GL5 2TB.
T/F:01453-731305. 'Naked Collection' of
80 items of MDF furniture for decoupage or
painting, available by mail order. They also
sell crackle paints, varnishes and glazes and
can hand-paint any item to order.

CONTEMPORARY FURNITURE & UPHOLSTERY

Aero
96 Westbourne Grove, London W2 5RT.
T:0171-221 1950. F:0171-221 2555.
Contract and wholesale services plus
Aeromail mail order catalogue. Orderline
T:0181-871 4030. F: 0181-870 8227.
Manufacturer and retailer of their own smart
range of tables, chairs, storage systems, loft
lights and accessories.

***denotes
trade suppliers.
Please phone
for retail outlets.** 51

Albrissi
1 Sloane Square, London SW1W 8EE.
T:0171-730 6119. F:0171-259 9113.
Antique and contemporary reproduction
designs combine to create an eclectic mix.
Good range of upholstered furniture.

Aram Designs
3 Kean St, London WC2B 4AT.
T:0171-240 3933. F:0171-240 3697.
Showroom at the forefront of modern design
with items like the Kama sofa and the Sutra
tables and Montana storage/ display units.

Ruth Aram Shop
65 Heath St, London NW3 6UG.
T:0171-431 4008.
F:0171-431 6755.
Three floors of 20th century classics from
the Twenties and Thirties to today. Original
collection including a reclaimed oak table
with a modern look. Mainly contemporary gift
items and tableware including designs by
Jasper Morrison, Philippe Starck, Eileen
Gray, Le Corbusier and lighting by Castiglione
and others.

Atrium
Centrepoint, 22-24 St Giles High St,
London WC2H 8LN.
T:0171-379 7288. F:0171-240 2080.
Stylish furniture for the home and office
by some top designers. Sole agents for
Moroso. Good lighting section and only
source in the UK for Madulight simulated
leather and Novasuede.

Carew Jones
188 Walton St, London SW3 2JL.
T:0171-225 2411. F:0171-225 2422.
Comprehensive range of coffee and lamp
tables in clear perspex and glass or bronze
metal and glass popular with interior
designers as they work well both in
traditional and contemporary interiors.

Coexistence
288 Upper St, London N1 2TZ.
T:0171-354 8817. F:0171-354 9610.
Modern designer classics, including Alvar
Aalto. Most of their work is contract but they
are happy to source any piece of furniture
from around 100 European manufacturers.

The Conran Shop
Michelin House, 81 Fulham Rd,
London SW3 6RD.
T:0171-589 7401. F:0171-823 7015.
Good selection of classic chairs, big sofas,
dining tables and chairs, metal and
cherrywood four poster beds. Plus
accessories, lighting, china and kitchenware
departments downstairs.

Design America
c/o Carter Green, 1 Knockhundred Row,
Midhurst, W.Sussex GU29 9DQ.
T:01730-817722. F:01730-817744.
Batman's chair, 'Mainstreet' and
'Chicago'sofas, stacking chairs, café chairs
and table - American contemporary look.

Designers Guild
267-271 King's Road, London SW3 5EN.
T:0171-243 7300. F:0171-243 7710.
Modern design emporium with contemporary
upholstery and furniture, painted furniture,
ceramics, tableware, glass, cushions,
lighting, beds and bedding and bathroom
accessories - all in the bold, bright look
made famous by Tricia Guild.

Domain
42 Newman St, London W1P 3PA.
T:0171-255 3264. F:0171-323 4051.
London retail outlet for high quality domestic
and contract furniture by the Italian
companies B & B Italia, Maxalto, Zanotta,
Bros, Casigliani, and many others. 20th
century furniture and lighting classics
including designs by Charles Rennie
Mackintosh, Mies van der Rohe, Le
Corbusier, Eileen Gray. Also 18th century
reproductions and modern rattan and woven
leather designs.

*Donghia
23 The Design Centre, Chelsea Harbour,
London SW10 0XE.
T:0171-823 3456. F:0171-376 5758.
Slick upmarket pieces designed by John
Hutton. Modern classics - sofas, club and
dining chairs, occasional and coffee tables,
Murano glass and platinum and gold finish
standard and table lamps. Furniture comes
in wood finishes in 20 colourways.

Christopher Farr

212 Westbourne Grove, London W11 2RH.
T:0171-792 5761. F:0171-792 5763.
Capellini furniture from Milan: dining tables, chairs, sofas, sofabeds, and shelving systems designed by luminaries like Tom Dixon, Terence Woodgate and Jasper Morrison. Plus the contemporary designer rugs for which Christopher Farr is known.

The Furniture Union

See entry under **TRADITIONAL UPHOLSTERED FURNITURE.**
Supplies British designed and British manufactured contemporary furniture, lighting and accessories to the trade and public. Excellent contract department including unit seating, café tables, chairs, stools, boardroom tables and tufted rugs.

*Hitch/Milius

Alma House, 301 Alma Rd,
Enfield, Middx EN3 7BB.
T:0181-443 2616. F:0181-443 2617.
Manufacturer of contemporary upholstered furniture for both contract and domestic markets. Commissioned designs by Nigel Coates, Fred Scott and others.

Inhouse

28 Howe St, Edinburgh EH3 6TG.
T:0131-225 2888. F:0131-220 6632.
And at: 24-26 Wilson St, Merchant City, Glasgow G1 1SS.
T:0141-552 5902. F:0141-552 5929.
The place to go for modern design in Scotland. Mainly Spanish and Italian furniture and accessories. Companies represented include Amat, Driade, Molteni, Cassina. They cater to both the contract and domestic market.

Jinan Furniture Gallery

17 Golden Square, London W1R 4JB.
T:0171-434 3463. F:0171-434 3463.
Exclusive UK outlet for American company Dialogica as well as the neo-baroque and 60s inspired work of British designer Orianna Fielding-Banks. One-off pieces by other British designers and an interesting range of rugs. Specialists in comfortable, modern upholstery.

Liberty

214-220 Regent Street, London W1R 6AH.
T:0171-734 1234. F:0171-573 9876.
Their department on the fourth floor commissions pieces from known and unknown designers.

Made of Waste

244 Grays Inn Rd, London WC1X 8JR.
T:0171-278 6971. F:0171-833 0018.
By appointment. Wacky furniture in plastic board made from recycled plastic bottles.

Mobili

T:0181-699 3626. F:0181-291 7937.
By appointment. Michael McMullen represents a vast selection of European designers of contemporary furniture and lighting for all domestic or contract projects. His range includes unusual slatted screens and blinds, design classics, modern Danish chairs, Italian lighting, contemporary Italian office systems, and clean, simple designs for modern interiors.

Charles Page Furniture

61 Fairfax Rd, London NW6 4EE.
T:0171-328 9851. F:0171-328 7240.
Showroom featuring mainly contemporary European designer furniture. They also manufacture a lot of their own designs. Good choice of shelving and storage units (including Banak's cherrywood TV/VCR cabinet), upholstered pieces and dining tables and chairs.

*denotes
trade suppliers.
Please phone
for retail outlets.

Purves & Purves
80-81 & 83 Tottenham Court Rd,
London W1P 9HD.
T:0171-580 8223. F:0171-580 8244.
One-stop shop for contemporary design,
selling everything from furniture to home
accessories.

Roche-Bobois
421-425 Finchley Rd, London NW3 6HJ.
T:0171-486 1614. F:0171-431 1611.
Best known for smart French leather,
suede and kilim-upholstered sectional
seating. Their innovative range includes
original shelving units, beds, a braided rattan
collection and painted furniture inspired by
Far Eastern designs.

*Roset
95A High St, Great Missenden,
Bucks HP16 0AL.
T:01494-865001. F:01494-866883.
Contemporary collection including
an aluminium occasional table
with a removeable tray top and a
wicker sofa.

SCP
135-139 Curtain Rd, London EC2A 3BX.
T:0171-739 1869. F:0171-729 4224.
Furniture by minimalist designers including
Jasper Morrison, Matthew Hilton, Terence
Woodgate, Nigel Coates, James Irvine and
Konstantin Grcic - from coffee tables to
public seating.

Space
214 Westbourne Grove, London W11 2RH.
T:0171-229 6533. F:0171-727 0134.
Tom Dixon's own designs in coloured
plastics and metals. Also paper and pyrex
glass lamps, chairs and bar stools made
from thin steel rods.

The Study
26 Old Church St, London SW3 5BY.
T:0171-376 7969. F:0171-795 0392.
Christopher Nevile's shop is dedicated to
promoting the best of British design. Items
include pebble door handles, 'Goliath' sofas
and the 'Camden' range of upholstered
furniture. Lighting by Hannah Woodhouse
and glass by Paul Clifford.

Viaduct
1-10 Summer's St, London EC1R 5BD.
T:0171-278 8456. F:0171-278 2844.
Huge selection of modern classics: designs
by Driade, Montis, Philippe Starck, Aleph and
Matthew Hilton to name a few.

Vitra
13 Grosvenor St, London W1X 9FB.
T:0171-408 1122. F:0171-499 1967.
London HQ for the Swiss design company
Vitra. Also selection by Charles Eames,
Philippe Starck, Antonio Citterio, Mario
Bellini and Frank Gehry's cardboard range.
New designs by Alberto Meda.

FURNITURE MAKERS

Nick Allen Studios
3 Shelgate Rd, London SW11 1BD.
T:0171-738 0050. F:0171-924 4901.
Designer in wood, glass and metal. His 'St.
George's Chair' is the first contemporary
piece of furniture in Westminster Cathedral's
St George's Chapel. Other unusual
commissions include a humidor in Cuban
mahogany and wenge and a botanical
cabinet in palm wood, bronze and glass.

Antaeus
3-11 Pensbury Pl, London SW8 4TP.
T:0171-622 1002. F:0171-498 0555.
Range of 16 designs by Alexander Brydon.
His furniture has a classical feel with
unusual combinations of wood like maple,
walnut and hornbeam. Collection includes
tables, bookcases, desks, chairs, some
pieces of garden furniture and lamps. He will
also design anything to commission.

Vanessa Benson
16 St Peters St, London N1 8JG.
T:0171-226 6875.
Mosaic artist who can undertake
special furniture commissions.

John Coleman
A-Z Studios, 3-5 Hardwidge St,
London SE1 3SY.
T:0171-403 0016. F:0171-378 8997.
Architectural look with veneer, glass, stone
and chrome in simple geometric shapes.

Contemporary Applied Arts
2 Percy St, London W1 9FA.
T:0171-436 2344. F:0171-436 2446.
Hold an index of furniture makers who can
be commissioned. They also display and
sell contemporary pieces in their gallery.

Kathy Dalwood
127 Fernhead Rd, London W9 3ED.
T/F:0181-968 4552.
Original modern designs including a glass
chair and glass and metal tables; some
encapsulate images of 18th French
paintings. There is also a velvet and silk pom
pom stool. Latest collection is a series of
tables covered in brightly coloured nylon
flocking. Re-interpretations of classical
chandeliers in ultra modern shaped clear
and coloured hand-blown glass; also mirrors.

Daubneys
10 Fifehead Business Centre, Fifehead
Magdalen, Gillingham, Dorset SP8 5RR.
T/F:01258-821234. Designers and makers
of classic contemporary furniture.

R & D Davidson
See entry under
REPRODUCTION FURNITURE.
Range of fine reproductions and
bespoke designs.

Mark Gabbertas
3 Normand Mews, London W14 9RB.
T/F:0171-381 1847.
Range of contemporary furniture including
chairs with upholstered seats and birch ply
backs (used in the 'Atelier' restaurant in
Beak St, London), a tall drawer unit in MDF
with leather handles, a wavy bookcase,
'Crab' coffee table and 'Spider' console
table. Plus one-off commissions.

Guy Lewis
See entry under
CHAIR & STOOL SPECIALISTS.

David Linley Furniture
60 Pimlico Rd, London SW1W 8LP.
T:0171-730 7300. F:0171-730 8869.
Range of furniture and accessories (desk
sets, key boxes, mirrors, humidors) in
beautiful native hardwoods, many featuring
marquetry. Larger pieces to order.

Longpré Cabinet Makers
Hatherleigh Farm, Wincanton,
Somerset BA9 8AB.
T:01963-34356. F:01963-31955.
Bespoke cabinet makers who cover most
styles - from fine replicas of antique furniture
to contemporary pieces.

John Makepeace
Parnham House,
Beaminster, Dorset DT8 3NA.
T:01308-862204. F:01308-863494.
One of the country's best known furniture
designers. He also runs Parnham College
which opened in 1977. Many of his designs
have become hallmarks and can be seen in
museums.

Guy Mallinson Furniture
Unit 7, The Coachworks,
80 Parsons Green Lane, London SW6 4HU.
T:0171-371 9190. F:0171-371 5099.
Guy Mallinson specialises in veneers:
sycamore, burr maple, vavona and lacewood
are among the unusual woods he uses. His
workshop makes coffee or kitchen tables,
kitchen cupboards, television cabinets and
any piece to order.

Simon Turner
5b Tenter Ground, London E1 7NH.
T:0171-426 0529. Furniture made to
commission from a combination of industrial
and reclaimed materials, including a kitchen
in painted MDF, aluminium and scaffolding;
tables in reclaimed oak; parquet flooring;
and tables in birch-faced ply with underlit
glass tiles.

Andrew Varah
Little Walton, nr Pailton,
Rugby, Warwicks CV23 0QL.
T:01788-833000. F:01788-832527.
Fine reproductions of period furniture
as well as one-off contemporary pieces.

METAL FURNITURE

Bisca Design
Shaw Moor Farm, Harome, York YO6 5HZ.
T:01439-771702. F:01439-771002.
Range of contemporary furniture, including

*denotes
trade suppliers.
Please phone
for retail outlets.

galvanised chairs and tables, tall ladderback 'Perky' chairs, beds, shelving and accessories.

Oliver Bonas
10 Kensington Church St, London W8 4EP. T:0171-368 0035. F:0171-938 4312. For mail order catalogue T:0171-627 4747. And branches in Fulham Rd and Battersea. Own range of metal furniture including simple dining chairs with very high backs and padded seats and coffee tables. Plus reproduction Indonesian and Indian wooden furniture.

Calmels
3/7 Southville, Wandsworth Rd, London SW8 2PR.
T:0171-622 6181. F:0171-498 2889.
Scrollwork metal chairs, wrought iron tables with glass, metal, wood or marble tops and any other furniture to order in all sorts of metals and finishes. They have done a lot of theatrical work, including the sets for Sunset Boulevard and the chandeliers for Phantom of the Opera.

Tom Faulkner Designs
13 Petley Rd, London W6 9SU.
T:0171-610 0615. F:0171-386 0797.
Wrought iron coffee, console, bedside and dining tables with a wide choice of tops - plain or bevelled glass, painted finish, natural wood, marble or stone. There are also five chair designs.

The Mark Francis Collection
The Blacksmith Shop, Stone St, Halmaker, Chichester, W.Sussex PO18 0NQ. T:01243-773431. Simple handmade chairs in Georgian, Victorian, Florentine styles, glass or wood topped tables, benches.

The Furniture Union
See entry under
TRADITIONAL UPHOLSTERED FURNITURE. Peter Leonard's 'Scroll Range' includes tables, bed, sofa, mirror, window seat and chair. They also carry his slightly more elaborate Rivoli range and the work of other talented British designers (Nick Allen and Adrian Reynolds).

Nicholas Herbert
118 Lots Rd, London SW10 0RJ.
T:0171-376 5596. F:0171-376 5572.
Practical folding tôle tables in polished steel, bronze, tortoiseshell or a plain painted finish.

The Heveningham Collection
Weston Down, Weston Colley, Micheldever, Winchester, Hampshire SO21 3AQ. T:01962-774990. F:01962-774790. Wrought iron furniture in simple lines for both interiors and exteriors. From chaises longues, dining tables and chairs to simple candlesticks. They are supplied in black or green paint finish with cream canvas cushions.

The Iron Design Company
Summer Carr Farm, Thornton-le-Moor, Northallerton, N.Yorks DL6 3SG. T:01609-778143. F:01609-778846. Glass topped tables, wide choice of chairs, benches and garden seats, even screens, elegant sun loungers, bar stools and curtain poles. All in iron and made to order.

McCloud & Co
269 Wandsworth Bridge Rd, London SW6 2TX.
T:0171-371 7151. F:0171-371 7186.
Hand-forged and hand-gilded furniture, mirrors and lighting made to order in any of twenty-seven standard finishes. Kevin McCloud's range includes curly chairs, unusual console tables and the heraldic-looking 'Regal Bench'. A lot of his work is commissions - the most unusual being all the lighting for the castle at Disneyland Paris (165 pieces in 65 different medieval designs).

Suzanne Ruggles
436 King's Rd, London SW10 0LJ.
T:0171-351 6565. F:0171-351 7007.
Original gothic and neo-classical style metal furniture with a curvy look. Her collection includes a polished steel bed and a basketweave metal tub chair.

Somerset House of Iron
See entry under
PAINTED/DECORATIVE FURNITURE.
Simple lines are the hallmark of this small
collection which includes a telephone seat,
chairs, a Gothic-look table, a four poster bed
and an iron and wood range.

Strawberry Steel
Broadway Studios, 28 Tooting High St,
London SW17 0RG.
T:0181-672 4465. F:0181-767 3247.
Everything from metal garden furniture to
rose arches to chairs and beds from this
young team.

Richard Taylor Designs
91 Princedale Rd, London W11 4NS.
T:0171-792 1808. F:0171-792 0310.
Richard Taylor supplies mainly interior
designers and architects from his collection
of unusual metal furniture featuring coffee,
console and side tables, dining chairs and
tables, standard lamps and metal pelmets.

Villiers Brothers
Fyfield Hall, Fyfield, Essex CM5 0SA.
T:01277-899680. F:01277-899008.
One-off furniture and lighting in iron for
interior designers, architects, films and
theatre. Recent work includes an unusual
chandelier for a church and fittings for the
Ralph Lauren shop.

*Young & D
Beckhaven House, 9 Gilbert Rd, London
SE11 5AA.
T:0171-820 3796/9403. F:0171-793
0537.
Mail order: *Colour Blue*, PO Box 69d, New
Malden, Surrey KT3 4PL.
T:0181-942 2525. F:0181-336 0803.
Hand forged café tables and taverna chairs.

DESKS

Antique Desks
36A Market Place, Warwicks CV34 4SH.
T:01926-499857.
Restored period desks: Edwardian roll tops,
partners and pedestal desks in solid oak,
mahogany or walnut.

Arthur Brett & Sons
See entry under REPRODUCTION
FURNITURE. Traditional desks and writing
tables, library tables, steps and pole
ladders. Also executive office furniture.

Budget Furniture
St Judes Church, Dulwich Rd,
London SE24 0PB.
T:0171-737 1371. F:0171-274 2023.
Low cost home/office furniture and
accessories including melamine desks
available in six finishes and several styles.
Delivery within a 40 mile radius.

Country Desks
78 High St, Berkhamsted, Herts HP4 2BW.
T:01442-866446. F:01442-872306.
Traditional reproduction desks, leather
covered chairs, computer cupboards,
bookcases, filing cabinets, and library steps.
Nationwide delivery.

IKEA
See entry under
PAINTED/DECORATIVE FURNITURE.
Furniture supermarket with good selection of
desks at moderate prices.

Just Desks
20 Church St, London NW8 8EP.
T:0171-723 7976. F:0171-402 6416.
Restored original and period reproductions
including styles for computers with
concealed keyboard, CPU, printer and fax.
Mail order.

LEATHER FURNITURE

*Connection Seating
Northfield Mills, Sharp Lane, Almondbury,
Huddersfield, W.Yorks HD4 6SR.
T:01484-514614. F:01484-547433.
Large range of contemporary leather
sofas and chairs for contract use.

Peter Dudgeon
See entry under
TRADITIONAL UPHOLSTERED
FURNITURE. Custom-built leather
furniture including a roll arm sofa, a
traditional Chesterfield, a wing chair, and a
button-backed chair.

***denotes
trade suppliers.
Please phone
for retail outlets.** 57

Howe's Designs
93 Pimlico Rd, London SW1W 8PH.
T:0171-730 7987. F:0171-730 0157.
Wonderful original leather sofas and chairs, when he can find them in good condition. Christopher Howe also supplies his own furniture upholstered in his exclusive range of goatskins which are aged and dyed in a wide range of colours. His workshops will also undertake leather re-upholstery and re-leathering of desktops.

M Pauw Antiques
606 King's Rd, London SW6 2DX.
T:0171-731 4022. F:0171-731 7356.
Antique dealer who specialises in period leather sofas and chairs, when available, and who also manufactures reproductions including a 1930s style Art Deco leather armchair and sofas to order. All the leathers are hand coloured and furniture is made in the traditional manner with handmade frames.

Roche-Bobois
See entry under **CONTEMPORARY FURNITURE & UPHOLSTERY.**
Furniture can be ordered in 30 colours of nubuck leather which is treated with a stain-resistant finish called 'DecoWash'.

Succession
See entry under
TRADITIONAL UPHOLSTERED FURNITURE. They occasionally have some old leather furniture, mainly brought over from France, but they will also supply all their own designs in leather.

PERSPEX FURNITURE & ACCESSORIES

Carew Jones
See entry under **CONTEMPORARY FURNITURE & UPHOLSTERY.**

Dauphin Display Oxford
PO Box 602, East Oxford OX44 9LU.
T:01865-343542. F:01865-343307.
Display stands, plinths, and cabinets in clear acrylic. Non-standard pieces to order. Glass or acrylic tables are a speciality: they can even incorporate tree trunks, statues, wooden horseheads, carved lions, or fossils, all encapsulated into a central base.

The Display Stand Company
5 Rickett St, London SW6 1RU.
T/F:0171-381 0255.
Specialise in acrylic display accessories but also undertake furniture commissions, such as coffee tables, bathroom furniture and shelving.

*Quadrant 4
Shakenhurst, Cleobury Mortimer, Kidderminster DY14 9AR.
T:01299-837406. F:01299-832676.
Acrylic furniture - selection of tables, showcases, wall brackets and mounts for artefacts.

ETHNIC FURNITURE & ACCESSORIES

Artichoke Interiors
D1 The Old Imperial Laundry,
71-73 Warriner Gardens,
London SW11 4XW.
T:0171-978 2439. F:0171-978 2457.
Agents for 19th century Chinese furniture by China Red: drinking and altar tables, stools, drums and rice buckets, wedding cabinets, chairs, blue and white porcelain and Chinese rugs.

Sebastiano Barbagallo Antiques
15-17 Pembridge Rd, London W11 3HL.
T:0171-792 3320. F:0171-232 1385.
Antiques from India and S.E. Asia, and a few from Africa: handicrafts, tables, cupboards,

and objects such as wooden spice and jewel boxes, vases, bronzes and stone sculptures.

Country & Eastern

8 Redwell St, Norwich, Norfolk NR2 4SN. T:01603-623107. F:01603-758108. And at: 3 Holland St, London W8 4NA. T:0171-938 2711. Antique and traditional furniture from India and S.E.Asia (coffee and dining tables, chests, cupboards etc). Plus cane furniture, wood carvings, hand printed and hand loomed tablecloths and bedspreads and copper and brass items. Good selection of ceramic, wood and metal lamps, Oriental rugs and kelims.

Jacqueline Edge

1 Courtnell St, London W2 5BU. T:0171-229 1172. F:0171-727 4651. Importer of colonial antiques from Burma. Specialist in old and new ceramics and antique lacquerwork. Also furniture (screens, chairs, tables), pots, pestles and garden planters and urns.

Exclusive Furnishings

34 Wigmore St, London W1H 0HU. T:0171-486 4748. F:0171-486 2667. Chinese furniture including dining suites, chests, low tables, screens, painted silks, statuary, cabinets and sideboards.

*Faraday Trading

Battersea Business Centre, 99 Lavender Hill, London SW11 5QL. T:0171-738 9420. F:0171-924 6260. By appointment. Cash & carry warehouse for Indian wooden and iron artefacts and furniture.

*In n Out Trading

Unit 1, Concord Rd, London W3 0TH. T:0181-993 1124. F:0181-993 9910. Cash and carry warehouse for old cupboards and apothecary chests, 'door' coffee tables, antique and reproduction chests and boxes mainly from northern and southern India.

The Kasbah

8 Southampton St, London WC2E 7HA. T:0171-240 3538. F:0171-379 5231. Moroccan furniture including mosaic-topped tables, iron and seagrass bookshelves and dark wood wardrobes, cabinets, and tables.

Orientique

40 Oak End Way, Gerrards Cross, Bucks SL9 8BR. T:01753-888361. F:01753-890105. Solid rosewood furniture imported from China: dining furniture, occasional and coffee tables, cabinets, Oriental screens, chests of drawers and TV cabinets. Some lacquer items as well.

Pukka Palace

174 Tower Bridge Rd, London SE1 3LR. T:0171-234 0000. F:0171-234 0110. Heavily-carved colonial furniture from India in exotic woods. There are day beds, divans, brass-bound merchants' boxes, cupboards, as well as coffee and dining tables made out of iron window grilles. The 'Pukka Pack' of 60 cards showing all the furniture and accessories available by mail order can be ordered on: 01345-666660.

William Sheppee

Old Sarum Airfield, Salisbury, Wilts SP4 6BJ. T:01722-334454. F:01722-337754. Largest importer of Indian reproduction and antique furniture in the UK, much of it hand finished here. Their premises are a World War I aircraft hangar which is a Grade II listed building.

Tansu

Skopos Mills, Bradford Rd, Batley, W.Yorks WF17 5LZ. T:01924-422391. F:01924-443856. Old Victorian mill chock-a-block with antique Japanese furniture. Most of it is from the Meiji period (1868-1912) and made from

*denotes trade suppliers. Please phone for retail outlets. 59

indigenous Japanese woods. There are tables, storage , clothing and shop chests, smaller boxes, as well as pottery, lanterns, screens and other smaller accessories.

*Tribal Traders
Marvin House, 279 Abbeydale Rd, Wembley, Middx HA0 1TW. T:0181-997 3303. F:0181-991 9692. Importers and wholesalers of furniture, antiques, crafts and decorative objects from Central Asia.

David Wainwright
61 Portobello Rd, London W11 3DB. T:0171-727 0707. F:0171-243 8100. And at: 28 Roslyn Hill NW3 6DT. T:0171-431 5900. An eclectic collection of artefacts from the ancient to the contemporary and ranging in price from £2 to £2000. Everything from colonial furniture to stone troughs and basins gathered from India and neighbouring countries.

SCREENS

*Altfield
See entry under REPRODUCTION FURNITURE. Range of about 70 reproduction 'antique' Japanese , Chinese and Korean screens, all hand painted. Plus others in lacquered leather with gold decoration.

Bery Designs
157 St John's Hill, London SW11 1TQ. T:0171-924 2197. F:0171-924 1879. Painted screens to order.

Besselink & Jones
99 Walton St, London SW3 2HH. T:0171-584 0343. F:0171-584 0284. Hand painted screens in leopard, tiger and zebra skin designs. Plus a bookcase-effect version and 20 different fire-screens.

The Dormy House
See entry under UNPAINTED/UNCOVERED FURNITURE. Five solid MDF screens and a pine-frame model in customers' own fabrics or supplied uncovered.

Gallery 19
19 Kensington Court Place, London W8 5BJ. T:0171-937 7222. Fireplace screen with panels which are reproductions of 17th century engravings.

Interiors Bis
60 Sloane Ave, London SW3 3DD. T:0171-838 1104. F:0171-838 1105. Modern cardboard screens by Interieur Carton and baroque cardboard furniture by Carton Massif.

Pukka Palace
See entry under ETHNIC FURNITURE & ACCESSORIES. Hand-painted 18th century-style screens in four designs; metal frame screen with jute panels.

Sinclair Melson
See entry under TRADITIONAL UPHOLSTERED FURNITURE. Upholstered screens.

Mobili
T:0181-699 3626. F:0181-291 7937. Danish curved room dividers with vertical slats or closed with fabric or linoleum. There is a matt aluminium version as well.

Take
715 Fulham Rd, London SW6 5UN. T:0171-736 7031. Shoji screens, futon sofabeds, covers, lighting, tables, chests of drawers, wardrobes and giftware - everything with a Japanese theme.

Viaduct
See entry under CONTEMPORARY FURNITURE & UPHOLSTERY. Corrugated cardboard screen.

David Wainwright
See entry under ETHNIC FURNITURE & ACCESSORIES. Wood and iron Jali screen from Rajasthan.

Alison White
Ground floor, Fitzpatrick Building, York Way, London N7 9AS. T:0171-609 6127. F:0171-609 6128. Smart screens with maple frames and opaque polypropylene panels.

Winston Yeatts of Warwickshire
See entry under PAINTED/DECORATIVE FURNITURE.

SHELVING

Aero
See entry under CONTEMPORARY FURNITURE & UPHOLSTERY.
Beech-veneered bookcase on wheels.

*Pavilion Rattan
Unit 4, Mill 2, Pleasley Vale Business Park,
off Outgang Lane, Pleasley,
Derbys NG19 8RL.
T:01623-811343. F:01623-810123.
Malacca shelf units combining rattan, steel
and glass; also traditional steel bakers'
shelves in antique black or antique green.

Rapid Racking
Unit 12, Spring Mill Estate, Avening Rd,
Nailsworth, Gloucs GL6 0BS.
T:01453-835431. F:01453-835127.
Easy to assemble chrome shelving, dividers
and baskets for shop displays or domestic
use. Optional glass shelves.

Slingsby Commercial and Industrial Equipment
Unit 8, Delta Pk, Smugglers Way,
London SW18 1EG.
T:0181-877 0778. F:0181-877 3063.
Nine branches nationwide. 'Super-Erecta'
adjustable wire shelving system made in
America from carbon steel and widely used
by retailers as display shelves.

Universal Providers
86 Golborne Rd, London W10 5PS.
T:0181-960 3736.
Usually has a good number of old French
bakers' shelves in stock in different sizes.

Viaduct
See entry under CONTEMPORARY FURNITURE & UPHOLSTERY.
'Pallucco'- a smart and adjustable
aluminum shelving system.

Vitsoe (UK)
85 Arlington Ave, London N1 7BA.
T:0171-354 8444. F:0171-354 9888.
Dieter Rams' flexible 'Universal Shelving
System' in anodized aluminium can be wall-
mounted or compressed between floor and
ceiling. It's been around for 35 years, and
can be taken with you when you move.

OFFICE FURNITURE

Ben Dawson Furniture
Eskmills, Musselburgh,
Edinburgh EH21 7UQ.
T:0131-665 9986. F:0131-653 6324.
Adaptable office system: conference tables,
desks and storage units in maple, oak,
cherry, madrona burr and walnut, with
veneering and inlay details if desired. Wide
range of shapes, finishes and sizes.

Directive Office
3 Rufus St, London N1 6PE.
T:0171-613 2888. F:0171-613 1506.
Everything from office furniture and modern
seating (for reception areas, cinemas or
auditoriums), to shelving and even wire
mannequins and coat hangers.

Domain
See entry under CONTEMPORARY FURNITURE & UPHOLSTERY.

Ergonom
365 Euston Rd, London NW1 3AR.
T:0171-387 8001. F:0171-387 4276.
Distributors for the Italian 'Unifor' range.
Also Wilkhahn seating and table systems
and Citterrio storage wall partitioning.

Knoll International
1 East Market, Lindsey St,
London EC1A 9PQ.
T:0171-236 6655. F:0171-248 1744.
Showroom for design classics by Florence
Knoll, Saarinen, Bertoia, Aulenti, Breuer,
Mics van der Rohe and Frank Gehry, as well
as complete office systems.

Haworth (UK)
10 New Oxford St, London WC1A 1EE.
T:0171-404 1617. F:0171-404 1607.
Traditional office system including reception
seating, filing and storage, boardroom
and executive furniture. Also distribute
the modern Ordo collection and Castelli
office systems.

Marcatre
143-149 Great Portland St, W1 5FB.
T:0171-436 1808. F:0171-436 1807.
Designer range of office furniture including a
collection by the architect Achille Castiglioni.

***denotes
trade suppliers.
Please phone
for retail outlets.** 61

Herman Miller

149 Tottenham Court Rd, London W1P 0JA.
T:0171-388 7331. F:0171-387 3507.
Classical American office collection.

Steelcase Strafor PLC

Newlands Drive, Poyle, Berks SL3 0DX.
T:01753-680200. F:01753-686918.
Consolidates Gordon Russell, Harvey
Furniture and Steelcase Strafor. Custom
built quality office furniture in wood, veneers,
inlays, coloured lacquers and glass. Also
standard range of office furniture in various
finishcs: oak, ash, beech, American black
walnut, American cherry and bird's-eye
maple. Steel filing and storage units. A
comprehensive range of office furniture
systems, storage and seating.

CONTRACT FURNITURE

Allemuir Contract Furniture

***denotes
trade suppliers.
Please phone
for retail outlets.**

Branch Rd, Lower Darwen, Lancs BB3 0PR.
T:01254-682421. F:01254-673793.
Contemporary contract tables and chairs
including smart stacking chairs and the
'Luna' aluminium bar stool.

Coexistence

288 Upper St, London N1 2TZ.
T:0171-354 8817. F:0171-354 9610.
Modern European designs including
anodized aluminium cafe tables and chairs.
Good range of bar stools and lighting.
Modern serving trays by Anaries Van
Onck and Antonio Citterio.

*The Conran Shop Contracts

22 Shad Thames, London SE1 2YU.
T:0171-357 7703. F:0171-357 7704.
Core range of products for architects and
designers to furnish office, hotel,
restaurant, theatre, boardroom
or airport. Furniture from Carlos
Jané, Indecasa,Vitra, Wilkhahn,
Hille, Fritz Hansen and others.
Good selection of chairs and
modern upholstered seating.
Also hi-fi systems and
contemporary door furniture
by leading designers.

Domain

See entry under **CONTEMPORARY
FURNITURE & UPHOLSTERY.**

*MAS Furniture Contracts

MAS House, 374-378 Old St,
London EC1V 9LT.
T:0171-739 6961. F:0171-739 2256.
Very large selection of standard and custom
made restaurant/hotel/leisure furniture
including 50s diner range.

*Primo Furniture

Baird Rd, Enfield, Middx EN1 1SJ.
T:0181-804 3434. F:0181-805 0606.
Designers and manufacturers of furniture for
the catering and leisure industry including
seating formed from steel, timber and GRP.

*Satelliet (UK)

Unit 14, Hazel Rd, Four Marks, Alton,
Hampshire GU34 5EY.
T:01420-561080. F:01420-561090.
Wood, rattan, metal and aluminium furniture
in modern and traditional styles for hotels,
clubs and other commercial areas.

SCP

See entry under **CONTEMPORARY
FURNITURE & UPHOLSTERY.**

*Sommer Allibert (UK)

Berry Hill Ind Estate,
Droitwich, Worcs WR9 9AB.
T:01905-795796. F:01905-794454.
High-grade resin furniture for contract use:
stackable poolside chairs and loungers.

*Target Furniture

Studland Rd, Kingsthorpe,
Northants NN2 6NE.
T:01604-792929 F:01604-792500.
Contract furniture for the leisure market,
primarily restaurants and pubs.

Andy Thornton

Ainleys Ind Estate, Elland, W.Yorks HX5 9JP.
T:01422-375595. F:01422-377455.
Huge range of furniture, lighting and
accessories for themed restaurants: bric-a-
brac, statuary, brasswork, bespoke joinery,
architectural metalwork - everything from
gazebos to bandstands. Plus vast stock of
architectural salvage and Design and
Contracting Department.

*Wychwood Design
Viscount Court,
Brize Norton, Oxon OX18 3QQ.
T:01993-851435. F:01993-851594.
Large selection of Louis XV, XVI,
Gainsborough, Sheraton, Chinese
Chippendale, Regency and Empire
reproduction furniture. Also modern designs
and reception and boardroom furniture
made to clients' specifications. Various
colours and wood finishes.

OTHER SUPPLIERS & SERVICES

Haddonstone
The Forge House, East Haddon,
Northants NN6 8DB.
T:01604-770711. F:01604-770027.
Manufacturers of the standard glass-
topped coffee table with stone supports
in the shape of lions, dolphins, scrolls or
Corinthian capitals.

The Handmade Wooden Tea Tray Company
Teignbridge Business Centre, Cavalier Rd,
Heathfield, Newton Abbot, Devon TQ12 6TZ.
T:01626-835174. F:01626-835186.
Wooden handmade trays available in antique
mahogany, pine or in coloured finishes. They
are sold separately or with a stand. The
company also makes trays to fit footstools.

LASSCo
St Michael's, Mark St,
off Paul St, London EC2A 4ER.
T:0171-739 0448. F:0171-729 6853.
The London Architectural Salvage & Supply
Company uses its marble off-cuts to make
mosaic and marquetry tables. A simple
chequerboard table with iron base costs
from £195 + VAT.

Roomservice Furnishing Group
28 Barwell Business Park, Leatherhead Rd,
Chessington, Surrey KT9 2NY.
T:0181-397 9344. F:0181-391 1800.
Rental service of furniture and accessories.
Fully inclusive 'Emergency Housepacks' so
you can move into a new house with only a
toothbrush. Nationwide service.

Screwdriver
15 Geraldine Rd, London W4 3PA.
T/F:0181-994 2920. Team of 120 men
nationwide (26 in London) who will assemble
flat-pack furniture for you at home or in
your office. Rates are £20 an hour. Time
necessary can be worked out in advance.

**For wicker, rattan,
and Lloyd Loom
furniture see
GARDENS chapter.**

4

BEDS & BEDDING

NEW BEDS

James Adam
24 Church St,
Woodbridge, Suffolk IP12 1DH.
T:01394-384471. F:01394-384520.
Wide selection of French reproduction beds
including a lit bateau, a Louis XV bed, a
Regency 'Put-U-Up', a Directoire bed and a
Jacobean four-poster.

And So To Bed
638-640 King's Rd, London SW6 2DU.
T:0171-731 3593. F:0171-371 5272.
Ten other branches nationwide. Good
selection of brass beds, but also wooden
bedsteads, mattresses and accessories.

Beaudesert
Old Imperial Laundry, London SW11 4XW.
T:0171-720 4977. F:0171-720 4970.
Specialists in four-poster beds. There are
seven hand carved styles, available in wood,
painted, or gilded, but any other design can
be made to order. Custom-made pocket
sprung mattresses and bed hangings.

Big Table Furniture Co-operative
56 Great Western Rd, London W9 3NT.
T:0171-221 5058. F:0171-229 6032.
Manufacturers of pine beds. There are
nine types on display, including bunks,
four-posters and stacking beds. Different
headboards and finishes available. Plus
handmade mattresses.

The Conran Shop
Michelin House, 81 Fulham Rd,
London SW3 6RD.
T:0171-589 7401. F:0171-823 7015.
'Travieso' metal four-poster, Matthew
Hilton's maple frame bed with a curved
laminated headboard, Tracey Byles' high-
framed cherrywood bed and an American
country-style four-poster in cherrywood.

*Deptich Designs
7 College Fields, Prince George's Rd,
London SW19 2PT.
T:0181-687 0867. F:0181-648 6515.
Manufacturers of traditional brass, metal
and wooden beds. Will also supply spare
brass or china knobs.

* denotes
trade supplier.
Please phone
for retail outlets. 65

Geoffrey Drayton

85 Hampstead Rd, London NW1 2PL.
T:0171-387 5840. F:0171-387 5874.
Contemporary beds by Cassina, Interlubke
and B&B Italia.

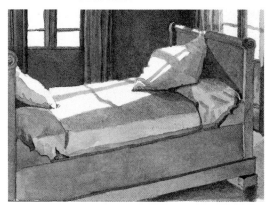

Simon Horn

117-121 Wandsworth Bridge Rd,
London SW6 2TP.
T:0171-731 1279. F:0171-736 3522.
Specialist in French and classical wooden
beds and daybeds. There are about 60
different designs, from a 'Dutch colonial'
four-poster to the simple 'Empire' bed - all in
a variety of woods or even 'in the raw', ready
for painting. Also antique beds, divans,
mattresses and other bedroom furniture.

The Iron Bed Company

Southfield Park, Delling Lane, Bosham,
Chichester, West Sussex PO18 8NN.
T:01243-574049. F:01243-573768.
And at:
580 Fulham Rd, London SW6 5NT.
T:0171-610 9903.
Branches in Puttenham and Harrogate. New
cast iron beds based on traditional designs
and available in black, acid yellow, orange,
purple, turquoise or bright pink. Mail order.

The Iron Design Company

Summer Carr Farm, Thornton Le Moor,
Northallerton, North Yorks DL6 3SG.
T:01609-778143. F:01609-778846.
Iron beds in both simple and swirly designs
and available as bedsteads, four posters,
or just as surrounds or headboards which
fit straight onto existing divans.

Litvinoff & Fawcett

281 Hackney Rd, London E2 8NA.
T:0171-739 3480. F:0171-738 1018.
And at:
238 Gray's Inn Rd, London WC1 8HB.
T:0171-278 5391. Specialists in pine beds:
there are 8 sizes and 40 different finishes.

Moriarti's Workshop

High Halden, Nr Ashford, Kent TN26 3LY.
T:01233-850214. F:01233-850524.
Pine furniture warehouse with at least
25 beds on display, in all styles and sizes.
Specialists in 'cabin' or 'study' beds which
incorporate a desk unit and drawer or a
cupboard.

Charles Page Furniture

61 Fairfax Rd, London NW6 4EE.
T:0171-328 9851. F:0171-328 7240.
Contemporary beds by Molteni: anything
from standard slatted bases to electrically
adjustable beds, with all sorts of different
headboards. Plus co-ordinating bedlinen.

Simon Poyntz

Kennel Lodge Rd, Bower Ashton,
Bristol BS3 2JT.
T/F:0117-963 2563. Hand-turned
and carved reproduction beds, from
Georgian four-posters to classic 'lits
bateau', in mahogany, walnut, oak, cherry,
gilt or hand-painted finishes. Large range
of bed canopies. Special commissions.

Purves & Purves

80-81 & 83 Tottenham Court Rd,
London W1P 9HD.
T:0171-580 8223. F:0171-580 8244.
Danish beds in cherrywood or beech, metal
beds by Ore Designs, cherrywood bed by
Tracey Byles, modern upholstered beds.

Renwick & Clarke

190 Ebury St, London SW1W 8UP.
T:0171-730 8913. F:0171-730 4508.
Niermann Weeks' range of beds and
headboards to order. Each piece is tailored
to your own requirements, so prices start
at about £1800.

*Roset (UK)

95a High St, Great Missenden,
Bucks HP16 0AL.

:01494-865001. F:01494-866883.
ontemporary beds: Pascal Mourgue's
Parallele' bed with upholstered headboard
nd attachable trays at the sides; Jean de
astelbajac's 'Astarac' metal four-poster
vith optional hangings; Peter Maly's
pholstered bed with removable back
ushions and side trays.

haker
5 Harcourt St, London W1H 1DT.
:0171-724 7672. F:0171-724 6640.
nd at:
22 King's Rd, London SW3 5UH.
:0171-352 3918. F:0171-376 3494.
encil post Queen-size four-poster in maple
r cherry. Plus a selection of bedding,
ashbags and accessories.

omerset House of Iron
79 Fulham Rd, London SW6 5HA.
:0171-371 0436. F:0171-371 0068.
our styles of iron bed as well as custom-
nade wooden beds, some painted.

tuart Interiors
arrington Court,
r Ilminster, Somerset TA19 0NQ.
:01460-240349. F:01460-242069.
eproduction Gothic and Elizabethan
ester and four poster beds in oak.

iaduct
-10 Summer's St, London EC1R 5BD.
:0171-278 8456. F:0171-278 2844.
he 'Palatino' beechwood bed by the Italian
ompany Driade has a curved beech
lywood headboard; Pallucco Italia's '3x3'
ed has a wooden slatted base and a solid
r upholstered headboard, and the
Acquariano' beechwood bed comes in 10
ifferent versions.

Vooden Tops and Tin Men
he Wheel Craft Workshops, Clifford St,
hudleigh, Devon TQ13 0LH.
:01626-852777. F:01626-852224.
ange of ten iron beds in single, double,
ingsize or four poster versions. Mail order.

Young & D
eckhaven House, 9 Gilbert Rd, London
E11 5AA. T:0171-820 3796/9403.
:0171-793 0537.

Mail order: *Colour Blue,* PO Box 69d, New
Malden, Surrey KT3 4PL. T:0181-942 2525.
F:0181-336 0803.
Elaborate iron beds in three styles called
Tree of Life, Swan and Morpheus. They are
available as singles, doubles and in rust or
black finishes.

ANTIQUE BEDS

After Noah
121 Upper St, London N1 1QP.
T/F:0171-359 4281.
And at: 261 King's Rd, London SW3 5EL.
T/F:0171-351 2610. Old wrought-iron beds.

Antique Beds
3 Litfield Place, Clifton, Bristol BS8 3LT.
T:0117-973 5134. F:0117-974 4450.
Mainly antique but also some reproduction
four-poster beds, drapes and custom-made
mattresses.

Bed Bazaar
The Old Station, Station Rd,
Framlingham, Suffolk IP13 9EE.
T:01728-723756. F:01728-724626.
Over 2000 old brass/brass & iron/all
iron beds. Their sister company Sleeping
Partners makes traditional mattresses in
any shape or size.

Brass Knight
Cumeragh House Farm, Cumeragh Lane,
Whittingham, Preston, Lancs PR3 2AL.
T/F:01772-786666. Stock of 1200 restored
and unrestored beds dating from 1840 to
1900.

Marilyn Garrow
6 The Broadway, White Hart Lane,
London SW13 0NY. T/F: 0181-392 1655.
Louis XV, Empire and other French beds.

Judy Greenwood Antiques
657 Fulham Rd, London SW6 5PY.
T:0171-736 6037. F:0171-736 1941.
French 'lits bateaux' and painted, iron
and cane beds.

Harriet Ann Sleigh Beds
Standen Farm, Smarden Rd,
Biddenden, Nr Ashford, Kent TN27 8JT.
T/F:01580-291220. 60-70 antique

* denotes
trade supplier.
Please phone
for retail outlets.

continental sleigh beds and Gustavian day beds in stock. Mattresses made to order.

Simon Horn
See entry under **NEW BEDS**.
Antique beds (cast iron, brass and wood) from all over Europe and occasionally the Far East. They restore and lengthen beds and make mattresses to fit.

House of Steel
400 Caledonian Rd, London N1 1DN. T/F:0171-607 5889. Victorian steel and brass beds plus any metal bed made to the client's own design.

Seventh Heaven
Chirk Mill, Chirk, Wrexham County Borough LL14 5BU. T:01691-777622/773563. F:01691-777313. Mid-Victorian cast iron bedsteads and four-posters restored and refinished in black, dark green, light cream, verdigris, pewter or bronze. Also British and European wooden beds dating 1860 to 1900.

The Victorian Brass Bedstead Company
Hoe Copse, Cocking,
Nr Midhurst, W.Sussex GU29 OHL. T:01730-812287. F:01730-815081. 200 restored traditional Victorian beds on display - plus another 2000 still unrestored ones to choose from.

OTHER BEDS

The Futon Company
138 Notting Hill Gate, London W11 3QG. T:0171-727 9252. F:0171-792 1165. Branches nationwide. Futon means mattress in Japanese and this company can make them in any size (they've just made one 18' wide). Also traditional Tatami mats made from solid rice straw with a seagrass cover for use as a sleeping platfom.

Futon Express
23-27 Pancras Rd, London NW1 2QB. T:0171-833 3945. F:0171-833 8199. And branches in Catford and Clapham. Claim to have the largest range of futons in the UK, and they certainly offer some of the cheapest.

GP Contracts
Suite 622, Linen Hall,
162-168 Regent St, London W1R 5TB. T:0171-434 4289. F:0171-287 2329. Horizontal and vertical wallbeds that fold away fully made up into fitted cupboards. The range includes a foldaway bunk bed and a wall-mounted couchette.

The London Wall Bed Company
430 Chiswick High Rd, London W4 5TF. T:0181-742 8200. F:0181-742 8008. Some forty different styles on offer - including one disguised as a bookcase.

London Waterbed Company
99 Crawford St, London W1H 1AN. T:0171-935 1111. F:0171-723 5846. The place to go if you want a nightly form of hydrotherapy. There are 20 models with 5 different mattress options.

Royal Auping
35 Baker St, London W1M 1AE. T:0171-935 3774. F:0171-935 3720. Manufacturers of the king of all adjustable beds, the 'Konfortabel Royal' model, which is £5,700 and custom-made to fit one's personal height and weight. It allows you to sit up, lie down, raise your feet above your head and the internal heating can be set so that, for instance, only your feet are warm.

Yakamoto Futons
Arch 4, Stables Market,
Chalk Farm Rd, London NW1 8AH. T:0171-284 2859. F:0171-485 5350. And at:
339B Finchley Rd, London NW3 6EP. T:0171-794 8034. Good quality futons in seven choices of frame and in pine, mahogany or black finishes.

MATTRESSES & DIVANS

*Dunlopillo (UK)
Pannal, Harrogate, N.Yorks HG3 1JL. T:01423-872411. F:01423-879232. Manufacturers of natural latex mattresses and pillows. Recommended for allergy sufferers as latex doesn't attract dust or fluff.

The Fairchild Company

arford Orchard, Parsonage Lane, Kingston
t Mary, Taunton, Somerset TA2 8AW.
:01823-451881. F:01823-451899.
Bespoke mattresses from the smallest
Moses to the largest king-size in either
uttoned or woven (with a removable cover)
ersions. Also pillows, duvets, quilts.

The Feather Bed Company

Crosslands House, Ash Thomas,
Tiverton, Devon EX16 4NU.
:01884-821331. F:01884-821328.
Densely-filled curled duck feather
mattresses for use over existing
eds for added warmth and comfort.

Foamplan Rubber & Plastics

450 Holloway Rd, London N7 6PA.
:0171-609 2700. F:0171-700 0275.
Made to measure foam, latex, pocket-sprung
r coil-sprung mattresses in standard or
nusual sizes. Plus foam in any size, grade
r shape cut to size on the spot.

GWB Products

Unit 10, Hanover Trading Estate,
orth Rd, London N7 9DH. T:0171-619
294. F:0171-609 1664. Manufacturers of
espoke mattresses, divans and bed bases.
pecial shapes and sizes, including cut-out
orners for four-posters.

Heal's

196 Tottenham Court Rd, London W1P 9LD.
:0171-636 1666. F:0171-637 5582.
wn factory for production of both
unstructured' hair mattresses (no springs)
nd sprung versions - the best known being
heir 'Jack Spratt' model, with two beds of
ifferent tensions joined together.

Lullaby Handmade Mattresses

8 Scrubs Lane, London NW10.
:0171-359 9413. Handmade coil, pocket
r open sprung mattresses in any shape
nd size. They pride themselves on their
peedy service: a new mattress takes
etween a couple of days and a week.

Mattison

110 -118 Romford Rd, London E15 4EH.
:0181-534 4474. F:0181-519 5358.
ontract and hotel mattresses, folding beds.

The Natural Furniture Company

192 Balls Pond Rd,
London N1 4AA.
T:0171-226 4477.
F:0171-704 0544.
Manufacturers of natural
fibre mattresses
in any size. There are
two versions: a
'Supernatural', which
consists of latex-covered
horsehair, coconut coir
fibre, and layers of cotton
encased in lambswool,
and a simpler 'Natural', in
cotton with layers of coir
fibre in the middle. They
make the cot mattresses
for the National Childbirth
Trust. Plus futon and sofa
bed frames to order.

RJ Norris

88 Coldharbour Lane, London SE5 9PU.
T:0171-274 5306. This family firm has
made bespoke natural fibre mattresses
since 1945. They make special sizes for
antique beds, foam-free cots and day
beds, thin mattresses for folding beds,
even triangular mattresses for boats.

*Relyon

Station Mills, Wellington, Somerset TA21
8NN. T:01823-667501. F:01823-666079.
Manufacturer of beds and sofabeds
in standard and special sizes.

*Rest Assured

Pontgwaith, Ferndale, Rhondda,
Mid Glamorgan CF43 3ED.
T:01443-730541. F:01443-756900.
Manufacturer of back-care and other beds
for both the contract and domestic market.

Savoy Bedworks

Unit 1, The Willows Centre,
17 Willow Lane, Mitcham, Surrey CR4 4NX.
T:0181-648 7701. F:0181-640 0087.
This company has made beds for the
Savoy Group's hotels and private clients
for over 60 years.

* denotes
trade supplier.
Please phone
for retail outlets.   69

*Sealy (UK)
Station Rd, Aspatria,
Carlisle, Cumbria CA5 2AS.
T:016973-20342. F:016973-22347.
The 'Posturepedic' is their most famous
bed. Wide range of beds for hotels, etc.

*Silentnight Beds
PO Box 9, Barnoldswick,
Colne, Lancs BB8 6BL.
T:01282-813051. F:01282-816803.
Beds for the domestic market, including
their 'no roll together' model with springs
adjusted so that the bed is firmer on one
side than the other.

*Sleepeezee
61 Morden Rd, Merton, London SW19 3XP.
T:0181-540 9171. F:0181-542 0547.
'Beautyrest' pocket-sprung mattresses.

Sleeping Partners
The Old Station, Station Rd,
Framlingham, Suffolk IP13 9EE.
T:01728-724944. F:01728-724626.
Traditional handmade mattresses in
any shape or size.

*Slumberland
Salmon Fields, Royton,
Oldham, W.Yorks OL2 6SB.
T:0161-628 2898. F:0161-628 2895.
Wide range of domestic and contract beds.

*Vi-Spring
Ernesettle, Plymouth PL5 2TT.
T:01752-366311. F:01752-355109.
Quality beds and mattresses sold through
major retailers. Contract division for hotels.

West London Bedding
The Old Church Warehouse,
220 North End Rd, London W14 9NX.
T/F:0171-385 7711/385 2000. Large
bed warehouse which supplies all the
leading makes and models at discounted
prices. Same day delivery for stock items.

**For advice on
buying a bed and
for other
manufacturers
contact The Sleep
Council, High Corn
Mill, Chapel Hill,
Skipton, North
Yorks BD23 1NL.
Their helpline is
on 01756-
792327.**

HEADBOARDS

A Barn Full of Sofas and Chairs
Furnace Mill, Lamberhurst, Kent TN3 8LH.
T:01892-890285. F:01892-890988.
Upholstered headboards to order.

Jane Clayton & Co
Unit 12, Old Mills,
Paulton, Bristol BS18 5SU.
T:01761-412255. F:01761-413558.
Any design to order, with prices from
£85 to £330.

Cover Up Designs
9 Kingsclere Park,
Nr Newbury, Berks RG20 4SW.
T:01635-297981. F:01635-298363.
16 different padded headboard designs
or any other to order.

The Dormy House
Sterling Park, East Portway Ind Estate,
Andover, Hampshire SP10 3TZ.
T:01264-365808. F:01264-366359.
Four styles of headboard supplied
uncovered or upholstered in any fabric.

Elizabeth Eaton
85 Bourne St, London SW1W 8HF.
T:0171-730 2262. F:0171-730 7294.
Bedheads in simulated bamboo; in pine for
painting; with two posts and upholstered;
and a copy of an 18th century design
with posts and a curtain suspended
from a brass rail.

PGI
Water-Ma-Trout,
Helston, Cornwall TR13 0LW.
T:01326-563868. F:01326-563491.
Manufacturers of padded headboards for
the big bed companies. Will also cover them
in customers' own fabric.

BEDLINEN & TOWELS

Antique Designs
4 Stretton Hall Mews, Hall Lane,
Lower Stretton, Cheshire WA4 4NY.
T:01925-730909. F:01925-730881.
Cotton and linen bedlinen and accessories
hand-embroidered in China, many
reproduced from Victorian designs.

Bedstock
26 Portobello Green Arcade,
281 Portobello Rd, London W10 5TZ.
T/F:0181-964 1547. Sheets, duvet covers,
pillowcases and pyjamas in stripes, checks

and bold red, orange or fuchsia roses. New designs based on Romantic poetry with different scripts and blocks of gold leaf. Their plain Egyptian cotton sheets and towels can be dyed in any one of 450 colours.

Cologne & Cotton
74 Regent St, Leamington Spa,
Warwicks CV32 4NS.
T:01926-332573. F:01926-332575.
London branches in Fulham Rd and Kensington Church St. Large range of pure cotton bedlinen in white, candy stripe, seersucker, gingham, self-stripe and flanellette. French honeycomb towels.

Courtaulds Textiles (Ashton)
PO Box 19, Carrfield Mills,
Hyde, Cheshire SK14 4NR.
T:0161-368 1961. F:0161-368 5148.
Manufacturers of Christy towels and co-ordinates. Minimum order £2000.

& N Davidson
52 Ledbury Rd, London W11 2AJ.
T:0171-243 2089. F:0171-243 2092.
Linen, toile, gingham, chambray and striped bedlinen; checked wool throws.

Delblanco Meyer
Portland House,
Ryland Rd, London NW5 3EB.
T:0171-468 3000. F:0171-468 3094.
Embroidered bedlinen and quality duvets and pillows.

Descamps
197 Sloane St, London SW1X 9QX.
T:0171-235 6957. F:0171-235 3903.
French collection which includes hemstitched, scalloped edged, and embroidered bedlinen, towels, bath hats and robes plus a children's range.

Designers Guild
267-271 King's Rd, London SW3 5EN.
T:0171-351 5775. F:0171-243 7710.
Printed and appliqué cotton bedlinen in bright checks, florals, and a new range in spicy colours.

Dorma
New Town Mill, PO Box 7, Lees St,
Swinton, Manchester M27 6DB.

T:0161-2514400. F:0161-2514404.
Manufacturer of a large range of patterned bed linen and towels.

Dreams
Knaves Beach, High Wycombe,
Bucks HP10 9QY.
T:01628-520520. F:01628-535350.
Claims to undercut comparable bedlinens by 10%.

Thomas Ferguson & Co
54 Scarva Rd, Banbridge, Co.Down
BT32 3AU, Northern Ireland.
T:018206-23491. F:018206-22453.
Weavers of Irish linen since 1854.
White linen sheets, pillowcases and duvet covers with natural or coloured trim and embroidered if desired. Plus linen damask towels and smart linen bathrobes. They also manufacture tablelinen.

*Fogarty
Havenside, Boston, Lincs PE21 0AH.
T:01205-361122. F:01205-353202.
Quilts, pillows, bathroom carpets, shower curtains and accessories. Curtains and quilts made up to order for contract sales.

*The French Linen Company
Unit 7, The Vale Ind. Centre, Southern Rd,
Aylesbury, Bucks HP19 3EW.
T:01296-394980. F:01296-394919.
Co-ordinated bedlinen, robes and towelling by Yves Delorme. Also manufacturers under licence of designs by Christian Lacroix, Kenzo, Chevignon and Pierre Frey. Brinkhaus duvets with natural fillings.

Frette
98 New Bond St, London W1Y 9LF.
T:0171-629 5517. F:0171-499 2332.
Top quality Italian bed and table linen and towels. Contract division for hotels.

*Heirlooms
Arun Business Park, Bognor Regis,
W. Sussex PO22 9SX.
T:01243-820252. F:01243-821174.
Manufacturers of table and bedlinen in Egyptian cotton, pure Irish linen and silk and polyester cotton percale. The range includes jacquard weave designs. Contract sizes made to order.

* denotes
trade supplier.
Please phone
for retail outlets. 71

The Irish Linen Company
35/36 Burlington Arcade, London W1 9AD.
T:0171-493 8949. F:0171-499 5485.
Traditional linens, hand-embroidered
in Madeira.

Ralph Lauren Home Collection
At Harvey Nichols, Selfridges, Harrods
and selected House of Fraser stores.
T:0171-495 5499 for other outlets and
trade enquiries. Collection includes the
'White Label' range in Egyptian cotton, the
'Denim Collection' in all shades of blue,
posy-printed 'Florals' and 'Aran Cottage'
with simple stripes and textures.

Linen and Lace Company
7 Greenwich Market, London SE10.
T:0181-293 9407. F:0181-317 3788.
White-on-white embroidered pillowcases,
duvet covers, sheets and bolster covers.
Patchwork, throws, bedspreads.

The Linen Cupboard
21 Great Castle St, London W1N 7AA.
T:0171-629 4062. Discounted towels
and bedlinen - including Irish linen and
Egyptian cotton.

Lunn Antiques
86 New King's Rd, London SW6 4LU.
T:0171-736 4638. F:0171-371 7113.
Antique and new bed and table linen, lace
bed covers, decorative cushions, bolsters,
accessories and embroidered muslin
curtain panels.

Monogrammed Linen Shop
168 Walton St, London SW3 2JL.
T:0171-589 4033. F:0171-823 7745.
Old fashioned quality linen. Sheets,
tablecloths and piqué bedspreads made
to measure in any size. The monogram
and embroidery service takes a week.

Old Town Bedlinen
32 Elm Hill, Norwich, Norfolk NR3 1HG.
T:01603-628100. Button-fastened duvet
covers and pillowcases in eight colours of
gingham, four tartans and five chambrays.

The Original Silver Lining
Workshop 29, Lenton Business Centre,
Lenton Boulevard, Nottingham NG2 7BY.
T:0115-955 5123. F:0115-962 3064.

By appointment. Range of heavily
embroidered bed linen in white and cream.

Peacock Blue
PO Box 11254, London SW11 5ZN.
T:0171-771 7400. F:0171-771 7401.
Mail order only. Bedlinen in simple
designs: chambray, stripes, plains and with
contrasting borders. Plus towels, bath robes
blankets, goose-down duvets and pillows.

'*Peter Reed Group
Springfield Mill, Lomeshaye,
Nelson, Lancs BB9 6BT.
T:01282-692416. F:01282-601214.
Manufacturers of Egyptian cotton bed
and tablelinen.

Renwick & Clarke
See entry under **NEW BEDS**. Embroidered
and plain linen and towelling by Bruno
Richard. Designs can be personalised to
order. Also mohair and cashmere blankets.

Seventh Heaven
Chirk Mill, Chirk, Wrexham County
Borough, Clwyd LL14 5BU.
T:01691-777622/773563.
F:01691-777313. Suppliers and restorers of
antique beds who also have their own range
of percale cotton/polyester bed linen in
standard, kingsize and emperor sizes. Plus
four-poster drapes, bolster cases, cushions
and bedding. Made to measure service.

Shaker
See **NEW BEDS.**
Red or blue plaid bedlinen, 'log-cabin'-style patchwork quilts, striped wool blankets, white honeycomb towels with Shaker motifs.

Silks of Copenhagen
32 Cannon Court Rd,
Maidenhead, Berks SL6 7QN.
T:07000-474557. F:01628-21074.
Machine-washable 100% silk bed linen in a wide range of sizes and colours and all available by mail order.

The Source
26-40 Kensington High St, London W8 4PF.
T:0171-820 2865. F:0171-820 2762.
And at:
Lakeside Retail Park, West Thurrock,
Essex RM16 1WS. T:01708-890253.
F:01708-890721.
And at: 10 Harbour Parade,West Quay,
Southampton SO16 1BA.T:01703-336141.
F:01703-336198. American style one-stop home store - the 'Sleeping' department offers both branded and own-label bedlinen, duvets, pillows, bedspreads and quilts.

*Turquaz
The Coach House, Bakery Place,
119 Altenburg Gardens, London SW11 1JQ.
T:0171-924 6894. F:0171-924 6868.
Indian cotton bedlinen in bold checks, stripes and plaids with ties and cloth covered buttons. Also tablelinen.
Mail order service.

*Webster Weave
Dock Ing Mill, Bradford Rd,
Batley, W.Yorks WF17 8HB.
T:01924-420024. F:01924-420350.
Towelling by the metre.

The White Company
Unit 19c, The Coda Centre,
189 Munster Rd, London SW6 6AW.
T:0171-385 7988. F:0171-385 2685.
Mail order firm offering classic cotton bedlinen (mainly white, but also in gingham), tablecloths, towels and blankets.

The White House
51-52 New Bond St, London W1Y 0BY.
T:0171-629 3521. F:0171-629 8269.

The finest bed and table linens (all the top names and their own collection), plus towels, quilts, nightshirts, slippers and layette gifts.

THROWS/BLANKETS/ BEDSPREADS

Anta Scotland
Fearn, Tain, Ross-Shire IV20 1XW.
T:01862-832477. F:01862-832616.
Large range of woollen checked furnishing throws and tartan rugs in various weights and sizes. Mail order.

*John Atkinson & Sons
Spring Valley Mills, Stanningley,
Pudsey, W.Yorks LS28 6DW.
T:0113-2553373. F:0113-2558187.
Manufacturer of wool, merino wool and cashmere blankets in all sorts of sizes, colours and styles.

The Blanket Box
Freepost LS6412,
Garforth, Leeds LS25 1YY.
T:0113-287 6057. F:0113-286 4438.
Mail order company with luxurious blankets in pure wool, merino, super merino or lambswool/cashmere mix. There are 22 colours to choose from and a new checked range. Also throws. Prices start at £46 for a bunk-bed sized blanket.

Chelsea Textiles
7 Walton St, London SW3 2JD.
T:0171-584 0111. F:0171-584 7170.
Custom-made bedcovers made from their wide range of hand embroidered fabrics, with hand woven checked or ticking backing cloths and several styles of hand quilting. Also Provencal-inspired quilted bedcovers, Chinoiserie spot motif embroidered bedcovers, cushions and fabrics reproduced from 18th and 19th century originals.

Damask
3-4 Broxholme House, Nr Harwood Rd,
New King's Rd, London SW6 4AA.
T/F:0171-731 3553. Cotton patchwork quilts, jacquard woven bedspreads, toile design quilts, linens and accessories.

*** denotes
trade supplier.
Please phone
for retail outlets.** 73

*Early's of Witney
Witney Mill, Witney, Oxon OX8 5EB.
T:01993-703131. F:01993-771513.
From cellular cotton to thick merino wool
blankets in all sorts of colours, and also
offered in flame retardant versions. Special
blanket embroidery service. Wool and cotton
throws and embroidered bed linen.

Ever Trading
12 Martindale,
East Sheen, London SW14 7AL.
T:0181-878 4050. F:0181-876 5757.
Luxurious imitation fur throws and
bedspreads lined with plain wool, coloured
linen or paisley cotton. Choose from lynx,
polar bear, leopard, sable, bear, wolf, or
brown and grey chinchilla. They are also
available by the metre. Plus plain or checked
linen throws.

Joss Graham Oriental Textiles
10 Eccleston St, London SW1W 9LT.
T/F:0171-730 4370. Narrow-strip indigo
dyed throws from Mali in Africa, made by a
70 year old man who is the last indigo dyer in
West Africa. They are available in very large
sizes and perfect as bedspreads.

*The Indian Collection
4 Castle St, Wallingford, Oxon OX10 8DL.
T:01491-833048. F:01491-839590.
And retail outlet at: *Bopsom & Son*,
34 High St, Kington, Herefordshire HR5 3BJ.
T/F:01544-231081. Very large range of
Indian bedspreads and quilts including hand-
blocked floral or geometric designs,
hand-woven and Ikat throws, blue and white
or indigo cotton-filled quilts, appliqué and
embroidered cushions. Plus tablecloths,
shawls, kimonos, dhurries.

Melin Tregwynt
Tregwynt Mill, Castlemorris, Haverfordwest,
Pembrokeshire, Wales SA62 5UX.
T:01348-891225. F:01348-891694.
Pure new wool blankets and throws in soft
shades, big bold checks or classic plains
and pinstripes. New gingham range in blue,
rose or spring green. The large fringed
throws are Teflon-coated to make them soil,
stain and water repellent.

Pembroke Squares
28 Westmoreland Place, London SW1V 4AE.
T/F:0171-834 9739. By appointment.
Crochet cotton bedspreads which are copies
of Victorian designs. Individually made or
stock sizes.

Shiuli Johanna
T:0171-794 6249. F:0171-916 4605.
By appointment. Ribbed cotton quilts from
NE India in bright orange, saffron and white.

*Sibona
Unit 12, Battersea Business Centre, 103
Lavender Hill, London SW11 5QL.
T:0171-924 5912. F:0171-738 0183.
Cotton quilts with appliqué or stitched
designs; reversible scallop border quilts;
white on white or white on cream fern motif
duvet covers; jacquard throws and cushions.

Sussex House
92 Wandsworth Bridge Rd,
London SW6 2TF.
T:0171-371 5455. F:0171-371 7590.
Thick cotton piqué bedspreads (in white,
ecru and pastel shades) and tapestries,
plus needlepoint and paisley cushions
and fabrics.

The White Company
See **SHEETS AND DUVETS.**
Portuguese cotton bedspreads; tartan,
plaid and large check blankets by mail order.

Zora
T:0181-675 7883. F:0181-673 5250.
By appointment. Hand block-printed quilted
bedspreads with pure cotton filling.

SPECIALIST SERVICES & PRODUCTS

*Arboretum Bespoke
16 South St, Leominster, Herts HR6 8JB.
T:01568-613396. F:01568-616815.
Design and make quilted throws and other
quilts to order.

Austrian Bedding Co
205 Belsize Rd, London NW6 4AA.
T/F:0171-372 3121.
The only specialist duvet shop in the UK.
Continental quilts and pillows in all sorts of

*** denotes
trade supplier.
Please phone
for retail outlets.**

sizes and weights in stock - anything more unusual is made up to order (like a recent request for a 10' wide quilt). Specialist cleaning and recovering of duvets and pillowcases.

Bedstock
See **BEDLINEN & TOWELS.**
Can dye Egyptian cotton towels and bedlinen in any one of 450 different colours.

Charlotte's Living Room
34 Edgware Rd, London W2 2EH.
T:0171-723 7808. F:0171-723 0178.
Can embroider monograms or emblems on anything - linen, towels, even upholstered leather dining chairs.

Cover Up Designs
See entry under **HEADBOARDS.**
Complete soft furnishing service, including quilt-making.

Eiderdown Studio
228 Withycombe Village Rd,
Exmouth, Devon EX8 3BD.
T:01395-271147. F:01395-267967.
Eiderdowns cleaned, restored or custom-made in any size.

Nomad
3-4 Wellington Terrace, Turnpike Lane,
London N8 0PX. T:0181-889 7014.
F:0181-889 9529. Trade and retail supplier of made-up mosquito nets in bell, box or wedge shapes. Mail order.

Nu-Life Upholstery Repairs
17 Chepstow Corner, 1 Pembridge Villas,
London W2 4XE.
T:0171-221 1515. F:0181-958 7515.
Divans, hair or wool mattresses remade and recovered. Can convert old mattresses into sprung mattresses.

Sundown Quilts
Northbridge House, Elm St,
Burnley, Lancs BB10 1PD.
T:01282-838887. F:01282-838213.
Make up non-standard bed linen and duvets in any size, filling and fabric. Their Sundown Marine division specialises in bedding for yachts.

*Textile Management Services
6 Ashlyns Court,
Berkhamstead, Herts HP4 3BU.
T:01442-872928. F:01442-877063.
Specialist supplier of a large selection of bedlinen and table nappery for the hotel and restaurant industry. Interior designers can call for expert advice.

For specialist cleaners of quilts and other textiles see also CRAFTSMEN & RESTORERS - Textiles and SPECIALIST SERVICES -Cleaners.

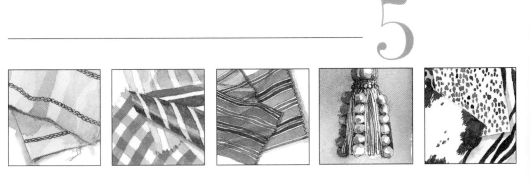

5

FABRICS

WHERE TO SEE A LARGE SELECTION

*Chelsea Harbour Design Centre
108 The Chambers, Chelsea Harbour,
London SW10 OXF.
T:0171-351 4433. F:0171-352 7868.
Trade centre for 29 different fabric and
trimmings companies, representing
hundreds of ranges.

Decorative Fabrics Gallery
278-280 Brompton Rd, London SW3 2AS.
T:0171-589 4778. F:0171-589 4781.
Showroom for GP & J Baker, Design
Archives, Fardis, Firifiss, Monkwell
and Parker Knoll.

A F Drysdale
35 North West Circus Place,
Edinburgh EH3 6TW.
T:0131-225 4686. F:0131-225 7100.
Major fabric companies are represented
including Osborne & Little, Warners,
Sanderson and Designers Guild - also
many American manufacturers.

John Lewis
Oxford St, London W1A 1EX.
T:0171-629 7711. F:0171-629 3449.
And :
Peter Jones, Sloane Square,
London SW1W 8EL. T:0171-730 3434.
Traditional English designs, French toiles,
silk damasks; high-tech fabrics as well in
their own collection. Most major companies'
ranges are represented.

Liberty
214-220 Regent Street, London W1R 6AH.
T:0171-734 1234. F:0171-573 9876.
Good fabric and needlecraft section.
Haberdashery section has braid woven
in France in heavy Russian style.

Sanderson
112-120 Brompton Rd, London SW3 1JJ.
T:0171-584 3344. F:0171-584 8404.
Own range of printed cottons, small weaves,
velvets, prints and wallpaper. Over 100
different companies represented on their
lower level. They distribute furniture by
Brigitte & Forestier and by Greengate.

*** denotes
trade supplier.
Please phone
for retail outlets.** 77

MAJOR FABRIC COMPANIES

*Abbott & Boyd
G8 Chelsea Harbour Design Centre,
Chelsea Harbour, London SW10 0XE.
T:0171-351 9985. F:0171-823 3127.
Distributors for Les Impressions Edition,
Créations Metaphores, Guell Lamadrid,
Color de Seda and Gaston y Daniela.

*Alton-Brooke / Brooke London
5 Sleaford St, London SW8 5AB.
T:0171-622 9372. F:0171-622 3010.
Alton Brooke distributes Gretchen Bellinger,
Bises Novità, Contempora, Cortis,
Deschemaker, The Humphries Weaving Co,
Luciano Marcato, J. Otten, J. Pansu,
Quadrille, Voghi, Zumsteg. Brooke London
distribute Shyam Ahuja.

Laura Ashley
27 Bagleys Lane, London SW6 2AR.
T:0171-880 5100. F:0171-880 5200.
Call this office for branches nationwide.
Traditional prints, stripes, checks and a
nursery collection.

G P & J Baker
See entry under Decorative Fabrics
Gallery in WHERE TO SEE A
LARGE SELECTION. Classic
florals, 'Warli' silks and an animal
print upholstery range.

Beaumont & Fletcher
261 Fulham Rd, London SW3 6HY.
T:0171-352 5553. F:0171-352 3545.
Fine wools, richly patterned chenilles
and prints on linen - mostly drawn from
historical collections. Opulent look.

*Bennison Fabrics
16 Holbein Place, London SW1W 8NL.
T:0171-730 8076. F:0171-823 4997.
'Tea-stained' linens printed with 18th
and 19th century designs.

*Brunschwig & Fils
10 The Chambers,
Chelsea Harbour Design Centre,
Chelsea Harbour, London SW10 0XF.
T:0171-351 5797. F:0171-351 2280.
Very large range of chintzes, stripes,
chenilles, paisleys, toiles, prints and plains.

*Manuel Canovas
2 North Terrace, Brompton Rd,
London SW3 2BA.
T:0171-225 2298. F:0171-823 7848.
Cotton prints and woven stripes; velvets,
damasks, jacquards and plains.

*Chelsea of London
Springvale Terrace, London W14 0AE.
T:0171-602 7250. F:0171-602 9221.
Consolidates Pallu & Lake, Christian
Fischbacher, Charles Hammond, Interior
Selection and Bassett McNab.

Jane Churchill
151 Sloane St, London SW1X 9BX.
T:0171-730 6379. F:0171-259 9189.
Collection of fresh printed fabrics with
matching papers and accessories.

*Claremont Furnishing Fabrics
29 Elystan Street, London SW3 3NT.
T:0171-581 9575. F:0171-581 9573.
Agents for Fortuny printed cottons. Also
silk damasks, wools, toiles and percales.

Colefax & Fowler
39 Brook St, London W1Y 2JE.
T:0171-493 2231. F:0171-355 4037.
And at:
110 Fulham Rd, London SW3 6RL.
T:0171-244 7427. F:0171-373 7916.
Traditional English chintzes, woven
fabrics and linen unions.

Design Archives
See entry under Decorative Fabrics
Gallery in WHERE TO SEE A LARGE
SELECTION. 'Manon' collection of 18th
century French damasks. 'Printed Room'
cameo design with a matching woven fabric.

Designers Guild
267-271, 277 King's Rd, London SW3 5EN.
T:0171-351 5775. F:0171-243 7710.
Tricia Guild's brightly coloured contemporary
designs and naturals. Distributors of Ralph
Lauren fabrics.

*Donghia
G23, Chelsea Harbour Design Centre,
Chelsea Harbour, London SW10 0XE.
T:0171-823 3456. F:0171-376 5758.
American classic contemporary designs;
mainly neutrals.

*Guy Evans
96 Great Titchfield St, London W1P 7AG.
T:0171-436 7914. F:0171-436 2980.
Top-of-the-range fabrics and trimmings:
wool damasks, prints and embroidery to
commission.

*Mary Fox Linton
1-8 Chelsea Harbour Design Centre,
London SW10 0XE.
T:0171-351 9908. F:0171-351 0907.
Woven silks, large range of plains, striped
and plain cotton velvets, woven fabrics
and natural cottons.

Anna French
343 King's Rd, London SW3 5ES.
T:0171-351 1126. F:0171-351 0421.
Brightly coloured prints with matching
borders and wallpapers. Cotton lace.

Pierre Frey
251-253 Fulham Rd, London SW3 6HY.
T:0171-376 5599. F:0171-352 3024.
Printed fabrics in vivid colours and a wide
selection of plains.

Nicholas Haslam
12 Holbein Place, London SW1W 8NL
T:0171-730 8623. F:0171-730 6679.
Glazed linens, printed cottons and
stonewashed fabrics including a zebra print.

*Hill & Knowles
2/15 Chelsea Harbour Design Centre,
Chelsea Harbour, London SW10 0XE.
T/F:0171-376 4686.
Plains, weaves and printed voiles including
a contemporary stencil motif. Distributor
for Dovedale and Galliards.

Hodsoll McKenzie
52 Pimlico Rd, London SW1W 8LP.
T:0171-730 2877. F:0171-823 4939.
Archival designs.

*JAB Anstoetz
1/15-16 Chelsea Harbour Design Centre,
London SW10 0XE.
T:0171-349 9323. F:0171-349 9282.
Extensive range including velvets. 2,000
designs in 23,000 colourways.

*Lelievre (UK)
101 Cleveland St, London W1P 5PN.
T:0171-636 3461. F:0171-637 5070.

Fur-effect cotton viscose, weaves, hand
woven silks, brocades, damasks, jacquards
and a vast selection of velvets; musical
instrument print. Distributors for Alcantara
fake suede.

*Malabar
Unit 31-33, South Bank Business Centre,
Ponton Rd, London SW8 5BL.
T:0171-501 4200. F:0171-501 4210.
Cotton plains, stripes and checks. Also
taffeta, raw jute, wild silk, Kashmir wool
and hand embroidered crewels.

Andrew Martin
200 Walton St, London SW3 2JL.
T:0171-584 4290. F:0171-581 8014.
Prints, weaves and a wallpaper collection.

*Marvic Textiles
1 Westpoint Trading Estate,
Alliance Rd, London W3 0RA.
T:0181-993 0191. F:0181-993 1484.
Classic woven upholstery fabrics. Art Deco
archival prints and a collection designed
by Henrietta Spencer Churchill.

Monkwell
See entry under Decorative Fabrics
Gallery in **WHERE TO SEE A LARGE
SELECTION.** Rough textured cottons in
hot, spicy colours. Chenille by the metre
and chenille throws.

Mrs Monro
16 Motcomb St, London SW1X 8LB.
T:0171-235 0326. F:0171-259 6305.
Traditional English chintzes.

*Mulberry Home Collection
76 Chelsea Manor St, London SW3 5QE.
T:0171-352 1871. F:0171-823 3886.
Classic English country-house style.

*Nobilis-Fontan
1/2 Cedar Studios,
45 Glebe Place, London SW3 5JE.
T:0171-351 7878. F:0171-376 3507.
Damasks, upholstery weaves, striped
and plain velvets; large designs including
animals, heraldic motifs and palm trees,
naturals and florals.

Osborne & Little
304 King's Rd, London SW3 5UH.
T:0171-352 1456. F:0181-673 8254.

* denotes
trade supplier.
Please phone
for retail outlets.   79

Some 12 new collections every year include prints, weaves, wallpapers, vinyls and trimmings. Distributors for Nina Campbell.

Parker Knoll
See entry under Decorative Fabrics Gallery. in **WHERE TO SEE A LARGE SELECTION.** Traditional plain velvets, chenilles and damasks. Contract fabrics.

*Percheron
97-99 Cleveland St, London W1P 5PN.
T:0171-580 5156. F:0171-631 4720.
And at:
G6, Chelsea Harbour Design Centre, Chelsea Harbour, London SW10 0XE.
T/F:0171-376 5992.
Top quality tapestries, voiles, lace, jacquards, weaves, prints, chintzes and linens. Wool twill (12 colours) to co-ordinate with the 'Horse Print' collection.

*RBI International
18 Chelsea Harbour Design Centre, Chelsea Harbour, London SW10 0XE.
T:0171-376 3766. F:0171-376 3763.
Distribute Kawashima, Vidivi, Missoni, George Franc, Le Murier, Alhambra, Atelier Casa.

*Ramm, Son & Crocker
Chiltern House, The Valley Centre, Gordon Rd, High Wycombe, Bucks HP13 6EQ.
T:01494-603555. F:01494-464664.
Geometric, damask and paisley prints. Plain linen and linen union in 90 colours. Documentary prints. Chenilles.

*Romo
Lowmoor Rd,
Kirkby-in-Ashfield, Notts NG17 7DE.
T:01623-750005. F:01623-750031.
Wide range of plain and woven fabrics in a good choice of colours.

*Sahco Hesslein (UK)
24 Chelsea Harbour Design Centre, Chelsea Harbour, London SW10 0XE.
T:0171-352 6168. F:0171-352 0767.
High quality silks, linens; and a large range of plain fabrics.

Sanderson
See entry under **WHERE TO SEE A LARGE SELECTION.**

*Ian Sanderson
Unit G13, Chelsea Harbour Design Centre, Chelsea Harbour, London SW10 0XE.
T:0171-351 2481. F:0171-351 7868.
Cut velvet upholstery fabrics, tickings, checks, prewashed cottons, woven damasks and more.

George Spencer Decorations
4 West Halkin St, London SW1X 8JA.
T:0171-235 1501. F:0171-235 1502.
Collection of printed and woven fabrics with matching trimmings and wallcoverings.

Bernard Thorp & Company
6 Burnsall St, London SW3 3ST.
T:0171-352 5745. F:0171-376 3640.
Hand-screen printed or woven upholstery fabrics to order in clients' own colourways and on cotton, voile union, silk etc.

*Titley & Marr
141 Station Rd, Liss, Hampshire GU33 7AJ.
T:01730-894351. F:01730-893682.
And at:
1/7 Chelsea Harbour Design Centre, Chelsea Harbour, London SW10 0XE.
T:0171-351 2913. F:0171-351 6318.
Designs inspired by 19th century documents. Toiles; woven fabrics.

*Turnell and Gigon
Unit G20, Chelsea Harbour Design Centre, Chelsea Harbour, London SW10 0XE.
T:0171-351 5142. F:0171-376 7945.
Damasks, weaves, silks, cottons, velvets, stripes, checks and jacquards. Also chintzes and linens.

*Warner Fabrics
Bradbourne Drive, Tilbrook,
Milton Keynes, Bucks MK7 8BE.
T:01908-366900. F:01908-370839.
Archive silk damasks. Wide selection of curtain and upholstery fabrics.

*Wemyss Weavecraft
Seaforth Works, East Wemyss,
Fife, Scotland KY1 4RZ.
T:01592-712255. F:01592-716348.
And at:
40 Newman St, London W1P 3PA.
T:0171-255 3305. F:0171-580 9420.
Distributors for Fadini Borghi and Boussac.

Dobby fabric in 16 colours.
Persian weaves in thirty colours.

*Brian Yates
Unit G26, Chelsea Harbour Design Centre,
Chelsea Harbour, London SW10 0XE.
T:0171-352 0123.F:0171-352 6060.
Designs by Sheila Coombes; they also
distribute Arte, Pepé Peñalver, Omexco,
and Taco Edition.

*Zimmer & Rohde (UK)
G15, Chelsea Harbour Design Centre,
Chelsea Harbour, London SW10 0XE.
T:0171-351 7115. F:0171-351 5661.
Silks, jacquards and lots of plains.

*Zoffany
Unit G12, Chelsea Harbour Design Centre,
London SW10 0XE.
T:0171-349 0043. F:0171-351 9677.
18th and 19th century reproductions
including damasks, stripes, sprigs, toiles,
florals and textured plains.

UTILITY FABRICS / TICKINGS / FELTS

The Berwick Street Cloth Shop
14 Berwick St, London W1V 3RG.
T:0171-287 2881.
Endless range of inexpensive fabrics.

JW Bollom
PO Box 78, Croydon Rd,
Beckenham, Kent BR3 4BL.
T:0181-658 2299. F:0181-658 8672.
Felts and basic utility fabrics.

Bourne Street Linen
T/F:0171-376 1113.
By appointment. Plain linens and stripes.

B Brown
Zoffany House, 74-78 Wood Lane End,
Hemel Hempstead, Herts HP2 4RF.
T:0990-117118. F:0990-329020.
Display fabrics and extra wide felts
in over 70 colours.

The Cloth Shop
290 Portobello Rd, London W10 5TE.
T:0181-968 6001.
Inexpensive fabrics: calico, muslin,
denim, lycra, cottons, wools and synthetics.

The Conran Shop
Michelin House, 81 Fulham Rd, London SW3
6RD. T:0171-589 7401. F:0171-823 7015.
Simple ethnic fabrics, checks and stripes.

Cover Up Designs
9 Kingsclere Park, Kingsclere,
Nr Newbury, Berks RG20 4SW.
T:01635-297981. F:01635-298363.
Simple printed chintzes, natural linens,
cottons and extra wide fabrics (280 cm).

Crucial Trading
The Market Hall, Craven Arms,
Shropshire
SY7 9NY.
T:01588-673666.
F:01588-673623.
And at:
Pukka Palace,
174 Tower Bridge Rd,
London SE1 3LF.
T:0171-234 0000.
F:0171-234 0110. 'Pukka cloth': a range
of 120 reasonably priced natural fabrics.

Elizabeth Eaton
85 Bourne St, London SW1W 8HF.
T:0171-730 2262. F:0171-730 7294.
Tickings, muslins, prints on linen
and complementary wallpapers.

Fibre Naturelle
51 Poole Rd, Bournemouth,
Dorset BH4 9BA T/F:01202-751750.
Fifteen colours of casement and over 100
hand loomed and hand dyed Indian cottons.

Final Curtain Company
T:0181-699 3626. F:0181-291 7937.
By appointment. Cottons, linens and
silks in natural colours.

GMW
22 Musgrave Crescent, London SW6 4QE.
T:0171-731 8704. F:0171-731 8634.
Linens and weaves.

Gerrietts GB
J412, Tower Bridge Business Complex,
Drummond Rd, London SE16 4EF.
T:0171-232 2262. F:0171-237 4916.
Fabrics for the stage, all flame-proofed.
Natural canvases in different weights,
nets, PVC, projection screens.

* denotes trade supplier. Please phone for retail outlets.

Image Line
13 Theobalds Rd, London WC1X 8SL.
T:0171-404 1494. F:0171-404 2428.
Display fabrics and PVC. Can make up
tablecloths.

MacCulloch & Wallis
25-26 Dering St, London W1A 3AX.
T:0171-409 0725. F:0171-491 9578.
Interlinings, ginghams, silks, velvets
and haberdashery.

Ian Mankin
109 Regents Park Rd, London NW1 8UR.
T:0171 722 0997. F:0171 722 2159.
And at:
271 Wandsworth Bridge Rd,
London SW6 2TX. T:0171-371 8825.
Good value plain, checked and striped
fabrics; tickings.

The Natural Fabric Company
Wessex Place, 127 High St,
Hungerford, Berks RG17 0DL.
T:01488-684002. F:01488-686455.
Ginghams, checks, calicos, toiles
and Indian cottons.

Nordic Style
109 Walton St, London SW3 2HP.
T:0171-581 8674.
Good selection of ticking stripes
for light upholstery or blinds.

Olicana Textiles
Brook Mills, Crimble, Slaithwaite,
Huddersfield HD7 5BQ.
T:01484-847666. F:01484-847735.
Washable cotton furnishing materials
in great colours - from white to brights;
also yachting cottons.

The Original Silver Lining
Workshop 29, Lenton Business Centre,
Lenton Blvd, Nottingham NG7 2BY.
T:0115-955 5123. F:0115-962 3064.
Natural, utility and plain fabrics,
especially linings.

*Porter Nicholson
Portland House, Norlington Rd,
London E10 6JX.
T:0181-539 6106. F:0181-558 9200.
Linings and utility fabrics for curtaining
and upholstery.

Russell & Chapple
23 Monmouth St, London WC2H 9DE.
T:0171-836 7521. F:0171-497 0554.
Artists' canvases, jutes, fine muslin,
hessian, polythene sheeting and pain
coloured canvas deckchair canvas.

Soho Silks
24 Berwick St, London W1V 3RF.
T:0171-434 3305. F:0171-494 1705.
Dress, furnishing and theatrical fabrics
and trimmings.

FR Street
Frederick House, Hurricane Way, Wickford
Business Park, Wickford, Essex SS11 8YB.
T:01268-766677. F:01268-764534.
Basic cloths like cotton duck, calico, linings;
traditional upholstery and curtaining fabrics.

Temptation Alley
See entry under TRIMMIMGS.
Plain calico, waffle calico, linen, cotton
drill, jute. Plus threads, buttons, ribbons
and stuffing for quilts.

Whaley
Harris Court, Great Horton,
Bradford, W.Yorks BD7 4EQ.
T:01274-576718. F:01274-521309.
Utility fabrics, silks, cottons, jutes,
linens - 400 different types.

SHEERS/VOILES/LACE

Bentley & Spens
Studio 25, 90 Lots Rd, London SW10 0QD.
T/F:0171-352 5685.
Hand painted sheers.

Celia Birtwell
71 Westbourne Park Rd, London W2 5QH.
T:0171-221 0877. F:0171-229 7673.
Hand printed sheers with dots, stars
and quirky animals.

*Brunschwig & Fils
See entry under MAJOR FABRIC
COMPANIES. Checked and plaid sheers.

*Manuel Canovas
See entry under
MAJOR FABRIC COMPANIES.
Cotton/linen mix voiles in white or cream
printed with floral or geometric designs.

Chelsea Textiles
See entry under **CREWEL**.

Jane Churchill
See entry under **MAJOR FABRIC COMPANIES.** Sheer checks and stripes.

Colefax & Fowler
See entry under
MAJOR FABRIC COMPANIES.
Thistle voile and spot muslin.

Cover Up Designs
See entry under **UTILITY & TICKINGS.**
Hand printed voiles.

*Anna French
See entry under **MAJOR FABRIC COMPANIES.** Lace and sheer collection.

Allegra Hicks
33 Bywater St, London SW3 4XH.
T:0171-589 8550. F:0171-589 2554.
By appointment. Hand blocked voiles printed in India. Motifs include vines, crescents and spheres. Also thick cotton upholstery fabrics.

Malabar
See entry under **MAJOR FABRIC COMPANIES.** Voiles in brilliant colours.

*Malthouse Fabrics
PO Box 5, Bingham, Nottingham NG13 8HS.
T:01949-831354. F:0115-9334284.
Striped cotton voile in several colours.

Material World
See entry under **OTHER SPECIALIST SUPPLIERS & SERVICES.** 100% cotton muslin with gold or white stars, trellis, flowers and other designs at £5.95 a yard.

Osborne & Little
See entry under **MAJOR FABRIC COMPANIES.** 25 different voiles, with trees, stars, pigs, hearts, giraffes, palm trees and many other designs.

Simon Playle
6 Fulham Park Studios, London SW6 4LW.
T:0171-371 0131.F:0171-384 2157.
Fine Swiss voiles in stripes or with embroidered motifs: sprigs of flowers, fern leaves, big spots and classical/Empire designs. Plain organdie and cotton cambric (290 cm wide). Fire-retardant voiles in Trevira.

Rose's Mill
76 Cowbridge Road East,
Canton, Cardiff CF1 9DW.
T:01222-667201.
F:01222-703690.
Traditional Nottingham lace by the panel or by the yard.

*Sahco Hesslein
See entry under **MAJOR FABRIC COMPANIES.**
Voiles and muslins in modern prints.

Silvan
21 Blandford St, London W1H 3AD.
T:0171-486 5883. F:0171-486 5887.
Lace trimmings and dress widths.
Plus gold and silver lace. Used for accessories, lampshades or window treatments.

*Tyrone Textiles
Arnell House, Marshgate Trading Estate,
Marshgate Lane London E15 2NG.
T:0181-519 0444.F:0181-519 1460.
Net, lace and embroidered voiles.

CREWEL

Chelsea Textiles
7 Walton St, London SW3 2JD.
T:0171-584 0111. F:0171-584 7170.
Crewel-work, needlepoint and embroidered fabrics reproduced from antique documents.
Co-ordinating checks and stripes and hand-embroidered voiles.

The Conran Shop
See entry under **UTILITY & TICKINGS.**

Fired Earth
Twyford Mill, Oxford Rd,
Adderbury, Oxon OX17 3HP.
T:01295-812088. F:01295-810832.
And 15 other branches nationwide.
Crewels; also chenilles, moirés, seersucker, plains, cotton checks and twills, wool tartans and velvets.

Graham & Green
4 Elgin Crescent, London W11 2JA.
T:0171-727 4594. F:0171-229 9717.
Three white on white crewels. They also distribute Malabar and Chelsea Textiles.

* denotes trade supplier. Please phone for retail outlets. 83

*JAB Anstoetz
See entry under **MAJOR FABRIC
COMPANIES.** 45 different crewels
with a cream background and multi-
coloured bird, floral or tree designs.

*Marvic Textiles
See entry under **MAJOR FABRIC
COMPANIES.** Two-ply elaborate crewelwork
hand woven in Kashmir in earthy colours;
traditional trellis design.

Nice Irma's
46 Goodge St, London W1P 1FJ.
T:0171-580 6921. F:0171-436 1567.
Indian hand loomed fabrics, including
ikats and crewel work.

*Paper Moon
Unit 4, Central Business Centre, Great
Central Way, London NW10 0UR.
T:0181-451 3655. F:0181-459 7445.
Cream on cream unbleached cotton
crewelwork with flower and vine motifs.

Valerie Wade
108 Fulham Rd, London SW3 6HS.
T:0171-225 1414. F:0171-736 5630.
Persian crewelwork design of abstract
flowers with circular embroidery in turquoise
and salmon on a cream background.

*Zoffany
See entry under
MAJOR FABRIC COMPANIES.
Crewelwork in various colours: buttercream,
pink, blue, green, pale yellow and red.

SILK

*Bennett Silks
Crown Royal Park, Higher Hillgate,
Stockport, Cheshire SK1 3HB.
T:0161-477 5979. F:0161-480
5385. Plain and printed silks, heavy
silk brocades, devoré velvet.

Bentley & Spens
See entry under
SHEERS/VOILES/LACE. Hand
painted silks.

*Henry Bertrand
11 Melton St, London NW1 2EA.
T:0171-383 3868. F:0171-383 4797.

Natural, dyed and
printed silks.

Bery Designs
157 St John's Hill,
London SW11 1TQ.
T:0171-924 2197.
F:0171-924 1879.
Hand painted silks
in large classical
designs: Italianate scrolls, heraldic themes,
and Empire and Aubusson motifs. They can
also paint on cotton or linen. Each design is
done to order.

*Brunschwig & Fils
See entry under **MAJOR FABRIC
COMPANIES.** Plain, striped and checked
silks and silk brocades.

*Manuel Canovas
See entry under **MAJOR FABRIC
COMPANIES.** Sumptuous silk damasks.

*Chase Erwin
22 Chelsea Harbour Design Centre.
Chelsea Harbour, London SW10 0XE.
T:0171-352 7271. F:0171-352 7170.
Hand woven Thai silks in many solid colours,
stripes and patterns. Also American
collection of hand woven chenilles and
'Ultrasuede' synthetic washable suede.

Jane Churchill
See entry under
MAJOR FABRIC COMPANIES. Colourful
striped and checked silks made in India.

*Gainsborough Silk Weaving Company
Alexandra Rd, Sudbury, Suffolk CO10 6XH.
T:01787-372081. F:01787-881785.
And at:
The Clocktower, 16 The Coda Centre,
189 Munster Rd, London SW6 6AW.
T:0171-386 7153.
Hand woven historical silks.

*Garin
1 Carlton Crescent, Luton, Beds LU3 1EN.
T:01582-37400. F:01582-415557.
Spanish silk brocades, traditional
damasks and jacquards.

The Humphries Weaving Company
DeVere Mill, Queen St, Castle Hedingham,
Halstead, Essex CO9 3HA.

T:01787-461193. F:01787-462701.
Hand loomed silk fabrics.

*JAB Anstoetz
See entry under
MAJOR FABRIC COMPANIES.
Maharadscha' silk in 90 colours.

*Lelièvre (UK)
See entry under **MAJOR FABRIC
COMPANIES.** 'Cantate' silk in 51
colours; 'Satin Stephanois' silk-look
fabric in 46 colours.

*Malabar
See entry under **MAJOR FABRIC
COMPANIES.** Raw silks, spun silks, silk
taffetas and cotton and silk jacquards in
classic and vivid colours.

Osborne & Little
See entry under **MAJOR FABRIC
COMPANIES.** Silks woven with
stars and checks; damask; taffeta.

*Percheron
See entry under **MAJOR FABRIC
COMPANIES.** 'Taffeta Ninon' in 129
colours. They also distribute Gamme which
has hundreds of silks in all weights.

Pongees
28-30 Hoxton Square, London N1 6NN.
T:0171-739 9130. F:0171-739 9132.
Silk specialists - enormous range of colours
and weights, all reasonably priced.

Carolyn Quartermaine
Chez Joseph, 26 Sloane St,
London SW1 7LQ.
T:0171-245 9493. F:0171-823 4604.
Specialises in hand painting silks with
calligraphy.

Shiuli Johanna
T:0171-794 6249. F:0171-916 4605.
By appointment.
Hand woven, embroidered and painted
Tussor silks.

*The Silk Gallery
G25 Chelsea Harbour Design Centre,
Chelsea Harbour, London SW10 0XE.
T:0171-351 1790. F:0171-376 4693.
100 shades of plain silk; silk damasks and
chenilles; woven curtain and upholstery
silks.

*Jim Thompson
G10 Chelsea Harbour Design Centre,
Chelsea Harbour, London SW10 0XE.
T:0171-351 2829. F:0171-351 0907.
Thai silks.

*Trade Eighty
63-65 Riding House St, London W1P 7PP.
T:0171-637 5188. F:0171-637 5187.
Over 100 colours in plain and shot wild silks.

Warris Vianni
85 Golborne Rd, London W10 5NL.
T:0181-964 0069. F:0181-964 0019.
Silks: dupion in 35 colours, organzas,
damasks, brocades. Hand loomed cottons
in 30 colourways; woollen paisleys; woven
linens. Also brushed cottons.

TARTANS & PLAIDS

Anta Scotland
Fearn, Tain, Ross-shire IV20 1XW. T:01862-
832477. F:01862-832616. 100% wool
tartan furnishing fabrics and accessories.

Brora
344 King's Rd, London SW3 5UR.
T:0171-352 3697. F:0171-352 1792.
Tartans and tweeds by the metre.

*The Isle Mill
12 West Moulin Rd, Pitlochry,
Scotland PH16 5AF.
T:01796-472390. F:01796-473869.
Large selection of wool tartans.

Ralph Lauren Home Collection
See entry under Designers Guild in **MAJOR
FABRIC COMPANIES.** Smart plaids.

*Malabar
See entry under **MAJOR FABRIC
COMPANIES.** Vibrant plaids.

Mikhail Pietranek
Saint Swithin St, Aberdeen,
Scotland AB10 6XB.
T:01224-310211. F:01224-312956.
Large range of traditional tartans in both
wool and cotton. Also 'Scottish Glen Checks'
and printed paisley and floral designs.

*Titley & Marr
See entry under **MAJOR FABRIC
COMPANIES.** Tweeds and plaids.

*** denotes
trade supplier.
Please phone
for retail outlets.** 85

VELVET/CORDUROY/ CHENILLE

G P & J Baker
See entry under Decorative Fabrics
Gallery in **WHERE TO SEE A LARGE SELECTION**. Good range of chenilles
and velvets.

Borgia Interiors
T/F:0171-581 8234.
By appointment. Printed and embroidered
velvets, dyed organzas and beaded fabrics
to commission.

*Brunschwig & Fils
See entry under **MAJOR FABRIC COMPANIES**. Striped, checked
and plain velvets.

*Manuel Canovas
See entry under **MAJOR FABRIC COMPANIES**. Silk and cotton velvets
in solid colours and stripes.

*Chanée Ducrocq
168 New Cavendish St, London W1M 7FJ.
T/F:0171-637 2910.
Orders and returnable samples:
T: 0171-631 5223.
French classical furnishing fabrics including
velvets and gaufrage.

*Donghia
See entry under **MAJOR FABRIC COMPANIES**. Mohair velvets in 25
colourways.

*Fitzroy Fabrics
Woodgrove Farm,
Fulbrook, Burford, Oxon OX18 4BH.
T:01993-824222. F:01993-822751.
Chenilles, checks and stripes - all reasonably
priced.

*Harris Fabrics
See entry under **OTHER SPECIALIST SUPPLIERS & SERVICES**.
Country corduroy.

Heal's
196 Tottenham Court Rd,
London W1P 0LD.
T:0171-636 1666.
'Velpor' velvets in a large selection of
strong colours and inexpensively priced.

*Mary Fox Linton
See entry under
MAJOR FABRIC COMPANIES. Distribute
chenilles by Glant in many colourways.

*JAB Anstoetz
See entry under
MAJOR FABRIC COMPANIES.
Velvet in 147 colours, corduroy,
and linen, velvet and cotton chenille.

*Lelièvre (UK)
See entry under
MAJOR FABRIC COMPANIES. Excellent
range of jewel toned velvets. Will gaufrage on
velvet from a catalogue of designs.

Andrew Martin
See entry under **MAJOR FABRIC COMPANIES**. Heavy upholstery corduroy.
Crushed velvet and embossed velvet stripes.

*Mulberry Home Collection
See entry under
MAJOR FABRIC COMPANIES.
Printed chenilles in paisley and Aubusson
designs; plain and gaufrage velvet.

*Nobilis-Fontan
See entry under
MAJOR FABRIC COMPANIES.
'Flanelle St Germain' range of velvets.

Osborne & Little
See entry under
MAJOR FABRIC COMPANIES.
'Patara' jumbo corduroy in eight colours.

*Percheron
See entry under
MAJOR FABRIC COMPANIES.
'Robespierre' and 'Mozart' corduroys;
exclusive range of patterned velvets.

*Ramm, Son & Crocker
See entry under
MAJOR FABRIC COMPANIES.
'Eclectic'printed geometric and 'Natural'
coloured chenilles.

*Sahco Hesslein (UK)
See entry under **MAJOR FABRIC COMPANIES**. 'Diplomat' range of plain
curtain velvets; 'Rubens' range of plain
upholstery velvets and 'Eroica' range of
solid colour striped velvets - all of them
in a wide range of colours.

Sanderson
See entry under **WHERE TO SEE A LARGE SELECTION.** 'Dressage' velvets in 40 colours.

*Ian Sanderson
See entry under **MAJOR FABRIC COMPANIES.** Damask and square patterned velvets.

*Turnell & Gigon
See entry under **MAJOR FABRIC COMPANIES.** Chenille in 12 colours.

Whaley
See entry under **UTILITY & TICKINGS.** Silk corduroy, uncoloured and prepared for dying and printing. It costs £11.88 per m for 10m or less and £9.98 per m for over 10m.

*Zoffany
See entry under **MAJOR FABRIC COMPANIES.** Velvets in wide and narrow stripes, and gaufrage in a sunflower design.

REAL & FAKE LEATHER/SUEDE

*Adcopa
5 Brookside, Sawtry,
Huntingdon, Cambs PE17 5SB.
T:01487-830830. F:01487-832518.
Naugahide contract vinyl upholstery fabric. Also fake suede in 50 colours.

Atrium
Centrepoint, 22-24 St Giles High St,
London WC2H 8LN.
T:0171-379 7288. F:0171-240 2080.
Only source in the UK for Madulight simulated leather and Novasuede - it comes in 80 colours and many finishes and is machine washable.

Bridge of Weir Leather Company
Clydesdale Works, Bridge of Weir,
Renfrewshire PA11 3LF.
T:01505-612132. F:01505-614964.
Scottish upholstery leather in over 90 colours.

*Chase Erwin
See entry under **SILK.** 'Ultrasuede' synthetic washable suede in 104 colours plus 8 more in the 'Jungle Collection".

Connolly
32 Grosvenor Crescent Mews,
London SW1X 7EX.
T:0171-235 3883. F:0171-235 3838.
Suppliers to Rolls Royce, Ferrari and Aston Martin; well known for fine leathers.

Christopher Howe
93 Pimlico Rd, London SW1W 8PH.
T:0171-730 7987. F:0171-730 0157.
Importer of goatskins in a great range of colours for upholstery.

*Kravet London
G17, Chelsea Harbour Design Centre,
London SW10 0XE.
T:0171-795 0110. F:0171-349 0678.
Fake suede in 248 colours.

*Lelièvre (UK)
See entry under **MAJOR FABRIC COMPANIES.** Distribute Alcantara - fake, washable suede in a wide array of colours.

Litchfield Clare
16 Horsleydown Lane, London SE1 3SX.
T:0171-403 6667. F:0171-403 6281.
Range of 300 leathers including calf, buffalo and suede. Printed horsehides in animal patterns like zebra or leopard; engraved cowhides with leaves, flowers and other designs.

Andrew Martin
See entry under **MAJOR FABRIC COMPANIES.** Fake suede.

Andrew Muirhead & Son
Dalmarnock Leather Works,
273-289 Dunn St, Glasgow,
Scotland G40 3EA.
T:0141-554 3724. F:0141-554 4741.
Leather tanners since 1840. Quality leathers for domestic, corporate, marine and aircraft upholstery, for wall panelling and desks.

Renwick & Clarke
190 Ebury St, London SW1W 8UP.
T:0171-730 8913. F:0171-730 4508.
Lutson's embossed, gilded and hand painted leather panels.

Kenneth Topp
T:0171-370 4344. F:0171-373 3099.
By appointment. Cowhides from America to order. Prices start at £250 for a 6'x 6' skin.

* denotes trade supplier. Please phone for retail outlets.

*Turnell and Gigon
See entry under **MAJOR FABRIC COMPANIES**. 'Glore Valcana' synthetic mix which resembles real suede, is washable, and comes in 31 colours

Whittle Brothers
89 Field Lane, Litherlands, Liverpool L21 9NA.
T:0151-928 6660. F:0151-949 0404.
Top quality upholstery leathers.
Bespoke colouring service.

ANIMAL PRINTS & IMITATION FUR

G P & J Baker
See entry under Decorative Fabrics Gallery in **WHERE TO SEE A LARGE SELECTION**. Good range of upholstery-weight fake animal skins.

*Brunschwig & Fils
See entry under **MAJOR FABRIC COMPANIES**. Leopardskin in printed cotton or linen mix.

*Manuel Canovas
See entry under **MAJOR FABRIC COMPANIES**.
Distributes Brochier's tiger and leopard prints on linen and zebra and cheetah on supple cotton velvet.

Colefax & Fowler
See entry under **MAJOR FABRIC COMPANIES**.
Spotty printed velvet.

Ever Trading
12 Martindale,
East Sheen, London SW14 7AL.
T:0181-878 4050. F:0181-876 5717.
Realistic imitation fur by the metre (lynx, polar bear, sable, leopard, wolf, bear and others), plus lined throws and bedspreads.

Pierre Frey
See entry under **MAJOR FABRIC COMPANIES**.
Range of furry fabrics most suitable for cushions and throws.

Nicholas Haslam
See entry under **MAJOR FABRIC COMPANIES**. Stonewashed fabrics including a zebra print.

*Lelièvre (UK)
See entry under **MAJOR FABRIC COMPANIES**. Lifelike animal skins suitable mainly for cushions.

Liberty
See entry under **WHERE TO SEE A LARGE SELECTION**. Leopard skin print.

*Percheron
See entry under **MAJOR FABRIC COMPANIES**.
Zebra, leopard, panther, tiger, and snake printed velvets.

Soho Silks
See entry under **UTILITY & TICKINGS**.
Fake fur prints including cotton and acrylic tiger, leopard and pony skin.

*Jim Thompson
See entry under **SILK**. Leopard print silk.

*Turnell and Gigon
See entry under **MAJOR FABRIC COMPANIES**. Giraffe, zebra, leopard, and tiger cotton velvet.

TRIMMINGS

*Abbott & Boyd
See entry under **MAJOR FABRIC COMPANIES**.
Fringe, tassel fringe, cord, flange cord, key tassels, and tassel tie backs in natural jute, cotton and various colours.

*British Trimmings
PO Box 46, Coronation St, Stockport SK5 7PJ.
T:01614-806122. F:01614-290476.
Trade suppliers of a wide selection of trimmings, tiebacks and accessories. The American 'King Cotton' range includes bobble fringes. Plus an extra long bullion fringe.

Chelsea Textiles
See entry under **CREWEL**.
'Onion bauble' fringe, tassels, and scallop trim in many colours.

Colefax & Fowler
See entry under
MAJOR FABRIC COMPANIES.
Excellent selection of trimmings to co-ordinate with their fabric collection: picot trim, fringe, tassels, tie-backs, flanged or unflanged cord in colours or in natural wool .

Cover Up Designs
See entry under UTILITY & TICKINGS.
Bobble fringe, brush fringe in different sizes, cut fringes (from 2" to 10"), flanged or unflanged cord, tassels and tie-backs.

Wendy Cushing Trimmings
Unit G7, Chelsea Harbour Design Centre, Chelsea Harbour, London SW10 0XE.
T:0171-351 5796. F:0171-351 4246.
Affordable stock range in chenille, jute, wool, linen and cotton. Custom made trimmings. Reproductions of 16th, 17th and 18th century wool passementerie and tassels.

Thomas Dare
See entry under OTHER SPECIALIST SUPPLIERS & SERVICES. Flanged or unflanged rope, fringe, moss fringe, key tassels, medallion tassels and tiebacks.

*Anna French
See entry under
MAJOR FABRIC COMPANIES. Hand-knotted fringe in their trimmings collection.

The Gallery of Antique Costume & Textiles
2 Church St, London NW8 8ED.
T/F:0171-723 9981. Period braids, fringes, tie backs and tassels in silk, cotton, linen or wool. Also ribbons.

*Mulberry Home Collection
See entry under MAJOR FABRIC COMPANIES. Flanged and unflanged rope, bobble and picot braid, tassels, tassels, bullion and cut fringe, clip fan-edged trim; tie backs in leather, velvet, jute or wood.

The Natural Fabric Company
See entry under UTILITY & TICKINGS.
Bobble fringe at £1.45 per metre.

*Henry Newbery & Company
18 Newman St, London W1P 4AB.
T:0171-636 2053. F:0171-436 6406.
Upholstery and curtain trimmings including bullion fringe, tie backs and tassels.

*Nobilis-Fontan
See entry under
MAJOR FABRIC COMPANIES.
Tassels and trims to match collection.

Christina Ojo
Studio 2, 90 Wandsworth Bridge Rd, London SW6 2TF. T/F:0171-371 9485.
By appointment. Vast range of handmade trimmings and accessories; tie backs and original fringes in linen, chenille and wool.

*Percheron
See entry under MAJOR FABRIC COMPANIES. Selection of top quality trimmings to match their fabrics.

VV Rouleaux
10 Symons St, London SW3 2TJ.
T:0171-730 4413. F:0171-730 3468.
Tassel, bullion, suede loop fringe; huge selection of braids, cords and fringes in cotton, chenille, wool and linen.

Frances Soubeyran
12 Atlas Mews,
Ramsgate St, London E8 2N.
T/F:0171-241 1064.
Makes special trimmings to order with fabrics and yarns dyed to match. Hand woven fringing and tassels in all sorts of unconventional shapes: pears, urns, pods and steeples. Also braid and gimp.

Specialist Needlework
Little Barrington, Burford, Oxon OX18 4TE.
T:01451-844433.
Handmade woollen cord for edging curtains and cushions available through mail order brochure (£1.95).

*Dr Brian J Taylor
Brunswick Mill, Bradford Rd, Manchester M40 7EZ.
T:0161-205 1977. F:0161-203 4280.
Designers and manufacturers of furnishing trimmings in chenille, cotton and wool.
Plus bespoke service.

Temptation Alley
361 Portobello Rd, London W10 5SA.
T:0181-964 2004. F:0171-727 4432.
Very large range of inexpensive trimmings, fringes, tassels, ribbons. Plus a good range of basic fabrics.

* denotes trade supplier. Please phone for retail outlets.

*Turnell and Gigon
See entry under **MAJOR FABRIC COMPANIES.** Their own range of trimmings plus Les Passementeries de l'Ile de France - a very large range in all colours, styles and textures.

*G J Turner & Co (Trimmings)
Fitzroy House, Abbot St, London E8 3DP.
T:0171-254 8187. F:0171-254 8471.
Braids, fringes, tassels and elaborate tie-backs in cotton, silk, wool and linen. Manufacturers since 1899. Pure silk spiral drop fringe, silk and wool cord, key tassels and colour matching service.

*Wemyss Houles
40 Newman St, London W1P 3PA.
T:0171-255 3305. F:0171-580 9420.
Best known for their natural range in cotton, wool and jute.

*A J Worthington (Leek)
Portland Mills, Queen St,
Leek, Staffs ST13 6LW.
T:01538-399600. F:01538-371968.
Braids, cords and trimmings including fan-edging and a natural cotton range.

OTHER SPECIALIST SUPPLIERS & SERVICES

Apenn Fabrics,
196 Kensington Park Rd, London W11 2ES.
T:0171-792 2457. F:0171-727 4719.
Hand printed cottons and linens inspired by old documents. Also smaller coordinates,patterned linings and voiles.

ARC
103 Wandsworth Bridge Rd,
London SW6 2TE. T:0171-731 3933.
F:0171-610 6591. Print room fabrics.

John Boyd Textiles
Higher Flax Mills,
Castle Cary, Somerset BA7 7DY.
T:01963-350451. F:01963-351078.
Specialist in horsehair fabrics for upholstery. The company was established in 1837 and is one of the last surviving horsehair fabric weavers in the world. Plain, striped, embroidered designs or any other to order.

Ciel Decor
187 New King's Rd, London SW6 4SW.
T:0171-731 0444. F:0171-731 0788.
Provencal fabrics; they carry their own range and are distributors for Les Olivades.

Connaught Flameproofing Services
25 Connaught Gardens, London N10 3LD.
T/F:0181-341 2000.
In situ flameproofing - minimum charge £75.

Belinda Coote Tapestries
3/14 Chelsea Harbour Design Centre,
Chelsea Harbour, London SW10 0XE.
T:0171-351 0404. F:0171-352 9808.
Tapestry and jacquard weave fabrics and borders by the metre.

Corcoran & May
157 and 161 Lower Richmond Rd,
London SW15 1HH.
T:0181-788 9556. F:0181-780 2178.
Branches in Ealing and Sevenoaks. Top quality fabrics at discount prices including designer names like G P & J Baker, Monkwell, Colefax & Fowler, Christian Fischbacher, Charles Hammond and Parkertex. Seconds, overstocks and clearance lines. Soft furnishing service.

Thomas Dare
341 King's Rd, London SW3 5ES.
T:0171-351 7991. F:0171-351 4150.
Large range of checks, stripes and plains.

*De Le Cuona Designs
1 Trinity Place, Windsor, Berks SL4 3AP.
T:01753-830301. F:01753-620455.
Luxurious hand loomed linen cloths in anything from muslin to upholstery weight. Also paisleys.

*J F Greenwood
Newhaven Business Park,
Barton Lane, Eccles M30 0TH.
T:0161-787 7464. F:0161-787 7613.
Manufacturers of cotton sheeting.

*Harris Fabrics
See entry under Warner Fabrics in
MAJOR FABRIC COMPANIES.
Contract division of Warner. Co-ordinating designs (mainly woven fabrics) which meet high abrasion and fire retardancy specifications.

* denotes trade supplier. Please phone for retail outlets.

Nicholas Herbert
118 Lots Rd, London SW10 0RJ.
T:0171-376 5596. F:0171-376 5572.
18th and 19th century French documentary prints.

Java Cotton Company
3 Blenheim Crescent, London S11 2EE.
T:0171-229 3212. F:0181-964 0758.
Batik fabrics.

KA International
60 Sloane Ave, London SW3 3DD.
T:0171-584 7352. F:0171-589 9534.
Spanish interior design shop with a large range of reasonably priced fabrics - prints, wovens, velvets, toiles, tapestry, chintz and voiles.

*Lienzo De Los Gazules
Cot Hill House, Elkington,
Northants NN6 6NH.
T:01858-575911. F:01858-575911.
Spanish collection which includes furnishing and sheeting fabrics in 280 cm widths.

Material World
256 Wimbledon Park Rd,
London SW19 6NL.
T:0181-785 3366. F:0181-780 1781.
Branches nationwide. Own ranges and discontinued fabrics. Roll after roll of inexpensive lines.

Christopher Moore Textiles
1 Munro Terrace, Cheyne Walk,
London SW10 0DL.
T:0171-792 3628.
F:0171-351 7644.
Reproductions of authentic toiles de Jouy and hand-blocked wallpapers.

Ornamenta
3-12 Chelsea Harbour Design Centre,
Chelsea Harbour, London SW10 0XE.
T:0171-352 1824. F:0171-376 3398.
Hand printed silks; gothic, chinoiserie and 'English Musick' designs.

*Plasticotter (UK)
Union Rd, Bolton, Lancs BL2 2HL.
T:01204-381991.
F:01204-528863.
PVC coating of fabric primarily for tablecloths; minimum quantity 40 metres.

Souleiado
39 rue Proudhon, 13150 Tarascon, France.
T:00-33-4909-15011.
F:00-33 4909-11760.
The best known Provencal fabrics. They no longer have a London showroom but will deal with UK orders directly from their head office in France.

Stuart Renaissance Textiles
Barrington Court, Barrington,
Nr Ilminster, Somerset TA19 0NQ.
T:01460-240349. F:01460-242069.
Design and weave accurate copies of English and European fabrics from the Byzantine period to the 19th century.

Timney Fowler
388 King's Rd, London SW3 5UZ.
T:0171-352 2263. F:0171-352 0351.
Famous for their black and white classical images of urns, columns, cameos and architectural details. New woven fabrics in pure wool worsted satin.

*Watts of Westminster
2/29 Chelsea Harbour Design Centre, Chelsea Harbour, London SW10 0XE.
T:0171-376 4486. F:0171-376 4636. Grand Gothic and Victorian fabrics and wallpapers based on archive designs.

*Webster Weave
Docking Mill, Bradford Rd,
Batley, W.Yorks WF17 8HB.
T:01924-420024. F:01924-420350. Towelling by the metre.

For more help:
Design Line's 'Directory of Fabric Suppliers' lists all the main UK manufacturers, distributors and specialists. There are 494 entries giving addresses, phone and fax numbers and a brief description. To order a copy send a cheque for £9.99 (inc p&p) to: Design Line, PO Box 300, London W11 3WE. Tel/Fax: 0171-221 6600.

6

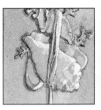

WALLPAPER

WHERE TO SEE A LARGE SELECTION

Baer & Ingram
273 Wandsworth Bridge Rd,
London SW6 2TX.
T:0171-736 6111. F:0171-736 8581.
Most top manufacturers of wallpapers are represented. They also have their own range including a fleur-de-lys design. Good choice of 'books','wood-effect', 'Staffordshire pottery', and children's papers. If a client brings in an old wallpaper they will try to match it.

Hamilton-Weston Wallpapers
18 St Mary's Grove,
Richmond, Surrey TW9 1UY.
T:0181-940 4850. F:0181-332 0296.
Specialists in archive wallpapers. Were involved in the reproduction of papers after the fire at Uppark.They hold books for many wallpaper manufacturers and provide a sourcing service for hard to find papers. Plus borders, fabrics, trimmings and decorative

accessories - many from unusual sources. Full interior design and soft furnishing service for both domestic and commercial projects.

John Oliver
33 Pembridge Rd, London W11 3HG.
T:0171-727 3735. F:0171-727 5555.
John Oliver will reproduce any of his own range of wallpapers in any colour way (nine roll minimum order). Large number of major manufacturers' pattern books. Plus more unusual papers: silk-stranded, metallic, huge damasks, fake paint effect, Japanese seagrass. They also provide a paper-backing service for fabrics.

Sanderson
112-120 Brompton Rd, London SW3 1JJ.
T:0171-584 3344. Showroom for over sixty different companies. The ground floor is devoted to Sanderson's own collection of papers including historic designs and the lower level is a good place to see papers from top British and European manufacturers.

Most major fabric companies have wallpaper collections, so see also: FABRICS - Major Fabric Companies.

ARCHIVE/HANDPRINTED WALLPAPER

Baer & Ingram
See entry under **WHERE TO SEE A LARGE SELECTION.** Will research and commission special orders.

*Alexander Beauchamp
2/12 Chelsea Harbour Design Centre, Chelsea Harbour, London SW10 0XE.
T:0171-376 4556. F:0171-376 3435.
Stock range of printed stripes, damasks and a 'Chinoiserie' collection inspired by Oriental ceramics, art and textiles. They specialise in screen-printed reproductions of historic papers from the 15th-18th century. If they don't have the screen for a specific design, they will make it.

*Manuel Canovas
2 North Terrace, Brompton Rd, London SW3 2BA.
T:0171-225 2298. F:0171-823 7848.
Two hand printed toile designs and another French document design called 'Merlin', with Mandarins and flutes in a trellis pattern. Plus stripes, dots and contemporary designs, all with matching fabrics.

*Cole & Son
144 Offord Rd, London N1 1NS.
T:0171-607 4288. F:0171-607 3341.
Historic wallpaper specialist. They hold the original lino blocks for Edward Bawden and John Aldridge's 'Bardfield' wallpapers; also the Cowtan collection which includes all the Crace & Son blocks by Pugin. There are Art Nouveau wallpapers as well. They own John Perry Wallpapers.

Colefax & Fowler
39 Brook St, London W1Y 2JE.
T:0171-493 2231. F:0171-355 4037.
And at:
110 Fulham Rd, London SW3 6RL.
T:0171-244 7427. F:0171-373 7916.
Historic range called the 'Musée Des Arts Décoratifs Designs'. They have a large collection of wallpapers co-ordinating with their fabrics in both traditional and contemporary designs.

de Gournay
14 Hyde Park Gate London SW7 5DF.
T:0171-823 7316. F:0171-823 7475.
Chinese export papers based on 18th century Chinese rooms in European and American homes. There are many scenes which can be painted on silk or paper in various colours and panel heights. Clients' own designs can be painted within 12 weeks.

*Guy Evans
96 Great Titchfield St, London W1P 7AG.
T:0171-436 7914. F:0171-436 2980.
Hand-blocked wallpaper designs from the 18th to the 20th century - from Revillon to Art Deco to contemporary designs. Hand-blocked papers from the old French firm of Mauny. Wallpapers by the American company Clarence House.

Farrow & Ball
33 Uddens Trading Estate, Wimborne, Dorset BH21 7NL.
T:01202-876141. F:01202-873793.
Showroom: 249 Fulham Rd, London SW3.
T:0171-351 0273. F:0171-351 0221.
Dragged and striped papers in the colours of their 'National Trust' range of paints.

Hamilton-Weston
See entry under **WHERE TO SEE A LARGE SELECTION.** Handmade and machine printed archival reproductions. They reproduced the wallpaper destroyed by the fire at Uppark. Historical specialists with a large selection of Victorian wallpapers. They can reproduce quality wallpapers from scraps and give advice on period detail.

Hodsoll McKenzie
52 Pimlico Rd, London SW1W 8LP.
T:0171-730 2877. F:0171-823 4939.
Archival papers to match their fabric range; mainly neo-classical designs and stripes in traditional colours like red, dark green, parchment, yellow, dusky pink, cream and beige.

Christopher Moore Textiles
1 Munro Terrace, London SW10 0DL.
T:0171-792 3628. F:0171-351 7644.
Hand blocked wallpapers in Toile de Jouy

designs based on 18th and 19th century documents.

John Oliver
See entry under **WHERE TO SEE A LARGE SELECTION.**

Osborne & Little
304 King's Rd, London SW3 5UH. T:0171-352 1456. F:0181-673 8254. Reproductions of papers from the Victoria & Albert's archive collection: they are boldly patterned designs in rich turquoise, purples and reds.

*John Perry Wallpapers
See entry above under Cole & Son. Founded in 1875, this company holds 3,000 wood blocks including Pugin's designs used in the restoration of the Houses of Parliament.

Sanderson
See entry under **WHERE TO SEE A LARGE SELECTION.** Arts and Crafts designs including William Morris reproductions. Also their original 1914 'Rose & Peony' design.

Silvergate Papers
Mount Orleans, Collingbourne Ducis, Marlborough, Wilts SN8 3EF. T:01264-850788. F:01264-850823. Range of 36 block-printed historical wallpapers to order. They all originate from restoration projects at Uppark, Osterley, Saltram, Blaise Castle, Temple Newsam and Oxburgh, to name only a few. New commissions undertaken.

*Warner Fabrics
Bradbourne Drive, Tilbrook, Milton Keynes, Bucks MK7 8BE. T:01908-366900. F:01908-370839. Archival range including the 'Malmaison' collection of 18th and 19th century designs. The many other period papers include 'Panelwork' (1810-1835) 'Madame Eugenia' (1828-1840) and 'Josephine Stripe'(1932).

*Watts of Westminster
2/9 Chelsea Harbour Design Centre, Chelsea Harbour, London SW10 0XE. T:0171-376 4486. F:0171-376 4636. Founded in 1874 by the three Victorian architects Bodley, Garner and Scott. Unique

archive of historic designs, including many by Pugin. New collection of handprinted reproductions of papers used in the great houses of Ireland from the 17th to the end of the 19th century.

*Zoffany
Unit G12, Chelsea Harbour Design Centre, Chelsea Harbour, London SW10 0XE. T:0171-349 0043. F:0171-351 9677. Archival prints developed originally for the redecoration of Temple Newsam House, Leeds. This collection includes over 50 papers in designs dating from the 16th to the early 19th century. Zoffany has also perfected a handprinted look by machine.

Zuber & Cie
42 Pimlico Rd, London SW1W 8LP. T:0171-824 8265. F:0171-824 8270. This company has been producing hand blocked wallpapers since 1797. The twenty five panoramic landscapes are the most famous designs, dating mainly from the Napoleonic and Restoration period in France. The spectacular 'Vues de Suisse', 'Vues d'Amerique du Nord' and 'Bresil' are printed using up to 1690 blocks, with 223 different colours.

TEXTURED WALLPAPER (FLOCK, HESSIAN, ANAGLYPTA)

*Akzo-Nobel
Hollins Rd, Darwin, Lancs BB2 1TU. T:01254-704951. F:01254-774414. Specialists in Lincrusta (with designs called 'Adelphi','Frieze','Italian Renaissance' and 'Art Nouveau') and Anaglypta.

*Altfield
G4 & 2/22 Chelsea Harbour Design Centre, Chelsea Harbour, London SW10 0XE. T:0171-376 5667. F:0171-351 5893.

* denotes trade supplier. Please phone for retail outlets.

Distributors for Maya Romanoff's textured and metallic papers.

C Brewer & Sons

327 Putney Bridge Rd, London SW15 2PG. T:0181-788 9335. F:0181-788 8285. Call for branches. Nationwide chain of specialist decorating shops with wallcoverings by Albany (woodchip, textured whites), Anaglypta, Coloroll, Crown, Euro, Fine Decor, Gallery, Graham & Brown, Harlequin, Kingfisher, Mayfair, Muraspec (wall hessian), Murella, Nairn, Sanderson, Sigma (woven textured fabric for wall which is hard-wearing and can be painted over), Venilia and Vymura. Also stencils, scumbles, crackle glazes, varnishes, paint and paint sundries.

*Cole & Son

See entry under ARCHIVE/ HANDPRINTED WALLPAPER. Traditional manufacturer of flocked damask and striped wallpapers drawn from historic designs in their archives.

*Donghia

Unit 23, Chelsea Harbour Design Centre, Chelsea Harbour, London SW10 0XE. T:0171-823 3456. F:0171-376 5758. Fabric-backed 'Raffia', paper-backed 'Grass Cloth' and 'Hemp' for walling.

Elizabeth Eaton

85 Bourne St, London SW1W 8HF. T:0171-730 2262. F:0171-730 7294. American range of 'Gracie' silk and grass cloths.

Muraspec

Zoffany House, 74-78 Wood Lane End, Hemel Hempstead, Herts HP2 4RF. T:0990-117118. F:0990-329020. Hessian wallcoverings, silk-strand papers, even paper-backed suede.

John Oliver

See entry under WHERE TO SEE A LARGE SELECTION. Japanese grass textured papers.

van Schelle & Gurland

1 Cambridge Rd, London SW11 4RT. T:0171-223 6485. F:0171-924 5651. Hand printed flocked wallcoverings.

FAUX-WOOD/ FAUX-STONE/FAUX-BOOK WALLPAPER

*Altfield

See entry under TEXTURED WALLPAPER (FLOCK, HESSIAN, ANAGLYPTA). Maya Romanoff's 'stone' and 'wood veneers'.

*Brunschwig & Fils

10 the Chambers, Chelsea Harbour Design Centre, Chelsea Harbour, London SW10 0XF. T:0171-351 5797. F0171-351 2280. Amongst their huge selection of wallpapers there are two wood-effect papers: 'Adirondack' and 'Faux Bois'. Their famous book paper is called 'Bibliothèque'. There's

also a stone block paper called 'Jackson Hall'.

Cath Kidston

See entry under OTHER SPECIALIST SUPPLIERS & SERVICES. Fake.wood wallpaper.

Andrew Martin International

200 Walton St, London SW3 2JL. T:0171-584 4290. F:0171-581 8014. 'Camelot/Stone' wallpaper.

*Nobilis-Fontan

1/2 Cedar Studios, 45 Glebe Place, London SW3 5JE. T:0171-351 7878. F:0171-376 3507. Faux-wood and faux-granite wallpapers.

Ornamenta

3-12 Chelsea Harbour Design Centre, Chelsea Harbour, London SW10 0XE. T:0171-352 1824. F:0171-376 3398. 'Ashlar block' and wood-effect wallpaper.

Osborne & Little

304 King's Rd, London SW3 5UH. T:0171-352 1456. F:0181-673 8254. Distribute Nina Campbell's 'tongue-and-groove' wallpaper.

*Brian Yates
G26 Chelsea Harbour Design Centre,
Chelsea Harbour, London SW10 OXE.
T:0171-352 0123. F:0171-352 6060.
Wood-effect wallcovering.

*Zoffany
See entry under ARCHIVE/
HANDPRINTED WALLAPER.
'Grand Ashlar Block' wallpaper.

TARTANS/PLAID WALLPAPER

Monkwell
Decorative Fabrics Gallery, 278-280
Brompton Rd, London SW3 2AS.
T:0171-589 4778. F:0171-589 4781.
Pastel plaid wallpapers.

*Paper Moon
Unit 4, Central Business Centre, Great
Central Way, London NW10 OUR.
T:0181-451 3655. F:0181-459 7445.
Best selection of traditional tartan
wallpapers including 'Black Watch' and
'Lindsay Claret'. Also good range of plaid
papers from American manufacturers like
Schumacher, Waverly and Imperial
Wallcoverings.

Today Interiors
Hollis Rd, Grantham, Lincs NG31 7QH.
T:01476-574401. F:01476-590208.
Small selection of plaid papers.

METALLIC PAPERS

*Altfield
See entry under TEXTURED
WALLPAPER (FLOCK, HESSIAN,
ANAGLYPTA). Maya Romanoff's clear
lacquered silver and bronze-leaf papers.

*Donghia
See entry under TEXTURED
WALLPAPER (FLOCK, HESSIAN,
ANAGLYPTA). Heavy metal wallcoverings.

John Oliver
See entry under WHERE TO SEE A
LARGE SELECTION. Stocks a good
selection of metallic papers.

PRINT ROOM PAPERS

National Trust Enterprises
P O Box 101, Melksham, Wilts SN12 8EA.
T:01225-705676. F:01225-790960.
'An Introduction to Print Room Borders'
(£7.95) comprises four sheets of decorative
borders and was inspired by the Print Room
at Blickling Hall in Norfolk.

Ornamenta
See entry under FAUX-WOOD/FAUX-
STONE/FAUX-BOOK WALLPAPER.
Print room designs like festoons and angels.

John Sutcliffe
12 Huntingdon Rd, Cambridge CB3 0HH.
T:01223-315858. By appointment.
Ornaments for print rooms comprising
frames, borders, corners, bows and
hooks in different sizes, plus festoons
of flowers and shells. Mail order.

Nicola Wingate-Saul Print Rooms
43 Moreton St, London SW1V 2NY.
T/F:0171-821 1577. Large range
of prints, friezes and borders for recreating
18th century print rooms.

OTHER SUPPLIERS & SPECIALIST SERVICES

*Manuel Canovas
See entry under ARCHIVE/
HANDPRINTED WALLPAPER.
Wallpapers with matching fabrics. There
are stripes in two widths and lots of smaller
motifs: dots, leaves, chevrons and stylised
stones and shells. Plus the large scale
florals and pomegranates for which Canovas
is famous.

Ciel Decor
187 New King's Rd, London SW6 4SW.
T:0171-731 0444. F:0171-731 0788.
Small collection of provencal print
wallpapers and borders by Les Olivades.

*Decor Shades
5 Brewery Mews Business Centre,
St John Rd, Isleworth, Middx TW7 6PH.
T/F:0181-847 1939. Paper-backing of
fabrics for wallcoverings.

*** denotes
trade supplier.
Please phone
for retail outlets.**

Designers Guild
267-271 & 277 King's Rd,
London SW3 5EN.
T:0171-351 5775.
F:0171-243 7710.
Tricia Guild's brightly coloured
contemporary designs. There
are floral prints, modern
interpretations of classical
themes, wide stripes, plain
pastel designs.

Nicholas Herbert
118 Lots Rd, London SW10 0RJ.
T:0171-376 5596. F:0171 376 5572.
Wallpapers designed by Nicholas Herbert
can be matched to one's fabric. Four roll
minimum - two week delivery.

Howard Chairs
30-31 Lyme St, London NW1 0EE.
T:0171-482 2156. F:0171-482 0068.
Can paper-back fabrics for wallcovering.

Cath Kidston
8 Clarendon Cross, London W11 4AP.
T:0171-221 4000. F:0171-229 1992.
Wallpapers with 1950s designs. Lots of
floral, rosy patterns, a 'Bath-time' paper and
a 'Fern Leaf' design based on an endpaper
from a 19th century pattern book.

Maecenas Decoration
13 Crescent Place, London SW3 2EA.
T:0171-581 1083. F:0171-584 5150.
Can hand-paint any design onto paper to
reproduce historical interiors or recreate
a client's own ideas.

Katherine Morris
2 Mathews Yard, Shorts Gardens,
London WC2H 9HR.
T/F:0171-379 0906. By appointment.
Hand-printed two colour papers in original
designs using lino-blocks. Katherine Morris
also designs bespoke wallpapers on a
particular theme in any two colours which
can be specifically matched to details in
a room.

John Oliver
See entry under **WHERE TO SEE A
LARGE SELECTION.** Will paper-back
fabrics to order.

Ornamenta
See entry under **FAUX-WOOD/FAUX-
STONE/FAUX-BOOK WALLPAPER.**
Cloud design wallpaper.

Osborne & Little
See entry under **ARCHIVE/
HANDPRINTED WALLPAPER.**
The 'Coloratura' collection includes metallic
gold and silver papers with splashed dots;
a crackle-glaze design in 8 colours, a
'distressed' paper in 12 colours, and
a 'paint-effect' paper in 32 colours.
Plus a large range of stripes and plains.
They distribute papers by Nina Campbell,
including 'Indore' with monkeys and birds,
'Tamarin', a flower motif and 'Nina's Garden'
with bees, beehives, flowers and shells.

Sandiford & Mapes
3B1 Cooper House,
2 Michael Rd, London SW6 2ER.
T:0171-384 3312. F:0171-736 5471.
Specialise in wallpaper and large paper
artwork conservation. Clients include
individuals, English Heritage and The
National Trust.

Timney Fowler
388 Kings Rd, London SW3 5UZ.
T:0171-352 2263. F:0171-352 0351.
Best known for their black and white Greco-
Roman designs of royal crowns, heraldic
symbols, stylised lettering and engraved
images, now also available in neutral tones
and pale colours.

Tones Specialist Decoration
29 Streatley Rd, London NW6 7LT.
T/F:0171-624 4936.
Specialist wallpaper hangers.

*Bruno Triplet
1/1 Chelsea Harbour Design Centre,
Chelsea Harbour, London SW10 0XE.
T:0171-795 0395. F:0171-376 3070.
Range includes a linen wallcovering.

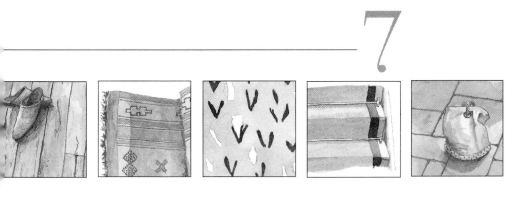

FLOORING

NATURAL MATTING

The Alternative Flooring Company
4 Anton Trading Estate,
Andover, Hants SP10 2NJ.
T:01264-335111. F:01264-336445.
Specialist trade supplier of natural flooring:
seagrass, coir, sisal. Also pure wool look-
alike. Basketweave seagrass, herringbone,
sisal and other patterns available.

Avery Designs
See entry under OTHER RUGS.
Handpainted sisal or wool/sisal
rugs in any design to order.

Country Weavers
The Long Barn, Eastnor,
Ledbury, Hereford HR8 1EL.
T:01531-631611. F:01531-631361.
Range of flatweave runners that start
at 24" wide.

Crucial Trading
Head/Sales office: The Market Hall,
Craven Arms, Shropshire SY7 9NY.
T:01588-673666. F:01588-673623.

London store:
Pukka Palace, 174 Tower Bridge Rd,
London SE1 3LF.
T:0171-234 0000. F:0171-234 0110.
Vast range of natural flooring from medieval
matting to coloured seagrass. Also flatweave
wools, cotton top and loop pile cotton
carpets.

The Deben Craftsmen
The Old Horseshoes, Lower
Tasburgh, Norwich NR15 1AR.
T:01508-471656. Rush matting handmade
in Norfolk from coarse and very hardwearing
Dutch rushes. The 3" strips are joined
together into mats of any size. This company
also makes willow baskets to order.

Fired Earth
See entry under TILE SHOPS
WITH A LARGE SELECTION.
Natural floorcoverings made from natural,
renewable plant fibre - grass, coir, jute and
sisal. Plus grass rugs in any length, in widths
up to 4m and with a choice of whipped
or braided edging.

* denotes
trade supplier.
Please phone
for retail outlets. 101

International Matting Company
2A Salter St, London NW10 6UL.
T:0181-964 2269. F:0181-960 8051.
And at:
555 Kings Road, London SW6 2EB.
T:0171-384 2773. F:0171-731 6568.
Sister company to Blenheim Carpets. Coir, jute, seagrass and sisal available from stock. Range of jute rugs with borders.

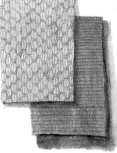

Natural Flooring Direct
Freepost LON1229,
London SE16 4BR.
T:0800-454721. F:0171-252 0073.
Bouclé pure wool flooring and natural matting: coir, sisal and jute. They also supply and fit wooden flooring, re-sand and seal wood floors and provide stain inhibition products for carpets and natural flooring.

Roger Oates Design
The Long Barn, Eastnor,
Ledbury, Hereford HR8 1EL.
T:01531-632718. F:01531-631361.
Specialist in seagrass, coir, abaca, sisal, jute, recycled wood pulp and pure cotton flooring. Good selection of linen and striped runners, decorative borders, carpet bindings and stair-rods. Pure wool felt and boucle floorcovering. 100% linen tape in ten colours for binding carpets and matting.

Many carpet specialists also supply natural matting - see Carpets & Stair-rods.

Rooksmoor Mills
Bath Rd, Stroud, Gloucs GL5 5ND.
T:01453-872577. F:01453-872420.
Specialists in seagrass, sisal, coir, jute, wool and wool/sisal flooring.

Sans Frontières
26 Danbury St, London N1 8JU.
T:0171-454 1230. F:0171-454 1231.
Wide range of natural matting plus contract needlepunch and 100% wool carpets.

Sinclair Till Flooring Company
See entry under LINOLEUM/VINYL/ RUBBER/CORK. Over 50 types of floor-coverings made from plant fibres. There are ribs, weaves, herringbones and stripes, some fine and elegant, others coarse and rustic. Plus 'The English Country' collection of painted sisal rugs and runners.

*Bruno Triplet
1/1 Chelsea Harbour Design Centre,
Chelsea Harbour, London SW10 0XE.
T:0171-795 0395. F:0171-376 3070. Pap
twine and cotton natural flooring.

Waveney Apple Growers
Aldeby, Beccles, Suffolk NR34 0BL.
T:01502-677345. F:01502-678134.
Specialists in medieval rush matting and basket-making.

CARPETS & STAIR-RODS

*Afia Carpets
11-12 Chelsea Harbour Design Centre,
Chelsea Harbour, London SW10 0XE.
T:0171-351 5858. F:0171-351 9677.
Decorative range of flat woven pure wool carpets, including a fake-leopard design. U
agents for Stark of New York, Flipo of Franc
and Van Besouw of Holland.

Anta Scotland
Fearn, Tain, Ross-shire IV20 1XW.
T:01862-832477. F:01862-832616.
Shetland tweed carpet in ten different tartan designs.

Blenheim Carpets
Unit 2A Salter St, London NW10 6UL.
T:0181-964 2700. F:0181-960 8051.
And at:
555 Kings Road, London SW6 2 EB.
T:0171-384 2773. F:0171-731 6568.
Stock range of wool carpets; bespoke carpets; tartan and herringbone jute collection and entrance matting.

*Bosanquet Ives
3 Court Lodge, 48 Sloane Square,
London SW1W 8AT.
T:0171-730 6241. F:0171-730 5341.
Comprehensive floorcovering service to interior designers from design to installatio
New exclusive range of Brussels weave an
wool naturals. Wide Belgian bindings which
are suited to natural matting and rugs.

Braquenié
Pierre Frey, 251-253 Fulham Rd,
London SW3 6HY.
T:0171-376 5599. F:0171-352 3024.

our ranges of custom made carpets
ncluding in Aubusson and Empire styles.

Brintons
O Box 16, Exchange St,
idderminster, Worcs DY10 1AG.
:01562-820000. F:01562-515597.
Voven Axminster and Wilton carpets;
eavyweight velvet carpets.

rora
44 Kings Road, London SW3 5UR.
:0171-352 3697. F:0171-352 1792.
ure wool tartan floor-covering and
artan rugs and blankets.

he Carpet Library
48 Wandsworth Bridge Rd,
ondon SW6 2UH.
:0171-736 3664. F:0171-736 7554.
raditional woven carpets: pure New Zealand
ool 'natural' range, Wilton twist pile and
xminster. Historical reproductions including
Villiam Morris designs. Excellent selection
nd top quality fitting service. Full range
f natural flooring. Stair-rods to order.
rade and retail.

Carpets International
oftshaw Lane, Bradford, W. Yorks BD4 6QW.
:01274-681881. F:01274-685161.
arpets for office/public projects.
Abingdon' stain free carpet in 100 colours.

hatsworth
27 Brompton Rd, London SW3 2EP.
:0171-584 1386. F:0171-581 3053.
arpet showroom with a good selection
f printed and plain woven carpets.
an custom make to any design or colour
nd plain carpets can be made in any width.
ood selection of colours and animal prints.

Curragh Tintawn
ewbridge, County Kildare, Ireland.
:01372-363393. F:01372-363374.
pecialist in natural woven and tufted
ool carpets.

Custom Carpet Company
0 Dymock St, London SW6 3HA.
:0171-736 3338. F:0171-731 2644.
ustom designed carpets: hand-tufted,
assmachine (to any width), wovens
nd tiles.

*Louis De Poortere
William House, Clarendon
Court, The Parade, Leamington
Spa, Warwicks CV32 4AH.
T:01926-431200.
F:01926-431525.
Their super deep pile
'Decorwool Prestige'
carpet comes in 22 colours.

*Hugh Mackay Carpets
PO Box 1, Durham City DH1 2RX.
T:0191-386 4444. F:0191-384 0530.
Axminster and Wilton tufted carpets
and carpet tiles.

E. Mills & Son
24-25 Shepherds Bush Market,
London W12 8DG.
T:0181-743 3891. F:0181-749 3660.
100% polypropylene carpet at £6.95 a
square yard. Specialist in unusual colours -
purples, bright yellows and greens.
Also lino in bright solid colours.

S & M Myers
100/106 Mackenzie Rd, London N7 8RG.
T:0171-609 0091. F:0171-609 2457.
Specialise in domestic quality twist
pile carpets (mostly in 80% wool) at
competitive prices.

Roger Oates Design
See entry under NATURAL MATTING.
Stair-rods in wood, metal and brass.

Stairrods (UK)
Unit 6, Park Road North Ind Estate,
Blackhill, Consett, County Durham DH8
5UN. T:01207-591176. F:01207-591911.
Stair-rods in brass, bronze, chrome, black -
any finish available.

*Steeles Carpets
Barford Rd, Bloxham, Oxon OX15 4HA.
T:01295-721000. F:01295-721743.
Brussels and Wilton carpets in an extensive
selection of colours and styles. Contract
specialist. Can incorporate a company logo
or your family crest into the carpet's design.

*Stockwell Carpets
3rd floor, 51/52 New Bond St,
London W1Y 0BY.
T:0171-629 0626. F:0171-409 2969.

**For additional help
try: British Carpet
Manufacturers'
Association, 5
Portland Place,
London W1N 3AA.
T:0171-580 7155.
F:0171-580 4854.**

**The National
Institute of Carpet
and Floor Layers,
4d St Mary's Place,
The Lace Market,
Nottingham
NG1 1PH.
T:0115-958 3077.
F:0115-941 2238.**

* denotes
trade supplier.
Please phone
for retail outlets.

Original 17th-19th century patterns reproduced to order. Range includes American style rugs and opulent carpets.

*Stoddard Templeton
Glenpatrick Rd, Elderslie, Johnston PA5 9UJ. T:01505-322538. F:01505-577107. Plain, textured or patterned carpets and borders. Axminster, Wilton and bonded ranges.

*Tomkinson Carpets
PO Box 11, Duke's Place, Kidderminster, Worcs DY10 2JR. T:01562-820006. F:01562-820030. Tufted and Axminster carpet specialist.

*V'soske Joyce (UK)
The Clocktower, Coda Centre, 189 Munster Rd, London SW6 6AW. T:0171-386 7200. F:0171-386 9220. Manufacturer and supplier of hand-tufted luxury carpets, dyed to match if required. New range of passmachine 'Merino Carpets' in any width.

*Woodward Grosvenor & Co
Stourvale Mills, Green St, Kidderminster, Worcs DY10 1AT. T:01562-820020. F:01562-820042. Established in 1790 this company specialises in accurate reproductions of archival designs in standard Wilton, Axminster or Brussels weave. They include original William Morris designs and Chlidema Masonic Squares.Traditional stock collection and range to order.

Wool Classics
41 Ledbury Rd, London W11 2AA. T:0171-792 8277. F:0171-792 0581. Large selection of pure wool carpets. 100% wool carpet in six colours from Australia, loop pile carpet from Prague, and Wilton Brussels rugs. Agents for Durkan patterned contract range.

NEEDLEPOINT RUGS

*Altfield
Units G4 and 2/22 Chelsea Harbour Design Centre, London SW10 OXE. T:0171-351 5893. F:0171-376 5667.

Needlepoint rugs (and cushions), with 'Melon, 'Floral', and 'Lattice' designs.

Deborah Rolt
Culworth Fields, Culworth, Banbury, Oxon OX17 2HN. T/F:01295-768353. Hand-stitched Portuguese needlepoint rugs in 300 designs.

Tindle
162-168 Wandsworth Bridge Road, London SW6 2UQ. T:0171-384 1485. F:0171-736 5630. Over twenty needlepoint rug designs including floral, Chinoiserie and dog motifs.

Valerie Wade
108 Fulham Road, London SW3 6HS. T:0171-225 1414. F:0171-589 9029. Handmade, 100% wool needlepoint rugs. Many in stock, but they can also be made to a specific size, design or colour.

AUBUSSONS/ ORIENTAL RUGS

Chandni Chowk
1 Harlequins, Paul St, Exeter EX4 3TT. T:01392-410201. F:01392-421095. Mainly contemporary Persian carpets.

Kennedy Carpets
9A Vigo St, London W1X 1AL. T:0171-439 8873. F:0171-437 1201. Handwoven new 'Agra' carpets which are fine replicas of antiques.

Orientalist
152 Walton St, London SW3 2JJ. T:0171-581 2332. F:0171-589 0760. Top of the range reproductions of Aubusson and Savonnerie carpets in over 150 designs available from stock or to order in any size; contemporary Persian and Turkish kelims; 17th to 20th century pieces, including Aubusson and Beauvais carpets.

Perez
199 Brompton Rd, London SW3 1LA. T:0171-589 2199. F:0171-589 2262. Well known for their antique Oriental and European carpets and rugs, their 'Antoinette Collection' is a range of replicas of 18th century French Aubussons.

BORDA
T:01753-623000. The British Oriental Rug Dealers Association, can give advice on good Oriental rug retailers across the country. They can also advise on cleaning, repairs and valuations.

Many antique rug specialists also carry a range of fine reproductions, so please refer to the chapter: ANTIQUES - Antique Carpets & Rugs.

Rezai Persian Carpets
123 Portobello Road, London W11 2DY.
T: 0171-221 5012. F:0171-229 6690.
Antique and modern oriental rugs, plus
Aubusson tapestry cushions made in
China to 18th century designs.

KELIMS/DHURRIES

David Black Oriental Carpets
96 Portland Rd, London W11 4LN.
T:0171-727-2566. F:0171-229 4599.
Kelims and rugs with natural dyes.

*Brooke London
5 Sleaford St, London SW8 5AB.
T:0171-622 9372. F:0171-622 3010.
Distributors for Shyam Ahuja's range: cotton
and wool dhurries (including fine weave and
hand-knotted Savonneries) and rag rugs with
fabric borders. They also carry a Chinese
collection comprising Soumaks (antique
washed copies of Persian designs), kelims,
washed needlepoint and Aubusson rugs.

Fired Earth
See entry under **TILE SHOPS WITH A
LARGE SELECTION.** Good range of hand-
knotted tribal rugs, kelims and Gabbehs.

Graham & Green
4 Elgin Crescent, London W11 2JA.
T:0171-727 4594. F:0171-229 9717.
Mainly Turkish kelims.

Habitat
196 Tottenham Court Rd, London W1P 9LD.
T:0171-255 2545. F:0171-255 6004.
For other branches call: 0645-334433.
Modern and ethnic rugs.

The Kilim Warehouse
28A Picketts St, London SW12 8QB.
T:0181-675 3122. F:0181-675 8494.
Wide selection of old and new decorative
kelims plus cleaning and restoration service.

Nice Irma's
46 Goodge St, London W1P 1FJ.
T:0171-580 6921. F:0171-436 1567.
Indian Jaldar rugs.

Oriental Rug Gallery
115-116 High St, Eton, Berks SL4 6AN.
T/F:01753-623000.

Hand-made Persian, Turkish,
Russian and Romanian kelims
and Turkish folk life rugs
(which incorporate scenes of
village life). Valuations and
cleaning.

The Persian Carpet Studio
Harrow St, Leavenheath,
Colchester, Essex CO6 4PN.
T/F:01787-210034.
Nearly 200 new and 70
antique Oriental rugs in stock.

CONTEMPORARY RUGS

A-Z Studios
3-5 Hardwidge St, London SE1 3SY.
T:0171-403 7114. F:0171-403 8906.
These studios carry a range of contemporary
crafts including Helen Yardley's hand-tufted
wool rugs.

Amanda Dakin
Flat B1, Lloyds Wharf,
2 Mill St, London SE1 2BD.
T/F:0171-232 2084.
Hand-made pile rugs including
designs for children.

Jack Fairman Carpets
218 Westbourne Grove, London W11 2RH.
T:0171-229 2262. F:0171-229 2263.
Contemporary tribal rugs from S.W.
Iran in bold designs; Caucasian and
Tibetan meditation rugs; plus selection
of antique rugs.

Christopher Farr
115 Regents Park Rd, London, NW1 8UR.
T:0171-916 7690. F:0171-916 7694.
And at:
212 Westbourne Grove, London W11 2RH.
T:0171-792 5761. F:0171-792 5763.
Handmade rugs by designers like Allegra
Hicks and Romeo Gigli. Custom design
service available. Also furniture and lighting.

Jinan Furniture Gallery
17 Golden Square, London, W1R 4JB.
T:0171-434 3464. F:0171-434 3463.
American 'Dialogica' collection and felted
rugs by Lamontage.

*** denotes
trade supplier.
Please phone
for retail outlets.**

Kappa Lambda
Studio 51, 2 Manor Gardens,
London N7 6JZ.
T:0171-263 4819.
F:0171-263 4909.
Good selection of modern
designs in pure wool and cotton.

Purves & Purves
80-81 & 83 Tottenham Court Rd,
London W1P 9HD.
T:0171-580 8223. F:0171-580
8244. Bright contemporary rugs
by designers like Kate Blee
and Susan Absolon.

OTHER RUGS

Appalachia
14A George St, St Albans, Herts AL3 4ER.
T:01727-836796. F:01992-467560.
American flat braided folk art rugs
and multi-coloured cotton rag rugs.

Bery Designs
157 St John's Hill, London SW11 1TQ.
T:0171-924 2197. F:0171-924 1879.
Handpainted sisal, wool/sisal, jute/sisal
or pure wool rugs. There is a range of 50
designs to choose from - anything from a
small border to a faded Aubusson. They
can all be painted in any colour or adapted.
Alternatively you can commission your very
own design.

Alain Rouveure Galleries
Todenham, Moreton-in-Marsh,
Gloucs GL56 9NU.
T/F:01608-650418.
Importer of hand-knotted traditional
Tibetan rugs and decorative textiles.

WOOD FLOORING

Agora London
328 Durnsford Rd, London SW19 8DX.
T/F:0181-946 2593.
Supply, design and install antique French
oak flooring in twelve classic styles including
strip, chevron and herringbone patterns and
the 'Versailles pad'.

Campbell & Young
16 Lettice St, London SW6 4EH.
T:0171-736 7191. F:0171-731 2431.
Supply and install hardwood flooring.
Restoration service.

Campbell, Marson & Company
Wimbledon Business Centre,
34 Riverside Rd, London SW17 0BA.
T:0181-879 1909. F:0181-946 9395.
This family business has been supplying
hardwood flooring for over 70 years.
Restoration service for old floors, particularly
parquet which they will match and fix in
areas where broken, then re-sand and
lacquer - this costs about £15-£20 per sq m.

*Bernard Dru Oak
Bickham Manor, Timberscombe,
Minehead, Somerset TA24 7UA.
T:01643-841312. F:01643- 841048.
High quality English oak floorboards, either
square edged or in tongue-and-groove.

Finewood Floors
Unit 5 Gibson Business Centre,
rear of 800 High Road, London N17 0DH.
T:0181-365 0222. F:0181-885 3860.
Specialists in wide plank floorboards (5"-8")
in American red elm, oak, maple, ash,
cherry, sycamore, walnut, chestnut and
beech. Also pre-finished flooring and kitchen
worktops.

The Hardwood Flooring Co
146-152 West End Lane, London NW6 1SD.
T:0171-328 8481. F:0171-625 5951.
Large selection of wood flooring including
pitch pine and white pigmented beech.
Distributors for Junckers, Kahrs, Tarkett
and Bruce. Also reclaimed flooring.

*Junckers
Wheaton Court Commercial Centre,
Wheaton Road, Witham, Essex CM8 3UJ.
T:01376-517512. F:01376-514401.
Manufacturer of a wide range of solid
hardwood flooring: boards, strips, blocks in
solid beech, oak, ash or elm.

The Natural Wood Floor Co
See entry under RECLAIMED WOOD
FLOORING. New flooring in oak, maple,
walnut, Burmese teak, beech and hickory.

Victorian Wood Works
See entry under RECLAIMED
FLOORING. Can also supply new floors.

RECLAIMED
WOOD FLOORING

Cardiff Reclamation
Tremorfa Ind. Estate,
Rover Way, Cardiff CF2 2SD.
T:01222-458995.
Well priced pine boards, mahogany blocks
and oak floorboards delivered nationwide.

Chauncey's
16 Feeder Rd, St Philips, Bristol BS2 0SB.
T:0117-971 3131. F:0117-971 2224.
Examples include mosaic oak jointed with
mahogany and padouk, wide plank
floorboards, oak, re-sawn pine, block and
strip flooring.

The Natural Wood Floor Co
20 Smugglers Way, London SW18 1EQ.
T:0181-871 9771. F:0181-877 0273.
Reclaimed English and French strip wood
flooring, parquet and boards in oak, pine,
pitch pine and Douglas fir. Plus new floors.

Pine Supplies
Lower Tongs Farm, Longshaw Ford Rd,
Smithills, Bolton, Lancs BL1 7PP.
T:01204-841416. F:01942-840505.
Tongue-and-groove floorboards in reclaimed
maple and pine. Samples on request.

LASSCo Flooring
101-108 Britannia Walk, London N1 7LU.
T:0171-251 5157. F:0171-336 7246.
Reclaimed flooring of all types - from
parquet to flagstones.

Shiver Me Timbers
Long Rock, Penzance, Cornwall TR20 8JJ.
T:01736-711338.
Old pine, oak, parquet, mahogany and teak
floors. Furniture made from old floorboards.

Solopark
The Old Railway Station, Station Road,
Near Pampisford, Cambs CB2 4HB.
T:01223-834663. F:01223-834780.
Huge reclamation yard with oak and
hardwood boards, parquet floors, oak
beams, period mouldings, old interior
panelling and much more.

Victorian Wood Works
Gliksten Trading Estate, 118 Carpenters Rd,
London E15 2DY.
T:0181-985 8280. F:0181-986 3770.
3/4 million pounds worth of reclaimed
timber in stock: oak, pine or jarrah
(Australian wood), reclaimed beams, flooring
and traditional bead and buck pub panelling.

Walcot Reclamation
The Yard, 108 Walcot Street, Bath BA1 5BG.
T:01225-444404. F:01225-448163.
Large selection of oak floorboards (mostly
over 100 years old) from industrial locations.
Also pit sawn medieval oak rescued from
decaying barns.

**For more
reclaimed timber
suppliers see
ARCHITECTURAL
SALVAGE.**

LINOLEUM/VINYL/
RUBBER/CORK FLOORING

*Altro Floors
Works Rd, Letchworth, Herts SG6 1NW.
T:01462-480480. F:01462-480010.
Good range of contract vinyl and rubber
flooring mainly for offices, hospitals and
shops. Also sporting surfaces for fitness
rooms and arenas.

*Amtico
Kingfield Road, Coventry CV6 5PL.
T:01203-861400. F:01203-861552.
Large range of quality vinyl tiles - wood

*** denotes
trade supplier.
Please phone
for retail outlets.**

effect, black and white checkerboard and many other designs. Inspiration from natural materials: marble, wood, slate, granite and ceramics. Amtico have even made a floor to look like a Monopoly board. Computer design service.

*Armstrong World Industries
Armstrong House, 38 Market Square, Uxbridge, Middx. UB8 1NG.
T:01895-251122. F:01895-231571.
Manufacturer of 'Rhinotex' mottled tiles for contract use in a huge range of colours.

*Bonar & Flotex
High Holborn Rd, Ripley, Derbys DE5 3NT.
T:01773-744121. F:01773-744142.
Easy-care vinyl flooring suitable for hospitals, offices, schools and nursing homes.

GW Brooks
Unit 19, Waterside Ind Estate, Edtringshall Rd, Wolverhampton, W.Midlands WV2 2RH.
T:01902-493675. F:01902-495707.
Supply and fit major brands of lino and vinyl.

J Brown & Son
Unit 19, Leyton Business Centre, Etloe Rd, London E10 7BT.
T:0181-556 9396. F:0181-539 6751.
Design, cut and install top quality lino floors.

DLW Floorings
Centurion Court, Milton Park, Abingdon, Oxon OX14 4RY.
T:01235-831296. F:01235-861016.
Suppliers of 'Marmorette' - a German lino made from linseed oil, cork, natural resins and jute. The marbled effect version comes in 38 colourways (£12-£14 per sq metre including laying) but there are also plain and speckled types.

*Dalsouple Direct
PO Box 140, Bridgwater, Somerset TA5 1HT.
T:01984-667233. F:01984-667366.
Smart and colourful rubber floors in smooth or textured finishes.

*J De Bruyn Flooring Services
Unit 7, Orient Ind. Park, London E10 7BN.
T:0181-558 4725. F:0181-539 7050.
Wholesalers of the entire range of Forbo-Nairn contract products. They also cut and design their own borders for Forbo-Nairn.

Custom design, cutting and installation using linoleum from any manufacturer.

Duro Lino
24 Trinity Rd, London SW17 7RE.
T:0181-672 3593. F:0181-672 7172.
Supply and installation of all sorts of floors: vinyl, lino, Amtico, rubber, even wood.

First Floor
174 Wandsworth Bridge Rd, London SW6 2UQ.
T:0171-736 1123. F:0171-371 9812.
Dalsouple rubber tiles, 'Marmoleum' lino by Forbo-Nairn; wool and wool/sisal mix natural-look flooring; wood flooring.

*Forbo-Nairn
PO Box 1, Kirkaldy, Fife KY1 2SB.
T:01592-643111/643777.
F:01592-643999.
Comprehensive range of vinyl in flexible sheets or tiles including slip resistant and heavy duty flooring. Britain's only remaining linoleum manufacturer. The 'Marmoleum' range comes in wonderful colours.

*Gerflor
Rothwell Rd, Warwicks CV34 5PY.
T:01926-401500. F:01926-401647.
French vinyl tiles and sheets in seven ranges, in plain colours, veined, marbled, speckled and chipped. From £10-£30 a square metre.

*James Halstead
New Road, Whitefield, Manchester M45 7NR.
T:0161-767 1111. F:0161-767 1100.
Heavy-duty vinyl sheet and tile flooring for retail, hospitality, leisure and commercial sites - even operating theatres. Customised inlaid motifs are cut by computerised water jets (£100-£150 for a bespoke pattern).

Harvey Maria
17 Mysore Rd, London SW11 5RY.
T:0171-350 1964. F:0171-738 1568.
By appointment. Very unusual cork based tiles bearing a photographic image. The range includes 'Meadow', 'Seashore', 'Rocks', and 'Tropical Seas' and costs from £29.50 per pack of nine tiles (each tile is 1sq ft). Plus any other design to order.

*Jaymart Rubber & Plastics
Woodlands Trading Estate, Eden Vale Rd,
Westbury, Wilts BA13 3QS.
T:01373-864926. F:01373-858454.
Hundreds of products: rubber flooring in
tiles, sheets or rolls (including the
'Marmolay' marbled range), vinyl flooring,
entrance mats, artificial grass, PVC
duckboarding, and much more.

*Kersaint Cobb
See entry under ENTRANCE MATS.
Smooth and profiled rubber flooring.

*Marley Floors
Dickley Lane, Lenham,
Maidstone, Kent ME17 2DE.
T:01622-854000. F:01622-854268.
Tile and sheet vinyl flooring in heavy duty or
general purpose weights and lots of colours.
Range which resembles stone, terrazzo,
marble and wood.

Martin & Frost
130 McDonald Rd, Edinburgh EH7 4NN.
T:0131-557 8787. F:0131-557 8045.
Supply and fit major brands of all flooring -
hardwoods, carpets, Eastern rugs, lino and
vinyl (including Amtico).

Millers Specialist Floorcoverings
177 Leith Walk, Edinburgh EH6 8NR.
T:0131-554 2408. F:0131-555 5346.
Scotland's only supplier of Dalsouple
rubber flooring. Specialist lino cutting and
installation. Also natural mattings and wood
floors.

Jennie Moncur
189 Bermondsey St, London SE1 3UW.
T:0171-407 5310. F:0171-403 5440.
By appointment. Will undertake large scale
commissions for the design, cutting and
installation of lino flooring.

*Nicholls & Clarke
Niclar House, 3-10 Shoreditch High St,
London E1 6PE.
T:0171-247 5432. F:0171-247 7738.
'Marble' or 'wood plank' luxury vinyl tiles.

Pentonville Rubber Company
104 Pentonville Rd, London N1 9JB.
T:0171-837 4582. F:0171-278 7392.
Sheets of plain black industrial rubber are in
demand for flooring. At £10.50 a square
metre it is one of the cheapest options.

Siesta Cork Tiles
Unit 21, Tait Rd, off Gloucester Rd,
Croydon, Surrey CR0 2DP.
T:0181-683 4055. F:0181-683 4480.
Cork tiles by mail order.

Sinclair Till Flooring Company
791-793 Wandsworth Rd, London SW8 3JQ.
T:0171-720 0031. F:0171-498 3814.
Can cut and inlay linoleum with any
geometric pattern, however intricate. You
can choose an all-over pattern or just a
border. Also wood flooring, mattings, carpets
and rugs (Chinese needlepoints, kelims).

*Sommer (UK)
Floorcoverings Division, Berry Hill Ind.
Estate, Droitwich, Worcs WR9 9AB.
T:01905-795004. F:01905-794306.
Sommer lino has been made in the Tuscan
city of Narni since the turn of the century.
There are 20 plain colours and two marbled
versions (from £15 a square metre including
laying). They also make a cork underlay for
sound-proofing.

*Tarkett
Poyle House, PO Box 173, Blackthorne Rd,
Colnbrook, Slough, Berks SL3 0AZ.
T:01753-684533. F:01753-684334.
Flexible sheet and tile vinyl flooring.
Also wood plank flooring in oak,
beech, birch, spruce, maple or
pine for commercial applications.

Chris Tipping
Clockwork Studios, 38b Southwell Rd,
London SW5 9PG.
T:0171-274 4116. F:0171-738 3743.
By appointment. Designer of intricate
lino floors.

*Wicanders
Amorim House, Star Road, Partridge Green,
Horsham, W.Sussex RH13 8RA.
T:01403-710001. F:01403-710003.
'Corkmaster' cork tiles; 'Wood-o-Cork' wood
and cork plank and strip floors in natural
colours or in grey, bright blue, crimson red or
charcoal; 'Wood-o-Floor' floating floors
(which can even be laid over carpets).

*** denotes
trade supplier.
Please phone
for retail outlets.** 109

TILE SHOPS WITH A LARGE SELECTION

Criterion Tiles

196 Wandsworth Bridge Rd,
London SW6 2UF.
T:0171-736 9610. F:0171-736 0725.
And at:
2A Englands Lane, London NW3 4TG.
T:0171-483 2608. F:0171-483 2609.
Specialise in hand-made English tiles.

European Heritage

48-52 Dawes Rd, London SW6 7EJ.
T:0171-381 6063. F:0171-381 9534.
Large selection of ceramic wall and floor
tiles, terracotta, slate, limestone and
sandstone.

Fired Earth

Twyford Mill, Adderbury, Oxon OX17 3HP.
T:01295-812088. F:01295-810832.
Fifteen branches nationwide. Colour
brochure with a good selection of ceramic,
encaustic, slate, new and reclaimed
terracotta and inset tiles. Plus natural
mattings, rugs and their own range
of fabrics and paints.

The Original Tile Company

23A Howe St, Edinburgh EH3 6TF.
T:0131-556 2013. F:0131-558 3172.
Manufacturer and distributor of terracotta,
limestone, slate, marble, Victorian geometric
and Moroccan encaustic floor tiles.

Paris Ceramics

583 Kings Rd, London SW6 2EH.
T:0171-371 7778. F:0171-371 8395.
And at:
4 Montpelier Walk, Montpelier St,
Harrogate, N.Yorks HG1 2RY.
T:01423-523 877. F:01423-523 911.
English and French limestone, 18th century
stone and terracotta floors, mosaics and
hand-painted ceramics.

The Reject Tile Shop

178 Wandsworth Bridge Rd,
London SW6 2UQ.
T:0171-731 6098. F:0171-736 3693.
Specialists in seconds, ends of lines and
good value first quality tiles. Good selection
of brightly coloured 10cm tiles, plus quarry
tiles, slate, terracotta and mosaics.

Terranova

22 Trinity Lane, Beverley, E.Yorks HU17 0DY.
T:01482-861301. F:01482-861472.
And branches in Nottingham, Chichester,
Chester and Lincoln. Traditional sandstones
and limestones, tumbled and polished
marble, slates, handmade terracotta and
stoneware tiles.

The Tile Gallery

1 Royal Parade, 247 Dawes Rd,
London SW6 7RE.
T:0171-385 8818. F:0171-381 1589.
Large selection of white tiles (Imperial Ivory
Victorian, Delft-like bluish-white, hand-glazed
Mexican) and good range of coloured
and patterned ceramics. Also mosaics
and terracotta.

The Tile Shop

4 & 6 Chamberlayne Rd,
London NW10 3JD. T:0181-968 9497.
Good selection of reasonably priced tiles.
One shop stocks hand-painted ceramic tiles,
handmade or glazed terracotta, sandstone
and limestone, slate, marble and marble
cobbles, the other shop has mosaics and all
the factory-made tiles.

West London Tiles

15 Portobello Rd, London W11 3DA.
T:0171-221 0033/7280.
F:0171-727 2848. And at: 119 Northfield
Ave, London W13 9QR. T:0181-567 1640.
Large choice available: ceramic, terracotta,
slate and marble tiles. Will hand paint tiles
to order.

World's End Tiles

British Rail Yard, Silverthorne Rd,
London SW8 3HE.
T:0171-720 8358. F:0171-627 1435.
And at: 9 Langton St, London SW10 0JL.
T:0171-351 0279. F: 0171-376 5533.
Claim to be the largest importers of Italian
ceramic tiles in the UK. Specialist in hand
painted tiles to order (to match a wallpaper
etc). The Langton Street branch specialises
in marble and glass mosaics and antique
terracotta.

CERAMIC TILES

*Candy Tiles
Heathfield, nr Newton Abbott,
Devon TQ12 6RF.
T:01626-832641. F:01626-834668.
Victorian 'Art Tiles' and 'Candy Core'
marble-effect range in pastel colours.

*Capital Fireplaces
The Old Grain Store, Nupend Business Park,
Old Knebworth, Herts SG3 6QJ.
IT:01438-821138. F:01438-821157.
Specialists in William Morris, Art Nouveau,
Art Deco and Victorian style tiles suitable for
walls or fireplace insets. Also 'tubelined'
hand-made tiles on which a client's own
designs can be produced at a fraction of
the usual cost.

Casbah Tiles
20 Wellington Lane,
Montpelier, Bristol. BS6 5PY.
T:0117-942 7318. F:0117-942 0037.
Traditional Moroccan encaustic tiles.
Some are plain, others decorated with
ornate patterns and borders.

Ceramica Blue
10 Blenheim Crescent, London W11 1NN.
T/F:0171-727 0288.
Hand-painted tiles, including a Sicilian range
(plus solid colour tiles to mix with them),
a Welsh range with farmyard designs
and a leaf pattern in relief. They are all
very suitable as splashbacks. Plus a
large range of hand-painted tableware.

Kenneth Clark Ceramics
The North Wing, Southover Grange,
Southover Road, Lewes, E.Sussex BN7 1TP.
T:01273-476761. F:01273-479565.
Wide range of hand-decorated and glazed
tiles in a good selection of colours.
Also Victorian and William de Morgan
reproductions.Special commissions.

De La Torre Tiles
The Courtyard Pottery, Old Rectory,
Stoke Lacy, Hereford HR7 4HH. T:01432-
820500. F:01432-820272.
Hand-made wall tiles with a clear glaze
over leaf impressions.

Domus Tiles
33 Parkgate Rd,
London SW11 4NP.
T:0171-223 5555.
F:0171-924 2556.
Italian ceramic
tiles and marble
mosaic in lots of
strong colours. Plus marble,
limestone and 'river-washed' marble
which is acid-etched and looks like the
floor of an Italian piazza.

Elon Tiles
66 Fulham Rd, London SW3 6HH.
T:0171-460 4600. F:0171-460 4601.
Hand-made floor and wall tiles from Mexico,
Italy, Spain and France. Good selection of
terracotta tiles.

Froyle Tiles
Froyle Pottery, Lower Froyle, Alton,
Hampshire GU34 4LL.
T:01420-23693. F:01420-22797.
Handmade vitrified stoneware and
earthenware tiles in all colours and
shapes and suitable for use inside or out.

In Situ
421 Fulham Palace Rd, London SW6 6SX.
T:0171-371 5677. F:0171-371 5979.
Moorish, encaustic and bespoke tiles.

*H & R Johnson Tiles
Highgate Tile Works, Tunstall,
Stoke-on-Trent ST6 4JX.
T:01782-575575. F:01782-577377.
Traditional encaustic, geometric and
vitrified tiles; large selection of floor and
wall ceramic tiles; cut tile murals for public
buildings; restoration of original 19th
century tiled floors.

Jones Tiles
Manor Barn, Orleton, Ludlow,
Shropshire SY8 4HR.
T:01568-780666. F:01568-780370.
Hand decorated tin-glaze tiles.

The Kasbah
8 Southampton St, London WC2E 7HA.
T:0171-379 5230. F:0171-379 5231.
Moroccan hand cut tiles in star, crescent
and oblong shapes. Also terracotta.

*** denotes
trade supplier.
Please phone
for retail outlets.** 111

The Life Enhancing Tile Company

31 Bath Buildings,
Montpelier, Bristol BS6 5PT.
T:0117-907 7673. F:0117-907 7674.
Encaustic inset tiles for floors and walls
in a wide range of designs - fish, stars,
geometric or to customer's own design.

*Original Style

Stovax, Falcon Rd, Sowton Ind Estate,
Exeter, Devon EX2 7LF.
T:01392-474011. F:01392-2119932.
Specialists in reproductions of Victorian
tiles, geometric hall tiles, plain and
decorated wall tiles, William de Morgan
designs.

Rustica

See entry under TERRACOTTA TILES.

*Wentworth Ceramics

Unit 2 Farnworth Business Park,
Gladstone Road, Farnworth, Bolton BL4 7EQ.
T:01204-795599. F:01204-577931.
Importers and distributors of Italian,
Spanish and German ceramic wall,
floor and mosaic tiles.

MARBLE/TERRAZZO TILES

Gove Marble

Dawson Rd,
Kingston-on-Thames, Surrey KT1 3AX.
T:0181-546 2023. F:0181-547 1315.
Can tackle marble bathrooms, granite
kitchens, marble or limestone floors,
marble topped tables or reception desks.

Geoffrey Pike

Garnet Close, Greycaines Ind. Estate,
Watford , Herts WD2 4JL.
T:01923-224884. F:01923-238124.
A team of draughtsmen, sawyers, polishers,
masons, marble workers, fixers and
restorers staff this vast marble and granite
centre. They've supplied the stone for many
commercial and residential buildings.

*Pisani

Transport Ave, Great West Rd,
Brentford, Middx TW8 9HF.
T:0181-568 5001. F:0181-847 3406.
Stock a vast selection of marbles (at least

64 varieties) and granites (at least 36) for
commercial jobs.Largest UK wholesaler.

*A Quiligotti & Co.

Newby Rd, Hazel Grove,
Stockport, Cheshire SK7 5DR.
T:0161-483 1451. F:0161-456 0209.
Manufacturers of terrazzo floor tiles
(a composite of natural marble chippings)
in a wide range of colours, shapes and sizes.
It is suitable for use in most commercial,
industrial and retail buildings.

Pallam Precast

187 West End Lane,
West Hampstead NW6 2LJ.
T:0171-328 6512. F:0171- 328 3547.
Manufacturers of terrazzo floor tiles.

Reed Harris

Riverside House,
27 Carnwath Rd, London SW6 3HR.
T:0171-736 7511. F:0171-736 2988.
Marble and granite from Italy, Portugal,
France, Spain and India. Ceramic floor tiles
from Italy, Switzerland, France and Germany
in four sizes and 44 plain and speckled
colours. Company logos can be incorporated
into tiled surfaces by water-jet cutting.

Vitruvius

Unit 20 Ransome's Dock,
35 Parkgate Rd, London SW11 4NP.
T:0171-223 8209. F:0171-924 3045.
Marble, slate, granite and stone specialists.
Everything from intricate detailed flooring
designs to marble vanity units.

Zarka Marble

41A Belsize Lane, London NW3 5AU.
T:0171-431 3042. F:0171-431 3879.
Marble and granite supply, restoration
and carving. Marble for wall cladding,
bathroom surfaces, furniture - either
large or small quantities.

STONE TILES

Artisans of Devizes

36 The Nursery, Bath Rd,
Devizes, Wilts SN10 2AG.
T:01380-720007. F:01380-728368.
Specialists in stone, slate, marble, granite.

For additional
help try:
The National
Federation of
Terrazzo, Marble and
Mosaic Specialists,
PO Box 50, Banstead,
Surrey SM7 2RD.
T:01737-360673.

The Contract Flooring
Association,
4C St. Mary's Place,
The Lace Market,
Nottingham
NG1 1PH.
T:0115-9411126.
F:0115-9412238.

Attica
543 Battersea Park Rd, London SW11 3BL.
T:0171-738 1234. F:0171-924 7875.
Reclaimed 'Biblical stone' from Jerusalem,
in characteristic rosy and sandy hues;
European and English limestones and
antique terracotta; hand painted wall tiles;
new 'fresco' range of tiles designed to look
like painted plaster (but more durable), in
designs ranging from Neolithic cave painting
to scenes from the Italian Renaissance.

Burlington Slate
Kirkby-in-Furness, Cumbria LA17 7UN.
T:01229-889661. F:01229-889466.
Natural slate in olive, blue black, light
green, silver and grey.

Classical Flagstones
Lyncombe Vale Farm,
Lyncombe Vale, Bath BA2 4LT.
T:01225-316759. F:01225-482076.
Very realistic reproduction limestone,
York stone, cobblestones and flagstones.

Cwt-y-Bugail Slate Quarries
Plas-y-Bryn, Wynne Rd, Blaenau Ffestiniog,
Gwynedd, Wales LL41 3DR.
T:01766-830204. F:01766-831105.
High quality natural Welsh slate mined
from 500 million year old Ordovician rock.
It is used for flooring, steps, hearths etc.

Delabole Slate
Pengelly Rd, Delabole, Cornwall PL33 9AZ.
T:01840-212242. F:01840-212948.
Riven tiles or traditional slate slabs suitable
for flooring, worksurfaces, cladding
or fireplaces.

Farmington Stone
Farmington, Northleach,
Cheltenham, Gloucs GL54 3NZ.
T:01451-860280. F:01451-860115.
Mellow Cotswold flagstones. This quarry
can supply building stone, architectural
dressings, fire surrounds and make
anything to order in stone.

*Fesco Tiles
Far East House, Carwood Rd,
Chesterfield S41 9QB.
T:01246-452495. F:01246-260727.
Natural stone flooring and slate roofing tiles.

Kirkstone Quarries
Skelwith Bridge, Ambleside,
Cumbria LA22 9NN.
T:015394-33296. F:015394-34006.
Volcanic stone traditionally known as
Westmoreland green slate - suitable for
flooring, cladding and work surfaces.

Limestone Gallery
2 Plimsoll Rd, London N4 2EW.
T:0171-359 4432. F:0171-359 5481.
Over 150 limestones to choose from -
possibly the widest selection in the UK -
some in antique finishes. Also 'Pyrolave'
volcanic lava slabs, French hand-made
ceramic tiles in over 500 colours and
reproduction 18th century antique terracotta
tiles from Normandy.

Manorhouse Stone
School Lane, Normanton-le-
Heath, Leics LE67 2TH.
T:01530-262999.
F:01530-262515.
Architectural stone
specialist - fireplaces,
window frames, door
surrounds. York stone flags.

Natural Stone Products
De Lank Quarry, St
Breward, Nr Bodmin,
Cornwall PL30 4NQ.
T:01208-850217.
F:01208-851328.
Sandstones, granites and limestones for
architectural masonry, flooring or walling.
Large selection of colours and finishes.

Naturestone
Crossway, Silwood Rd,
Sunninghill, Ascot, Berks SL5 OPZ.
T:01344-27617. F:01344-873185.
Range includes African slates, Indian
sandstone and yellow Brazilian quartzite.

Geoffrey Pike
See entry under
MARBLE/TERRAZZO TILES.

F W Poole
12 Larkhall Lane, London SW4 6SP.
T:0171-622 5154. F:0171-622 4232.
Slate, marble and granite specialist.

* denotes
trade supplier.
Please phone
for retail outlets. 113

Realstone
Wingerworth,
 Chesterfield, Derbys S42 6RG.
T:01246-270244. F:01246-220095.
Eight different limestones, four types of
granite, six marbles for internal or outdoor
flooring and wall cladding. Quartzite for
external flooring and cladding.

Reed Harris
See entry under
MARBLE/TERRAZZO TILES.

Stone Age
19 Filmer Rd, London SW6 7BU.
T:0171-385 7954/5. F:0171-385 7956.
Over 40 types of limestone and sandstone.

Stonell
521-523 Battersea Park Rd,
London SW11 3BN.
T:0171-738 0606. F:0171-738 0660.
Sandstone, limestone, slate, marble and
granite tiles for interior and exterior use.

TERRACOTTA TILES

Acorn Ceramic Tiles
17 Beech Business Park,
Tillington Rd, Hereford HR4 9QJ.
T:01432-355132. F:01432-355134.
Specialists in glazed and
traditional terracotta tiles.

Antique Terracotta
Laurel Cottage, Main Street,
Peasmarsh, Nr Rye,
E.Sussex TN31 6SX.
T:01797-230559.
F:01797-230743.
Antique French terracotta
tiles rescued from a shipwreck
lost off Hastings in The Great
Storm of 1861.

Corres Tiles
1a Station Rd, Hampton Wick,
Kingston, Surrey KT1 4HG.
T:0181-943 4142. F:0181-943 4649.
Handmade Mexican floor
and wall terracotta tiles.

The Good Flooring Company
T:01892-516411. F:01892-510820.

By appointment. 'Antica Umbria' ceramic
floor tiles which look just like terracotta but
are easy to maintain.

*Marlborough Tiles
Elcot Lane, Marlborough, Wilts SN8 2AY.
T:01672-512422. F:01672-515791.
Handmade terracotta wall tiles, both plain
and glazed. Individual hand-painted tiles and
special panels to order.

Robus Ceramics
Evington Park, Hastingleigh,
Ashford, Kent TN25 5JH.
T/F:01233-750330.
English terracotta tiles made to any size or
specification. Plus hand-glazed medieval and
delft-inspired designs.

Rustica
154C Milton Park, Abingdon,
Oxon OX14 4SD.
T:01235-834192. F:01235-835162. French
and Spanish terracotta in subtle shades.
Glazed ceramic floor tiles in 28 shapes and
40 colours.

MOSAIC

Attica
See entry under **STONE TILES.**

Roman mosaic specialist.

Vanessa Benson
16 St Peter's Street,
London N1 8JG.
T:0171-226 6875.
Vanessa Benson
teaches mosaic design
and undertakes mosaic
commissions in marble,
glass or both.

*Certikin International
Wittan Park, Avenue 2,
Station Lane Ind Estate,
Witney, Oxon OX8 6FH.
T:01993-778855. F:01993-778620.
Vitreous glass mosaic sheet.

Marjorie Knowles
80 High St, Long Crendon,
Nr Aylesbury, Bucks HP18 9AL.
T:01844-208435.

Undertakes commissions - anything from animals to classical figures.

Marabout
Unit 27, Town Mead Business Centre, William Morris Way, London SW6 2SZ. T/F: 0171-736 5755. Moroccan mosaics.

Mosaic Arts
18 Buckland Crescent, London NW3 5DX. T:0171-722 1505. F:0171-722 9674. By appointment. Largest UK stock of materials for mosaic design - stone, glass, porcelain, marble, gold and silver leaf . Tailored designs for interiors, exteriors, walls, floors, swimming pools, bathrooms, kitchens and special features.

Mosaic Workshop
Unit B, 443-449 Holloway Rd, London N7 6LJ. T/F: 0171-263 2997. Designed the mosaic in Conran's Quaglino restaurant, but much of their work is for private clients - mosaics for floors, kitchen splashbacks and swimming pools. They work in glass, smalti, marble and glazed and unglazed ceramic.

Mosaik
10 Kensington Square, London W8 5EP. T/F:0171-795 6253. Parisian mosaicist Pierre Mesguich experiments with new forms and styles but uses traditional paste, ceramic, Venetian glass or gold leaf tiles applied with flour and water. Will undertake a single panel or decorate a whole bathroom or swimming pool. Mosaik also supplies Venetian glass tiles.

Paris Ceramics
See entry under **TILE SHOPS WITH A LARGE SELECTION.** Mosaics based on ancient Roman designs (many of them are in the British Museum) in subtle, natural colours. There are a number of border designs and individual wall and floor panels.

Edgar Udny
314 Balham High Rd, London SW17 7AA. T:0181-767 8181. F:0181-767 7709. Huge selection of mosaic tiles, including swimming pool tiles.

World's End Tiles
See entry under **TILE SHOPS WITH A LARGE SELECTION.**

ENTRANCE MATS

*Afia Carpets
See entry under **CARPETS & STAIR-RODS.** 'Pur' floor coverings in flax, coir, paper or thread with non-slip backing for smart entrance mats.

*Kersaint Cobb
Unit A02, Tower Bridge Business Complex, Clements Rd, London SE16 4DG. T:0171-237 4270. F:0171-252 0073. Coir entrance matting in a selection of colours which can be made to incorporate company logos.

OTHER SPECIALIST SUPPLIERS & SERVICES

Bill Amberg
The Workshops, 23 Theatre Street, London SW11 5ND. T:0171-924 4296. F:0171-924-4002. Handbag designer Bill Amberg can install leather floors - they are warm and soft underfoot and as easy to look after as wood. Prices start at £250 per square metre.

Art on Tiles
8 Royal Parade, Dawes Road, London SW6 7RE. T:0171-386 7774. F:0171-381 1589. Can hand paint any design on any tile.

Intec
16 Shrivenham Hundred Business Park, Watchfield, Swindon, Wilts SN6 8TZ. T:01793-783999. F:01793-783053. Can provide a protector for natural flooring, carpet and fabrics.

*H & R Johnson Tiles
See entry under **CERAMIC TILES.** Restoration of original 19th century tiled floors.

* denotes trade supplier. Please phone for retail outlets. 115

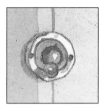

8

LIGHTING

TRADITIONAL

Ann's
34a & b Kensington Church St,
London W8 4HA.
T:0171-937 5033. F:0171-937 5915.
Good range of traditional lighting,
especially porcelain lamp bases.
Handmade lampshades. Rewiring service.

BHS
252-258 Oxford St, London W1N 9DC.
T:0171-629 2011.
For branches nationwide call:
0171-262 3288.
Inexpensive range in all styles.

Beaumont & Fletcher
261 Fulham Rd, London SW3 6HY.
T:0171-352 5553. F:0171-352 3545.
Hand-carved and gilded wall lights
based on Georgian and Regency originals.

Bella Figura
Decoy Farm, Old Church Rd,
Melton, Suffolk IP13 6DH.
T:01394-461111. F:01394-461199.
Large range of decorative lighting including
ceramic table lamps, reading lamps in
antique brass or silver and Italian gilded
tole wall lights and chandeliers.
Lampshade making service.

Besselink & Jones
99 Walton St, London SW3 2HH.
T:0171-584 0343. F:0171-584 0284.
Excellent choice of table lamps (column,
glass, candlestick, tea caddies, ceramic,
etc), desk lamps, floor lamps, wall lights
(including library lights), picture lights,
hanging lamps, storm lanterns and
candlesticks.

*Best & Lloyd
William Street West,
Smethwick, Warley, W.Midlands B66 2NX.
T:0121-558 1191. F:0121-565 3547.
Designers and manufacturers of the
classic 'Bestlite' range which has been in
continuous production for over 60 years.
The company also produces a wide range
of brass fittings, including swing arm wall
brackets, picture lights (including one for use

* denotes
trade supplier.
Please phone
for retail outlets.   117

in bathrooms), Dutch pendants and wall brackets.

*Thomas Blakemore
Atlas Works, Sandwell St, Walsall, West Midlands WS1 3DR.
T:01922-25951/613230.
F:01922-611330.
Large range of ornate marbled and ormolu, gilded and crackle-effect lamp bases. Plus clock, globe and gift collections.

*Brunschwig & Fils
10 The Chambers, Chelsea Harbour Drive, London SW10 OXF.
T:0171-351 5797. F:0171-351 2280.
American fabric company with a sideline in smart reproduction lamp bases - Biedermeier, Chinese and classical urns plus tôle and découpage ranges.

*Chelsom
Heritage House, Clifton Rd, Blackpool, Lancs FY4 4QA.
T:01253-791344. F:01253-791341.
London showroom at:
Unit 4, Hurlingham Business Park, Sulivan Rd, London SW6 3DU.
T:0171-736 2559. F:0171-384 2024.
Manufacturer of office, hotel and contract lighting. The range is vast - from brass column bases, Georgian lanterns, French empire styles and brasserie ranges to bathroom, corporate and public area lighting, spotlights and exterior fittings.

Elizabeth Eaton
85 Bourne St, London SW1W 8HF.
T:0171-730 2262. F:0171-730 7294.
Large choice of pretty light fittings, including one-off antique lamp bases, hanging lanterns, chandeliers, water-lily wall lights and outside lanterns made in any size. Also lampshades in plain card or pleated fabric.

Charles Edwards
582 King's Rd,London SW6 2DY.
T:0171-736 8490. F:0171-371 5436.
Very smart Gothic, Regency and French brass and painted lanterns, glass star lanterns, pretty wall or swing arm glass hurricane lamps, marble Ionic columns, clear glass urns and many others.

Howe's Designs
93 Pimlico Rd, London SW1W 8PH.
T:0171-730 7987. F:0171- 730 0157.
Hanging lanterns, table lamps, outdoor wall lanterns, silver columns based on antique designs.

*Christopher Hyde
Unit 4, Vulcan Business Centre, 18 Vulcan Way, Croydon, Surrey CR0 9UG.
T:01689-844020. F:01689-844021.
Quality hand-made brass lighting in a selection of finishes. Also 'marbleised', terracotta and ceramic table lamps, lanterns, an 'Empire' range and outdoor lighting.

Isis Ceramics
The Old Toffee Factory, 120A Marlborough Rd, Oxford OX1 4LS.
T:01865-722729. F:01865-727521.
Blue and white hand-painted ceramic lamp bases based on English delftware designs.

McCloud & Co
269 Wandsworth Bridge Rd, London SW6 2TX.
T:0171-371 7151. F:0171-371 7186.
Range of 85 hand-forged, brass or resin lighting, furniture and mirrors which are all hand-finished by gilding or painting. There are unusual chandeliers (crowns and armillary spheres), lanterns, fleur de lys, laurel, acanthus and urn sconces, directoire table lamps and much more. There are 26 standard finishes and any other, including matching a client's existing finish, to order.

*William Mehornay Porcelain
Studio 7, 13-17 Princes Rd, Richmond, Surrey TW10 6DQ.
T:0181-940 5051.
Large porcelain lamp bases colour-matched to order or in lacquered, japanned, gilded or chinoiserie finishes. Also available as vases and jars.

Mr Light
279 King's Rd, London SW3 5EW.
T:0171-352 8398. F:0171-351 3484.
And at:
275 Fulham Rd, London SW10 9PZ.
T:0171-352 7525. F:0171-376 8034.

Good selection of contemporary lighting - from star-shaped Moroccan lanterns to wrapped silk lampshades in exotic colours.

Peter Place at I & JL Brown
632-636 King's Rd, London SW6 2DU.
T:0171-736 4141. F:0171-736 9164.
Copies of 17th and 18th century lights in iron or pewter and converted lamps.

*Porta Romana
Lower Froyle, Nr Alton,
Hampshire GU34 4LS.
T:01420-23005. F:01420-23008.
Carved and painted candlestick, column and urn lampbases in many finishes; Biedermeier and wrought iron range.

Red Mud
Units C&D,
Lower Ground Floor, Linton House,
39-51 Highgate Rd, London NW5 1RS.
T:0171-267 1689. F:0171-267 9142.
Large range of ceramic pots in all sizes - they can all be converted into lamps on request.

*Carlos Remes Lighting Company
10 New Quebec St, London W1H 7DD.
T:0171-262 9963. F:0171-262 9227.
Wholesaler of ceiling fittings, wall sconces and table lamps made in the UK, Italy, China and Asia. Star lantern range.

Renwick & Clarke
190 Ebury St, London SW1W 8UP.
T:0171-730 8913. F:0171-730 4508.
Large selection of large and small table, standard lamps and wall lights in painted or gilded wood, metal, china and silver. Plus chandeliers and bespoke lampshades.

*R & S Robertson
36 Bankhead Drive, Edinburgh EH11 4EQ.
T:0131-442 1700. F:0131-442 4356.
One-stop light shop for the contract market. Four main collections which include anything from brass chandeliers, lanterns, plain turned wood lamp bases and Art Nouveau-style fittings to low energy bulkheads, lighting for offices and shops, even emergency lighting.

Rogier Antiques
20a Pimlico Rd, London SW1W 8LJ.
T:0171-823 4780.

Range of decorative lanterns, wall sconces and table lamps reproduced from antiques, most of them in tôle.

Edward Stoddart
68 Oxford Gardens, London W10 5UN. T/F:0181-969 1403.
Small range of beautifully carved and gilded candlesticks and lamps. There is a griffin, a lion, a sphynx, a Regency and a Renaissance column. Also gilding, restoration and one-off pieces to order.

Richard Taylor Designs
91 Princedale Rd, London W11 4NS.
T:0171-792 1808. F:0171-792 0310.
Decorative lighting including oak leaf, bamboo and rustic leaf metal chandeliers, a swirly Rococo wall light and tôle, terracotta and carved wooden urn lamp bases.

Tempus Stet
Trinity Business Centre, 305-309 Rotherhithe St, London SE16 1EY.
T:0171-231 0955. F:0171-252 3820.
Reproduction wall lights, chandeliers and lamp bases moulded from resin. They can be supplied in many finishes: three gilts, three woods, verdigris or Chinese red.

Tindle
162-168 Wandsworth Bridge Rd,
London SW6 2UQ.
T:0171-384 1485. F:0171-736 5630.
Hand painted armorial porcelain lamps, hand decorated wooden bases, large selection of candlestick lamps (including glass or lacquered), tea canisters, floor lamps, wall and picture lamps.

*Vaughan
156-160 Wandsworth Bridge Rd,
London SW6 2UH.
T:0171-731 3133. F:0171-736 4350.
Manufacturers and wholesalers of a large range of reproduction light fittings. The ceramic range includes Imari porcelain bases, classical urns, armorial porcelain and Majolica pottery vases. There are also lamps in unlacquered brass, tôle and distressed paintwork.

* denotes trade supplier. Please phone for retail outlets. 119

Woolpit Interiors

The Street, Woolpit, Bury St Edmunds,
Suffolk IP30 9SA.
T:01359-240895. F:01359-242282.
Large selection of hand painted 'Tea
canister' lamps with wild animals, exotic
birds and a Chinese theme. Faux-bamboo
range, natural and painted wood columns
and standard lamps. New mahogany and
tôle Chinese style wall lantern after Thomas
Chippendale. Lampshades.

Christopher Wray

600 King's Rd, London SW6 2YW.
T:0171-371 0077. F:0171-731 3507.
Christopher Wray first set up 25 years ago
and now has the largest traditional lighting
showroom in the UK. Anything from
Bohemian chandeliers to small oil lamps.
Cleaning and restoration service. 500
different glass shades available. Bulb
boutique and spare parts for oil/gas lamps.

William Yeoward

336 King's Rd, London SW3 5UR.
T:0171-351 5454. F:0171-351 9469.
Range of simple metal table, standard and
wall lights with tilt top or conical shades in
several finishes.

CHANDELIERS

*Best & Lloyd

See entry under TRADITIONAL.
Manufacturers of crystal chandeliers, table
lamps and wall lights - most of it bespoke.
Plus brass chandeliers in Dutch, Colonial,
Queen Anne and Jacobean styles.

Chandelier Cleaning & Restoration Services

Guppy Mead, Fyfield, Essex CM5 0RB.
T:01277-899444. F:01277-899642.
Glass making and bending, specialist
decorative chains and roses, polishing
and lacquering, winch installations and
valuations. Chandeliers made to order.

Elizabeth Eaton

See entry under TRADITIONAL.
Decorative French chandelier chains
in brass.

Kensington Lighting Company

59 Kensington Church St, London W8 4HA.
T:0171-938 2405. F:0171-937 5915.
And at:
17 High St, Newmarket CB8 8LX.
T:01638-667541. F:01638-561663.
Good range of crystal and metal chandeliers
and wall fittings.

Lion, Witch and Lampshade

See entry under LAMPSHADES.
Agents for several chandelier makers.
Rewiring and restoration of chandeliers.
Can look for a particular piece for you.

Period Brass Lights

9A Thurloe Place, London SW7 2RZ.
T/F:0171-589 8305.
Old and new crystal chandeliers, plus some
in brass or bronze; reproduction Tiffany table
lamps; large selection of wall lights; picture
lights; desk lamps; silk lampshades. You
can bring in your chandelier and they will
wash each piece by hand and do any
necessary repairs. Large jobs done in situ.
Full cleaning and restoration service for
other light fittings.

Renwick & Clarke

See entry under TRADITIONAL.
Chandeliers in crystal, painted wood,
metal, gilded, 'antiqued' and bespoke.

*Starlite (Chandeliers)

127 Harris Way, Windmill Rd,
Sunbury-on-Thames, Middx TW16 7EL.
T:01932-788686. F:01932-780283.
Manufacturer of bespoke crystal
chandeliers.

Richard Taylor Designs

See entry under TRADITIONAL.
Very pretty range of metal chandeliers,
ranging from the simple 'Naive' to the leafy
'Bamboo' version. Also an unusual wall-
mounted chandelier.

Tindle

See entry under TRADITIONAL.
Dutch brass chandeliers, Georgian glass
or antiqued brass and glass chandeliers.
Also classic scroll chandeliers, antique
gold ribbon and bow, rope and tassel
and wheatsheaf chandeliers.

See also
ANTIQUES-
Antique Lighting
and RESTORERS
& CRAFTSMEN-
Glass

Wilchester County

The Stables, Vicarage Lane, Steeple Ashton, Trowbridge, Wilts BA14 6HH.
T:01380-870764.
Simple tin lights based on designs of 17th and 18th century settlers in America. There are chandeliers and wall-lights (with matching chains, hook links and ceiling roses). Mail order only.

Wilkinson

5 Catford Hill, London SE6 4NU.
T:0181-314 1080. F:0181-690 1524.
And at:
1 Grafton St, London W1X 3LB.
T:0171-495 2477. F:0171-491 1737.
Large range of reproduction crystal chandeliers: copies of all English styles from 1730 to 1890. Some brass and metal chandeliers. Glass chandelier restorers. They also supply replacement glass drops.

Woolpit Interiors

See entry under TRADITIONAL. Faux-bamboo chandeliers. 'Le Clos' collection of metal wall sconces and chandeliers inspired by French Provencal designs and available in black, antique or semi-bright finishes.

Christopher Wray

See entry under TRADITIONAL.
From heavy Gothic-style to Murano glass.

LAMPSHADES

*Acres Farm

Bradfield, Reading, Berks RG7 6JH.
T:01734-744305. F:01734-744012.
One thousand candle shades, carriers and associated products.

Ann's

See entry under TRADITIONAL.
Handmade lampshades to order and rewiring service.

*BCG Shades

Unit G11, Avonside Enterprise Park, Melksham, Wilts SN12 8BS.
T:01225-707079. F:01225-707926.
Trade fabric and laminate lampshade makers. Plus wooden and ceramic lamp bases.

Besselink & Jones

See entry under TRADITIONAL.
Wide range of lampshades in stock sizes and colours or in customers' own fabrics or wallpapers.

*Suzie Clayton

2 St Margarets Business Centre, Moor Mead Rd, Twickenham TW1 1JS.
T:0181-607 9704. F:0181-607 9705.
Designers, manufacturers and wholesalers of lamps and shades. There are candle shades in card (with dozens of designs), cutwork, and filigree brass or silver plate. The handmade shades come in silk, tartan, unbleached calico, gingham, toile or lace.

*Lucy Cope Designs

Fox Hill House, Allington, Chippenham, Wilts SN14 6LL.
T:01249-650446. F:01249-444936.
Antique and period style lighting. Specialist lampshade maker. Restoration of antique lamps and lampshades.

Elizabeth Eaton

See entry under TRADITIONAL.
Any card or fabric shade to order.

Lion, Witch and Lampshade

89 Ebury St, London SW1W 9QU.
T:0171-730 1774.
And at:
Broxborne Barn, High St, Northleach, Cheltenham G9 54 9EW. T:01451-860855.
F:01285-750430.

Claim to be able to make 'literally any lampshade'- recent commissions include one in the shape of a Russian dome with teardrop windows and another, like an elaborate Chinese lantern, 4' high. Also chandeliers and other lighting.

Patrick Quigly

Benbow House,
24 New Globe Walk, London SE1 9DR.
T/F:0171-633 9933. By appointment.
Eccentric lampshades, in parchment, crushed velvet and fake fur, including an Erotica Collection.

* denotes
trade supplier.
Please phone
for retail outlets.

Renwick & Clarke
See entry under TRADITIONAL.
Handmade lampshades - anything from laminated fabric, silk and devoré velvet to cut-out and découpage.

*Simon & Simon
Fitzwarren St, Salford,
Greater Manchester M6 5JF.
T:0161-745 7985. F:0161-745 9856.
Lampshade frame manufacturers and wireworkers. Handmade iron scroll light fittings.

John Sutcliffe
12 Huntingdon Rd, Cambridge CB3 0HH.
T:01223-315858. By appointment.
Paper candle shades designed to complement his range of paper borders for print rooms. There are four black and white designs: Cupid & Psyche, Capriccio, Gardeners and Music in Venice.

Tindle
See entry under TRADITIONAL .
Large selection of parchment and silk shades and a made to order service.

Robert Wyatt
13 The Shrubbery,
Grosvenor Rd, London E11 2EL.
T/F:0181-530 6891.
Lampshades with 1950s shapes to order, in suede, parchment with overstitching, or in customers' own fabric which can be laminated.

CANDLES, CANDLESTICKS & STORM LANTERNS

Angelic
194 King's Rd, London SW3 5ED.
T/F:0171-351 1557 and 7 other branches. Candlesticks in 300 designs and all sorts of candles.

Ethos Candles
Quarry Fields, Mere,
Wilts BA12 6LA.
T:01747-860960. F:01747-860934.
Manufacturers of church candles, hand-dipped table candles in 40 colours, as well as outdoor candles and flares.

*Golfar & Hughes
Unit C1, The Old Imperial Laundry, 71 Warriner Gardens, London SW11 4XW.
T:0171-498 0508. F:0171-622 4970.
Tôle candlesticks and reproductions of student and bouillotte lamps.

Howe's Designs
See entry under TRADITIONAL.
Handmade storm lanterns on square bases with different styles of glass.

Price's Patent Candle Co
110 York Rd, London SW11 3RU.
T:0171-228 2001. F:0171-738 0197.
Dinner candles, church candles, chunky garden candles in terracotta or tôle pots, scented candles, garden flares.

William Sheppee
See entry under WROUGHT-IRON CANDLESTICKS & CANDELABRA.
Storm lanterns and glass Hundi lamps.

The Tôle Candle Company
PO Box 36, Battle, E.Sussex TN33 0ZS.
T:01424-775708. F:01424-775545.
Their unique 'everlasting candle' burns for up to 6 hours using safe and odourless lamp oil. They also do brass and silver candle shades, hurricane lamps, wall brackets and sconces, candlesticks and night lights.

Wax Lyrical
61 Hampstead High St, London NW1 1QH.
T:0171-435 5105 and branches nationwide.
Pewter and iron candelabra, lanterns, church candles, shaped and scented candles.

*Young & D
See UNUSUAL LIGHTING .
Clear or blue glass hanging and table top night-light holders.

WROUGHT-IRON CANDLESTICKS & CANDELABRA

Stuart Buglass
Clifford Mill House,
Little Houghton, Northants NN7 1AL.
T:01604-890366. F:01604-890372.
Simple hand forged candelabra for candles or wired for electricity.

The Heveningham Collection
Weston Down, Weston Colley, Micheldever,
Winchester, Hampshire SO21 3AQ.
T:01962-774990. F:01962-774790.
Elegant wrought-iron three-armed standard
candlestick.

Interior Art Metalworks
Camborne Forge, Trevu Rd, Camborne,
Cornwall TR14 8SR. T:01209-719911.
Blacksmiths who produce a small range of
iron candlesticks, candelabra and curtain
poles plus anything else to order.

Kensington Lighting Company
See entry under CHANDELIERS. Wrought-
iron chandeliers, hand forged to order to the
customer's own size requirements.

Marston & Langinger
192 Ebury St, London SW1W 8UP.
T:0171-824 8818. F:0171-824 8757.
Large wrought-iron electric chandelier (1m
high x 1m wide), a pineapple chandelier in a
verdigris and rust finish, Cottage, Coptic and
Ship's lanterns, a Moorish lantern and a flat
star lantern.

*Porta Romana
See entry under TRADITIONAL. Italian
wrought iron chandeliers and wall lights in
gold leaf or leaded black with gold leaf.

William Sheppee
Old Sarum Airfield, Salisbury, Wilts SP4 6BJ.
T:01722-334454. F:01722-337754.
Hand wrought candlesticks, candelabra
and chandeliers.

Stuart Interiors
Barrington Court, Barrington,
Ilminster, Nr Somerset TA19 0NQ.
T:01460-240349. F:01460-242069.
Iron chandeliers, wall sconces and a
candletree based on Elizabethan and
Jacobean originals. They can be powered
by electricity or, for the purists, fitted
with candles.

*Tribal Traders
Marvin House, 279 Abbeydale Rd,
Wembley, Middx HA0 1TW.
T:0181-997 3303. F:0181-991 9692.
Three sizes of wrought-iron candlesticks,
plus wall sconces and other candle holders.

Wooden Tops and Tin Men
The Wheel Craft Workshops,
Chudleigh, Devon TQ13 0LH.
T:01626-852777. F:01626-852224.
Large range of wrought-iron items:
candlesticks, floor-standing candelabra,
wall sconces, chandeliers (for candles or
electricity), plus chairs, wooden-topped
tables, benches, pot hangers and much
else. All available by mail order.

UNUSUAL

DZ Designs
The Old Mill House, Stanwell Moor,
Staines, Middx TW19 6BJ.
T:01753-682266. F:01753-685440.
Blackamoor lamps and bronze fist wall lights
with silk, card or glass 'flambeau' shades.

Egyptian Touch
28 Goldhawk Rd, London W12 8HA.
T:0181-749 8790. F:0181-749 9145.
Hanging lanterns and wall lights in filigree
brass and coloured glass.

Liberty
214-220 Regent St, London W1R 6AH.
T:0171-734 1234. F:0171-573 9876.
Large range of ethnic lamp bases -
Moroccan ceramic, Indian iron, copper and
bronze, Indian coloured glass, plus
Murano chandeliers.

Ochre
T:0171-244 7082. F:0171-244 7082.
By appointment. Lamps (and mirrors,
clocks and console tables) in contemporary
designs decorated with traditional precious
metal leaf work.

The Original Book Works
1 Wilkinson Rd,
Cirencester, Gloucs GL7 1YT.
T:01285-641664. F:01285-641705.
Fake book lamps.

Anthony Redmile
533 King's Rd, London SW10 0TZ.
T:0171-351 3813. F:0171-352 8131.
Antler chandeliers and wall lights with
sconces in silver, brass or antique brass
made to order. Also antler furniture.

*** denotes
trade supplier.
Please phone
for retail outlets.** 123

Ghislaine Stewart Designs
110 Fentiman Rd, London SW8 1QA.
T/F:0171-820 9440. By appointment.
Lamp bases covered in plain or animal-skin
printed leather or even in upholstery fabrics
to order; silver plated, resin or bronze lamps.
Special commissions.

Robert Wyatt
See entry under LAMPSHADES.
Bamboo floor and table lamps.

*Young & D
Beckhaven House,
9 Gilbert Rd, London SE11 5AA.
T:0171-820 3796. F:0171-793 0537.
Retail shop:
Belle du Jour, 13 Flask Walk,
London NW3 IHJ. T:0171-431 4006.
Aluminium or coloured Greek fishermen's
lamps in 4 sizes.Mail order: *Colour Blue*,
PO BOx 69d, New Malden, Surrey KT3 4PL.
T:0181-942 2525. F:0181-336 0803.

CONTEMPORARY/ LOW VOLTAGE

Aero
96 Westbourne Grove,London W2 5RT.
T:0171-221 1950. F:0171-221 2555.
Tripod, spots and loft lights.
Also modern wall, pendant and floor lights.

*Aktiva Systems
8 Berkley Rd, London NW1 8YR.
T:0171-722 9439. F:0171-722 4748.
Manufacturer of low voltage display
lighting, downlighters and wall lights.
Design and development service.

*Anglepoise
Unit 51, Enfield Ind.Area,
Redditch, Worcs B97 6DR.
T:01527-63771. F:01527-61232.
Manufacturers of a wide range of
domestic and office task lighting.

Aram Designs
3 Kean St, London WC2B 4AT.
T:0171-240 3933. F:0171-240 3697.
The lighting side includes ranges by
Arteluce, Artemide, Best & Lloyd, Candle,
Flos, Fontana Arte, Ingo Maurer, Oluce.

Ruth Aram Shop
65 Heath St, London NW3 6UG.
T:0171-431 4008. F:0171-431 6755.
New lighting department with the main
Italian ranges and new English designers.

*Artemide GB
323 City Rd, London EC1V 1LJ.
T:0171-833 1755. F:0171-833 1766.
Low voltage modern tracking systems
& fluorescent lighting in a range of vivid
colours. Unconventional spotlights in several
styles. Futuristic table lamps, floor lamps,
wall lights and ceiling lamps by top Italian
designers. Also suspended lamps and
fluorescent tubing.

Atrium
22-24 St.Giles High St, London WC2H 8LN.
T:0171-379 7288. F:0171-240 2080.
Carry ranges by 12 or 13 different European
manufacturers - anything from hand-blown
glass fittings to low voltage downlighters.

Babylon Design
Unit 4b, 9 Hoxton Square, London N1 6NU.
T:0171-729 3321. F:0171-729 3323.
Simple and sculptural modern lighting
by Peter Wylly, Ross Menuez and
Roland Simmons.

*Best & Lloyd
See entry under TRADITIONAL.
Manufacturers of the classic 'Bestlite'
which has been in continuous production
for 50 years. It comes in desk, wall and
floor versions.

Box Products
Unit 2.28, 2nd Floor, Oxo Tower Wharf,
Bargehouse St, London SE1 9PH.
T:0171-401 2288. F:0171-928 1188.
Limited edition range of 25 wall and
ceiling lights in metal and glass.
Custom-designed specials.

*Candell Lighting
20/22 Avenue Mews, London N10 3NP.
T:0181-444 9004. F:0181-444 5232.
UK distributors for the B'Lux range by Jorge
Pens, for Porsche, Gianfranco Frattini and
Toshyuki Kita. There are freestanding
uplighters, wall lights, table lamps, pendants
and uplighters.

*Catalytico
25 Montpelier St, London SW7 IHF.
T:0171-225 1720. F:0171-225 3740.
Agents for Foscarini Murano Spa, Luceplan,
Ingo Maurer.

*Chad Lighting
James Rd, Tyseley, Birmingham B11 2BA.
T:0121-707 7629. F:0121-707 9431.
Up-lighters, table lamps and wall lights
in wood, metal, ceramics and glass.

*Concord Sylvania
174 High Holborn, London WC1V 7AA.
T:0171-497 1400. F:0171-497 1404.
And at:
Avis Way, Newhaven, E.Sussex BN9 OED.
T:01273-515811. F:01273-512688.
Manufacturers of spots, floodlights,
lighting tracks and recessed downlighters
for commercial and domestic use.

John Cullen Lighting
585 King's Rd, London SW6 2EH.
T:0171-371 5400. F:0171-371 7799.
Wide range of discreet interior and garden
fittings for 'effect' lighting, mainly low
voltage. Demonstration studio which can
simulate almost any lighting effect you
want and design advisory service.

Deck 2 Lighting
37 Alexandra Rd, London W4 1AX.
T:0181-995 9539. By appointment.
Smart range of desk lamps in chrome
and black with leather, wood or glass.

Designer Light Shop
4 Kennington Rd, London SE1 7BL.
T:0171-928 0097. F:0181-674 9612.
Design, planning and completion of
lighting projects. Suppliers of Flos, Arteluce,
Foscarini, Optelma, Reggiani and others.

*Erco Lighting
38 Dover St, London W1X 3RB.
T:0171-408 0320. F:0171-409 1530.
Manufacturers and distributors of recessed
downlighters, spots, lighting tracks, task
lighting and exterior fittings for commercial
and domestic projects.

Christopher Farr
212 Westbourne Grove, London W11 2RH.
T:0171-792 5761. F:0171-792 5763.

Lighting by the Spanish company
Santa & Cole - free-standing,hanging
and wall lights mainly in wood with
card or raffia shades.

*Flos
31 Lisson Grove, London NW1 6UV.
T:0171-258 0600.
F:0171-723 7005. Modern
lighting by designers like
Philippe Starck and Castiglioni.
Arteluce range from Italy.

The Furniture Union
46 Beak St, London W1R 3DA.
T/F:0171-287 3424.
Trade office at: Mandeville Courtyard,
142 Battersea Park Rd, London SW11 4NB.
T:0171-498 1570. F:0171-498 1012.
Lighting by contemporary British designers:
Patrick Quigly, Peter Wylly, Dan Maier and
Jonathan Rothenberg.

Haute Deco
556 King's Rd, London SW6 2DZ.
T:0171-736 7171. F:0171-736 8484.
Small range which includes cast bronze
lamps, the tall and skinny 'Betta' lamp
in pewter and gold, and a resin design
suitable for children's rooms.

*iGuzzini
Unit 3, Mitcham Ind.Estate,
85 Streatham Rd, Mitcham, Surrey CR4 2AP.
T:0181-646 4141. F:0181-640 6910.
Architectural lighting for internal and
external uses.

Inhouse
24-26 Wilson St, Glasgow G1 1SS.
T:0141-552 5902. F:0141-552 5929.
And at :
28 Howe St, Edinburgh EH3 6TG.
T:0131-225 2888. F:0131-220 6632.
The best place for modern lighting in
Scotland.

*La Conch Lighting
4 The Chase Centre, Chase Rd,
London NW10 6QD.
T:0181-961 0313. F:0181-961 0337.
Manufacturers and suppliers of a wide range
of internal and external lighting in all styles
for hotel, catering and office environments.

* denotes
trade supplier.
Please phone
for retail outlets. 125

Light Projects

23 Jacob St, London SE1 2BG.
T:0171-231 8282. F:0171-237 4342.
Showroom with access to over 600
architectural, display and garden light
fittings, including their own designs. As
well as providing a complete lighting design,
supply and installation service, the company
also specialises in Fine Art lighting, in
manufacturing one-off products, and in
advising architects and designers on any
aspect of a lighting project.

The Light Store

11 Clifton Rd, London W9 1S2.
T:0171-286 0233/8033.
F:0171-266 2009.
Good one-stop shop for modern lighting:
bathroom and shower lights, fluorescent
tubing, standard lamps, spots, ceiling
lamps, picture lights.

London Lighting Co

135 Fulham Rd, London SW3 2RT.
T:0171-589 3612. F:0171-581 9652.
Large showroom with a big selection of
modern European designs.

*Microlights

Elcot Lane, Marlborough, Wilts SN8 2BG.
T:01672-515611. F:01672-513816.
Manufacturers of energy efficient lighting
used mainly in retail outlets.

*Optelma Lighting

14 Napier Court, The Science Park,
Abingdon, Oxon OX14 3NB.
T:01235-553769. F:01235-523005.
Swiss manufacturers of low voltage track
lighting including the award-winning 'Civa'
and 'Canal' systems.

Optime Lighting

156 Ladbroke Rd, London W10 5NA.
T/F:0181-964 9711. Good selection
of spots, switches, sockets, etc

*Prolumena

Unit 1, Townmead Business Centre,
William Morris Way, London SW6 2SZ.
T:0171-736 4879. F:0171-736 4859.
Designers and manufacturers of display
lighting and uplighters for retail, domestic
and contract applications.

Purves & Purves

80-81 & 83 Tottenham Court Rd,
London W1P 9HD.
T:0171-580 8223. F:0171-580 8244.
Interesting selection of colourful
contemporary lighting by British
and continental designers.

Radiant Distribution

The Pall Mall Deposit, Unit 68,
124-128 Barlby Rd, London W10 6BL.
T:0181-964 0211. F:0181-964 0288.
By appointment. Large range of stylish
aluminium pendants, spotlights, work,
table and floor lamps made in Italy in a small
factory set up after the Second World War.
The shapes (by an anonymous designer)
remain unchanged; some were used in the
1940s on Italian railway stations.

SKK

34 Lexington St, London W1R 3HR.
T:0171-434 4095. F:0171-287 0168.
Lighting company run by designer Shiu-Kay
Kan. Smart low voltage spots and barewire
systems as well as low voltage post modern
chandeliers, customised IP rated bathroom
fittings, energy-saving office lighting, even
jacuzzi and underwater lighting.

The Study

26 Old Church St, London SW3 5BY.
T:0171-376 7969. F:0171-795 0392.
Christopher Nevile's shop promotes the best
of young British design. Lighting by Hannah
Woodhouse, Charlotte Packe, Michael Young
and many others.

*Targetti

6 Stanton Gate, Mowney Rd,
Romford, Essex RH7 7H3.
T:01708-741286. F:01708-742060.
One of the largest Italian architectural
lighting companies. Their range includes
the 'Mondial' precision directional
projectors in diecast aluminium.

Viaduct

1-10 Summers St, London EC1R 5BD.
T:0171-278 8456. F:0171-278 2844.
Agents for Foscarini, Flos, Artemide,
Arteluce, Ingo Maurer. Can source
products for clients.

Villiers Brothers
Fyfield Hall, Fyfield, Essex CM5 OSA.
T:01277-899680. F:01277-899008.
Range of non-standard standard lamps
in nickel finishes, some with stainless
steel shades. Commissions.

OFF-BEAT

Inflate
3rd Floor, 5 Old St, London EC1V 9HL.
T:0171-251 5453. F:0171-250 0311.
Inflatable 'UFO' pendant light and a table
light. Plus inflatable picture frames, egg
cups, fruit bowls and mirrors.

Mathmos
179 Drury Lane, London WC2B 5QF.
T:0171-404 6605. F:0171-404 6606.
The full range of Lava-lamps in all colour
combinations and sizes.

Patrick Quigly
See entry under LAMPSHADES.

Sculptures-Jeux
31 Lisson Grove, London NW1 6UV.
T:0171-258 0600. F:0171-723 7005.
Sell the French 'Clips' lamp which clamps
on to any drinks can.

SKK
See entry under
CONTEMPORARY/LOW VOLTAGE.
Range includes eccentric designs like
dinosaur lamps and illuminated rocks.

Katrien Van Liefferinge
13 Armstrong St, Leeds LS28 5BZ.
T/F:0113-2570241. Inflatable conical
lights, some decorated with little fairy lights.

Villiers Brothers
See entry under
CONTEMPORARY/LOW VOLTAGE.
Brightly-coloured flexible velvet cactus lamps.

OUTSIDE LIGHTING

*Chelsom
See entry under TRADITIONAL.
Large range of die-cast aluminium street and
wall lanterns in traditional and contemporary
styles and external flood lights.

*Concord Bega
See entry under
CONTEMPORARY/LOW VOLTAGE.
Smart exterior lighting for every situation:
road and garden luminaires, floodlights,
downlighters, pathway lighting and swimming
pool fittings.

John Cullen Lighting
See entry under
CONTEMPORARY/LOW VOLTAGE.

*Dorothea
Pearl House, Hardwick St,
Buxton, Derbys SK17 6DH.
T:01298-79121. F:01298-70866.
Architectural metalwork, from cast iron or
aluminium street lighting in traditional styles
to litter bins, bollards, signposts, brackets,
balustrades, canopies and shop fronts.

*Erin-Gardena
Dunhams Lane,
Letchworth Garden City, Herts SG6 1BD.
T:01462-475000. F:01462-482456.
Wide range of products available from
garden centres.

**Garden & Security Lighting/Lightscape
Projects**
67 George Row, London SE16 4UH.
T:0171-231 5323. F:0171-237 4342.
Two other divisions of the Light Projects
Group (see entry under Contemporary/Low
Voltage). The latter provides architectural,
landscape and underwater lighting; the
former lighting and security for the town and
country garden. The company offers a range
of over 600 exterior lighting products from
general purpose low voltage systems to
underwater lighting and powerful fittings to
light mature trees and architectural features.

Hozelock
Haddenham, Aylesbury, Bucks HP17 8JD.
T:01844-291881. F:01844-290344.
Helpline on 01844-292002. Low voltage DIY
outdoor lighting systems which are very
easy to install.

The Light Store
See entry under CONTEMPORARY/LOW
VOLTAGE. Exterior floodlights, spotlights
and traditional lanterns.

*** denotes
trade supplier.
Please phone
for retail outlets.** 127

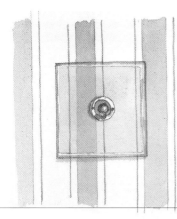

For more help:
The Lighting
Association,
Stafford Park 7,
Telford, Shropshire
TF3 3BQ. T:01952-
290905.
F:01952-290906. Has
some 300 members
nationwide who supply
decorative lighting.

The Lighting
Industry Federation,
207 Balham High Rd,
London SW17 7BQ.
T:0181-675 5432.
F:0181-673 5880.
Trade association for
commercial and
industrial lighting
manufacturers, with
about 92 members.

London Lighting Co
See entry under
**CONTEMPORARY/
LOW VOLTAGE.**
Good selection of
outdoor light fittings.

*Optelma Lighting
See entry under
**CONTEMPORARY/
LOW VOLTAGE.**
Good range of
garden light fittings.

Outdoor Lighting (OLS)
6 Kingston Business
Centre, Fullers Way South, Chessington,
Surrey KT9 1DQ.
T:0181-974 2211. F:0181-974 2333.
Spotlighting, floodlighting, buried uplighting,
path, underwater, garden and festoon
lighting. Design service. Suppliers to the
trade and public.

SKK
See entry under **CONTEMPORARY/LOW
VOLTAGE.** Low voltage garden lighting with
scene setting controls which, they claim,
'makes the garden look like a living room'.

*DW Windsor
Marsh Lane, Ware, Herts SG12 9QL.
T:01920-466499. F:01920-460327.
Traditional and contemporary street
lanterns, a wide range of street furniture,
plus custom replication and refurbishment.

SPECIALIST FITTINGS

Architectural Components
4-8 Exhibition Rd, London SW7 2HF.
T:0171-581 2401. F:0171-589 4928.
Good selection of switches and sockets
including chrome fittings and dolly switches.

JD Beardmore & Co
3-4 Percy St, London W1P OEJ.
T:0171-637 7041. F:0171-436 9222.
Traditional brass rocker and dolly switches,
dimmer units and matching sockets.

Chelsea Lighting Design
Unit 1, 23a Smith St, London SW3 4EJ.
T:0171-824 8144. F:0171-823 4812.

Stock a flexible lighting strip called the Rope
Light which is useful for lighting alcoves.

Forbes & Lomax
205b St.John's Hill, London SW11 1TH.
T:0171-738 0202. F:0171-738 9224.
Nickel, silver and brass switches and
sockets; 'invisible' perspex switches for
use on walls with patterned wallpapers.

*R Hamilton & Co
Unit G, Quarry Ind.Estate,
Mere, Wilts BA12 6LA.
T:01747-860088. F:01747-861032.
Wholesalers of wooden and brass light
switches and sockets in four different
finishes and others to order.

Light Projects
See entry under **CONTEMPORARY/LOW
VOLTAGE.** Fixed-frame picture lights which
are adjustable in height.

Olivers Lighting Company
6 The Broadway,
Crockenhill, Swanley, Kent BR8 8JH.
T/F:01322-614224.
Fluted and plain brass domed switches with
a choice of backplate in antique mahogany
and oak or natural oak. Matching sockets.

Preferred Electrical
18 Lettice St, London SW6 4EH.
T:0171-731 0805. F:0171-731 0623.
Manufacturers and distributors of the
'Reolite' picture frame lights which come in
frame-mounted or wall-mounted versions.
There are eight sizes and several arm
lengths so they can be tailored exactly to the
height of the picture. The company is also a
general electrical wholesaler.

SKK
See entry under
CONTEMPORARY/LOW VOLTAGE.
Switches and sockets in any colour or metal
finish to order; 'invisible' infra-red switching
system, customised IP rated bathroom
fittings; discreet low voltage picture lights.

William Sheppee
See entry under **WROUGHT-IRON
CANDLESTICKS & CANDELABRA.**
Antique brass toggle switches imported
from India.

NT Sussex Brassware
Napier Rd, Castleham Ind.Estate,
St.Leonards on Sea, E.Sussex TN38 9NY.
T:01424-440734. F:01424-853862.
Satin and polished brass, stainless steel,
nickel, bronze and black hammered iron
switches and sockets.

Touch of Brass
210 Fulham Rd, London SW10 9PJ.
T:0171-351 2255. F:0171-352 4682.
Stockists of brass light switches in ten
different patterns; they are also available
to order in 10 other finishes, including
pewter, verdigris and satin nickel.

Wandsworth Electrical
Albert Drive, Sheerwater,
Woking, Surrey GU21 5SE.
T:01483-740740. F:01483-740384.
Metal plate sockets and switches in
nine finishes.

Christopher Wray
See entry under **TRADITIONAL**.
Wide range of accessories, including candle
tubes, oil lamp chimneys and wicks, ceiling
hooks, silk flex and plain brass toggle
switches.

LIGHTING CONSULTANTS

Peter Burian Associates
Hillview, Vale of Health, London NW3 1AN.
T:0171-431 2345. F:0171-435 2294.
Lighting schemes for domestic and
commercial situations. Low voltage lighting.

Chelsea Lighting Design
See entry under **SPECIALIST
FITTINGS**. Will tackle up-market
domestic projects in any style.
Have developed their own range
of low voltage fittings suitable
for domestic use.

John Cullen Lighting
See entry under
**CONTEMPORARY/
LOW VOLTAGE**.
Full consultancy or hourly advisory
service. Showroom demonstrations
to experiment with different effects.

Seminars on lighting themes, from
garden & conservatory lighting to
lighting a period interior.

Into Lighting Design
2 St George's Court, 131 Putney Bridge Rd,
London SW15 2PA.
T:0181-877 1707. F:0181-877 1506.
There are five professional lighting designers
in this company whose projects range from
residential to large scale retail (Habitat, The
National Gallery). They don't carry out the
work themselves, but work closely with
recommended contractors.

Isometrix
Exmouth House,
3 Pine St, London EC1R OJH.
T:0171-833 8888. F:0171-833 2202.
Specialise in high-profile jobs: hotels, shops,
large condominiums.

Light Projects
See entry under **CONTEMPORARY/
LOW VOLTAGE**. Complete lighting design,
supply and installation service, including
professional advice for architects and
designers.

SKK
See entry under
CONTEMPORARY/LOW VOLTAGE.
Lighting consultants who can come up
with almost any customised fitting.

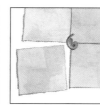
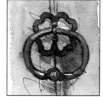

9

DOORS & WINDOWS

OLD DOORS

Havenplan
The Old Station, Station Rd, Killamarsh,
Sheffield S31 8EN. T/F: 0114-2489972.
Hundreds of period doors, housed in an
old railway station. Mainly Victorian and
Edwardian plain panelled doors, or with
leaded and stained glass. Plus fireplaces,
bathroom fittings and church fittings.

In Doors
Beechin Wood Farm, Beechin Wood Lane,
Platt, Nr Sevenoaks, Kent TN15 8QN.
T:01732-887445. F:01732-887446.
Sell restored interior, exterior and cupboard
doors. Manufacture doors in old timber. Also
cleaning and restoration of windows, door
frames, wainscotting and floors and supply
of etched glass panels. Stripping service.

In-Situ Architectural Antiques
607 Stretford Rd, Old Trafford, Manchester
M16 0QJ. T/F:0161-848 7454.
500 period doors on display and
reproductions to order in any size. Period

panelled front doors with glass inserts;
internal and external panelled doors. All
sorts of other salvage as well: fireplaces,
bathroom fittings, garden ornaments.

Old Door & Fireplace Company
67-69 Essex Rd, London N1 2SF.
T/F:0171-226 0910.
Doors and fireplaces, as the name suggests,
but also window shutters, stained glass
windows and old parquet flooring. Plain
stripped doors cost between £50 and £65,
one with stained glass around £350.

Original Door Specialists
298 Brockley Rd, London SE4 2RA.
T:0181- 691 7162.
Over 1000 interior and exterior reclaimed
doors in stock, some of them with their
original stained glass windows intact. Also
room dividers, shutters, kitchen cupboards,

Stiffkey Antiques
The Chapel, Stiffkey,Norfolk NR23 1AJ.
T:01328-830099. F:01328-830005.
Claim to have the biggest range of Victorian
doors and fittings in the country.

See also
**ARCHITECTURAL
SALVAGE.** 131

NEW & REPRODUCTION DOORS

British Gates & Timber
Biddenden, Nr Ashford, Kent TN27 8DD.
T:01580-291555. F: 01580-292011.
Traditional Tudor oak doors with antique iron fittings.

*John Carr
Watch House Lane,
Doncaster, S.Yorks DN5 9LR.
T:01302-783333. F:01302-787383.
Britain's biggest joinery manufacturer. There are over 10,000 products - anything from staircases to windows. Doors of all types, in hardwood, softwood, plywood, aluminium and steel. All products are available through builders' merchants.

Cotswood Doors
5 Hampden Way, London N14 5DJ.
T:0181-368 1664. F:0181-368 9635.
Good selection of standard interior, exterior, garage and security doors. Hardwood doors, frames, screens, skirting and architraves made to order.

County Hardwoods
Creech Mill, Mill Lane, Creech St Michael,
Taunton, Somerset TA3 5PX.
T:01823-443760. F:01823-443940.
Softwood and hardwood ledged, braced and boarded doors sold in kits. All their wood is from managed estates.

Darwin Bespoke Furniture Makers
38A Darwin Rd, London W5 4BD.
T/F:0181-560 0424.
Specialist in handmade period reproduction doors, usually in mahogany or oak with hand carved mouldings if required.

Deacon & Sandys
Hillcrest Farm Oast, Hawkhurst Rd,
Cranbrook, Kent TN17 3QD.
T:01580-713775. F:01580-714056.
Oak planked and panelled doors based on 17th and 18th century designs, some with moulded frames and hand carvings. Deacon & Sandys will tackle all sorts of architectural woodwork, including wall panelling, floors, windows and balustraded staircases.

Dor-O-Matic
Berrington Rd, Sydenham Ind Estate,
Leamington Spa, Warwicks CV31 1NB.
T:01926-334231. F:01926-450330.
Doors for commercial sites including automatic, swing and folding doors.

Grandisson
The Mill, Alansway,
Ottery St.Mary, Devon EX11 1NR.
T/F:01404-812876.
Range of 14 hand carved doors available in mahogany, rosewood, oak and walnut. Any other size or design to order.

The Handmade Door Company
12-14 Brook Rd, Redhill, Surrey RH1 6DL.
T/F:01737-773133.
Custom made interior and exterior doors either painted or stained with etched or stained glass panels. They also manufacture reproduction pine fireplaces.

*JB Kind
Shobnall St, Burton-on-Trent,
Staffs DE14 2HP.
T:01283-564631. F:01283-511132.
Importer and distributor of timber and luxury internal panel doors.

London Door Company
153 St John's Hill, London SW11 1TQ.
T:0171-801 0877. F:0171-223 7296.
And at:
263 New North Rd, London N1 7AT.
T: 0171-704 8068. Victorian style doors in solid pine or with leaded lights, but also any other sort of door, French window or room divider to order.

WH Newson & Sons
61 Pimlico Rd, London SW1W 8NF.
T:0171-730 6262. F:0171-924 1682.
For other branches call 0171-978 5000.
Timber merchants with a large range of internal and external softwood and hardwood doors by Bolton & Paul.

*Pella at WHN Distributors
1 The Quadrant, Howarth Rd,
Maidenhead, Berks SL6 1AP.
T:01628-773353. F:01628-773363.
Top-hung sliding or folding doors, partitions and moveable walls.

The Period House Group
Main St, Leavening, N.Yorks YO17 9SA.
T/F:01653-658554.
Planked ledged doors made from reclaimed
timber with rose head nails and a hand-
waxed patina. Also hand forged door
and window furniture.

*John Porter
St Lawrence Rd,
Newcastle-upon-Tyne NE6 2HP.
T:0191-265 6016. F: 0191-276 1378.
Fire-rated, smoke sealed, X-ray rated
and sound-proofed doors.

*Premdor Crosby
Stephenson Rd, Groundwell Ind. Estate,
Swindon, Wilts SN2 5BQ.
T:01793-708200. F:01793-708300.
One of the largest specialist timber door
manufacturers in Europe, with 1000s of
designs and sizes available.

Stuart Interiors
Barrington Court, Barrington,
Nr Ilminster, Somerset TA19 0NQ.
T: 01460-240349. F: 01460-242069.
Internal and external 16th and 17th century-
style panelled or planked doors. Handmade
latches and ironwork.

The Yorkshire Pine Company
Clarke House, Keighley Rd,
Bingley, W.Yorks BD16 2RD.
T:01274-568532. F:01274-551573.
Period style doors to order, as well as free-
standing and fitted pine furniture. They also
sell an 'Antiquator' staining kit to give your
doors an antiqued look.

TRADITIONAL DOOR & CABINET FITTINGS

Antique Restorations
The Old Wheelwright's Shop,
Brasted Forge, Brasted, Kent TN16 1JL.
T:01959-563863. F: 01959-561262.
Some 800 'Brass and Foundry Castings' for
furniture, doors and clocks reproduced
(down to the blemishes) from 17th to 20th
century fittings. They are available polished,
'aged' or unlacquered. Mail order only.

Architectural Components
4-8 Exhibition Rd, London SW7 2HF.
T:0171-581 2401. F:0171-589 4928.
Period and contemporary door fittings,
furniture hinges and handles, letter boxes,
espagnolettes, locks and barrier bolts.
French enamel house numbers.

Ashfield Traditional
Cricketers, Forward Green,
Stowmarket, Suffolk IP14 5HP.
T/F:01449-711273.
Authentic hand forged reproductions of
period window catches and stays, door
latches and pulls, bolts, nails and hinges.

Bath Knob Shop
2-4 Hot Bath St, Bath, Avon BA1 1SJ.
T: 01225-469606. F: 01225-443081.
From inexpensive Indian hardware to top
quality Birmingham-made knockers, letter
boxes, etc. Mail order service.

JD Beardmore & Co
3-4 Percy St, London W1P 0EJ.
T: 0171-637 7041. F: 0171-436 9222.
300 items of traditional hardware, including
brass door bells, ceramic and glass knobs
and decorative grilles. They will also copy
other designs to order.

Brass Tacks Hardware
177 Bilton Rd, Perivale, Middx UB6 7HG.
T:0181-566 9669. F:0181-566 9339.
Locks, hinges and door fittings in brass,
aluminium, china, iron, perspex and
stainless steel.

John Churchill
The New Forge, Capton,
Nr Dartmouth, Devon TQ6 0JE.
T:01803-712535. F:01803-712470.
Blacksmith who produces his own range
of hand-forged door and window furniture.

Clayton Munroe
Kingston, Staverton, Totnes, Devon TQ9 6AR
T:01803-762626. F:01803-762584. Turned
steel fittings by Feron: there are traditional
French handles, a black-finish 'Celtic' range
plus their own 'Rough at
the Edges' collection of aged iron hinges
and latches; crackle-glaze china knobs.
Mail order only.

* denotes
trade supplier.
Please phone
for retail outlets. 133

Charles Collinge Architectural Ironmongery
44 Loman St, London SE1 0EH.
T:0171-928 3541. F:0171-620 1326.
Suppliers of door furniture including locks,
hinges, knockers.

Elizabeth Eaton
85 Bourne St, London SW1W 8HF.
T:0171-730 2262. F:0171-730 7294.
Import traditional French ranges, including
a brass and black iron door knocker in the
shape of a woman's hand.

Forgeries
108 Brassey Rd,
Winchester, Hants SO22 65A.
T/F:01962-842822.
Rustic-style door furniture including hinges,
nails and window latches. Mail order only.

Knobs & Knockers
561 King's Rd, London SW6 2EB.
T: 0171-384 2884. F: 0171-371 8244.
Branches in Wolverhampton and Edinburgh.
Large range of door and window furniture in
chrome, brass, porcelain, black iron and
special finishes. Also decorative grilles
and china pull cords.

*MacKinnon & Bailey
72 Floodgate St, Birmingham B5 5SL.
T:0121-773 5827. F:0121-766 6072.
Manufacturers of door fittings in polished
brass or chromium plate: lever and pull
handles, finger plates and brass boxes
for catching post.

*Martin & Company
119 Camden St, Birmingham B1 3DJ.
T:0121-233 2111. F: 0121-236 0488.
Large range of reproduction cabinet
hardware: plate handles, ring and
drop handles, backplates, knobs,
castors, hinges.

The Period House Group
See entry under NEW &
REPRODUCTION DOORS. Hand forged
iron latches and hinges for doors and
windows and rose head nails. New range of
hand cast brassware and one-off designs.

The Repro Shop
108 Walcot St, Bath BA1 5BG.
T: 01225-444404. F: 01225-448163.

Hand forged or cast iron hooks, pulls,
hinges, brackets.

Romany's Architectural Ironmongers
52-56 Camden High St, London NW1 0LT.
T:0171-387 2579. F:0171-383 2377.
Good place to see a big range -
from traditional designs to modern
aluminium fittings.

Shiners
8 Windmill St, London W1P 1HF.
T: 0171 636 0740. F: 0171-580 0740.
Open Mon-Fri from 6.45am to 3pm.
Charming old-fashioned shop catering
mainly for the antique restoration trade.
Good selection of escutcheons and
handles. Desk leathers and shelf edgings.

NT Yannedis
Riverside House,
Woodford Trading Estate, South End Rd,
Woodford Green, Essex IG8 8HQ.
T:0181-550 8833. F:0181-551 0026.
Traditional ironmongery, radiator grilles
and specials to order.

MODERN DOOR
& CABINET FITTINGS

By Design
Studio 702, The Big Peg,
120 Vyse St, Birmingham BA18 6NF.
T:0121-6043300. F:0121-6043311.
Mail order. Lever and cabinet handles cast
in brass or aluminium and shaped like
wriggly 'squirms', stars and suns. One-off
designs available on the contract side.

*Cooper Dryad
Omega House, Blackbird Rd, Leicester LE4
0AJ. T:0116-2538844. F:0116-2513623.
Manufacturers and distributors of
architectural hardware and handrails in
stainless steel, anodised aluminium, brass
and nylon-coated steel in lots of colours.

FSB Design Hardware
Allgood Hardware,
297 Euston Rd,London NW1 3AQ.
T:0171-387 9951. F:0171-380 1232.
Branches in Birmingham, Glasgow and
Manchester. Over fifty styles of door handle

or contract and domestic applications
from designers like Jasper Morrison
and Philippe Stark.

Glover & Smith
4 London Rd, Overton,
Basingstoke, Hants RG25 3NP.
T/F: 01256-773012.
Unusual range of hand cast solid pewter
door handles, pulls and robe hooks in a
variety of finishes and shapes - ammonites,
sea horses, star fishes and snails.

Handles & Fittings
HAF House, Mead Lane,
Hertford, Herts SG13 7AP.
T: 01992-505655. F: 01992-505705.
Smart range of modern handles in
steel, chrome and brass; brushed steel,
bronze, chrome and brass switchplates;
mortice and rim locks and other
architectural ironmongery.

Haute Deco
556 King's Rd, London SW6 2DZ.
T:0171-736 7171. F:0171-736 8484.
Unusual and colourful range of metal and
resin knobs including a Moorish collection
in gold or silver finishes.

Hewi (UK)
Scimitar Close, Gillingham Business Park,
Gillingham, Kent ME8 0RN. T:01634-
377688. F:01634-370612. Known for their
simple lever and pull handles in nylon on a
steel core - they come in twelve colours.

NT Laidlaw
Pennine House, Carrs Rd,
Cheadle, Cheshire SK8 2BW.
T: 0161-491 4343. F: 0161-491 4355.
And at:
124-126 Denmark Hill, London SE5 8RX.
T:0171-733 2101. F:0171- 737 2743.
And branches nationwide. Contemporary
door furniture in a variety of finishes and
supplied mainly to the contract market.

McKinney & Co
Wandon Rd,London SW6 2JF.
T:0171-384 1377. F:0171-736 1196.
Chunky brass, wood and resin door and
cupboard knobs and pulls. There are
beehive, studded, Roman, fossil, sea

urchin and sea horse designs, plus
escutcheons and door knockers.

Ornamental Arts Trading
Unit 1-7, Chelsea Harbour Design Centre,
Chelsea Harbour, London SW10 0XE.
T:0171-351 0541. F:0171-351 3034.
Range of 10 solid brass and bronze
cupboard handles and one door handle
available in any one of six finishes. Their
designs are based on natural forms:
acorns, berries, waves and beehive.

Ghislaine Stewart Designs
110 Fentiman Rd, London SW8 1QA.
T/F: 0171-820 9440.
Unusual door and cupboard knobs in
burnished bronze or exotic woods which
could fit into a modern or classic setting.

The Study
26 Old Church St, London SW3 5BY.
T:0171-376 7969. F:0171-795 0392.
Real pebble door knobs and glass knobs.

Turnstyle Designs
Village St, Bishop's Tawton,
Barnstaple, Devon EX32 0DG.
T:01271-25325. F:01271-328248.
Unusual reconstituted stone knobs and
handles shaped like shells, fish, moons,
frogs, cats, pelicans and many others.

CERAMIC AND GLASS FITTINGS

*Bullers
Albion Works,
Uttoxeter Rd,
Longton, Stoke-on-
Trent, ST3 1PH.
T:01782-599922.
F:01782-598037. Manufacturers of fine
English porcelain door and cupboard
furniture, finger plates and light switches.
They are available In white, black, ivory
or decorated.

Charles Harden
14 Chiltern St, London W1M 1PD.
T:0171-935 2032.
Specialist in plain and painted ceramic
door knobs.

*** denotes
trade supplier.
Please phone
for retail outlets.** 135

Merlin Glass
Barn St, Station Rd, Liskeard,
Cornwall PL14 4BW.
T/F:01579-342399.
Glass with brass mortice and cupboard
knobs in 6 colours plus opaque and clear.

*Top Knobs
4 Brunel Buildings, Brunel Rd,
Newton Abbot, Devon TQ12 4PB.
T:01626-63388. F:01626-332383.
Twelve styles of ceramic knobs in five sizes.
Range of plain colours or with contrasting
bands. Also brass knobs and handles.

David Wainwright
61-63 Portobello Rd, London W11 3DB.
T:0171-727 0707. F:0171-243 8100.
And at:
251 Portobello Rd, London W11 1LT.
T: 0171-792 1988. F:0171-243 8100.
And at:
28 Roslyn Hill, London NW3 6DT.
T:0171-431 5900.
Brass-mounted 19th century Indian ceramic
knobs; modern Indian glass and bone
cupboard knobs.

WINDOWS/ROOFLIGHTS/ FANLIGHTS

*Andersen Windows & Patio Doors
Black Millwork, Andersen House, Dallow St,
Burton-on Trent, Staffs DE14 2PQ.
T:01283-511122. F:01283-510863.
Vast range of windows, encompassing
6000 combinations of shapes and sizes,
including oval, casement, circular and sash.

Bylaw (Ross)
The Old Mill, Brookend St,
Ross-on-Wye, Hereford HR9 7EG.
T:01989-562356. F:01989-768145.
Oak mullioned windows to order.

Clement Brothers
Clembro House, Weydown Rd,
Haslemere, Surrey GU27 1HR.
T:01428-643393. F:01428-661369.
Manufacturers of steel windows and
doors. Also cast rooflights, lantern lights
and leaded lights.

Crittall Windows
Springwood Drive,
Braintree, Essex CM7 2YN.
T:01376-324106. F:01376-349662.
This company invented the original steel
window and still make them for new or
period properties (they can now be double-
glazed). Also aluminium windows and
curtain walling.

*Don Forbes Sash Fittings
Cottarton, Logiealmond,
Perthshire PH1 3TJ.
T/F:01738-880329.
Wholesale supplier of sash and casement
window fittings: pulleys, fasteners, sash
screws, cast iron or lead weights. Can
refurbish existing fittings and supply
matching replacements.

Lattice Windows
Fiddington Farm, Monks Lane,
Fiddington, Tewkesbury, Gloucs GL20 7BJ.
T:01684-299222. F:01684-299223.
Traditionally crafted windows: leaded lights,
metal casements in wrought iron or black
steel, oak frames. Copying of existing
windows. Renovation and replacement of
period windows.

The Metal Window Company
The Old Stables, Oxleaze Farm, Filkins,
Lechlade, Gloucs GL7 3RB.
T/F:01367-850313.
Manufacturers of 'the Conservation

Rooflight', which is a faithful reproduction of the Victorian cast-iron originals, but in steel and with modern insulation. Other sized and shaped rooflights made to measure.

Mumford & Wood
Hallsford Bridge Ind. Estate,
Ongar, Essex CM5 9RB.
T:01277-362401. F:01277-365093.
Specialist manufacturer of replacement sliding sash windows. Their conservation sash window combines double glazing with finely moulded glazing bars. They also make French doors and door frames.

The Original Box Sash Window Company
The Joinery, Unit 10,
Bridgewater Way, Windsor, Berks SL4 1RD.
T:01753-858196. F:01753-857827.
Double glazed versions of period originals, fully draught-proofed and with timber treated to last for 60 years.

Oxford Sash Window Company
Eynsham Park Estate Yard, Cuckoo Lane,
North Leigh, Oxon OX8 6PS.
T:01993-883536. F:01993-883027.
Manufacturers of individually made sash windows for domestic, commercial and listed buildings; they install them nationwide. Restoration service.

Refurb-a-Sash
The Old Station Works,
119-123 Sandycombe Rd,
Richmond, Surrey TW9 2EP.
T:0181-332 9352. F:0181-332 6366.
Refurbishment, full or part replacement and double glazing of sash windows. French windows and casements also available.

John Sambrook
Park House, Northiam, E.Sussex TN31 6PA.
T: 01797-252615.
Makes exact copies of fanlights to order, as well as rooflights or metal windows to match 18th century designs.

The Sash Window Workshop
Unit 2, Mayfield Farm Ind.Estate,
Hatchet Lane, Cranbourne,
Nr Windsor, Berks SL4 2EG.
Freephone: 0500-652653.
F:01344-893034.

Georgian and Victorian sash window renovation and repair; French windows; bespoke commissions.

Sashy and Sashy
46 Grosvenor Rd,
Tunbridge Wells, Kent TN1 2AS.
T:01892-514145. F:01892-514221.
Custom made windows, internal and external doors, shutters, staircases, kitchen units. Nationwide window restoration and consultancy service, including replacement fittings, frames and sashes and re-glazing.

Sibley & Son
PO Box 315, Guildford, Surrey GU1 4NW.
T:01426-949346.
Manufacturers and restorers of windows. They have a draught-proof invisible sealing system to stop windows from rattling.

Ventrolla
11 Hornbeam Square South,
Hornbeam Business Park,
Harrogate, N.Yorks HG2 8NB.
T:01423-870011. F:01423-873399.
Franchises in most parts of the country. Renovation service for windows (especially period and traditional). Their perimeter sealing system for weatherproofing can be applied to both sash windows and casement windows.

SHUTTERS

American Shutters
72 Station Rd, London SW13 OLS.
T:0181-876 5905. F:0181-878 9548.
Custom made in America in a wide range of styles and louvre sizes. Can also supply Shoji window screens to order in Synskin (synthetic ricepaper which is as tough as leather) as well as solid window shutters.

Lindman
Tower Lane, Warmley, Bristol BS15 2XX.
T:0117-961 0900. F:0117-961 0901.
External shutters in PVC which are maintenance-free and carry a 40 year guarantee. Sizes to fit almost any window. Ten solid colours to choose from.

For security shutters see CURTAINS & BLINDS & SOFT FURNISHINGS - Blinds

* denotes trade supplier. Please phone for retail outlets.

London Shutter Company
18 Brockenhurst Rd,
South Ascot, Berks SL5 9DL.
T:01344-28385. F:01344-27575.
Interior and exterior shutters custom made
in cedar. Installation service. Paint matching
if required.

London's Georgian Houses
291 Goswell Rd, London EC1V 7LA.
T/F:0171-833 8217.
Specialists in recreating 18th and 19th
century fitted woodwork, including internal
boxed shutters, alcove bookcases,
cupboards and front doors.

The Shutter Shop
Queensbury House, Dilly Lane, Hartley
Wintney, Hampshire RG27 8EQ.
T:01252-844575. F:01252-844718.
Hardwood shutters made to measure
and supplied painted or stained,
panelled or louvred.

GLASS MANUFACTURERS & SUPPLIERS

The Birmingham Guild
Guild House, Cradley Rd, Netherton,
Dudley, W.Midlands DY2 9TH.
T:01384-411511. F:01384-411234.
General glass merchants who also supply
toughened safety glass, double glazing,
coloured panels and curtain walling.

Philip Bradbury Glass
83 Blackstock Rd, London N4 2JW.
T:0171-226 2919. F:0171-359 6303.
Bespoke service for anyone who needs to
reproduce a period acid-etched design.
Lead lights.

Ray Bradley
3 Orchard Studios, London W6 7BU.
T:0171-602 1840.
Can tackle anything to do with architectural
glass, on any scale, from the dome in a
Nash house to a glass floor. Enamelling,
silvering, acid embossing and stained glass.

Chelsea Glass
650 Portslade Rd, London SW8 3DH.
T:0171-720 6905. F:0171-978 2827.
Domestic and contract glazing; mirrors;
glass cutting while you wait; bevelling;
table-tops and shelves cut to size;
24 hour emergency service.

HW Cooper & Co
Page House,
33 Pages Walk, London SE1 4SF.
T:0171-237 1767. F:0171-237 6480.
UK distributor for the German-made Gerrix
glass blocks, paving lights for highway or
patio use (incl. repairs to old ones), remote
control window gear (for that roof-light 20ft
above your desk). Plus solar control, anti-
shatter and blackout films for glass (by the
roll or in cut lengths).

Daedalian Glass
The Old Smithy, Cold Row, Carr Lane,
Stalmine, Poulton-le-Flyde, Lancs FY6 9DW.
T:01253-702531. F:01253-701532.
Glass bending, sandblasting, etching and
photo-etching (which enables them to
transpose anything on to glass - even a
photo of the family dog) and glass fusing
(which produces a layered textured look).
Leaded lights, stained glass, all sorts of
architectural glass, with nationwide delivery
and installation if required.

James Hetley & Co
Glasshouse Fields, Schoolhouse Lane,
London E1 9JA.
T:0171-790 2333. F:0171-790 2682.
Etched glass specialists - range of stock
designs available in 2 sizes and 2
thicknesses. Can send photocopies of their
designs and deliver all over the country.

T&W Ide
Glasshouse Fields, London E1 9JA.
T:0171-790 2333. F:0171-790 2682.
Supplier of stained glass and hand blown
cylinder sheet glass.

The London Crown Glass Company
Twin Archway, Elizabeth Rd,
Henley-on-Thames, Oxon RG9 1RJ.
T:01491-413227. F:01491-413228.
Hand blown glass for the renovation of
period windows and furniture. Clients include
English Heritage, The National Trust and the
Crown Estates. The skill for blowing true

For more
suppliers or other
specialists
contact The Glass
and Glazing
Federation, 44-48
Borough High St,
London SE1 1XB.
T:0171-403 7177.
F:0171-357 7458.
They give advice
on glass, choosing
windows or
conservatories,
and can send a
list of members in
138   your area.

Crown Glass died out in the 30s, but London Crown have developed a replacement for it called Vauxhall Glass. It is made using traditional techniques.

London West Ten Glass

485-491 Latimer Rd, London W10 6RD.
T:0181-969 5682. F:0181-969 4574.
General glass merchants who provide glass cut to size, safety glass, table tops, mirrors in any size, coloured glass and 24 hour emergency glazing and boarding.

Luxcrete

Premier House, Disraeli Rd,
Harlesden, London NW10 7BT.
T:0181-965 7292. F:0181-961 6337.
Glass blocks in 29 different patterns and sizes for both commercial and domestic use. The company also manufactures sand-blasted and chemically-etched blocks as well as bullet-proof and bullet-resistant blocks.

Nero Signs (Glass/Designs)

332-334 Brixton Rd, London SW9 7AA.
T:0171-737 8021. F:0171-733 8589.
Decoration of glass and mirrors using acid-etching, sand blasting, brilliant cutting, bevelling, gilding and sign writing. Design and manufacture stained glass and leaded lights. Advice given on all flat glass projects.

*Pilkington Glass Products

Prescot Rd, St. Helens,
Merseyside WA10 3TT.
T:01744-28882. F:01744-613049.
Specialists in textured glass. They have other divisions for mirror manufacturing and for laminating designs into security glass.

Preedy Glass

Lamb Works, North Rd,London N7 9PA.
T:0171-700 0377. F:0171-700 7579.
Coloured mirror and glass, antique finishes, extra clear glass. They have a division called Prefit which deals in glass-related ironmongery (hinges, clips and clamps).

Radford & Ball

R&B Studios,
Glasshouse Fields, London E1 9JA.
T:0171-790 1799. F:0171-790 1899.
Architectural glass, enamelled and sand-blasted to individual commissions.

Rankins

23-24 Pearson St, London E2 8JD.
T:0171-729 4200. F:0171-729 7135.
Manufacturers and distributors of all flat glass including fire resistant, non-reflective, shock-proof, sculptured and white vitrolite.

SW82 Glass & Design

29 Commissioner St,
Crieff, Perthshire PH7 3AY.
T:07000-782074. F:01764-655201.
Designers and manufacturers of decorative glass and mirror for doors, showers, mirrors, windows and table tops.

*Shades (Screenprint)

Spur Mill, Broadstone Hall Rd South,
Reddish, Stockport, Cheshire SK5 7BY.
T:0161-477 4688. F:0161-474 7629.
Glass printing which achieves the look of stained glass murals with the use of transparent printing inks.

*Solaglas

Herald Way, Binley, Coventry CV3 2ND.
T:01203-458844. F:01203-636473.
65 outlets throughout the country.
Manufacturers of laminated safety glass, fire resistant glazed doors, glass partitions and glass for furniture. Also bevelling, etching and screenprinting.

Tatra Glass (UK)

2a Loughborough Rd, Quorn, Leicester LE12 8DX. T:01509-620661. F:01509-620305.
Importers of 'mouth-blown antique glass' from Poland, widely used in restoration. Can match any pre- First World War glass.

* denotes trade supplier. Please phone for retail outlets.

STAINED GLASS SUPPLIERS & ARTISTS

Mark Angus
144 North Rd, Combe Down, Bath BA2 5DL.
T:01225-834530.
Stained glass artist who uses traditional ecclesiastical iconography in innovative ways - his chancel window for Eardisley Church near Hereford depicts a choir which has been screen-printed on to the glass. Can be commissioned for abstract secular designs as well.

Alexander Beleschenko
43 Jersey St, Hafod, Swansea SA1 2HF.
T:01792-462801. F:01792-480281.
Architectural glass installations which combine all sorts of techniques: stained glass, acid etching, sand-blasting, enamel printing and painting.

Glass Heritage
Reynolds Warehouse, The Docks, Gloucester GL1 2EN.
T:01452-503803. F:01452-504803.
Design, manufacture, installation or repair of stained glass and leaded lights. They stock coloured and textured sheet glass. Hand-blown glass. Courses.

Goddard & Gibbs Studios
41-49 Kingsland Rd, London E2 8AD.
T:0171-739 6563. F:0171-739 1979.
Established over 100 years ago. Stained and leaded glass refurbishment and design - both traditional and contemporary.

Nero Signs (Glass/Designs)
See entry under GLASS MANUFACTURERS. Designers and manufacturers of stained glass.

ES Phillips
99 Portobello Rd, London W11 2QB.
T:0171-229 2113. F:0171-229 1963.
And at:
John Hardman's Studios
Light Woods Park, Hagley Rd, W.Birmingham B67 5DP.
T:0121-429 7609. F:0121-429 5696.
Antique stained glass window specialists, from small mosaic fragments to entire windows (dating from 1820 to 1950). The Birmingham studio was originally established as a metal workshop in 1838, making ecclesiastical and domestic plate to designs by Pugin. This branch now handles the restoration and conservation side and new designs.

Tomkinson Stained Glass Windows
87 Portobello Rd, London W11 2QB.
T/F:0171-267 1669.
Victorian stained glass windows. Restoration service.

Sasha Ward
19 Salisbury Rd, Marlborough, Wilts SN8 4AD.
T:01672-515638. F:01672-516738.
Painted and printed glass in strong colours with geometric shapes. She has recently completed a screen for the Sheriff's Court in Edinburgh.

Whiteway & Waldron
305 Munster Rd, London SW6 6BJ.
T/F:0171-381 3195.
Victorian stained glass, mostly religious.

OTHER SPECIALIST SERVICES & SUPPLIERS

Franco-file
PO Box 31, Tiverton, Devon EX16 4YU.
T/F: 01884-253556.
French enamelled house numbers.

The Keyhole
Pilgrim's Progress, Far Back Lane, Farnsfield, Newark, Notts NG22 8JX.
T:01623-882590.
Repair and supply of antique and period locks and keys.

The Letterbox Company
Tebworth, Leighton Buzzard, Bedfordshire LU7 9QG.
T:01525-874599. F:01525-875746.
Steel post boxes for exterior use, ranging from the genuine US Mail Box to the ornate 'Postillion' decorated with a crown and a post horn. They also do hand painted house signs, which can be supplied with or without extra decorative motifs.

* denotes trade supplier. Please phone for retail outlets.

Quality Lock Co
Leve Lane, Willenhall,
W.Midlands WV13 1PS.
T/F:01653-658554. Manufacturers of
traditional locks. They can refurbish and re-
key locks dating from the early 1800s to the
present day, and can even produce new
locks to match your existing one exactly.

Richard Quinnell
Rowhurst Forge, Oxshott Rd,
Leatherhead, Surrey KT22 0EN.
T:01372-375148.
Will cast, forge, cut or engrave
door numbers to measure.

Techniform Graphics
156 Camberwell Rd, London SE5.
T:0171-701 1070.
Sign writers who can cut letters and numbers
to almost any size in a range of materials,
from perspex to stainless steel. Ideal if
you want an oversized house number.

Our settlement terms are 0 days.

The goods on this invoice remain the property of ART BOOKS INTERNATIONAL LTD until payment is received in full

1 STEWART'S COURT 220 STEWART'S ROAD LONDON SW8 4UD TEL: 0171 720 1503 FAX 0171 720 3158
A LIMITED COMPANY REGISTERED IN THE UK No.: 2608288 VAT No.: 548 1215 52

TOTAL

14.99

CURTAINS & BLINDS & SOFT FURNISHINGS

CURTAIN MAKERS

Adams & Co
Ground Floor, 14 Cottenham Park Rd,
London SW20 0RZ.
T:0181-946 2743. F:0181-879 0584.
Full range of soft furnishings and related
services, including bed canopies,
headboards and bedcovers, curtains, soft
blinds, pelmets, valances, swags,
lambrequins, cushions, lampshades, cot
quilts, valances and layette baskets. Full
fitting and hanging service for curtains
to include the supply of tracks and
pelmet boards. They also offer a fabric
walling service.

*Arboretum Bespoke
16 South Street,
Leominster, Hereford, HR6 8JB.
T:01568-613396. F:01568-616815.
Design and make custom dyed silk throw-
overs, soft furnishings and accessories.
They also make quilts to commission, and
curtains and blinds in customers' own fabric.

Morse Ashworth
The Studio, 77 Kingsmead Rd,
London SW2 3HZ.
T:0181-671 1114.
Specialists in soft furnishings including
curtains, blinds, cushions, bedspreads,
bed-hangings,valances, screens - both
to the trade and the general public.

Cover Up Designs
9 Kingsclere Park, Kingsclere,
Nr Newbery, Berks RG20 4SW.
T:01635-297981. F:01635-298363.
Complete soft furnishing service:
bedheads, bedcovers, dressing tables
and TV cabinets. Good range of fabrics,
including printed voiles, chintzes and
curtain linings. They have a quilting service
and there's an upholsterer on site.

Curtains Complete
See entry under
SECOND-HAND CURTAINS.

The Final Curtain Company
T:0181-699 3626. F:0181-291 7937.
By appointment. Brochure available. Natural

*** denotes
trade supplier.
Please phone
for retail outlets.** 143

fabric specialists. Full range of soft furnishings to order: curtains, loose covers, upholstery, cushions. Known for their soft, unstructured, contemporary look. Mail order service throughout the UK.

*From The Top
29 Blenheim Gardens, London SW2 5EU. T:0181-671 7629. F:0181-674 0375. High quality curtain making and complete soft furnishing service to the trade.

Gallery of Antique Costume & Textiles
2 Church St, London NW8 8ED. T/F:0171-723 9981. Antique curtain making service. They also stock antique fabrics for curtains and upholstery.

Ketcher & Moore
41 North Road, London N7 9DP. T:0171-609 7067. F:0171-700 3701. Top quality makers of curtains, blinds and soft furnishings who also provide a complete interior design service if required. They can supply upholstered pieces such as a copy of an 18th century window seat. Trade and retail.

Let It Loose
6 Methley Street, London SE11 4AJ. T:0171-582 1437. F:0171-582 4448. From one small cushion to a complete soft furnishing service. A team will cut loose covers on site - they then make them up in their workrooms and return them in a week. Curtain deliveries can be promised within two weeks.

Ann Lister Historic Furnishings
Cam Laithe, Far Lane, Kettlewell, Skipton, N.Yorks BD23 5QY. T:01756-760809. F:01756-760857. Authentic replication of original furnishings, particularly fabrics and trimmings. Handmade window treatments, bed hangings, wall coverings, furniture covers: all traditionally hand sewn with historical accuracy. Clients include major private houses and English Heritage.

The Loose Cover Company
PO Box 140, High Wycombe, Bucks HP13 6YF. T:01494-471226. Custom make loose covers within a 100 mile radius of London.

The Original Silver Lining
Workshop 29, Lenton Business Centre, Lenton Blvd, Nottingham NG7 2BY. T:0115-955 5123. F:0115-962 3064. Range of natural fabrics, linings (including blackout and thermal) and a making-up service for curtains and cushions.

D M Philp
137-139 Queens Road, Watford, Herts WD1 2QL. T:01923-222363. F:01923-239925. Exclusive curtain makers. Specialise in swags and tails and bed hangings. They have their own upholsterer on site. All hand made, bespoke designs.

Jon Rhodes
The Old Cinema, Stalham, Norwich, Norfolk NR12 9DG. T:01692-582748. F:01692-580154. Top-of-the-range custom made, hand sewn, lined and interlined curtains; also upholstery, fabric walling, tented ceilings, bed drapes - anything to do with fabric in the home.

Ruffle & Hook
Florence Works, 34 1/2 Florence Street, London N1 2DT. T:0171-226 0370. F:0171-226 5285. Simple curtains made to order and hessian and jute blinds. Also loose covers, flooring and decorative accessories. They carry a good range of natural fabrics.

Sayers & Bays
50 Pembroke Rd, London W8 6NX. T:0171-602 6555. F:0171-371 3672. Handmade curtains and upholstery. They can supply fabrics and trimmings and provide a full fitting service.

Margaret Sheridan
36 Market Place, Hingham, Norwich NR9 4AF. T:01953-850691. F:01953-851447. Soft furnishing workrooms for upholstered furniture, curtains and bed hangings. Full interior design service.

The Workroom

10 Addington Square,
London SE5 7JZ. T/F:0171-708 1920.
Makers of headboards, slipcovers and
curtains as well as cushions, pads,
tablecloths, eiderdowns, bedspreads,
valances and window seats. They also
provide dressing tables and unpainted table
bases with customized skirts and stools.

CURTAIN POLES

Artisan

Unit 4a, Union Court, 20 Union Road,
London SW4 6JP.
T:0171-498 6974. F:0171-498 2989.
Iron curtain rails including a double bracket
to hang sheers and curtains from one fixing.
Finials in oak, frosted glass, resin, wire and
wrought iron. New poles in English oak and
steel. Wrought iron range includes hooks,
brackets, portière rods and poles.

Bisca Design

Shaw Moor Farm, Harome, York YO6 5HZ.
T:01439-771702. F:01439-771002.
Chunky knotted black metal poles and tie
backs. Will undertake large commercial
commissions and design to special order.

*Boulet Frères

Boulet House 142a Canbury Park Rd,
Kingston-Upon-Thames, Surrey KT2 6LE.
T:0181-974 5695. F:0181-974 5635.
3000 products - tracks (including tracks for
the stage), poles in acrylic, nickel, gunmetal,
wood and brass. Cord weights, control rods,
tie backs, hooks and curtain clips.

Byron & Byron

Thane Works, Thane Villas,
off Seven Sisters Rd, London N7 7NU.
T:0171-700 0404. F:0171-700 4111.
Wide range of lacquered and gilded wooden
and metal curtain poles and finials - some
with heraldic motifs. Biedermeier range.

Clayton Munroe

Kingston West Drive, Staverton,
Totnes, Devon TQ9 6AR.
T:01803-762626. F:01803-762584.
The 'Celtic' range of curtain poles and
accessories (rings, brackets and tie backs).
Finials in a basket weave design.

*Cope & Timmins

Angel Road Works, Angel Rd, Edmonton,
London N18 3AY.
T:0181-803 6481. F:0181-887 0910.
Trade suppliers of a wide range of curtain
poles, tracks and fittings. They have a made
to measure collection if you need a pole
of 12 ft or more or custom-bent brass
poles for swept or angled bays.
8000 stockists nationwide.

Danico Brass

31-33 Winchester Rd, London NW3 3NR.
T:0171-483 4477. F:0171-722 7992.
Agents for Blome: modern curtain poles,
tracks and high tension wire used for
minimalist window dressing.

*Hallis Hudson

Bushel Street, Preston, Lancs PR1 2SP.
T:01772-202202. F:01772-883555.
Made to measure curtain poles mainly
in wood with gilded, brass or wood finials
in a large range of traditional designs.
Plus some chunky deluxe models.

Edward Harpley

Crownings, Buxhall Rd, Brettenham,
Ipswich, Suffolk IP7 7PA.
T:01449-737999. F:01449-736111.
Range of walnut, oak, painted pine, gilded
wood and wrought iron poles and finials.
Special custom-made orders undertaken.
They have a wooden pole for swept bays.

*Harrison Drape

Bradford St, Birmingham B12 0PE
T:0121-766 6111. F:0121-772 0696.

*** denotes
trade supplier.
Please phone
for retail outlets.** 145

Curved track system which can be fitted around a bay window. Pre-corded tracks and valances. Wood poles in many finishes, an 'Ironworks' collection and an antique brass-effect range.

Haute Deco
556 King's Road, London SW6 2DZ.
T:0171-736 7171. F:0171-736 8484.
Curtain poles, brackets, finials and tie-backs in modern cast bronze, nickel plate or any finish to order.

The Holbein Collection at Titley & Marr
Unit 7, 1st floor, Chelsea Harbour Design Centre, London SW10 0XE.
T:0171-351 6383. F:0171-351 6318.
Resin hand painted finials and curtain tassel ends which look and feel like wood. Also painted brackets.

*Hunter Hyland
201-205 Kingston Rd,
Leatherhead, Surrey KT22 7PB.
T:01372-378511. F:01372-370038.
Agents for Rufflette (curtain tapes, hook rings), Kirsch (rods, rails and accessories), wrought iron cornice poles, ombras and curtain bands, brass poles and brackets, wood poles and an excellent range of finials and swing arms for dormer windows. 'Swish' tracks, poles and accessories.

Interior Art Metalworks
Camborne Forge, Trevu Rd,
Camborne, Cornwall TR14 8SR.
T:01209-719911.
Blacksmiths who produce a small range of iron candlesticks, candelabra and curtain poles plus anything else in iron to order.

The Iron Design Company
Summer Carr Farm, Thornton Le Moor,
Northallerton, N.Yorks DL6 3SG.
T:01609-778143. F:01609-778846.
Iron poles, finials, tie-backs, custom made in any length or to fit bay windows and corners.

McKinney & Co
1 Wandon Rd, London SW6 2JF.
T:0171-384 1377. F:0171-736 1196.
Huge selection of antique and reproduction poles, rings, finials and tiebacks, in wood, resin or metal. Brass items can be antiqued, bronzed, chrome or nickel plated. Specials made to order. Pelmets and coronas in wood, gilt or paint finishes. Unusual glass poles and glass finials which can also be used with wood and metal bases. Special poles for bay windows. Wood or brass tie backs.

Merchants
Olmar Wharf, Olmar St, London SE1 5AY.
T:0171-237 0060. F:0171-237 8204.
Poles, finials, brackets in lacquered steel or bamboo with raffia or copper details. They also do simple and reasonably priced metal poles.

Resina Designs
Unit 6a, Cox's Green, Wrington,
Bristol, N.Somerset BS18 7QU.
T:01934-863535. F:01934-863536.
Decorative finials in metal leaf or coloured glass. Painted, wooden and gilded poles; also brackets and hold-backs.

*Rockingham
Earlstrees Rd, Corby, Northants NN17 4AZ.
T:01536-260001. F:01536-408473.
Manufacturers and distributors of wooden and brass curtain poles, plastic tracks and curtain accessories.

*Silent Gliss
Star Lane, Margate, Kent CT9 4EF.
T:01843-863571. F:01843-864503.
Manual and electrically operated blinds and curtain tracks; solar control conservatory blinds and dim-out systems.

Tempus Stet
Trinity Business Centre,
305-309 Rotherhithe St, London SE16 1EY.
T:0171-231 0955. F:0171-252 3820.
Selection of bed coronas, gilded and wooden classical tie-backs and curtain finials with elephant heads, rams heads, palms, acanthus and many other designs. Also gilded and wooden pelmets.

Villiers Brothers
Fyfield Hall, Fyfield, Ongar, Essex CM5 0SA.
T:01277-899680. F:01277-899008.
Designers of one-off iron furniture and lighting. They have also been commissioned to make smart iron curtain poles.

SECONDHAND CURTAINS

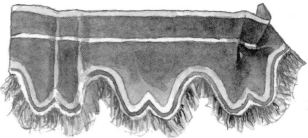

The Curtain Agency
231 London Rd, Camberley, Surrey.
T:01276-671672. The Curtain Agency
has a large stock of secondhand curtains,
blinds, cushions, bedcovers and rugs.

Curtain Exchange
133 Stephendale Rd, London SW6 2PG.
T:0171-731 8316/7 and branches
nationwide. An Aladdin's cave of high quality
curtains at under half the price of made-to-
order. Prices from £20-£1000.

The Curtain Rack
25 High Street, Pershore, Worcs WR10 1AA.
T:01386-556105. F:01386-462344.
Secondhand curtains and a range of
brocade and damask fabrics at very
competitive prices. Selection of ready
made curtains and made to measure
curtains and blinds.

The Curtain Ring
5 Perry Rd (Park Row), Bristol BS1 5BQ.
T:0117-9292844. Fine quality secondhand
curtains, matching bedheads, bed canopies
and small fabric related accessories.
Approximately 500 pairs in stock,
most of them interlined.

The Curtain Shop
12 Goods Station Rd,
Tunbridge Wells, Kent TN1 2BL.
T:01892-527202. F:01892-522682.
Top quality secondhand curtains. They
also stock a range of designer (and some
antique) fabrics and offer a curtain making,
track fitting and interior design service.

The Curtain Trading Centre
24 Baker St, London W1M 1DF.
T:0171-224-2006. Good choice of used
curtains, new interior decorators' and
showhouse samples, blinds and bedspreads
at a fraction of the original price.

Curtains Complete
The Stables, East Farndon Hall,
Market Harborough, Leics LE16 9SE.
T:01858-466671. F:01858-432112.
Open only Tues 9:30-3:00 or by
appointment, including Sat and Sun

mornings. Apart from the 150-250
secondhand curtains available there's also
a reasonably priced range of new curtains in
toiles, damasks or fleur-de-lys with different
headings to order in any combination of
details. The owner worked in Colefax &
Fowler's workrooms for five years and
is well qualified to alter curtains in stock.

The London Curtain Shop
298 Sandycombe Rd, Kew, Surrey TW9 3NG.
T:0181-940 5959. F:0181-977 4415.
Over 300 pairs of curtains from hotels,
showhouses, interior designers and
private homes.

Well Hung
137 Northcote Rd, London SW11 6PQ.
T:0171-924 4468. F:0171-924 4134.
Wide range of curtains and blinds in fabrics
by Colefax & Fowler, Osborne & Little,
Bennison and other top companies.

BLINDS & AWNINGS

Actel Sunblinds
32 Wilson Road, Chessington,
Surrey KT9 2HE.
T:0181-397 4737.
Blinds of all types. Free home visits
in London and the Home Counties.

Andersons Blinds
Penrhewl Works, St Asaph, Clwyd LL17 0NH.
T:01745-583410. F:01745-584860.
Manufacturers of vertical, roller,
blackout, venetian and conservatory
blinds and awnings.

Appeal Blinds
6 Vale Lane, Bedminster, Bristol BS3 5SD.
T:0117-9637734. F:0117-9666216.
Specialists in conservatory blinds with the

**All these
secondhand
curtain shops
have different
opening hours.
Please ring first**

*** denotes
trade supplier.
Please phone
for retail outlets.** 147

option of motor operation by remote or thermostatic control. Their mini-pinoleums are made of flat strips of hardwood which can be stained, painted or left natural.

*Avenue Technology
PO Box 140, Gloucester GL2 5ZN.
T:01452-302924. F:01452-302903.
Automatic or motorized blinds for solar shading in museums, offices and galleries.

*Blind Fashion by Sander-Shade
Unit 8, Treadaway Tech Centre, Loudwater, High Wycombe, Bucks HP10 9RS.
T:01628-529676. F:01628-521684.
Laminated roller blinds, Austrian, cascade, festoon or roman soft blinds, woodslat venetians and lambrequins. Blinds made from customers' own fabric or from the choice in stock.

*The Blinds Company
Unit 2, London Stone Business Estate, Broughton Street, London SW8 3QR.
T:0171-627 0909. F:0171-498 7305.
Complete blind manufacturing service. Laminated roller blinds, Swedish, Scottish Holland, Roman,Vertical, Austrian, Velux, aluminum and wooden venetians, pinoleums plus selection of base trims and pelmets. Also conservatory blinds.

Breezeway
The Avenue, Bletsoe, Bedford MK44 1QF.
T:01234-781000. F:01234-781372.
Internal and external insect screens in kit form for doors and windows. There are different styles to suit most types of openings - hinged and lift-out versions or roller screens. They will mail order anywhere in the EEC.

Continental Awnings
Unit 14, Torbay Trading Est,
New Road, Brixham, Devon TQ5 8NF.
T:01803-859996. F:01803-859994.
Tailor-made exterior window, conservatory and patio awnings.

*Contravent Regal
5 Cowley Mill Trading Est, Longbridge Way, Uxbridge, Middx UB8 2YG.
T:01895-257766. F:01895-257860.
Branch in Croydon. Manual or motorized

venetians, vertical, roller, Roman and other soft blinds and curtains.

*Decor Shades
5 Brewery Mews Business Centre, St John Rd, Isleworth, Middx TW7 6PH.
T/F:0181 847 1939. Specialises in making up shades in customer's own fabric.

*Faber Blinds
Kilvey Rd, Brackmills,
Northampton NN4 7PB.
T:01604-766251. F:01604-768802.
Faber manufacture venetians in various slat widths, including one with a rounded headrail. They also make roller, vertical, pleated and blackout blinds, blinds for audio-visual use, rooflight and conservatory blinds. Specialists in external blinds and the 'Mechoshade' sunscreening system. Stocked by major department stores.

Fiesta Blinds
72-76 Yarm Lane,
Stockton-on-Tees, Cleveland TS18 1EW.
T:0800-591539. F:0191-617846.
Conservatory and roof blind specialist. Also manufacture venetians, pleated, roller and vertical blinds to order.

HDB
South Wonston,
Winchester, Hants SO21 3HN.
T:01962-885700.
Suppliers of 'Pli-sol' pleated blinds in 13 different fabrics (including transparent, metallised, blackout) for any type of window; 'Visio-lux' louvre blinds, 'Timberdrape' pinoleum blinds and 'Woodweave' for natural insulation.

*Hunter Douglas
Mersey Ind Estate, Heaton Mersey, Stockport, Cheshire SK4 3EQ.
T:0161-432 5303. F:0161-431 5087.
Call for branches nationwide. Specialist in 'Luxaflex' venetian blinds, roller blinds in an assortment of finishes and vertical, pleated, and light- blocking blinds in all colours. They can manufacture from the customer's own or a large range of in-house fabrics. Plus fly screens, security shutters and curved blinds for bays. John Lewis is a stockist.

For additional information try the British Blind and Shutter Association, 42 Heath Street, Tamworth, Staffs B79 7JH. T:01827-52337. F:01827-310827. There are 250 blind and shutter manufacturers on their books nationwide.

Shades
2B Chingford Road, Bell Corner,
Walthamstow E17 4PJ.
T:0181-527 3991. F:0181-523 4476.
Specialize in interior blinds - roller, vertical,
aluminum and wood venetians, soft roman,
woodweaves, blinds for velux windows
and conservatories.

*Silent Gliss
See entry under **CURTAIN POLES.**
Roller, venetian and vertical blinds as
well as conservatory and dim-out systems.

Tidmarsh & Sons
Transenna Works,
1 Laycock St, London N1 1SW.
T:0171-226 2261. F:0171-226 4115.
Designers, manufacturers and installers
of blinds since 1828. Roller blinds from
customers' own materials; venetian blinds
for odd shaped windows or sloping
rooflights; wood slat blinds in a big range
of colours; blackout blinds, roller flyscreens,
projection screens and most other
specialist blinds.

Venetian Blind Manufacturing Co
45-47 Lawley Middleway,
Aston, Birmingham B4 7XH.
T:0121-359 6941. F:0121-359 5758.
Metal, wood and eco-wood venetians,
vertical and roller blinds, awnings
and canopies.

Alison White
Ground floor, Fitzpatrick Building,
York Way, London N7 9AS.
T:0171-609 6127.F:0171-609 6128.
Unusual pierced roller blinds in Swedish
cotton with aluminum fittings.

RE-UPHOLSTERY

Abbott Upholstery
12 York Way, London N1 9AA.
T:0171-278 0118. F:0171-833 0870.
Traditional upholstery and specialist
contract work - pub seating, restaurant
chairs, even car seats. They can copy
existing upholstered furniture. Specialists
in leather re-upholstery.

Antique Leathers
Unit 2 Bennetts Field Trading Est,
Wincanton BA9 9DT.
T:01963-33163. F:01963-33164.
Specialist in leather re-upholstery.
They will re-do table and desk tops in
leather (with gold tooling), install or refurbish
wall panelling and padded doors.

Antique Restorations
The Old Wheelwright's Shop,
Brasted Forge, Brasted, Kent TN16 1JL.
T:01959-563863. F:01959-561262.
Traditional and modern re-upholstery
and leather covering.

Albert E Chapman
17 Crouch Hill, London N4 4AP.
T:0171-272 2536. F:0171-263-1033.
Traditional firm (established in 1930)
of upholsterers and curtain makers.
Also restoration service, fabric wall
covering and tented ceilings.

Classic Upholstery
Estate Yard, Upper Harlestone,
Northampton NN7 4EH.
T:01604-584556.
Upholstery of antique furniture:
loose covers and all aspects of re-
upholstery tackled, including leatherwork.

Jane Clayton & Co
Unit 12, Old Mills,
Paulton, Bristol BS18 5SU.
T:01761-412255. F:01761-413558.
Specialist soft furnishing workrooms.
Upholstered headboards in customers'
own fabrics.

Cover Up Designs
See entry under **CURTAIN MAKERS.**

The Easy Chair Co
30 Lyndhurst Rd, Worthing,
Sussex BN11 2DF.
T:01903-201081.F:01903-237840.
Specialist in re-upholstery, curtain making
and interior design. Mail order catalogue for
all sorts of upholstery and curtain sundries.

The Furnishing Workshop
146 Stanley Park Rd,
Carshalton, Surrey SM5 3JG.
T/F:0181-773 3950.

*** denotes
trade supplier.
Please phone
for retail outlets.** 149

Re-upholstery and soft furnishings; curtain-making; loose covers; traditional and modern upholstery.

Howard Chairs
30-31 Lyme St, London NW1 0EE.
T:0171-482 2156. F:0171-482 0068.
Provide a top quality re-upholstery and curtain making service. They manufacture an exclusive range of handmade upholstered furniture and will also undertake fabric walling or paper backing of fabrics.

Christopher Howe
93 Pimlico Rd, London SW1W 8PH.
T:0171-730 7987. F:0171-730 0157.
Antique dealer who has his own workshop which specialises in leather re-upholstery and re-making of desk tops.

Daniel Newlyn
11 West Street, London WC2H 9NH.
T/F:0171-379 8680.
Re-upholsterer who can tackle more unusual or modern designs.

Paine & Company
47-51 Barnsbury St, London N1 1TP.
T:0171-607 1176. F:0171-609 6201.
Interior designers and architects who have a retail showroom and can provide an in-house curtain making and re-upholstery service.

Charles Pateman and Company
2 Bittern Place, Coburg Road, London N22 6TP.
T:0181-889 1144.F:0181-889 0156.
Upholsterers who will also copy existing pieces and who can tackle all aspects of soft furnishings - curtain making, fabric walling .

The Revival Company
The Old Stores, The Green, Great Milton OX44 7NT.
T:0800-393689. F:01844-279080.
Branches covering W/SW/NW London, Middx, West Surrey, Berkshire, Bucks and Oxon. Traditional re-upholstery and leather work. Also curtain making and upholstery and carpet cleaning service.

Revival Upholstery
22 All Saints Rd, London W11 1HG.
T/F:0171-727 9843.
Traditional upholstery and loose covers.

David Richardson Oriental Carpets
26 Southgate, Chichester, Sussex PO19 1ES.
T:01243-533025. F:01243-782010.
Can cover a customer's chair in old or modern kelims or in any fabric. They also do kelim or fabric-covered stools.

Jill Saunders
46 White Hart Lane, London SW13 0PZ.
T:0181-878 0400. F:0181-876 2103.
Traditional re-upholstery and stockist of DIY upholstery sundries. They have a selection of fabrics to choose from for upholstery and curtains and also provide furniture restoration and repair of Lloyd Loom and wickerwork.

Upholstery Express
Unit 33, Liberty Close, Woolsbridge Ind Park, Three Legged Cross, Wimborne, Dorset.
T:01202-814500. F:01202-814600.
Known for speedy service, they will tackle commercial, office and domestic re-upholstery for anything from hotel groups and supermarket chains to domestic jobs. Also leather re-upholstery.

*Zodiac Upholstery
Unit F, 260-261 Riverside Business Centre, Haldane Place, London SW18 4UQ.
T/F:0181-874-4738.
Trade only upholsterers who also make headboards, pelmets,loose covers and manufacture sofas and chairs to order using traditional methods.

FABRIC WALLING

Adams & Co
See entry under CURTAIN MAKERS.

Albert E Chapman
See entry under RE-UPHOLSTERY.

The Holbein Collection at Titley & Marr
See entry under
CURTAIN POLES.
Reproduction 18th century carved wood fillets used to edge silk damask wallcoverings - they can be ordered in wood, hand painted or metallic finishes and cost from £25 per metre.

For additional help try the Association of Master Upholsterers & Soft Furnishers, Frances Vaughan House, 102 Commercial St, Newport, Gwent NP9 1LU. T:01633-215454. F:01633-244488.

* denotes trade supplier. Please phone for retail outlets.

Howard Chairs
See entry under RE-UPHOLSTERY.

Stephen La Grange and Justin Manley
556A King's Rd, London SW6 2DZ.
T:0171-736 6121. F:0171-352 7069.
Batoned fabric walling and tented
ceiling specialists.

Charles Pateman and Company
See entry under RE-UPHOLSTERY.

Jon Rhodes
See entry under RE-UPHOLSTERY.

Pierre Vuillemenot
56A Emmanuel Rd, London SW12
0HP.T/F:0181-673 2455. By appointment.
Trained in France in traditional fabric walling.

OTHER SPECIALIST SERVICES

Cadogan Company
95 Scrubs Lane, London NW10 6QU.
T:0181-960 8020. F:0181-960 4037.
Specialist cleaners who also repair
and re-make curtains.

Pilgrim Payne & Co
290-294 Latimer Rd, London W10 6QU.
T:0181-960 5656. F:0181-964 0598.
Specialist cleaning, repairs or re-making
of curtains.

Tracking and Hanging
5 Copthorne Ave, Clapham Park,
London SW12 0JZ.
T:0181-674 9142/0860-330191.
Specialists in just the tracking and
hanging of curtains - from one
window to a whole hotel.

HEATING & COOLING

ANTIQUE & NEW FIREPLACES

Robert Aagaard
Frogmire House, Stockwell Road,
Knaresborough, N.Yorks HG5 0JP.
T:01423-864805. F:01423-869356.
18th and 19th century fire surrounds plus
period reproductions and bespoke designs.
Restoration/installation service.

Amazing Grates
61-63 High Road, London N2 8AB.
T:0181-883 9590. F:0181-365 2053.
Georgian, Victorian, Edwardian and Art Deco
fireplaces in marble, stone or wood.
Restoration service and reproductions.

The Antique Fireplace Warehouse
194-202 Battersea Park Road,
London SW11 4ND.
T:0171-627 1410. F:0171-622 1078.
18th and 19th century wood, marble, cast-
iron and stone fireplaces plus reproductions
in marble and stone displayed in an 18,000
sq ft warehouse.

Arbon Interiors
102 Golborne Road, London W10 5PS.
T:0181-960 9787. Period and reproduction
fireplaces, in wood, stone and marble.
There are usually about fifty in stock.
Plus gas effect fires.

Architectural Antiques
1 York Street, Bedford, MK40 3RJ.
T:01234-213131. Early Georgian to
Edwardian fireplaces and surrounds.

Architectural Antiques
351 King Street. London W6 9NH.
T:0181-741 7883. F:0181-741 1109.
A selection of 300 marble and stone
fireplaces, mainly from the turn of the
century. Commissions undertaken.

Architectural Heritage
Taddington Manor, Taddington, Nr Cutsdean,
Cheltenham, Gloucs GL54 5RY.
T:01386-584414. F:01386-584236.
Specialists in stone fireplaces from the
16th -19th century. They also buy and sell
fine quality marble and mahogany antique
mantelpieces when available.

* denotes
trade supplier.
Please phone
for retail outlets. 153

Ashburton Marbles
Great Hall, North St,
Ashburton, Devon TQ13 7QD.
T/F:01364-653189.
6,000 sq ft showroom with 18th and 19th
century fireplaces in marble, wood and cast
iron. Fully restored surrounds, inserts,
firebaskets and coal and gas fires supplied.
In-house restoration. Export world-wide.

Nigel Bartlett
67 St Thomas Street, London SE1 3QX.
T:0171-378 7895. F:0171-378 0388.
Specialist in early English chimneypieces
and architectural antiques.

*Capital Fireplaces
The Old Grain Store, Nupend Business Park,
Old Knebworth, Herts SG3 6QJ.
T:01438-821138. F:01438-821157.
Wooden or cast iron reproduction
mantelpieces. Victorian, Arts & Crafts
(including William Morris designs), Art
Nouveau and Deco tiles; cast iron insets.

Clarke's of Buckfastleigh
rear of 32 Fore St,
Buckfastleigh, Devon TQ11 OAA.
T:01364-643060. Georgian and Victorian
marble and timber fireplaces, as well as a
reproduction range.

Crowther of Syon Lodge
Busch Corner, London Road,
Isleworth, Middx TW7 5BH.
T:0181-560 7978. F:0181-568 7572.
Period English and French mantelpieces.
Plenty of imposing Georgian, Regency and
Early Victorian examples. They recently sold
a rare English Rococo marble surround for
close to half a million pounds.

For antique fireplaces see also ARCHITECTURAL SALVAGE.

Cwt-y-Bugail Slate Quarries
Plas-y-Bryn, Wynne Rd, Blaenau Ffestiniog,
Gwynedd, Wales LL41 3DR.
T:01766-830204. F:01766-831105.
Full fireplaces or a simple hearth in
Welsh slate.

Design Fireplaces
113 Walnut Tree Close,
Guildford, Surrey GU1 4UQ.
T:01483-503333. F:01483-570013.
Manufacture their own range of marble,
cast iron and brick fireplaces; also French
quarried stone mantelpieces .

Dyfed Antiques and Architectural Salvage
The Wesleyan Chapel, Perrots Rd,
Haverfordwest SA61 2JD.
T:01437-760496. Chapel filled with
architectural salvage, Georgian, Victorian
and Art Deco fireplaces and slate surrounds.

Elgin and Hall
Adelphi House, Hunton nr Bedale,
N.Yorks DL8 1LY.
T:01677-450712. F:01677-450713.
Reproduction fire surrounds made of
hand-carved wood in a range of finishes,
including marble, stone and Swedish effect.

Farmington Fireplaces
Farmington Stone, Northleach,
Cheltenham, Gloucs GL54 3NZ.
T:01451-860280. F:01451-860115.
Bath stone and Cotswold stone
fireplaces, some custom designed
and intricately carved.

The Fire Place
31-35 Welford Rd, Leics LE2 7AD.
T/F:0116-254 6361. Large selection of
period reproductions and contemporary
surrounds in cast iron, timber, marble,
stone; gas fires installed.

Firecraft
1159 Melton Road, Syston, Leics LE7 2JS.
T:0116-2697030. F:0116-2697031.
Ten basic designs in Derbyshire or French
limestone. Specials can be made to the
customer's own specifications.

The Fireplace
Old Fire Station, Charnham Street,
Hungerford, Berks RG17 OEP.

T:01488-683420. Specialists in period fenders, irons and old pine surrounds.

Focal Point Original Fires
135 Eardley Road,
London SW16 6BB. T:0181-769 5496.
F:0181-769 8758. Specialists in original and reproduction Edwardian and Victorian fireplaces in cast iron, marble and wood.

H & D Fireplace Company
61 Essex Road, London N1 2SF.
T:0171-359 8179. F:0171-704 6891.
Antique Georgian, Victorian, Regency and some French fireplaces. Most are marble and start at around £400. Reproduction range in Carrara or Aquina marble.

Hallidays
The Old College, Dorchester on Thames, Wallingford, Oxon OX10 7HL.
T:01865-340028. F:01865-341149.
Traditional fine hand-carved pine mantelpieces.

Hayles & Howe
Picton House 25 Picton Street, Montpelier, Bristol BS6 5PZ.
T:01179-246673. F:01179-243928.
High quality reproductions of period fire surrounds in ornamental plaster.

Inglenook Canopy Company
5 Park View Close, Exhall, Warwicks CV7 9GN.
T:01203-319640. Canopies, fire baskets and chimney lining systems.

*Jetmaster Fires
Dimplex UK, Millbrook, Southampton SO15 0AW.
T:01962-841341. F:01703-771096.
Jetmaster supply fires that will burn solid fuel - either coal, gas or peat; also natural gas and liquid petroleum. Their Dimplex division manufactures electric and gas fires.

La Maison
410 St John Street, London EC1V 4NJ.
T/F:0171-837 6522.
Antique French (particularly Louis XV and XVI) marble mantelpieces; also period beds, mirrors, gilded provincial furniture and architectural details.

Manorhouse Stone
School Lane, Normanton-Le-Heath, Leics LE67 2TH.
T:01530-262999. F:01530-262515.
Stone fireplaces, reclaimed quarry tiles and old flagstones for hearths.

Marble Hill Fireplaces
70-72 Richmond Road, Twickenham, Middx TW1 3BE.
T:0181-892 1488. F:0181-891 6591.
Antique French marble fireplaces; also English and French reproductions in painted wood or marble. Plus bespoke mantelpieces.

Old Door and Fireplace Company
67-69 Essex Road, London N1 2SF.
T/F:0171-226 0910.
Period and reproduction cast iron, stone, marble and wood surrounds.

Old World Trading Company
565 Kings Road, London SW6 2EB.
T:0171-731 4708. F:0171-731 1291.
French 18th and 19th century marble, stone and wood examples plus grates, tongs and fire baskets.

Roger Pearson
Springwood House, Hockley Lane, Wingerworth, Chesterfield, Derbys S42 6QG.
T:01246-276393. Hand-carved marble chimneypieces and accessories.

H W Poulter & Son
279 Fulham Road, London SW10 9PZ.
T:0171-352 7268. F:0171-351 0984.
18th and 19th century marble, wood and stone chimneypieces and accessories.

Real Flame
80 New Kings Road, London SW6 4LT.
T:0171-731 2704. F:0171-736 4625.
Specialists in gas fires, reproduction fireplaces, grates and accessories. Fireplaces include Adam, Georgian hob-grate, Victorian inset and modern hole-in-the-wall styles.

Mark Ripley Antiques and Forge
Bridge Bungalow, Northbridge Street, Robertsbridge, E. Sussex TN 32 5NY.
T/F:01580-880324. Canopies, firebacks

For additional help try: The National Fireplace Association, 8th floor, Bridge House, Smallbrook Queensway, Birmingham B5 4JP. T:0121-643 1133. They supply a list of members and publish technical leaflets on chimneys and fireplaces (£2 each). Or 0800-521611 for the NFA Yearbook (£3) which includes a guide to fireplaces and recommended suppliers.

NASCO (National Association of Chimney Sweeps): 0800-833464. Can provide information about sweeps in your area.

* denotes trade supplier. Please phone for retail outlets. 155

and accessories for ingle-nook fireplaces, all made up from original patterns.

*Stovax
See entry under STOVES.
Faithful Victorian reproductions and excellent selection of tiles.

Thornhill Galleries
Rear of 78 Deodar Road, London SW15 2NJ.
T:0181-874 2101. F:0181-877 0313.
English and French reproduction wood fireplaces. High quality 16th-19th century antique chimneypieces in wood, stone or marble.

Townsend's
81 Abbey Road, London NW8 OAE.
T:0171-624 4756. F:0171-372 3005.
Antique fire surrounds - from stone to 'Chinoiserie'. Art Nouveau tiles; reproduction mantelpieces.

Troika Architectural Mouldings
Troika House, 41 Clun Street,
Sheffield S4 7JS.
T:01142-753222. F:01142-753781.
Reproduction fire surrounds manufactured from non-combustible plaster, suitable for gas, electric or open fires. Can be supplied with marble hearths and back panels.

Welcome Fireplace Company
44-46 Seaward Street, Glasgow G41 1HJ.
T:0141-429 8242. F:0141-429 1067.
Large selection of period originals salvaged from old houses including cast iron pieces. 50-60 reproduction marble and stone mantels on display at any given time. 'Living flame' fires as well as modern designs.

*Winther Browne
Nobel Road, Eley Estate, London N18 3DX.
T:0181-803 3434. F:0181-807 0544.
Range of carved wood reproduction fire surrounds in pine, oak, and a mahogany-effect.

GAS FIRES

AA Coal & Log Fires
63A Langford Road, London SW6 2LF.
T:0171-371 5070. F:0171-371 0883.
Neville Stephens designs amazingly realistic gas log fires as well as surreal versions like burning wads of 'money'.

Bower & Child
91 Wakefield Road, Huddersfield HD5 9AB.
T:01484-425416. F: 01484-517353.
Large range of gas fires; Aga and Rayburn specialists and selection of fireplace accessories.

Focus
Diligence International,
Highbank House, Upper Somborne,
Stockbridge, Hants SO20 6QZ.
T/F: 01794-388335.
Avant garde, ultra modern fireplaces designed by Dominique Imbert.

Petit Roque
5A New Road, Croxley Green,
Rickmansworth, Herts WD3 3EJ.
T:01923-779291/720968.
F:01923-896728. For over 20 years Petit Roque has been installing coal-effect gas fires.Their showroom has 13 different fires on view. They also make surrounds in marble, slate or stone. Prices are from £170 to £4000.

The Platonic Fireplace Company
40 Peterborough Road, London SW6 3BN.
T:0171-610 9440. Designers of the first decorative gas fire for contemporary interiors. Instead of fake logs there are geologs - ceramic spheres, cubes, cones and prisms. Also available is a chrome-finished grate to hold them.

Real Flame
See entry under
ANTIQUE & NEW FIREPLACES.

*Stovax
See entry under STOVES.

Town and Country Fires (Pikering)
See entry under STOVES.
Manufacturers of coal-effect gas fires.

*Trident Systems (UK)
Industrial Unit 12, Lea Hall Enterprise Park,
Armitage Road, Rugeley, Staffs WS15 1PG.
T:0500-400403. F:01889-578542.
'Reality' power-flue gas fires for chimneyless sites. Unique system allows installation without an outside wall.

CLUB FENDERS

Acres Farm
Acres Farm, Bradfield,
Reading, Berks RG7 6JH.
T:01734-744305. F:01734-744012.
Selection of fenders made to order.

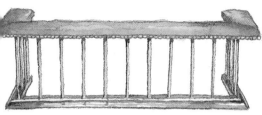

Architectural Components
4-8 Exhibition Road, London SW7 2HF.
T:0171-581 2401. F:0171-589 4928.
Selection of brass fenders in a variety of
styles, club fenders and iron fireside
accessories.

Robin Gage
Unit 7, Talina Centre,
23 Bagley's Lane, London SW6 2BW.
T:0171-610 6612. F:0171-736 1020.
Custom made fenders - five basic
designs in a variety of materials,
finishes, columns and upholstery.

STOVES

*Aga-Rayburn
P O Box 30, Ketley,
Telford, Shropshire TF1 4DD.
T:01952-642000. F:01952-641961.
Coalbrookdale cast-iron stoves in a range
of sizes and a variety of fuel options.

*Arrow Fires
The Fireworks, North Mills,
Bridport, Dorset DT6 3BE.
T:01308-427234. F:01308-423441.
Large range of wood burning multi-fuel
and gas stoves.

The Ceramic Stove Company
4 Earl St, Oxford OX2 0JA.
T/F:01865-245077. Tall Scandinavian tile-
clad stoves based on 18th century designs.
Plus antique stoves imported from Sweden.

They also have a new English-made range
which includes stoves, bread ovens, pizza
ovens and barbecues.

John Churchill
The Forge, Capton, Nr Dartmouth, Devon.
T:01803-712535. Blacksmith who
specialises in making multi-heating stoves
with extras like hot plates
or towel rails.

Clearview Showroom
Dinham House,
Ludlow, Shropshire SY8 1EH.
T:01584-878100.
F:01584-872010.
Range of four stoves with
glass doors so you can see the flames.
Unique smoke-control systems means
they can burn wood in smokeless zones
like London.

Country Stoves
Lower Rd, Cookham, Berks SL6 9EH.
T:01628-528262. F:01628-528265.
Stock the tiny cast-iron Morso Squirrel
stove made by the Danish company NA
Christensen, as well as Clearview, Godin,
Charmwood, Vermont Castings, Stovax,
Jotul, Yeoman, Euroheat and Calfire Stanley.

Dovre Castings
Unit 1, Wefton Works, Wefton Lane,
Tyseley, Birmingham B11 3RP.
T:0121-706 7600. F:0121-706 9182.
Wood-burning and multi-fuel stoves in
simple styles.

Fuelmizas A.T.
Bee Mill, Preston Rd,
Ribchester, Nr Preston, Lancs PR3 3XJ.
T/F:01254-878368. Showroom for over 50
multi-fuel stoves, cookers, gas coal-effect
fires, surrounds, flues and accessories.

Gazco
Osprey Rd, Sowton Ind Estate,
Exeter, Devon EX2 7JG.
T: 01392-444030. F:01392-444148.
Coal and log effect gas fires for almost any
fireplace including made to measure designs
and a version for houses with no chimney or
flue. Closed cast iron gas stoves and
canopied convector fires.

* denotes
trade supplier.
Please phone
for retail outlets. 157

House of Stone
Redroof, Huncote Road,
Croft in Leics LE9 3GU. T:01455-286150.
F:01455-286151.
Reproductions of 19th century
French stoves and attractive
gas heaters which can operate
without a flue.

Kedddy-Poujoulat
Silverlands, Holloway Hill,
Chertsey, Surrey KT16 OAE.
T:01932-570620. F:01932-570702.
English and Swedish contemporary
and traditional stoves. Also
complete chimney lining systems,
chimney fans and other parts for
fireplaces.Agents for other stove
manufacturers.

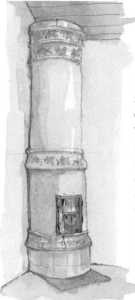

Kyte Marketing
Unit 1, Golden Acres, Woolfords
Lane, Elstead, Surrey GU8 6LL.
T:01252-702351.
F:01252-519267. Sole UK
distributors for the Swedish ceramic
wood burning stoves by Cronspisen.
They are energy-efficient and approved
for use in smokeless zones. Prices range
from £1998 to £4000.

LHA-SCAN
28 Darmonds Green,
West Kirby, Wirral L48 5DU.
T/F: 0151-625 0504.
Modern Danish stoves by SCAN production.
There are 20 designs in wood or multi-fuel
burning versions.

Modus Design
16 The Warren, Radlett,
Herts WD7 7DX.
T:01923-210442. F:01923-853486.
Modern wood burning stoves. Fireplace
designs in glass, steel, brass, marble, or
metal - either free-standing, suspended
or wall based.

Morley Marketing
Marsh Lane, Ware, Herts SG12 9QB.
T:01920-468002. F:01920-463893.
Good choice of enamel wood burning or fuel
stoves including the Morley cast-iron range

which is equipped with a hot-plate.
French 'Petit Godin' range.

*Morso
4 Wychwood Court, Cotswold Business
Village, Moreton-in-Marsh, Gloucs GL56 0JQ.
T:01608-652288. F:01608-652255.
Large selection of cast iron multi-fuel stoves
including the famous 'Squirrel' from this
company which has been in business for
over a hundred years.

Norfolk Stove Company
Street Farm House, Fakenham Rd,
Morton on thc Hill, Norwich NR9 5SP.
T:01603-860762. Showroom for many
stove manufacturers including the traditional
cast iron multi-fuel 'Long-life' range.

*Ouzledale Foundry Company
PO Box 4, Barnoldswick near Colne, Lancs
BB8 6BN. T:01282-813235. F:01282-
816876. Traditional cast-iron stoves.

*Stovax
Falcon Rd, Sowton Ind Estate,
Exeter, Devon EX2 7LF.
T:01392-474011. F:01392-219932.
Reproduction Victorian cast-iron fireplaces
which can be installed with Gazco 'living
flame' gas fires (see Gazco); plus nine styles
of surrounds, reproduction Victorian tiles
and a range of fireplace care products.
Distributor of Norwegian Jotul stoves.

W. Tierney
Pither Products, 7 Berkeley Close,
Moor Lane, Staines, Middx TW19 6ED.
T/F:01784-457896.
Their Pither Studio Stove was designed
in the 1920s but looks contemporary.

Town & Country Fires (Pikering)
128-129 Eastgate,
Pickering, N.Yorks YO18 7DW.
T:01751-474803. F:01751-475205.
Manufacturer of coal-effect gas stoves and
suppliers of fuel stoves by Clearview and
Franco Belge. Fireplaces, installations
and site visits.

Vermont Castings
VCW International, Unit 3a, Osprey Court,
Hawkfield Business Park, Whitchurch,
Bristol BS14 0BB.

T:0117-9641234.F:0117-9647714.
Cast iron wood stoves for coal, multi-fuel and natural gas. There is also an environmentally friendly catalytic version.

Wye Valley Stoves and Fireplaces
Station Street, Ross-on-Wye HR9 7AG.
T:01989-565870. F:01989-567003.
At least 70 varieties of stoves and fireplaces on display in this showroom which was once an old Victorian brewery,

*Yeoman Stoves
20 Trusham Rd, Exeter EX2 8DF.
T:01392-425252. F:01392-413519.
Over 300 stockists nationwide carry Yeoman's traditional steel stoves in wood burning, multi-fuel or gas versions.

RADIATORS

*AEL (Acoustics & Environmetrics)
1 Berkeley Court, Manor Park,
Runcorn, Cheshire WA7 1TQ.
T:01928-579068. F:01928-579523.
Sectional radiators in aluminium.
They can be made as long as you like.

Benson Environmental
47 Central Ave, West Molesey,
Surrey KT8 2QZ. T:0181-783 0033.
F:0181-783 0140. Perimeter and underfloor heating for domestic or contract use.

Bisque
15 Kingsmead Square, Bath, Avon BA1 2AE.
T:01225- 469244. F:01225-444708.
And at: 244 Belsize Rd, London NW6 4BT.
T:0171-328 2225. F:0171-328 9845.
Specialists in designer radiators in more than 2000 colours as well as metallic and nickel-plated finishes. Anything from slim panels that run along the skirting boards to floor to ceiling tubular versions. The most sculptural is the X-tream which consists of sweeping pipes in the shape of an X.

*Caradon Stelrad
Stelrad House, Marriott Rd, Swinton,
Mexborough, S Yorks S64 8BN.
T:01709-578878. F:01709-572200.
Steel panel radiators, tubular towel rails and combined radiators and rails.

Clyde Combustions
Head Office, Cox Lane,
Chessington, Surrey KT9 1SL.
T:0181-391 2020. F:0181-397 4598.
Industrial boilers are one side of their business. They also manufacture traditional cast iron column radiators and tubular contemporary styles.

Edwins Plumbing and Heating Supplies
21 All Saint's Rd, London W11 1HE.
T:0171-221 3550. F:0171-243 0206.
Good one-stop shop for radiators and plumbing items.

Faral Radiators
Tropical House, Charlwoods Rd, East Grinstead, W.Sussex RH19 2HJ.
T:01342-315757. F:01342-315362.
Manufacturers and distributors of a large range of die-cast aluminium and steel Italian radiators in a variety of styles, colours and heights.

Gunning Engineering
16 Radford Crescent,
Billericay, Essex CM12 0DG.
T:01277-652177. F:01277-650320.
Manufacturers of industrial heater coils in steel, warm air curtains for factories and the 'Package' heater for commercial use. They also manufacture and distribute steel gilled-tube radiators for domestic sites.

*Hudevad
Hudevad House, 130-132 Terrace Rd,
Walton-on-Thames, Surrey KT12 2EA.
T:01932-247835. F:01932-247694.
Manufacturers of radiators for domestic, commercial and industrial use, the majority of which are individually made for each installation. Radiators can be made straight, curved or angled, to be used in any location - up a stairwell, on a ceiling or around a column.

ICC (Internal Climate Control)
Unit 1, Walnut Tree Park, Walnut Tree Close,
Guildford, Surrey GU1 4TR.
T:01483-37000. F:01483-37500.
Manufacture the 'Heat Profile Skirting Heating System' fueled either by electricity or hot water.

* denotes
trade supplier.
Please phone
for retail outlets. 159

MHS Radiators

35 Nobel Square, Burnt Mills Ind Estate,
Basildon, Essex SS13 1LT.
T:01268-591010. F:01268-728202.
Simple and ornate Victorian style cast iron
column radiators (assembled to virtually any
length), slab-column radiators with smooth
'linear' or 'fleck' textures, radiators with an
open construction to be used even in front
of windows and bathroom towel radiators.

Old Door and Fireplace Company

67-69 Essex Rd, London N1 2SF.
T/F: 0171-226 0910. Stock old cast
iron radiators, both plain and ornate.

*PMP

Stanton Square, Stanton Way,
London SE26 5AB.
T:0181-676 0911. F:0181-659 1017.
Range of Victorian style column radiators in
cast iron. Also tubular steel, aluminium and
flat faced high-output mild steel radiators.

*Potterson Myson

Eastern Ave, Team Valley Trading Estate,
Gateshead, Tyne & Wear NE11 0PG.
T:0191-491 4466. F:0191-491 7330.
Four types of radiators: round top, seam
top, the 'LST' flat-face and the 'Plan' flat
convector radiator for kickspaces.

Radiating Style

Unit 15, Derby Road Ind. Estate,
Hounslow, Middx TW3 3UQ.
T:0181-577 9111. F:0181-577 9222.
Radiators with visual appeal, including
leaping dolphin designs and Matisse or
Picasso-inspired brass and copper tubing.

Strebel

1F Albany Park Ind. Estate, Frimley Rd,
Camberley, Surrey GU15 2PL.
T:01276-685422. F:01276-685405.
One of the largest selections of column
radiators in the country.

Zehnder

Unit 6, Invincible Road,
Farnborough, Hants GU14 7QU.
T:01252-515151. F:01252-522528.
Classical multi-column radiators in mild
steel. Also low skirting and either horizontal
or vertical panel radiators.

UNDERFLOOR HEATING

Flo-Rad Heating Systems

Subsidiary of Radiant Surfaces, Unit 1
Horseshoe Business Park, Lye Lane,
Brickett Wood, Herts AL2 3TA.
T:01923-893025. F:01923-670723.
Warm water, low pressure underfloor
'Thermoboard' heating.

Kampmann

47 Central Avenue,
West Molesey, Surrey KT8 2QZ.
T:0181-783 0033. F:0181 783 0140.
Suppliers of underfloor heating, floor
and sill-line grilles, and perimeter heating.
They can also recommend installers.

Invisible Heating Systems

PO Box 50, Ullapool,
RossShire, Scotland IV26 2ZD.
T:01854-613161. F:01854-613160.
Total heating system from boilers to Grohe
taps and valves. Underfloor and wall heating
specialists. They also supply specially
adapted units to integrate with solar panels.

Marston & Langinger

192 Ebury Street. London SW1W 8UP.
T:0171-824 8818. F:0171-824 8757.
Have developed an underfloor heating
system for their conservatories. Warm air
comes through smart cast-iron grilles which
are also available separately. The system
costs between £150-£200 per metre
complete.

Multibeton

15 Oban Court, Hurricane Way,
Wickford, Essex SS11 8YB.
T:01268-561688. F:01268-561690.
Underfloor and perimeter heating for the
commercial and residential sector. Full
service to include supply and installation.
They also manufacture and sell their own
convector heater.

ThermoFloor (GB)

32 Cavendish Road,
Bognor Regis, W.Sussex PO21 2JN.
T:01243-864581. F:01243-860379.
Water-borne or electric underfloor
heating systems.

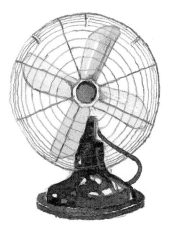

FANS & AIR CONDITIONING

Aero
96 Westbourne Grove, London W2 5RT.
T:0171-221 1950. F:0171-221 2555.
Stainless steel 'Tornado' fan.

The Air Improvement Centre
23 Denbigh St, London SW1V 2HF.
T:0171-834 2834. F:0171-630 8485.
Humidifiers for furniture, dehumidifiers for
damp, air purifiers and ionisers, mobile air
conditioners.Range of non-electric
humidifiers designed to hang on radiators.

Fans and Spares Group
Peartree House, Peartree Lane,
Dudley, W Midlands DY2 0QU.
T:01384-481015. F:01384-70435.
Air conditioning supplier with a limited
selection of white colonial-type ceiling fans
and kitchen, bathroom and toilet fans.

Fantasia
Unit B, The Flyers Way,
Westerham, Kent TN16 1DE.
T:01959-564440. F:01959-564829.
Large selection of wood and cane, white
and brass or chrome ceiling fans. Some
incorporate light fittings.

Freud
198 Shaftesbury Ave, London WC2H 8JL.
T:0171-831 1071. F:0171-831 3062.
Italian-style fans by the Indian company
National Winder. The range is called Cinni
after the daughter of one of the makers.
Desk, ceiling and pedestal versions.

Ocean
Freepost LON811, London SW8 4BR.
Orderline: 0800-132 985.
F:0171-498 8898. Mail order only.
High-powered (and smart) American
air circulators which can be free-
standing or wall-mounted.

Out of Time
21 Canonbury Lane, London N1 2AF.
T/F:0171-354 5755.
1920s to 1950s reconditioned
American and British fans - floor,
standard and desk models.

Themes & Variations
231 Westbourne Grove,
London W11 25E. T:0171-727 5531.
F:0171-221 6378. Original 1930s
fans by industrial manufacturers
Marelli, in black bakelite and brass.

Xpelair
PO Box 220, Deykin Ave,
Witton, Birmingham B6 7JH.
T:0121-327 1984. F:0121-327 8292.
Ventilation, heating and air circulation
specialists. Range of cooker hoods.

OTHER SPECIALIST SERVICES & SUPPLIERS

Cadogan Company
95 Scrubs Lane, London NW10 6QU.
T:0181-960 8020.F:0181-960 4037
Can restore marble fireplaces.

J & R Marble Company
9 Lammas Road, Leyton,
London E10 7QT. T:0181-539 6471.
F:0181-539 9264. Restorers of
marble, granite and slate.

H W Poulter & Son
See entry under **ANTIQUE & NEW
FIREPLACES.** Restorers of antique
marble fireplaces.

The Specialist Chimney People
61A Horseshoe Lane, Garston,
Herts WD2 7HH.
T:01923-211072.
Reline and reseal chimney flues.

**The Solar Trade
Association,
Pengillan, Lerryn,
Lostwithiel,
Cornwall
PL22 0QE.
T/F:01208-873518
can give help and
information on
solar heating
suppliers and
installers.**

*** denotes
trade supplier.
Please phone
for retail outlets.** 161

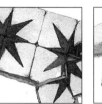

12

RESTORERS & CRAFTSMEN

BUILDING RESTORERS

Abbey Heritage
Dartford House, Two Rivers Ind. Estate,
Station Lane, Witney, Oxon OX8 6BH.
T:01993-709699. F:01993-709959.
Facade cleaning and restoration; they will
undertake new projects in terracotta,
faience, granite and marble.

David Ball Restoration
104A Consort Rd, London SE15 2PR.
T:0171-277 7775. F:0171-635 0556.
Building facade cleaning and restoration.

London Brick Cleaning Service
2 King James Ave, Cuffley, Herts EN6 4LR.
T/F:01707-875303. Restoration and
cleaning of brick and stone facades.

Rattee & Kett
Purbeck Rd, Cambs CB2 2PG.
T:01223-248061. F:01223-412869.
Conservators and restorers of historic
buildings: stonemasonry, carving
and sculpture, leadwork, joinery
and letter cutting.

Renaissance Partnership
Queen Anne House,
Charlotte St, Bath BA1 2NE.
T:01225-314426/331254.
F:01225-311362. Conservation consultants
who specialise in the repair and alteration of
old buildings: structural engineering, quantity
surveying, timber frame joinery, stone
masonry and painting in authentic colours.
They also advise on finance applications
to the state for VAT relief for
protected buildings.

St. Blaise
Westhill Barn, Evershot,
Dorchester DT2 0LD.
T:01935-83662. F:01935-83017.
Consultants on the best process for the
restoration and conservation of stonework,
ornamental plasterwork, fine joinery and
leadwork. They use traditional materials
to repair old buildings.

Stonehealth
73 London Rd, Marlborough, Wilts SN8 2AN.
T/F:01672-511515. This company advises

* denotes
trade supplier.
Please phone
for retail outlets. 163

on building restoration and markets environmentally friendly, biodegradable products to use for the cleaning of brick, stone, concrete and timber. One of their products removes paint in flakes without damaging plants on the exterior of buildings.

Stonewest
Lamberts Place,
St. James Rd,
Croydon CR9 2HX.
T:0181-684 6646.
F:0181-684 9323.
Masonry cleaning and restoration service - both brick and stone; also cleaning and restoration of internal marble, granite and stone. Will execute commissions in London and the South East of England.

S & J Whitehead
Derker St, Lower Moor,
Oldham OL1 4EE.
T:0161-624 4395.
F:0161-627 2952. Specialist conservation and restoration of stonemasonry and leadwork in the North West of England. Clients include The National Trust.

STONE/MARBLE

Anthemion
PO Box 6, Teddington, Middx TW11 8XU.
T/F:0181-943 4000.
Team of craftsmen - masons, sculptors, silversmiths, blacksmiths and gilders. Recent commissions include the restoration of an 18th century marble Rococo chimneypiece and the replicas of 19th century carved Bath stone brackets.

Plowden & Smith
190 St. Ann's Hill, London SW18 2RT.
T:0181-874 4005. F:0181-874 7248.
This company's 40 restorers and conservators can turn their hands to almost anything: ancient and modern metal, marble and stone, sculpture, bronzes, miniatures, porcelain, paintings, furniture, gilding, enamel, ivory, lacquer, pietra dura, mother of pearl - even a frescoed ceiling. They can also deal with other specialist areas like the restoration of fire damaged objects.

HW Poulter & Son
279 Fulham Rd, London SW10 9PZ.
T:0171-352 7268. F:0171-351 0984.
Restorers of antique marble table tops, sculpture and fireplaces. They can also make new stone or marble table tops and bases.

The Scagliola Company
Chapeltown Business Centre,
231 Chapeltown Rd,
Leeds, W.Yorks LS7 3DX.
T:0113-262 6811. F:0113-262 5448.
Manufacturers and restorers of scagliola artefacts like tazzas and urns, as well as table tops, columns, panels, floors and inlays.

Southern Stone Restorations
Unit 59, Smithbrook Kilns,
Cranley, Surrey GU6 8JJ.
T:01483-277969. F:01483-268141.
Stonemasons who specialise in historic repair and conservation. Commissions include monuments for English Heritage and for the Church. They will also build new stone stairs or carve fireplaces.

POTTERY & PORCELAIN

China Repairers
64 Charles Lane, London NW8 7SB.
T:0171-722 8407. There are four experts at this workshop which has been trading for over 40 years. They also run one or two month china restoration courses.

Rosemary Hamilton
44 Moreton St, London SW1V 2PB.
T:0171-828 5018. F:0171-828 1325.
Porcelain and pottery repair.

Brett Manley and Ann Sams
Basement, 183 Ladbroke Grove,
London W10 6HH.
T:0181-969 8683. Will tackle all kinds of china repairs from pottery to fine porcelain. Minimum charge of £18 per item. Free quotes on all jobs. Open between 1-6 p.m.

Cynthia McNair China Restoration
17 Elm Park Gardens,
Selsdon, Surrey CR2 8RW.
T/F:0181-651 1890. By appointment.
Will visit to give estimates locally.
Nationwide service by post.

Rose Hill Restorations of Chobham
See entry under METAL/SILVER.

LIGHTING

**Chandelier Cleaning
& Restoration Services**
Gypsy Mead, Fyfield, Essex CM5 0BB.
T:01277-899444. F:01277-899642.
Restorers of fine period chandeliers. Their
team of glass blowers, cutters and gilders
can restore all glass and metalwork, down to
the smallest replacement drops. Customers
include royal households and British
embassies worldwide. They recently
catalogued all the chandeliers in the White
House. They also make chandeliers in
composition, glass, gilt and wood.

Fritz Fryer Antique Lighting
12 Brookend St,
Ross-on-Wye, Hereford HR9 7EG.
T:01989-567416. F:01989-566742.
Specialist in antique lighting. Will restore
customers' own antique lighting in their
workshops.

**London Glassblowing Workshop
(Peter Layton Associates)**
See entry under GLASS.

Period Brass Lights
9A Thurloe Place, London SW7 2RZ.
T/F:0171-589 8305. Old and new crystal
chandeliers, plus some in brass or bronze;

reproduction Tiffany table lamps; large
selection of wall lights; picture lights; desk
lamps; silk lampshades. You can bring in
your chandelier and they will wash each
piece by hand and do any necessary repairs.
Large jobs done in situ. Full cleaning and
restoration service for other light fittings.

W Sitch & Co
48 Berwick St, London W1V 4JD.
T:0171-437 3776. Restoration of 19th
century lighting; they convert vases into
lamps, restore glass chandeliers and will
silver-plate any fitting.

Wilkinson
See entry under GLASS.
Rewiring and restoration of chandeliers.
Replacement glass drops.

METAL/SILVER

Anthemion
See entry under STONE.
They have reinstated the armature of an
18th century lead statue of Mercury.

Antique Restorations
The Old Wheelwright's Shop, Brasted Forge,
Brasted, Westerham, Kent TN16 1JL.
T:01959-563863. F:01959-561262.
Manufacturers of 800 reproduction 'Brass
and Foundry Castings' for furniture, doors
and clocks reproduced (down to the
blemishes) from 17th to 20th century
fittings. Antique Restorations are specialists
in metalwork repair, but they also tackle re-
upholstery and French and wax polishing.

Casting Repairs
Marine House, Hipper Street South,
Chesterfield S40 1SS.
T:01246-277656. F:01246-206519.
Cracked and damaged castings repaired -
from bollards to pumps, including decorative
and structural ironwork.

Paul Dennis & Sons
Penllwyn-yr-Hendy, Heol Senni,
Nr Brecon, Powys LD3 8SU.
T:01874-636696. F:01874-638970.
Specialist in the restoration of antique cast
and wrought ironwork. Nationwide service.

See also
Antique Lighting.

*** denotes
trade supplier.
Please phone
for retail outlets.** 165

Rupert Harris
Studio 5C, 1 Fawe St, London E14 6PD.
T:0171-987 6231/0171-515 2020.
F:0171-987 7994. Conservators for all the metalwork for National Trust properties. Recent commissions include restoration of the lions in Trafalgar Square. They restore anything from arms and armour to monumental sculptures, bronzes, silver, lead and decorative ironwork.

Langfords
Vault 8-10, The London Silver Vaults, Chancery Lane, London WC2A 1QS. T:0171-242 5506. F:0171-405 0431. Specialise in repairing, replating, embossing and engraving silver. Supply replacement blue glass liners for salt cellars. Silver matching and hire service.

Plowden & Smith
See entry **STONE/MARBLE.** Ancient and modern metalwork restoration including gold, silver, bronze and iron. Removal of encrustation from ancient bronzes. Uncrushing and repair of ancient metal. They will also make small castings as replacements for missing furniture fittings.

Richard Quinnell
Rowhurst Forge, Oxshott Rd, Leatherhead, Surrey KT22 0EN. T:01372-375148. F:01372-386516. Restores wrought iron, cast iron, bronze, brass and other base metals.

Rose Hill Restorations of Chobham
T/F:01276-858171. By appointment. Silver restored and replated and small copper and brass items tackled. Porcelain and china repairs. They will also clean glass decanters, repair stoppers and chipped glass. Collection and delivery in the Home Counties.

Verdigris
Arch 290, Crown St, London SE5 0UR. T:0171-703 8373. F:0171-708 5740. Metalwork restoration including colouring, patination, plating and repairs of bronzes, chandeliers, ormolu, pewter, copper and brass. They also undertake gilding and lacquering.

For other restorers and cleaners of textiles and carpets see also SPECIALIST SERVICES - Specialist Cleaners and ANTIQUE DEALERS - Textiles and Carpets & Rugs

**or contact:
The Rug Restorers' Association
T:01935-816479.**

**BORDA
(The British Oriental Rug Dealers' Association)
T:01753-623000
gives advice on
Oriental rug dealers
across the country
and on cleaning,
repairs and
valuations.**

TEXTILES & CARPETS

David Bamford Marketing
The Workhouse, Presteign Ind. Estate, Powys LD8 2UF. T:01544-267849 F:01544-260530. Cleaners, restorers and conservators of Oriental rugs and textiles including needlepoint and petit point. They also weave bespoke handmade carpets. Clients include The National Trust.

Behar Profex
St. Albans Place, Upper St, London N1 0NX. T:0171-226 0144. F:0171-359 4795. Skilled cleaning of antique carpets and tapestries with purified water; all repairs and weaving undertaken, including mending cigarette burns.

Jen Jones
Pontbrendu, Llanybydder, Ceredigion, Wales SA40 9UJ. T:01570-480610. F:01570-480112. Quilt washing and restoration service.

John Maclean
112 Thirlestane Road, Edinburgh EH9 1AS. T:0131-447 4225. Specialist in the conservation of hand woven carpets and rugs. He has worked on historic houses for The National Trust of Scotland and also undertakes private commissions anywhere in Britain and Ireland.

The Royal School of Needlework
Apartment 12A, Hampton Court Palace, East Molesey, Surrey KT8 9AU. T:0181-943 1432. F:0181-943 4910. Restorers of tapestries, embroidery and canvas work.

The Textile Restoration Studio
2 Talbot Rd, Bowdon, Altrincham, Cheshire WA14 3JD. T/F: 0161-928 0020. This company will tackle anything from small embroideries and samplers to large Aubussons. On site consultations. Mail-order catalogue of materials related to textile conservation: non-ionic detergents, iron mould removers, finely curved needles and thread, acid-free tissue paper, storage boxes and other items

LEATHER

Antique Leathers
Unit 2, Bennetts Field Trading Estate,
Wincanton BA9 9DT.
T:01963-33163. F:01963-33164.
Traditional leather re-upholstery including
horsehair-filled cushions; re-lining of leather
desk tops, writing boxes and bureau falls
and restoration of bellows and screens.

Brighton Regency Leathers
The Parade, Valley Drive,
Brighton BN1 5FQ.
T:01273-557418. F:01273-561169.
Can provide by mail order nine shades
of standard coloured desk leather,
with a choice of 30 designs that
can be tooled in gilt.

Restorations
See entry under **FURNITURE**.

The Leather Conservation Centre
34 Guildhall Rd, Northampton NN1 1EW.
T:01604-232723. F:01604-602070.
Recent commissions have included the
conservation of an 18th century leather
screen from Highclere Castle in Berkshire
and a number of carriages owned by the
National Trust. They can tackle wallhangings,
decorative screens, furniture, upholstery,
costumes - even harnesses and saddlery.

FURNITURE

Anita Marquetry
Unit 7, Ddole Road Ind. Estate,
Llandrindod Wells, Powys LD1 6DF.
T:01597-825505. F:01597-824484.
Restores marquetry and veneers and
repairs metal banding and brass and
metal inlays on furniture.

Antique Restorations
See entry under **METAL/SILVER**.

Ballantyne Booth
Cadogan House,
Hythe Rd, London NW10 6RS.
T:0181-960 3255. F:0181-960 4567.
Restoration, waxing and polishing of cabinet-
work, and repair of veneers, leatherwork,
carvings, gilding and metalwork.

Beechams Furniture
Unit 2 Romside Commercial Centre,
149 North St, Romford, Essex RM1 1ED.
T:01708-745778. F:01708-764328.
Makes chair frames, tables and cabinets to
order and undertakes furniture restoration
and French polishing.

Jean Burhouse Furniture
The Old Sawmill, Inver,
Dunkeld, Perth PH8 0JR.
T:01350-727723. F:01350-727261.
Bespoke furniture makers and restoration
specialists. They also supply materials for
restoration including over 80 types of timber,
brass cabinet hardware, wood-finishing
products and wood-carving and gilding tools,
even environmentally-friendly floor polishes.

The Cane Store
207 Blackstock Rd, London N5 2LL.
T/F:0171-354 4210. Restorers of
canework. They supply bamboo and cane
poles, sheets of woven cane, chair cane,
basket cane, seagrass, rush, raffia
and willow.

Canework and Rush Restoration
53 Macfarlane Rd, London W12 7JY.
T:0181-749 7615. Restorers of period cane
furniture, modern pieces with pre-woven
loom cane and chairs with natural rush.

Carvers & Gilders
9 Charterhouse Works,
Eltringham St, London SW18 1TD.
T:0181-870 7047. F:0181-874 0470.
Specialists in wood carving and gilding.
Traditional techniques are used for both
restoration work (at the Royal Palaces,

* denotes
trade supplier.
Please phone
for retail outlets. 167

Uppark and Harewood House) and for new commissions. The workshop tackles fireplaces, doors, cornices, architraves, mirror frames and furniture.

A Dunn
The White House, 8 Wharf Rd, Chelmsford, Essex CM2 6LU. T:01245-354452. F:01245-494991. Specialist work in Boulle and marquetry.They have restored the marquetry panels for the Orient Express; they also produce a large range of inlays for cabinet makers.

Cliff Fuller
7 Kingsmere Park, London NW9 8PJ. T:0181-205 0329. Repairwork of traditional and modern cane furniture, including rush seating. Specialist restoration of Danish 'Muller' chairs.

Joan Gilbert Cane & Rush Seating
50 Ashbourne Rd, Derby DE22 3AD. T:01332-344363. Will undertake all cane, rush and seagrass repairs including work to chairs, settees and bedheads. All patterns of cane can be reproduced (single set, double set, sunset patterns, hanging medallions, blind holes and French close caning) using split cane from Indonesia and English rush.

J A Harnett Antique Restoration
4 Lancaster Stables, Lambolle Place, Hampstead, London NW3 4PH. T:0171-722 2470. Mainly restoration of 18th and 19th century furniture; marquetry, carvings, French polishing, gilding, leather and baize table lining; repair of tortoiseshell and mother-of-pearl inlay. Also metal craft objects and furniture.

HJ Hatfield & Son
42 St. Michael's St, London W2 1QP. T:0171-723 8265. F:0171-706 4562. Restorers of English and French 17th-19th century antique furniture (including lacquer work). They also have metal workers, wood-turners and upholsterers.

K Restorations
2A Ferdinand Place, London NW1 8EE. T:0171-482 4021. F:0171-284 2806 Antique furniture repair including re-upholstery, French polishing and gilding. They have seven shades of hand dyed leather in eight tooled designs which they can supply by mail order. Also oil painting restoration.

W Lusty & Sons
Hoo Lane, Chipping Camden, Gloucs GL55 6AU. T:01386-841333. F:01386-841322. Manufacturers of Lloyd Loom Furniture since 1922, they can also strip old pieces using a special technique which avoids wetting (from £30 a chair) and have a repainting service.

M & F Caners
22 Inks Green, London E4 9EL. T:0181-527 5797. For the past 30 years M & F Caners have been re-rushing and re-caning bergères, Regency and modern chairs and Bentwood rockers.

Roger Newton & Company
Studio 52, Warriner House, 140 Battersea Park Rd, London SW11 4NE T:0171-498 1798. F:0171-207 2992. Specialist in the restoration of gilded, lacquered or painted furniture for the antique trade and for private clients.He also runs courses on furniture painting, gilding and lacquering.

Ossowski
83 Pimlico Rd, London SW1W 8PH. T:0171-730 3256/731 0334. F:0171-823 4500. Restoration of giltwood mirrors and furniture, including carvings.

Oxley's Furniture
Lapstone Barn, Westington Hill, Chipping Camden, Gloucs GL55 6UR. T:01386-840466. F:01386-840455. This manufacturer of decorative metal garden furniture can also verdigris any piece

Charles Perry Restorations
Praewood Farm, Hemel Hempstead Rd,
St. Albans, Herts AL3 6AA.
T:01727 853487. F:01727-846668.
This workshop can restore most English and
Continental furniture using gilding, carving,
marquetry, polishing, lacquerwork, marble,
caning and re-rushing and traditional re-
upholstery. Also globes, clock cases, ship's
models and rocking horses.

Camilla Redfern
24 Abbey Business Centre,
Ingate Place, London SW8 3NS.
T:0171-627 0935. F:0171-352 1805.
Specialises in the conservation of painted,
lacquered, gilded and japanned furniture.
Designs and makes mirror/picture frames.

Jill Saunders
46 White Hart Lane, London SW13 0PZ.
T:0181-878 0400. Repair of furniture, re-
upholstery, recaning and refurbishment of
Lloyd Loom chairs. Stockist of DIY
upholstery sundries.

Titian Studio
318 Kensal Rd, London W10 5BN.
T:0181-960 6247. F:0181-969 6126.
Restoration of transfer, water and oil gilding,
lacquering and other decorative finishes
using traditional methods. Broken carvings
can also be precisely copied and replaced.

Clifford J Tracy
6-40 Durnford St, Seven Sisters Rd,
London N15 5NQ.
T:0181-800 4773/4. F:0181-800 4351.
Cabinetmakers and antique furniture
restorers. Repertoire includes marquetry,
Boulle work, wood carving, wax and
French polishing; repairs to clock cases,
leather desk tops and refurbishment
of keys and locks.

Jo van Gerbig & Co
Unit 32 Charter House Works,
Eltringham Rd, London SW18 1TD.
T:0181-874 3767. Maker and restorer
of fine gilded furniture and frames. Jo
van Gerbig can design to commission
contemporary mirrors, sconces, beds,
chairs or ottomans.

E & A Wates
82 & 84 Mitcham Lane, London SW16 6NR.
T:0181-769 2205. F:0181-677 4766.
French polishing, inlay repairs, marquetry
restoration, re-caning and re-rushing.
Also re-upholstery and loose covers.

GLASS

Living Art
35 Kenway Rd, London SW5 0RE.
T/F:0171-370 2766. Silver, pewter
and glass engraved to commission
with initials, crests or badges - for
corporate or individual clients.

**London Glassblowing Workshop
(Peter Layton Associates)**
7 The Leather Market,
Weston St, London SE1 3ER.
T:0171-403 2800. F:0171-403 7778.
Commissions include the blown glass
luminaires and lighting for the Art
Deco restoration of the Savoy Theatre.
Consultants and makers of bespoke
glasswork: windows, screens, sculptures,
fountains for architectural applications.

Clare Mosley
66 Camberwell Grove, London SE5 8RF.
T:0171-708 3123. Has pioneered the
revival of 'verre eglomisé' - the art of
applying silver or gold-leaf onto glass.
She uses it to great effect for decorative
wall panels and lamp bases.

Rose Hill Restorations of Chobham
See entry under METAL/SILVER.

Wilkinson
Workshop: 5 Catford Hill, London SE6 4NU.
T:0181-314 1080. F:0181-690 1524.
Showroom: 1 Grafton St, London W1X 3LB.
T:0171-495 2477. F:0171-491 1737.
This company has restored glass for three
generations and holds a royal warrant.
Services offered include putting a new
foot on a wine glass or grinding down chips,
finding or re-making stoppers and liners
(in blue or clear glass) and cleaning stained
glass. They also rewire and restore
chandeliers and antique mirrors.

The Guild of
Antique Dealers and
Restorers
(T:01743-271852)
has between 300-
400 members
nationwide, covering
anything from china
restoration to
resilvering.

* denotes
trade supplier.
Please phone
for retail outlets.   169

PAINTINGS

Bourlet
32 Connaught St, London W2 2AY.
T:0171-724 4837. Restore oils,
watercolours, photographs and carved
and gilded woodwork. They will also
undertake lamp conversions.

Sebastian D'Orsai
8 Kensington Mall, London W8 4EA.
T:0171-229 3888. Restoration of oil
paintings and cleaning of watercolours.
Can also 'de-fox' prints.

Paul Mitchell
99 New Bond St, London W1Y 9LF.
T:0171-493 8732. F:0171-409 7136.
Restoration of paintings of all periods and
mediums - treatments include canvas lining
(for the repair of tears, flaking paint and
water damage), panel stabilisation (where
the painting and frame is reinforced with
keys and batons), cleaning, and varnishing
(to protect against discolouration).
Conservation specialists.

Plowden & Smith
See entry under **STONE/MARBLE.**
Cleaning and restoration of oil paintings
on canvas or on wood panels; also
miniatures, frescoes, carved
statues and painted furniture.

The Rowley Gallery
115 Kensington Church St, London W8 7LN.
T:0171-727 6495.
Bespoke framers who will repair mirror
frames and undertake gilding and
veneering. They can restore oil paintings,
prints and watercolours.

OTHER SPECIALISTS

The Abbey Bookbindery
5A Frimhurst Farm, Deepcut, Bridge Rd,
Deepcut, Camberley, Surrey. GU16 6RF.
T/F:01252-837580.
Bookbinding workshop for private collections
and libraries (clients include The British
Museum and London University colleges).
They also bind university theses.

The Association of
British Picture
Restorers (ABPR)
T/F:0181-948 5644
has some 360
members: mainly oil
painting restorers,
but there are some
wall painting
experts as well.

The British
Horological Institute
(T:01636-813795)
has a list of 3500
qualified restorers for
clocks, watches,
barometers,
chronographs,
musical boxes,
sundials. Their
museum in Upton,
Newark, Notts, is
open Easter to Sept.

* denotes
trade supplier.
Please phone
for retail outlets.

Buck & Ryan
101 Tottenham Court Rd, London W1P 0DY.
T:0171-636 7475. F:0171-631 0726.
This busy tool merchant has been
established since 1824. They will sharpen
all garden implements: lawnmower
blades, garden shears, shovels, spades,
forks and hoes.

The Clock Clinic
85 Lower Richmond Rd,
London SW15 1EU. T:0181-788 1407.
F:0181-780 2838. Specialists in clocks and
barometers, particularly 17th-19th century
longcase clocks. Dial restoration, cabinet
repairs and any other sort of restoration
carried out on the premises.

Crispin & Son
92-96 Curtain Rd, London EC2A 3AA.
T:0171-739 4857. F:0171-613 2047.
Makers of veneers, inlays and marquetry.

*H & R Johnson Tiles
Highgate Tile Works, Tunstall,
Stoke-on-Trent ST6 4JX.
T:01782-575575. F:01782-577377.
Restoration of original 19th century
tiled floors.

Derek and Tina Rayment Antiques
Orchard House, Barton Rd, Barton,
Nr Farndon, Cheshire SY14 7HT.
T:01829-270429.
Dealers in 18th and 19th century
English and Continental barometers.
Repairs, restoration and valuations.

St. Blaise
See entry under
BUILDING RESTORERS.
Architectural woodcarving is one of the many
skills offered by this conservation company
specialising in the repair of historic
buildings. They replaced some of the carving
at Uppark using oak and pine, but they will
also work in lime and other woods.

ANTIQUES

LONDON ANTIQUES ARCADES

Please call for opening hours.

Alfie's Antiques Market

13-25 Church St, London NW8 8DT.
T:0171-723 6066. F:0171-724 0999.
The largest covered antique market in
the UK. Jewellery, ceramics, Art Nouveau,
furniture, books, prints and several
Art Deco dealers.

Antiquarius

131-141 King's Rd, London SW3 4PW.
T:0171-351 5353.
Over 120 specialist dealers - anything
from netsukes and ivories to Clarice Cliff
ceramics, silverware and prints.

The Antiques Market

155a Northcote Rd, London SW11 6QB.
T:0171-228 6850. Around 30 dealers
in Art Deco, old advertising, prints,
Victoriana, kitchenalia, clocks and
furniture, 1950s ephemera.

Antiques Pavilion

175 Bermondsey St,
entrance in Newham's Row,
London SE1 3UW.
T/F:0171-403 2021. One of 20 furniture
warehouses on and around Bermondsey
Street. This one has some 20 dealers
with anything from school chairs to
chaises longues.

Chelsea Antiques Market

245a-253 King's Road, London SW3 5EL.
T:0171-352 5689. F:0171-823 3449.
The oldest of the King's Road arcades, with
stalls selling film and theatre memorabilia,
prints, jewellery and antiquarian bookseller
Harrington Brothers whose strengths are
travel and children's books.

Chenil Galleries

181-183 King's Rd,
London SW3 5EB.
T:0171-351 5353.
Under the same ownership as Antiquarius.
Good for Art Nouveau and Art Deco but there
are also dealers in 18th and 19th century

paintings, prints, jewellery and Victorian and early 20th century period costumes.

The Furniture Cave

533 King's Rd, London SW10.
T:0171-352 4229.
30,000 square feet (and 15 independent dealers) with antique and decorative furniture of all periods and styles.

Grays Antique Market

58 Davies St, London W1 1AR and 1-7 Davies Mews, London W1Y 2LP.
T:0171-629 7034.
F:0171-493 9344.
Large and eclectic range of stalls. Silverware, Oriental and Islamic ceramics, tribal art, Toby jugs, books, prints, even a specialist in antique medical instruments.

LONDON ANTIQUES MARKETS

Bermondsey (New Caledonian) Market

Bermondsey Sq, London SE1.
Open Fri 5am-2pm. Portobello's great rival (see below). But on different days so most dealers get to both. Some 250 traders, some indoors, some outside.

Camden Passage

The Angel, Islington, London N1.
For more information call the Camden Passage Traders Association.
T:0171-359 9969.
A paved pedestrian precinct dating from the 18th century. There are over 200 shops and 150 stalls in the area selling all types of antiques, furniture and collectors' items. Most shops are open Tues to Sat, and market days are Wed (7am to 2pm) and Sat (9am to 3.30pm). On Thurs mornings there are secondhand and antiquarian book stalls.

Portobello Road Market

Portobello Road and Westbourne Grove, London W11. World famous antiques market (Sat only). Nothing you can't find among the hundreds of stalls, shops and arcades. The

antique shops on neighbouring Westbourne Grove and Ledbury Road are open weekdays as well. For more information contact The Portobello Antiques Dealers Association on 0171-229 8354.

THE 'BIG FOUR' LONDON AUCTION HOUSES

Bonhams

Montpelier St,
London SW7 1HH.
T:0171-393 3900. F:0171 393 3905.
And at: Bonhams Chelsea,
65-69 Lots Rd, London SW10 0RN.
T:0171-393 3999. F:0171-393 3906.
Wide range of specialised sales - anything from contemporary ceramics to Tribal art. Less expensive items are sold at the Lots Road branch.

Christie's

8 King St,
London SW1 6QT.
T:0171-839 9060. F:0171-839 1611.
And at: Christie's South Kensington,
85 Old Brompton Rd, London SW7 3LD.
T:0171-581 7611. F:0171-321 3321.
Major sales held at King St, less grand items and collectors' items (antique toys, teddy bears, pop memorabilia etc) at South Kensington.

Phillips

New Bond St,
London W1Y 0AS.
T:0171-629 6602.
F:0171-629 8876.
And at: Phillips West,
10 Salem Rd, London W2 4DL.
T:0171-229 9090. F:0171-792 9201.
Conventional auctions at New Bond St, with weekly antique and modern furniture sales in Bayswater.

Sotheby's

34-35 New Bond St, London W1A 2AA.
T:0171-493 8080. F:0171-408 5989.
Only one London branch, but their smaller sales are held in their 'Colonnade' gallery, with prestigious ones in the main galleries.

For detailed information on auctions in London and all over the country, see the Antiques Trade Gazette, published weekly by Metropress (T:0171-930 9958). Also available at some newsagents.

ENGLISH & CONTINENTAL EARLY COUNTRY FURNITURE

Antiquus
90/92 Pimlico Rd, London SW1W 8PL.
T:0171-730 8681. F:0171-823 6409.
Early works of art: European textiles,
furniture, glass, sculpture and antiquities.

Beedham Antiques
PO Box 4, Bakewell, Derbys DE45 1ZU.
T/F:01629-584753. By appt. and at antique
fairs. English and Continental 16th and 17th
century oak furniture and works of art.

I & JL Brown
632-636 King's Rd, London SW6 2DU.
T:0171-736 4141. F:0171-736 9164.
Large selection of French provincial and
country furniture, decorative lighting (plus a
big reproduction range) and French pottery.

Peter Bunting
238 Higham Lane, Werneth Low,
Hyde, Cheshire SK14 5LW.
T:0161-368 5544. F:0161-368 1488.
By appointment. 17th and 18th century oak
and country furniture, portraits, carvings.

Manuel Castilho
53 Ledbury Rd, London W11 2AA.
T:0171-221 4928. Early continental
furniture (mainly Portuguese and Spanish) -
lots of painted furniture, mirrors,
candlesticks from churches and chapels.

Denzil Grant
Hubbards Corner, Felsham Rd,
Bradfield St George,
Nr Bury St Edmunds, Suffolk IP30 0AQ.
T:01449-736576. F:01449-737679.
By appointment. 17th to 19th century
country furniture, especially French.

Heritage Antiques
112 Islington High St, Camden Passage,
London N1 8EG. T:0171-226 7789.
F:01273-326850. Oak and country
furniture, 17th to 19th century European
metalwork and decorative objects.

Thomas Kerr at #12
12 Cale St, Chelsea Green,
London SW3 3QU.

T:0171-581 5022. F:0171-581 3966.
And at: *L'Encoignure,*
517 King's Rd, London SW10 0TX.
T:0171-351 6465. F:0171-351 4744.
Extensive stock of French fruitwood and
walnut provincial furniture, including
armoires, chests, extending tables. Plus gilt
mirrors, pairs of fauteuils and bergères,
confit pots.

Daniel Mankowitz
208a Westbourne Grove, London W11 2RH.
T:0171-229 9270. F:0171-229 4687.
Unusual early and decorative furniture,
sculpture, textiles, paintings, works of art.

Angela Page Antiques
Tunbridge Wells, Kent. T:01892-522217.
At antique fairs and by appointment. 18th
and 19th century English and European
country and painted furniture, folk art,
spongeware pottery and some textiles.

Alistair Sampson
120 Mount St, London W1Y 5HB.
T:0171-409 1799. F:0171-409 7717.
Early and fine English furniture, pottery,
Oriental works of art, pictures, needlework.

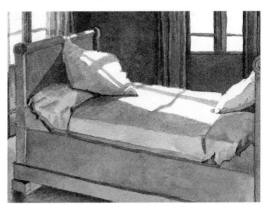

M&D Seligmann
37 Kensington Church St, London W8 4LL.
T:0171-937 0400. F:0171-722 4315.
17th to 18th century English country
furniture, pottery, treen and objets d'art.

Robert Young Antiques
68 Battersea Bridge Rd, London SW11 3AG.
T:0171-228 7847. F:0171-585 0489.
Mid 17th to mid 19th century good country
furniture, folk art, wrought iron candleholders.

ENGLISH & CONTINENTAL FURNITURE & DECORATIVE ITEMS

Robert Barley Antiques
48 Fulham High St, London SW6 3LQ.
T/F:0171-736 4429.
Unusual precious objects dating from
2000BC to 1940. Grand Tour items,
classical engravings, lots of statuary
and bronzes of animals.

John Bird Antiques
Norton House, Iford,
Lewes, E.Sussex BN7 3EJ.
T/F:01273-483366. By appointment.
Eclectic mix of decorative furniture and
accessories; painted and lacquered
furniture; garden antiques.

Alasdair Brown
24 Chelsea Wharf, 15 Lots Rd,
London SW10 0QP.
T:0171-351 1477. F:0171-351 1577.
19th century Gothic furniture, blond
woods, chairs and chunky decorative
items, mirrors, lamps.

Antoine Chenevière Fine Arts
27 Bruton St, London W1X 7DP.
T:0171-491 1007. F:0171-495 6173.
18th and 19th century furniture, paintings
and objets d'art from Russia, Italy, Austria,
Sweden and Germany.

Colefax & Fowler
39 Brook St, London W1Y 2JE.
T:0171-493 2231. F:0171-355 4037.
18th and 19th century English and
continental furniture (especially painted),
decorative objects, tôle cachepots, baskets.

Charles Edwards
See entry under **ANTIQUE LIGHTING.**

Peter Farlow
189 Westbourne Grove, London W11 2SB.
T:0171-229 8306. F:0171-229 4297.
19th century Gothic revival, Arts & Crafts,
Aesthetic period. 'The Coach House' behind
the shop houses another three dealers (in
equestrian and marine art; campaign
furniture; and glass) and between them they
claim to offer 'the best of the 19th century'.

Harvey Ferry & William Clegg
At The Country Seat,
Huntercombe Manor Barn, Huntercombe,
Nr Henley on Thames, Oxon RG9 5RY.
T:01491-641349.
F:01491-641533.
Specialists in architect/artist-designed
19th century furniture, but their large
showrooms also have whole panelled
rooms, other 17th to 19th century
furniture, art pottery and metalwork,
antique Chinese furniture and antiquities.

Great Brampton House Antiques
Madley, Hereford HR2 9NA.
T:01981-250244. F:01981-251333.
Large collection of quality 18th and 19th
century English and French antiques
displayed in the rooms of a stately home.
Interior design service.

Guinevere
See entry under
OTHER ANTIQUE DEALERS.

Hallidays
The Old College, High St,
Dorchester-on-Thames, Oxon OX10 7HL.
T:01865-340028/68.
F:01865-341149. Twenty-eight rooms of
late 17th-early 19th century furniture (with a
predominance of Georgian), porcelain and
decorative objects. Also bespoke furniture
and panelling in 'antique' carved pine or
limed oak.

Jonathan Harris
T:0171-602 6255. F:0171-602 0488.
In a temporary office at the time of going to
press, after 30 years in Kensington Church
St. Should soon have new showrooms in the
West End. High quality European & Oriental
furniture & works of art.

Carlton Hobbs
46 Pimlico Rd, London SW1W 8LP.
T:0171-730 3640/3517.
F:0171-730 6080. Museum-quality English
and Continental furniture, chandeliers,
pictures and works of art.

Christopher Howe
93 Pimlico Rd, London SW1W 8PH.
T:0171-730 7987. F:0171-730 0157.
17th to 20th century furniture and lighting:
from a whole Jacobean style panelled room
made in 1830 to a 1970s desk used in
The Avengers.

Mallett & Son
141 New Bond St, London W1Y 0BS.
T:0171-499 7411. F:0171-495 3179.
Top quality 18th century English furniture,
works of art, glass.

Mallett at Bourdon House
2 Davies St, London W1Y 1LJ.
T:0171-629 2444. F:0171-499 2670.
Decorative and continental furniture
and works of art.

McCEd
8 Holbein Place, London SW1W 8NL.
T:/F:0171-730 4025.
19th century architecturally inspired
furniture, objects and lighting.

McClenaghan
69 Pimlico Rd, London SW1W 8NE.
T/F:0171-730 4187. Grand antiques,
big chandeliers, lots of gilt and ormolu.

McVeigh and Charpentier
498 King's Rd, London SW10 OLE.
T:0171-352 6084. 18th and 19th
century French furniture and objets d'art.

Sylvia Napier
554 King's Rd, London SW6 2DZ.
T/F:0171-371 5881. Eclectic mix of
antiques from Europe and the East
including painted and gilded furniture,

screens, mirrors, statuary, lots of
chandeliers and wall sconces.

George Sherlock
588 King's Rd, London SW6 2DX.
T:0171-736 3955. F:0171-371 5179.
Very decorative furniture: lots of gilt mirrors,
bookcases, chandeliers, desks. On a recent
visit they even had a 7ft convex mirror.

*Keith Skeel
94-98 Islington High St, London N1 8EG.
T:0171-226 7012. F:0171-226 0935.
All sorts of antiques and eccentricities.
Trade and export only.

Stair & Company
14 Mount St, London W1Y 5RA.
T:0171-499 1784. F:0171-629 1050.
18th century English furniture, works
of art, mirrors, chandeliers, lamps.

Talisman
The Old Brewery,Wyke, Gillingham,
Dorset SP8 4NW. T:01747-824423.
F:01747-823544. Vast stock of interesting
furniture and decorative items.

OF Wilson
3-6 Queens Elm Parade,
Old Church St, London SW3 6EJ.
T:0171-352 9554.
F:0171-351 0765.
18th and early 19th century furniture,
French marble and stone fireplaces, painted
and gilded mirrors (mainly continental),
architectural items and decorative objects.

*** denotes
trade supplier.
Please phone
for retail outlets.** 177

FRENCH DECORATIVE FURNITURE & ACCESSORIES

Bazar
82 Golborne Rd, London W10 5PS.
T:0181-969 6262.
Decorative French country pieces. Kitchen antiques, painted furniture, beds, mirrors.

Nicholas Chandor and Andrew Hirst
See entry under **ANTIQUE LIGHTING**. Mirrors, beds, sofas from all over Europe.

Decorative Living
55 New King's Rd, London SW6 4SE.
T/F:0171-736 5623. Interesting mix of European, colonial and ethnic furniture (from places as diverse as Vietnam, Morocco and Czechoslovakia) and decorative items, plus pieces they have designed themselves incorporating old elements and crafted in a traditional way.

Nicole Fabre
See entry under **ANTIQUE TEXTILES**. 18 th and 19th century French provincial furniture and textiles.

Marilyn Garrow
See entry under **ANTIQUE TEXTILES**. French painted furniture including desks, chairs and chests of drawers.

Judy Greenwood
See entry under **ANTIQUE TEXTILES**. Painted wood and metal beds, pretty lighting and lots of decorative accessories.

La Maison
410 St.John St, London EC1V 4NJ.
T/F:0171-837 6522.
Antique beds, provincial furniture, 18th and 19th century fireplaces, gilded mirrors and architectural items.

Mark Maynard
651 Fulham Rd, London SW6 5PU.
T:0171-731 3533. A good source of affordable big painted cupboards, armchairs, chairs, bookcases and decorative bits.

Rogier Antiques
20a Pimlico Rd, London SW1W 8LJ.
T:0171-823 4780. Continental (mainly French) decorative antiques, lighting, mirrors and objects, especially in tôle. Plus a large range of reproduction tôle and wood (painted or gilded) lanterns, wall sconces, lamps.

Universal Providers
86 Golborne Rd, London W10 5PS.
T:0181-960 3736. French metal café chairs, beds and other bedroom furniture, large wardrobes, mirrors and old shop fittings.

SWEDISH/NEO-CLASSICAL/ BIEDERMEIER

The Blue Door
77 Church Rd, London SW13 9HH.
T:0181-748 9785. F:0181-563 1043. Always have some pieces of Swedish furniture in stock (plus reproductions), and are happy to hunt for particular pieces on request.

Rupert Cavendish
610 King's Rd, London SW6 2DX.
T:0171-731 7041. F:0171-731 8302. Early and late 19th century Biedermeier and Empire birch wood bookcases, sofas, tables and chairs, cupboards.

Hermitage Antiques
97 Pimlico Rd, London SW1W 8PH.
T:0171-730 1973. F:0171-730 6586. Early 19th century Biedermeier, Empire and Russian furniture, chandeliers, bronzes, paintings.

Jorgen Antiques
38 & 40 Lower Richmond Rd,
London SW15 1JP.
T/F:0181-789 7329. Open Tue-Fri or by appointment. 18th and 19th century Swedish and Danish furniture, mirrors, china, candlesticks, lamps.

ARTS & CRAFTS/ 20TH CENTURY DESIGN

20th Century Renaissance
Camden Stables Market, Chalk Farm Rd, London NW1. T:0171-603 1431. Open Sat & Sun only or by appointment. Designer furniture and lighting 1950-1970.

The Facade
196 Westbourne Grove,
London W11 2RH.
T:0171-727 2159.
Lighting from 1910 to 1950.

David Gill
60 Fulham Rd, London SW3 6HH.
T:0171-589 5946. F:0171-584 9184.
20th century and contemporary furniture
and objects. Contemporary designers
include Garouste & Bonetti, Oriel Harwood
and Donald Judd.

Haslam and Whiteway
105 Kensington Church St, London W8 7LN.
T:0171-229 1145. F:0171-221 7065.
British furniture and decorative arts dating
from 1850 to 1930.

Hemisphere
173 Fulham Rd, London SW3 6JW.
T:0171-581 9800. F:0171-581 9880.
Specialists in 1940s and 1950s French
furniture; 20th century decorative arts.

John Jesse
160 Kensington Church St, London W8.
T:0171-229 0312. Decorative arts 1880-
1950, especially Art Nouveau and Art Deco
silver, glass, bronzes and jewellery.

Liberty
214-220 Regent St,
London W1R 6AH. T:0171-734 1234.
Has a department that specialises in the
Arts & Crafts period, plus new furniture (to
order) based on Arts & Crafts traditions.

New Century
69 Kensington Church St,
London W8 4BG. T/F:0171-937 2410. Arts
& Crafts furniture, pottery and metalwork,
with a lot of designs by Christopher Dresser.

Pruskin Gallery
73 Kensington Church St, London W8 4BG.
T:0171-937 1994. F:0171-376 1285.
Specialise in French Art Deco bronze and
ivory figurines and glassware, but there are
also a few paintings, furniture and ceramics.

The Studio
18 Church St, London NW8 8EP.
T:0171-258 0763. Original Arts & Crafts, Art
Deco, Aesthetic Movement as well as early

Heals pieces. Can also produce precise
replicas of architect-designed furniture.

Themes & Variations
231 Westbourne Grove, London W11 2SE.
T:0171-727 5531. F:0171-221 6378.
Post-war and pop-art design. Exclusive
agents for the Italian company Fornasetti.
Contemporary artists include André
Dubreuil, Danny Lane, Carl Hahn, Deborah
Thomas and Tom Dixon.

Tomtom
42 New Compton St, London WC2H 8DA.
T:0171-240 7909. Post-war decorative arts,
furniture and glass.

Twentieth Century Design
274 Upper St, London N1 2UA.
T/F:0171-288 1996.
Furniture and lighting from 1935 to today.
Classics by Charles Eames, Alvar
Aalto, George Nelson,
Pierre Paulin and many others.

Gordon Watson
50 Fulham Rd, London SW3 6HH.
T:0171-589 3108. F:0171-584 6328.
Art Deco furniture, silver, lighting, jewellery
1920-1940. Plus custom made carpentry,
carved wood or metalwork in any style.

ANTIQUE TEXTILES

Joanna Booth
247 King's Rd, London SW3 5EL.
T:0171-352 8998. F:0171-376 7350.
16th to 18th century tapestry, cushions,
European sculpture, old master drawings
and French antiquarian books.

Decorative Textiles of Cheltenham
7 Suffolk Parade,
Cheltenham, Gloucs GL50 2AB.
T:01242-574546. F:01242-578495.
18th to 20th century textiles, tapestry,
hangings, trimmings, bell pulls, needlework
pictures, samplers and curtains.

Nicole Fabre
592 King's Rd, London SW6 2DX.
T:0171-384 3112. F:0171-610 6410.
18th and 19th century French textiles and
provincial furniture.

The Gallery of Antique Costume and Textiles

2 Church St, London NW8 8ED.
T/F:0171-723 9981. 19th century Durham, Welsh, Provencal and patchwork quilts, antique velvets, brocades, silks, needlepoints and other textiles. They provided costumes for Sense & Sensibility.

Marilyn Garrow

6 The Broadway, White Hart Lane, London SW13 0NY.
T/F:0181-392 1655. 17th and 18th century European, Asian, Islamic textiles.

Joss Graham Oriental Textiles

10 Eccleston St, London SW1W 9LT.
T/F:0171-730 4370. New and antique textiles from India, Afghanistan, Central Asia, Middle and Near East, Africa and South East Asia. Large selection of fine kilims in lighter weaves suitable for upholstery, curtains and covering stools.

Judy Greenwood

657 Fulham Rd, London SW6 5PY.
T:0171-736 6037. F:0171-736 1941.
French beds, small chandeliers and a large stock of plain and patchwork antique quilts dating from 1850 to 1920.

Linda Gumb

9 Camden Passage, London N1 8EA.
T:0171-354 1184. F:0171-359 0103.
17th-19th century tapestry, cushions, objects.

Heraz

2 Halkin Arcade, London SW1X 8JT.
T:0171-245 9497. F:0171-235 7416.
Specialists in 17th to 19th century tapestry cushions, antique carpets and tapestries.

Jen Jones

Pontbrendu, Llanybydder, Ceredigion, Wales SA40 9UJ.
T:01570-480610. F:01570-480112.
Some 300 antique quilts (including many Welsh ones), divided into four groups: designer, cottage, collector and flannels. Blankets are also divided into 19th century coarse weaves and plaids and stripes. Plus linen and cotton sheets and edged pillowcases.

Lunn Antiques

86 New King's Rd, London SW6 4LU.
T:0171-736 4638. F:0171-371 7113.
Antique and new bed and table linen, bedcovers, cushions, bolsters.

Pavilion Antiques

Freshford Hall, Freshford, Bath BA3 6EJ.
T/F:01225-722522.
By appointment. Huge stock (over 1000) of 19th century linen/hemp sheets and yardage; trimmings and period haberdashery (including mother of pearl buttons); French mattress tickings, bed-hangings and curtains; French rustic linen clothes and domestic linen (tea towels etc) as well as charming painted furniture and folk art.

Peta Smyth Antique Textiles

42 Moreton St, London SW1V 2PB.
T:0171-630 9898. F:0171-630 5398.
Specialist in 17th to 19th century textiles, needlework, tapestry fragments, cushions, braids, fringes, tassels.

Bryony Thomasson

283 Westbourne Grove, Portobello Rd, London W11 (Sat mornings only).
And at : 19 Ackmar Rd, London SW6 4UP.
T:0171-731 3693 (by appointment). Rustic hand-woven textiles. Linen/hemp sheets, sacks and agricultural working clothes.

Tobias and The Angel

68 White Hart Lane, Barnes, London SW13 0PZ.
T:0181-878 8902. Patchwork and Durham quilts, handwoven Welsh throws in checks and plaids, pillows and bolsters in French ticking, linen sheets, towels and lengths.

ANTIQUE CARPETS & RUGS

Majid Amini, Persian Carpet Gallery

Church St, Petworth, W.Sussex GU28 0AD.
T:01798-343344. F:01798-342673.
Has access to over 10,000 antique and new carpets, including modern gabbeh. His team can tackle any restoration, from frayed edges to huge holes. Plus valuations and lectures.

Atlantic Bay Carpets
5 Sedley Place, London W1R 1HH.
T:0171-355 3301. F:0171-355 3760.
Antique Oriental and European rugs and
carpets including Aubussons and textiles.
Plus Islamic pottery and artefacts.

Benardout & Benardout
7 Thurloe Place, London SW7 2RX.
T:0171-409 1234. F:0171-584 7658.
Oriental and European carpets, needlepoint,
tapestry and Aubussons. Cleaning,
restoration and valuations.

David Black Oriental Carpets
96 Portland Rd, London W11 4LN.
T:0171-727 2566. F:0171-229 4599.
Decorative carpets from Persia, Turkey,
Russia and Europe. Excellent selection of
tribal rugs and Arts & Crafts designs. Also
antique Indian dhurries.

Jack Fairman Carpets
218 Westbourne Grove, London W11 2RH.
T:0171-229 2262. F:0171-229 2263.
Antique rugs, hand knitted contemporary
rugs, flat-woven rugs, restoration & cleaning.

Gallery Yacou
127 Fulham Rd, London SW3 6RT.
T:0171-584 2929. F:0171-584 3535.
Antique and decorative Oriental and
European carpets. Large range of room-size
ond oversized carpets always in stock.

Gallery Zadah
29 Conduit St, London W1R 9TA.
T:0171-493 2622. F:0171-629 6682.
Antique Oriental and European rugs, carpets
and tapestries. Plus 120 designs in any size
in their new Abadjian range.

Joss Graham Oriental Textiles
See entry under **ANTIQUE TEXTILES.**
Lighter weave kelims and grain sacks and
saddle bags for cushions and floor cushions.

Alastair Hull
The Old Mill, 4 The Green,
Haddenham, Ely, Cambs CB6 3TA.
T:01353-740577. F:01353-740688.
Buys kelims from Central Asia, Afghanistan
and Iran to sell from home or through
galleries and tribal art exhibitions. Advice,
valuations and maintenance.

C John
70 South Audley St, London W1Y 5FE.
T:0171-493 5288. F:0171-409 7030.
Antique carpets & rugs from the 17th
to the 19th century, with a large selection
(about 100) of Aubusson rugs.

The Kilim Warehouse
28a Picketts St, London SW12 8QB.
T:0181-627 3122. F:0181-627 8494.
Wide selection of old and new decorative
kelims plus cleaning and restoration service.

Christopher Legge Oriental Carpets
25 Oakthorpe Rd, Oxford OX2 7BD.
T:01865-557572. F:01865-554877.
Old and new carpets (the latter are in hand-
spun wool with vegetable dyes, from
Western Turkey), village and tribal pieces,
from small bags to large rugs, runners,
kelims. Hand cleaning and reweaving.

Clive Loveless
29 Kelfield Gardens, London W10 6NA.
T:0181-969 5831. F:0181-969 5292.
By appointment. Consultant and dealer in
18th and 19th century Oriental tribal rugs
and 17th to 19th century Ottoman, Central
Asian, African and Pre-Columbian textiles.

Mansour Carpets
56 South Audley St, London W1Y 5FA.
T:0171-499 5601. F:0171-355 3662.
Antique and new handmade Persian and
European carpets and rugs.

The Odiham Gallery
78 High St, Odiham, Hampshire RG25 1LN.
T:01256-703415. F:01256-704548.
Old kelims from Anatolia, Persia, the
Caucasus. Specialists in Oriental carpets.

The Gordon Reece Gallery
24 Finkle St, Knaresborough,
N.Yorks HG5 8AA. T:01423-866219
Old kelims from Afghanistan, Persia and
Pakistan. Permanent exhibition of 200 rugs
and Gabbehs, plus changing exhibitions of
tribal and primitive art, including furniture,
textiles, masks, sculpture, jewellery.

David J Wilkins
27 Princess Rd, Regents Park,
London NW1 8JR.
T:0171-722 7608. F:0171-483 0423.

Oriental rugs. Specialist in unusual sizes, both old and new (the majority are Persian). Restoration and cleaning.

ANTIQUE LIGHTING

The Antique Lighting Company
The Old Rectory, Danehill, Kennett, Newmarket, Suffolk CB8 7QL. T:01638-751354. Wide range of antique light fittings, from 19th century to Art Deco.

Nicholas Chandor & Andrew Hirst
42 and 61a Ledbury Rd, London W11 2AB. T:0171-221 6707 and 0171-221 1643. Interesting selection of lighting from all over Europe: chandeliers (some with drops and some in wrought iron), lanterns, Venetian chandeliers and matching wall lights. Plus mirrors and French decorative furniture, and any other interesting finds from their monthly trip to France, Italy and Spain.

Fergus Cochrane and Leigh Warren
570 King's Rd, London SW6 2DY. T:0171-736 9166. F:0171-736 6687. Antique lanterns, table lamps, lampbases - anything from Regency to Art Deco.Plus decorative items.

Mrs ME Crick Chandeliers
166 Kensington Church St, London W8 4BN. T:0171-229 1338. F:0171-792 1073. Large range of cut glass and ormolu chandeliers, candelabra and wall lights.

Tulissio de Beaumont
283 Lillie Rd, London SW6 7LL. T:0171-385 0156. Period lighting, especially 1850s onwards. Chandeliers, wall lights. Rewiring service.

Delomosne & Son
Court Close, North Wraxall, Chippenham, Wilts SN14 7AD. T:01225-891505. F:01225-891907. Period glass fittings, including chandeliers, candelabra and candlesticks. Restoration.

Charles Edwards
582 King's Rd, London SW6 2DY. T:0171-736 8490. F:0171-371 5436. Good selection of antique lighting, especially lanterns; unusual 19th century English furniture, sculpture and objects. Interesting reproduction range as well, including lighting, ceiling roses, furniture.

Hector Finch Lighting
88 Wandsworth Bridge Rd, London SW6 2TF. T/F:0171-731 8886. The whole spectrum of antique lighting, from chandeliers and lanterns to alabaster bowls and Spanish ironwork.

Fritz Fryer Antique Lighting
12 Brookend St, Ross-on-Wye, Hereford HR9 7EG. T:01989-567416. F:01989-566742. Has some 500 restored and rewired lamps in stock. Will restore customers' own antique lighting in their workshops.

Christopher Howe
See entry under ENGLISH & CONTINENTAL FURNITURE & DECORATIVE ITEMS. Anything from small candlesticks to huge hall lanterns. He has supplied antique light fittings for the Brighton Pavilion and the Soane Museum. Also a range of reproduction lighting.

Jones
194 Westbourne Grove, London W11 2RH. T/F:0171-229 6866. Vast selection of original Victorian, Edwardian, Art Nouveau and Art Deco fittings and replacement glass shades.

W Sitch & Co
48 Berwick St, London W1V 4JD. T:0171-437 3776. Soho shop crammed with old light fittings. They restore 19th century lighting, convert vases into lamps and will silver-plate any fitting and restore glass chandeliers.

Stiffkey Lamp Shop
Townshend Arms, Wells Rd, Stiffkey, Norfolk NR23 1AJ. T:01328-830460. F:01328-830005. Victorian and Edwardian light fittings, table

lamps, wall brackets and oil lamps. 15% of their stock is reproduction - bathroom lighting, glass shade rise-and-fall lamps, ceramic ceiling roses and switches.

PAINTINGS

Agnew's
43 Old Bond St, London W1X 4BA.
T:0171-629 6176. F:0171-629 4359.
Old Master paintings and drawings; English paintings and watercolours; prints, sculpture, works of art and 20th century British and continental works of art.

Colnaghi
15 Old Bond St, London W1X 4JL.
T:0171-491 7408. F:0171-491 8851.
Old Master and English paintings and Master Drawings, sculpture and works of art.

The Fine Art Society
148 New Bond St, London W1Y 0JT.
T:0171-629 5116. F:0171-491 9454.
19th and early 20th century paintings, watercolours, drawings, sculpture and furniture.

Richard Green
39 & 44 Dover St, London W1X 4JQ.
T:0171-493 3939. F:0171-629 2609.
And at: 4 & 33 New Bond St, London W1.
The four showrooms cover paintings from the 17th to the 20th century: Old Masters, Victorian & European, sporting & marine, French Impressionists and modern British.

Iona Antiques
PO Box 285, London W8 6HZ.
T:0171-602 1193. F:0171-371 2843.
By appointment. English 19th century paintings of animals.

The Mallett Gallery
141 New Bond St, London W1Y 0BS.
T:0171-499 7411. F:0171-495 3179.
Victorian paintings, watercolours, drawings and prints; late 19th and early 20th century Western applied arts.

David Messum
8 Cork St, London W1X 1PB.
T:0171-437 5545. F:0171-734 7018.
British Impressionism and contemporary art.

Richard Philp Gallery
59 Ledbury Rd, London W11 2AA.
T:0171-727 7915. F:0171-792 9073.
16th & 17th century English portraits and Old Master drawings and paintings. Early furniture. Antiquities. Medieval and Renaissance sculpture. 20th century paintings and drawings.

Charles Plante
T:0171-834 3305. F:0171-828 3499.
By appointment. 18th and 19th century neoclassical watercolours and drawings, plus neoclassical objects and French and English Empire and Regency porcelain.

Spink Leger Galleries
13 Old Bond St, London W1X 4HU.
T:0171-629 3538. F:0171-493 8681.
English paintings, drawings and watercolours from the 17th to the 20th century.

Rafael Valls
11 Duke St, London SW1Y 6BN.
T:0171-930 1144. F:0171-976 1596.
17th century Dutch and Flemish Old Master paintings. And at: 6 Rider St, London SW1Y 6QB. T:0171-930 0029. 18th century flower, bird and topographical pictures.

Waterhouse & Dodd
110 New Bond St, London W1Y 0RJ.
T:0171-491 9293. F:0171-491 9669.
Late 19th and early 20th century British and European oils, watercolours and pastels.

ANTIQUE PRINTS & MAPS

Norman Blackburn
32 Ledbury Rd, London W11 2AB.
T:0171-229 5316. F:0171-229 2269.
Decorative prints (17th to 19th century) on all subjects - botanical, sporting, marine, portraits and views. First editions in period frames.

Julia Boston
The Old Stores, The Gasworks,
2 Michael Rd, London SW6 2AD.
T:0171-610 6783. F:0171-610 6784.
Specialist in 19th century tapestry cartoons, the full-size designs from which Aubussons

and other tapestries were copied. Plus other antique decorative prints and 18th and 19th century English and continental furniture. Open Tue,Wed, Thurs and by appointment.

Lucy B Campbell Gallery
123 Kensington Church St, London W8 7LP. T:0171-727 2205. F:0171-229 4252. Antiquarian decorative prints.

Dinan & Chighine
PO Box 266, Kew, Surrey TW9 3QR. T:0181-948 1939. F:0181-255 6986. By appointment. 17th to 19th century decorative prints and watercolours and handmade frames.

Andrew Edmunds
44 Lexington St, London W1R 3LH. T:0171-437 8594. F:0171-439 2551. 18th and early 19th century caricature and decorative prints and drawings.

The Map House
54 Beauchamp Place, London SW3 1NY. T:0171-589 4325. F:0171-589 1041. Antique maps, atlases, engravings and globes, ranging in price from £20 to several hundred thousand.

The O'Shea Gallery
120a Mount St, London W1Y 5HB. T:0171-629 1122. F:0171-629 1116. 15th to 19th century English county maps and maps from other countries and continents; natural history prints and engravings (good stock of botanicals and birds); 18th/19th century political and social caricatures; architectural and sporting prints.

Jonathan Potter
1st Floor, 125 New Bond St, London W1Y 9AF. T:0171-491 3520. F:0171-491 9754. Maps and atlases, some dating from as early as 1500. Plus facsimile globes from £110 upwards.

The Schuster Gallery
14 Maddox St, London W1R 9PL. T:0171-491 2208. F:0171-491 9872. Decorative and rare maps and prints, especially botanicals and topographical.

Trowbridge Gallery
555 King's Rd, London SW6 2EB. T:0171-371 8733. F:0171-371 8138. Specialists in 17th and 18th century natural history and botanical subjects. Large range of reproduction prints and framing service.

ANTIQUE ORIENTAL CERAMICS & WORKS OF ART

Antique West
140 142 Kensington Church St, London W8 4BN. T:0171-229 4115. Chinese pottery and porcelain, neolithic to early 20th century; early 19th century Chinese and Tibetan rugs; some Chinese furniture.

Beagle Gallery
303 Westbourne Grove, London W11 2QA. T:0171-229 9524. F:0171-792 0333. Chinese furniture in elmwood and red lacquer. Some Tibetan chests and bronzes.Oriental sculpture.

Barry Davies Oriental Art
1 Davies St, London W1Y 1LL. T:0171-408 0207. F:0171-493 3422. Japanese works of art, netsuke, lacquer and bronzes.

Eskenazi
10 Clifford St, London W1X 1RB. T:0171-493 5464. F:0171-499 3136. Early Chinese ceramics, bronzes, sculptures works of art.

Michael Goedhuis
116 Mount St, London W1Y 5HD. T:0171-629 2228. F:0171-409 3338. Asian art, ancient and contemporary, from 500BC to the 20th century.

Japanese Gallery
66d Kensington Church St, London W8 4BY. T/F:0171-229 2934. Japanese wood-cut prints and works of art.

The Oriental Gallery
4 Davies St, London W1Y 1LG. T:0171-499 7009. F:0171-409 0122. Chinese and Japanese ceramics and works of art.

Kevin Page Oriental Art
2-6 Camden Passage, London N1 8ED.
T:0171-226 8558. F:0171-354 9145.
Room after room of antique Japanese and
Chinese ceramics in excellent condition.
18th and 19th centuy blue and white
porcelain, famille rose, Satsuma, export
ware and works of art (ivory, bronze,
gold lacquer).

Spink & Son
5-7 King St, London SW1Y 6QS.
T:0171-930 7888.
F:0171-839 4853.
Chinese, Japanese, Indian, South
East Asian and Islamic art.

ANTIQUE POTTERY & PORCELAIN

Andrew Dando
4 Wood St, Queen Sq, Bath BA1 2JQ.
T:01225-422702. F:01225-310717.
17th to early 19th century English,
Continental and Oriental pottery and
porcelain; local topographical and decorative
engravings.

Brian & Angela Downes
PO Box 431, Chippenham, Wilts SN14 6SZ.
T:01454-238134. By appointment.
19th century porcelain, mainly English,
including dinner and dessert services.

Brian Haughton Antiques
3b Burlington Gardens, London W1X 1LE.
T:0171-734 5491. F:0171-494 4604.
British and European porcelain and pottery,
18th and 19th century.

Heirloom and Howard
Manor Farm, West Yatton,
Chippenham, Wilts SN14 7EU.
T:01249-783038. F:01249-783039.
Armorial Chinese porcelain and other
armorial antiques.

Jonathan Horne
66b & 66c Kensington Church St,
London W8 4BY.
T:0171-221 5658.
F:0171-792 3090.
Early English pottery and works of art.

Libra Antiques
131d Kensington Church St, London W8 7PT.
T:0171-727 2990. 19th century blue
and white pottery, lustreware and early
European ceramics.

Mercury Antiques
1 Ladbroke Rd, London W11 3PA.
T:0171-727 5106. 18th and early 19th
century English pottery, porcelain and glass.

Jacqueline Oosthuizen
23 Cale St, London SW3 3QR.
T:0171-352 6071. Large selection of
Staffordshire figures, animals,cottages,
Toby Jugs.

The Gordon Reece Gallery
See entry under
ANTIQUE CARPETS & RUGS.
Large stock of non-European ceramics,
ranging from 3000BC Chinese neolithic to
20th century Nigerian pots. Good selection
of large decorative pieces, including huge
16th century storage jars from Burma.

Alistair Sampson
see entry under
ENGLISH & CONTINENTAL EARLY
COUNTRY FURNITURE.

Jean Sewell Antiques
3 Camden St, London W8 7AP.
T:0171-727 3122. F:0171-229 1053.
English, Continental and Oriental porcelain
and pottery.

Simon Spero
109 Kensington Church St, London W8 7LN.
T:0171-727 7413. F:0171-727 7414.
18th century English and French porcelain.

Stockspring Antiques
114 Kensington Church St, London W8 4BH.
T/F:0171-727 7995. Pre-1830 English and
Oriental porcelain.

Carolyn Stoddart-Scott
London W11.
T:0171-727 5045. F:0171-243 1278.
By appointment and at antiques fairs. 19th
century decorative pottery and porcelain,
mainly English.

Oliver Sutton
34c Kensington Church St, London W8 4HA.
T:0171-937 0633. Staffordshire portrait
figures, animals and cottages.

ANTIQUE GLASS

Christine Bridge Antiques
78 Castelnau, Barnes, London SW13 9EX.
T:0181-741 5501. F:0181-255 0172.
18th century collector's and 19th century
decorative glass, lighting and chandeliers.

WGT Burne Antique Glass
PO Box 9465, London SW20 9ZD.
T:0374-725834. T/F:0181-543 6319.
English and Irish 18th and 19th century
glass and chandeliers. Valuations
and restoration.

Delomosne & Son
See entry under
ANTIQUE LIGHTING.
18th and 19th century English and
Irish glass.

Guinevere
See entry under
OTHER ANTIQUE DEALERS.

Jeanette Hayhurst
32a Kensington Church St, London
W8 4HA. T/F:0171-938 1539.
18th century drinking glasses,
19th and 20th century cut coloured
and engraved glass.

Mark J West (Cobb Antiques)
39a High St, Wimbledon Village,
London SW19 5BY.
T/F:0181-946 2811. 18th and 19th
century glass and a very large stock of
decanters and glasses. Regency decanters

(at £200-£300) are no more expensive than
good modern examples.

ANTIQUE SILVER

ADC Heritage
95a Charlwood St, London SW1V 4PB.
T:0171-976 5271. F:0171-976 5898.
By appointment. Silver and old
Sheffield plate.

Bond Street Silver Galleries
111-112 New Bond St, London W1Y 0BQ.
T:0171-493 6180. F:0171-495 3493.
16 dealers in silver, old Sheffield plate
and jewellery.

Garrard & Co
112 Regent St, London W1A 2JJ.
T:0171-734 7020. F:0171-734 0711.
Garrard The Crown Jewellers was founded in
1735. Their neoclassical flagship store in
Regent Street has a vast selection of new
and antique silver and old Sheffield plate.
Also clocks and barometers, jewellery,
bijouterie and snuff boxes.

How of Edinburgh
1st Floor, 41 St.James' Place,
London SW1 1NS.
T:0171-408 1867. Pre-1800 English silver.

Langfords
Vault 8/10, London Silver Vaults,
53-64 Chancery Lane, London WC2A 1QS.
T:0171-242 5506. F:0171-405 0431.
Large selection of antique and modern silver
and silver plate. Household silver includes a
huge range of cutlery, centrepieces,
condiment sets etc. Their specialist services
include replating and repairs, embossing
and engraving, matching of family heirlooms,
custom made pieces and trophies.

MP Levene
5 Thurloe Place, London SW7 2RR.
T:0171-589 3755/3785.
F:0171-589 9908. Antique and secondhand
silver, services of table cutlery and old
Sheffield plate; insurance valuations.

The London Silver Vaults
Chancery House,
53-64 Chancery Lane, London WC2A 1QT.

T:0171-242 3844. There are 40 dealers in these subterranean vaults, selling silver, silver plate and jewellery at prices ranging from £20 to £20,000.

SJ Phillips
139 New Bond St, London W1A 3DL.
T:0171-629 6261. F:0171-495 6180.
18th and 19th century English & continental silver. Claim to have the largest selection of antique jewellery in the world, spanning the 16th to the 20th century.

Tessier
26 New Bond St, London W1Y OJY.
T:0171-629 0458. F:0171-629 1857.
18th and 19th century silver and jewellery. Repairs, valuations.

ANTIQUE CLOCKS & BAROMETERS

The Clock Clinic
85 Lower Richmond Rd, London SW15 1EU.
T:0181-788 1407. F:0181-780 2838.
Clocks and barometers, particularly 17th-19th century longcase clocks. Dial restoration, cabinet repairs and any other sort of restoration carried out on the premises.

Derek and Tina Rayment Antiques
Orchard House, Barton Rd, Barton,
Nr Farndon, Cheshire SY14 7HT.
T:01829-270429. Specialists in 18th and 19th century English and Continental barometers. Repairs and restoration; valuations.

Strike One (Islington)
48a Highbury Hill, London N5 1AP.
T/F:0171-354 2790. Longcase, bracket,lantern, carriage and wall clocks, barometers and music boxes, dating from 1700 to 1860. Occasional catalogue.

OTHER ANTIQUE DEALERS

Peter Adler
191 Sussex Gardens, London W2 2RH.
T:0171-262 1775. F:0171-262 1321.
Traditional African and Oceanic art, textiles, furniture, sculpture and jewellery.

Maria Andipa
162 Walton St,London SW3 2JL.
T:0171-589 2371. F:0171-225 0305.
Greek, Russian, Byzantine, Coptic and Syrian icons from the 14th to the 19th century, plus other ecclesiastical objects like oil lamps, crosses, candlesticks.

The Bacchus Gallery
Lombard St, Petworth,
W. Sussex GU28 0AG.
T:01798-342844. F:01798-342634.
Old and new wine related artefacts. Among the antique items are mahogany cellarettes on stands, silver bottle labels, 18th century glass, and hundreds of corkscrews.

Blunderbuss Antiques
29 Thayer St, London W1M 5LJ.
T:0171-486 2444. F:0171-935 1127.
Arms and armour.

Adam Bray
63 Ledbury Rd, London W11 2AD.
T:0171-221 5820. F:0171-792 4558.
On our last visit the eclectic mix included a bone chandelier, an African mask, a 1930s chair, an Arts & Crafts table and a continental chest.

Jack Casimir
23 Pembridge Rd, London W11 3HG.
T:0171-727 8643. 16th to 19th century British and European brass, copper and pewter.

The Dining Room Shop
64 White Hart Lane,
London SW13 0PZ.
T:0181-878 1020. F:0181-876 2367.
Specialists in anything to do with dining - from antique tables to dinner sets in the customer's own design. They also offer a china finding service.

Christopher Gibbs
8 Vigo St, London W1X 1LG.
T:0171-439 4557. F:0171-287 9961.
Pictures of all periods, decorative furniture and works of arts.

Guinevere
574-580 King's Rd, London SW6 2DY.
T:0171-736 2917. F:0171-736 8267.
Antiques ranging from Chinese neolithic to

For other antique dealers see also GARDENS- Antique Garden Furniture, BEDS & BEDDING- Old Beds and KITCHENS - Kitchen Antiques.

Art Deco, all inspiringly displayed. Large selection of 17th to 19th century continental furniture and objets d'art, but also Chinese and Anglo-Indian furniture, a room-full of antique crystal, antique Chinese ceramics and much more.

Halcyon Days
14 Brook St, London W1Y 1AA.
T:0171-629 8811.
F:0171-409 0280. Antique enamel boxes, tea caddies, candlesticks. Plus treen, tortoiseshell, shagreen and objects of vertu.

The Lacquer Chest
75 Kensington Church St, London W8 4BG.
T:0171-937 1306. F:0171-376 0223. Interesting selection of decorative antiques. Upstairs there is a vast collection of kitchenalia and props for hire for photographic shoots etc.

The Lacy Gallery
203 Westbourne Grove, London W11 2SB.
T:0171-229 6340. F:0171-229 9105. Three floors of period frames, ranging from 15th/16th century Italian to 1920s and 1930s examples.

Langfords Marine Antiques
The Plaza, 535 King's Rd, London SW10 0SZ.
T:0171-351 4881. F:0171-352 0763. Sextants, compasses, telescopes, chronometres and ship models of all kinds.

Maggs Bros
50 Berkeley Square, London W1X 6EL.
T:0171-493 7160. F:0171-499 2007. Antiquarian books, modern first editions & private presses, autographs, illustrated manuscripts, natural history, travel.

Arthur Middleton
12 New Row, Covent Garden, London WC2N 4LF.
T:0171-836 7042/7062.
F:0171-497 2486.
Period globes, marine, scientific, surveying instruments and telescopes.

*denotes trade supplier. Please phone for retail outlets.

188

Paul Mitchell
99 New Bond St, London W1Y 9LF.
T:0171-493 8732. F:0171-409 7136. Extensive stock of antique frames on four floors of an 18th century town house. Framing consultants to collectors, dealers and museums all over the world. Can reproduce frames of all styles and periods. Expert cleaning, conservation and restoration of oil paintings on canvas or panel.

Pairs
202 Ebury St, London SW1W 8UN.
T:0171-730 1771/1881.
F:0171-730 1661. Dealers exclusively in pairs of decorative objects - anything from bookends to marble fireplaces. Will also search for missing halves or have copies made.

Peter Petrou
195 Westbourne Grove, London W11 2SB.
T/F:0171-229 9575. Furniture, works of art and eccentricities, plus Tribal and Oriental art, Black Forest carvings and Vienna bronzes.

Pew Corner
Artington Manor Farm, Old Portsmouth Rd, Artington, Guildford, Surrey GU3 1LP.
T:01483-33337. Old pews, pulpits, choir stalls and lecterns - some of them reworked into benches and other furniture.

Risky Business
44 Church St, London NW8 8EP.
T:0171-724 2194. F:0171-724 3409. Early 20th century luggage and sports goods (old golfing equipment, riding gear, butterfly nets, etc). They are used a lot for fashion and advertising shoots.

Dyala Salam
174a Kensington Church St, London W8 4DP. T:0171-229 4045.
F:0171-229 2433. Decorative 18th and 19th century Ottoman antiques.

Manfred Schotten
109 High St, Burford, Oxon OX18 4RH.
T:01993-822302. F:01993-822055. Sporting antiques and library and club furniture.

*Keith Skeel
See entry under
**ENGLISH & CONTINENTAL
FURNITURE & DECORATIVE ITEMS.**

Spink & Son
See entry under **ANTIQUE ORIENTAL.
CERAMICS & WORKS OF ART.**
Also English paintings, drawings and
watercolours; textiles, coins (from Greek &
Roman to the present day), numismatic
books, medals and decorations.

Robin Symes
3 Ormond Yard, Duke of York St,
London SW1Y 6JT.
T:0171-930 9856/7. F:0171-930 1077.
One of the main dealers in near
Eastern, Egyptian, Greek and Roman
antiquities. From small amulets to
life-size marble sculptures.

Whiteway & Waldron
305 Munster Rd, London SW6 6BJ.
T/F:0171-381 3195.
Ecclesiastical furniture, Victorian
stained glass, candlesticks.

SPECIALIST SUPPLIERS & SERVICES

PAINT

Auro Organic Paint Supplies
Unit 1, Goldstone Farm, Ashdon,
Saffron Walden, Essex CB10 2L7.
T:01799-584888. German range of
organic paints in 30 shades of emulsion,
more in gloss. Available by mail order
or from suppliers around the country.

JW Bollom
PO Box 78, Croydon Rd,
Beckenham, Kent BR3 4BL.
T:0181-658 2299. F:0181-658 8672.
Decorative, industrial,flame retardant paints.

Brats
281 King's Rd, London SW3 5EW.
T:0171-351 7674. F:0171-349 8644.
And at: 624c Fulham Rd, London SW6 5RS.
T:0171-731 6915.

Stockists of 'Mediterranean palette' - a
Turkish range of concentrated paint in 25
colours. It can be diluted with water or mixed
with white emulsion for a softer effect.

C Brewer & Sons
327 Putney Bridge Rd, London SW15 2PG.
T:0181-788 9335. F:0181-788 8285
and many branches in the South East.
Suppliers of standard paint brands (Albany,
Classidur from Switzerland, Dulux) and
specialist paints: flame retardant, anti-
condensation, metallic. Also varnishes,
scumbles, glazes, woodstains and
decorating equipment.

Lawrence T Bridgeman
1 Church Rd,
Roberttown, W.Yorks WF15 7LS.
T:01924-412453. F:01924-410578.
The Stulb Company's historic buttermilk
paint colours from America with colours like
'Steeple White' and 'Loyalist Green'.

Jane Churchill
See entry under **FARROW & BALL.**
Range of undercoat, matt emulsion,
gloss and eggshell paints designed to
co-ordinate with their fabrics and
manufactured by Farrow & Ball.

**Most of the paint
companies listed
will send colour
charts on request,
or give details
of stockists and
mail order.**

*** denotes
trade supplier.
Please phone
for retail outlets.** 191

Cole & Son
144 Offord Rd, London N1 1NS.
T:0171-607 4288. F:0171-607 3341.
Range of 22 historic 'Colours of Distinction'.

Colourman Paints
Pine Brush Products,
Coton Clanford, Stafford ST18 9PB.
T:01785-282799. F:01785-282292.
Water-based paints which reproduce the look
of 18th and 19th century buttermilk paint.

Craig & Rose
172 Leith Walk, Edinburgh EH6 5EB.
T:0131-554 1131. F:0131-553 3250.
Manufacturers of traditional paints since
1829. Their red oxide used on the Forth
Bridge north of Edinburgh is a smart
alternative to the green paintwork used so
much in gardens. It contains linseed so
weathers well. They also do a chlorinated
paint for swimming pools (it could be
used in a bathroom instead of tiles).

Crown
Customer advice centre on
01254-704951 for stockists nationwide.
Major paint manufacturer.

Dulux
Retail Advice Centre:01753-550555.
Trade:01753-534225.
Literature:01420-23024.
Manufacturer of a wide range of paints, retail
and trade, including the 'Heritage Colours'
reproduced from original Georgian, Regency,
Victorian, Edwardian and Art Deco paint
schemes. Also floor paint, blackboard
paint and tile paint.

Farrow & Ball
33 Uddens Trading Estate,
Wimborne, Dorset BH21 7NL.
T:01202-876141. F:01202-873793.
Paint charts and mail order.
Showroom at:
249 Fulham Rd, London SW3.
T/F: 0171-351 0273.
Manufacturers of 'The National Trust Range',
available in 57 colourways and 7 paint
types: dead flat oil, oil eggshell, oil full gloss,
estate emulsion, oil bound distemper, soft
distemper and traditional lead (with names

like Ointment Pink, Dead Salmon and
Mouse's Back). Very good range of off-whites.

Fired Earth
Twyford Mill, Oxford Rd,
Adderbury, Oxon OX17 3HP.
T:01295-812088. F:01295-810832.
Many other branches. Range of paints
developed with the V&A and available in
dead flat oil, distemper, eggshell and
emulsion. The 'Historic Colours'are based
on earth pigments in use before 1820,
whereas the vivid Pugin colours are from an
1840s palette used in the decoration of The
Palace of Westminster (chemical pigments
were by then available).

Foxell & James
57 Farringdon Rd, London EC1 3JB.
T:0171-405 0152. F:0171-405 3631.
Good one-stop paint shop. Large range
of specialist products and the main outlet
for Ardenbrite paint.

*Hammerite Products
Prudhoe, Northumberland NE42 6LP.
T:01661-830000 for stockists.
Paints for metal - radiators, old beds,
garden furniture. Available in three
finishes and lots of colours. They
also make car care products.

Heart of the Country
Home Farm, Swinfen,
Nr Lichfield, Staffs WS14 9QR.
T:01543-481612. F: 01543-481684.
Import and sell by post the'Heritage Village
Colours' by the American company Gryphin.

Holman Specialist Paints
15/16 Central Trading Estate,
Signal Way, Swindon, Wilts SN3 1PD.
T:01793-511537. F:01793-431142.
Outlet for Valtti (from Finland) and Jotun
(from Norway) - ranges of interior and
exterior paints and finishes, including
floor paints and industrial coatings.
Also 'Tintex' furniture paints and
stains and fire-retardant coatings.

The Kasbah
8 Southampton St, London WC2E 7HA.
T:0171-240 3538.F:0171-379 5231.
Colours of Morocco are water-based paints

made with natural pigments. There are 13 rich colours including Bleu Kasbah and Rouge Marrakech.

Nutshell Natural Paints
Hamlyn House, Mardle Way, Buckfastleigh, Devon TQ11 0NR.
T:01364-642892. F:01364-643888.
Paints made to traditional and ecologically sound recipes used for restoration work. Their Casein Milk Paint is a hard-wearing alternative to conventional distemper.

John Oliver
33 Pembridge Rd, London W11 3HG.
T:0171-727 3735. F:0171-727 5555.
Has been creating paint colours for clients since the early Sixties. Good on strong shades as well as authentic colours for historic houses. Colourmatching service available.

Paint Library
25 Draycott Place, London SW3 2SH.
T:0171-823 7755. F:0171- 823 7766.
Handmade paints and glazes - 112 colours and 12 finishes. Plus metallic and pearlescent colours.

Paint Service Company
19 Eccleston St, London SW1W 9LX.
T:0171-730 6408. F:0171-730 7458.
Glazes, stains, and specialist brushes.

Paper and Paint Effects
17 Holywell Hill, St Albans, Herts AL1 1EZ.
T:01727-836338.
For mail order: T:01727-834353.
F:01727-845353.
Range of emulsions and oil colours based on 18th and 19th century colours. Plus pigments, glazes and specialist brushes.

Papers and Paints
4 Park Walk, London SW10 0AD.
T:0171- 352 8626. F:0171-352 1017.
Have been selling paints for 40 years and colour-matching to order. For the past ten years historic paint colours have been added to their range.

Potmolen Paint
27 Woodcock Ind Estate, Warminster,Wilts BA12 9DX.
T:01985-213960. F:01985-213931.

Traditional paints: distempers, limewashes and linseed oil paints.

Rose of Jericho
At: St Blaise, Westhill Barn, Evershot, Dorchester, Dorset DT2 0LD.
T:01935-83662. F:01935-83017.
Manufacturers of traditional mortars and paints.

Sanderson
T:0171-584 3344 for stockists.
Spectrum range of 1350 colours.

Shaker
322 King's Rd, London SW3 5UH.
T:0171-352 3918. F:0171-376 3494.
And at:
25 Harcourt St, London W1H 1DT.
T:0171-724 7672. F:0171-724 6640.
Suppliers of the 'Old Village' colonial colours by Stulb.

*Simoniz International
Treloggan Ind Estate, Newquay, Cornwall TR7 2SX.
T:01637-871171. F:01637-878627.
Manufacturers of car-care products like high-tech spray paints, including matt-black and chrome finishes.

*Tor Coatings Group
Portobello Ind Estate, Birtley, Chester-Lee St, County Durham DH3 2RE.
T:0191-4106611. F:0191-492 0125.
Manufacturers of Ardenbrite gold, silver and other metallic paints used widely in the redecoration of churches, theatres, museums and embassies.

WOOD FINISHES

Dulux
Advice Centre on 01753-550555 for stockists. Wood stains, preservatives and varnishes to cater for most projects.

Liberon Waxes
Mountfield Ind Estate, Learoyd Rd, New Romney, Kent TN28 8XU.
T:01797-367555. F:01797-367575.
Wood products for sealing and colouring, as well as restoration products, metal cleaners and polishers, gilt creams and varnishes.

* denotes trade supplier. Please phone for retail outlets. 193

Ostermann & Scheiwe (UK)

Osmo House, 26 Swakelys Drive,
Ickenham, Middx UB10 8QD.
T:01895-234899. F:01895-252171.
Exterior and interior colour wood finishes
based on natural oils and waxes which
keep the wood elastic and water-repellent.

Sadolin (UK)

Sadolin House, Meadow Lane,
St Ives, Cambs PE17 4UY.
T:01480-496868. F:01480-496801.
Complete range of wood preservatives,
stains and varnishes in attractive colours.
Their technical advisory service provides
written specifications or samples.

Valtti Specialist Coatings

Unit B3, South Gyle Crescent Lane,
Edinburgh EH12 9EG.
T:0131-334 4999. F:0131-334 3987.
Importers of a range of interior and exterior
paints and finishes from Finland. Particularly
good for their opaque and translucent wood
finishes (in Scandinavian blues and greys)
for use on weatherboarding or other exterior
sawn or smooth timber.

STENCILS / PIGMENTS & SPECIALIST SUPPLIERS

Brodie & Middleton

68 Drury Lane, London WC2B 5SP.
T:0171-836 3289. F:0171-497 8425.
Theatrical suppliers of everything from
ultra-violet powder to brushes and
fireproofing materials. They also sell French
enamel varnishes (used to create the look of
stained glass windows) and supply pigments
by post.

L Cornelissen & Son

105 Great Russell St, London WC1B 3RY.
T:0171-636 1045. F:0171-636 3655.
Pigments and artists' supplies. Materials
for gilding. Worldwide mail order service .

The English Stamp Company

Sunnydown, Worth Matravers,
Dorset BH19 3JP.
T:01929-439117.F:01929-439150.
Print your own decorative effects on walls,
paper, fabric or ceramics. The sturdy stamp
kits include a roller and ink pad and a carved
wooden stamp in two sizes. There is a mail
order catalogue with dozens of designs.

Green and Stone

259 King's Rd, London SW3 5EL.
T:0171 352 0837. F:0171-351 1098.
Artists' supplies and restoration materials
like liquid soap for cleaning stone (e.g. for
removing ingrained dirt in marble), textiles
and oil paintings, as well as lacquers and
glazes for china.

*LG Harris & Co

Stoke Prior, Bromsgrove, Worcs B60 4AE.
T:01527-575441. F:01527-575366.
Quality brushes and decorating tools.

Lyn le Grice

The Flowerloft, Trereife,
Penzance, Cornwall TR20 8TJ.
T:01726-812389.
For the large-scale designs used in the
original Stencilled House created by Lyn le
Grice phone the studio on 01736-64193.
Catalogue available also for smaller
scale designs.

Mad Hatters

26 High St, Otford, Kent TN14 5PQ.
T:01959-525578. Stencils, heat pens for
cutting stencils and other home decorating
products including water-based emulsions.

Paint Magic

Head office:
79 Shepperton Rd, London N1 3DF.
T:0171-354 9696. F:0171-226 7760.
Branches in Richmond, Notting Hill,
Islington, Arundel, Belfast and abroad. Mail
order. Jocasta Innes' book 'Paint Magic'
started the craze for paint finishes 10 years
ago. Her shops sell all you need: stencils,
stamps, wood and colour washes, verdigris
and liming kits, varnishes, découpage
equipment as well as books and videos on
techniques. Courses offered.

Pavilion Originals
6a Howe St, Edinburgh EH3 6TD.
T:0131-225 3590. F:0131-225 9913.
Suppliers of paints, glazes and stencilling
materials, including a varnish to cover newly-
stencilled ceramic tiles.

E. Ploton
273 Archway Rd, London N6 5AA.
T: 0181-348 0315. F:0181-348 3414.
One of London's widest and best-priced
sources for gilding and artist's materials.

Reeves Dryad Craft Centre
178 Kensington High St, London W8 7NX.
T:0171-937 5370.
Fabric paints, lacquers for stained glass
effects, china paints and much else in
this emporium of artist's supplies.

Relics of Witney
35 Bridge St, Witney, Oxon OX8 6DA.
T/F:01993-704611.
Distributors of decorative painter Annie
Sloan's range of paints and pigments, as
well as mail order suppliers of products and
brushes for stencilling, découpage, gold leaf.

The Stamping Ground
PO Box 1364, London W5 5ZE.
T:0181-758 8629. F:0181-758 8647.
Range of stamps for printing motifs
onto walls, floors, fabrics etc.

The Stencil Library
Stocksfield Hall, Stocksfield,
Northumberland NE43 7TN.
T:01661-844844. F:01661-843984.
Mail order catalogue with almost 1000
stencil designs. Courses & commissions.

The Stencil Store
20-21 Heronsgate Rd,
Chorleywood, Herts WD3 5BN.
T:01923-285577. F:01923-285136.
And at:
89 Lower Sloane St, London SW1W 8DA.
T:0171-730 0728.
Mail order catalogue with over 300 stencil
designs, plus specialist equipment.

Stuart Stevenson
68 Clerkenwell Rd, London EC1M 5QA.
T:0171-253 1693. F:0171-490 0451.
Artist's, gilding and restoration materials.

Whistler Brush Co
128 Fortune Green Rd, London NW6 1DN.
T:0171-794 3130. F:0171-435 2346.
Manufacturer of specialist brushes for
graining, marbling and faux finishes.

DECORATIVE PAINTERS

Adam Calkin
Albion House, 47 Bath Rd,
Atworth, Wilts SN12 8JT.
T/F:01225-702177.
Trompe l'oeil landscapes, panelling,
neo-classical decoration and even wood-
coffered ceilings. Design, consultation
and supervision of projects.

Belinda Canosa
38 St Mary's Grove, London W4 3LN.
T:0181-747 0436. F:0181-995 1099.
Will commision murals, trompe l'oeil,
frescos and fine copies of paintings from a
wide range of artists on their books.
Anything from a Tiepolo to the neo-classical
design for the domed ceiling of the Soane
Museum's new Picture Room.

David Carter
109 Mile End Rd, London E1 4UJ.
T/F:0171-790 0259.
All aspects of interior decoration with special
emphasis on paint finishes such as trompe
l'oeil and faux effects. He also has a range
of unusual furniture and accessories
including a trompe l'oeil fireplace painted
on canvas which can be ordered in any
size or shape.

Davies Keeling Trowbridge
3 Charterhouse Works,
Eltringham Street, London SW18 1TD.
T:0181-874 3565. F:0181-874 2058.
Large group of specialists who will tackle
all sorts of decorative finishes including
plasterwork, murals, trompe l'oeil,
stencilling and gilding and also hand
painting of tiles and fabrics.

Flaminia Murals
T:0171-727 2900. By appointment.
Murals and trompe l'oeil are Amanda
Glossop's forte. She paints fake columns,

* denotes
trade supplier.
Please phone
for retail outlets. 195

bookshelves, niches with statues, even Persian rugs or oak floorboards.

The Francesca Di Blasi Company

37 Portland Road, London W11 4LH. T:0171-221 1312. F:0171-221 1295. Specialist in plaster finishes: 'Marmorina' is like finished stone - either polished or rough-patterned. Their stucco finish is an alternative to marble. They actually fly specialists in from Morocco for the Moroccan wall finish.

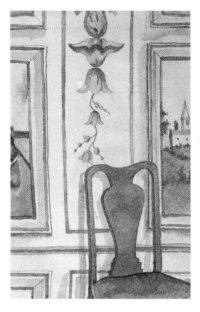

Friend or Faux

28 Earsham St, Bungay, Suffolk NR35 1AG. T:01986-896170. F:01502-714246. Specialize in hand-painted furniture, headboards, wardrobes and cabinets. They can also be commissioned for paint finishes, mural work and custom reproductions.

Hampstead Decorative Arts

2/20 Highgate High Street, London N6 5JG. T:0181-348 2811.Harry Levinson runs this training workshop for specialist painters but also undertakes commissions in marbling, graining, exotic finishes and trompe l'oeil.

Touchstone Design

10 Dollis Park, London N3 1HG. T:0181-349 0195. By appointment. Traditional and avant-garde trompe l'oeil and murals. Fine quality faux-marbre and faux-bois. Stencil work and all decorative effects. Impressive client list includes English Heritage.

Sebastian Wakefield

Cam Laithe, Far Lane, Kettlewell, Skipton, N Yorks BD23 5QY. T:01756-760809. F:01756-760857. Highly skilled paint finish specialist covering London as well as Northern England. He undertakes oil and water gilding, distressing and ageing, mural and trompe l'oeil and all other special effects. He can also provide top quality decorators for special jobs. He's worked for Mary Fox Linton and David Hicks.

RESTORATION MATERIALS

Berrycraft

Swansbrook Lane, Horam, Sussex TN21 0LD. T:01435-812383. Suppliers of raffia, fibre rush and sea-grass. They stock chair caning materials including Danish cord (twisted paper tape). If they can't do the re-caning themselves they can put you in touch with someone who can.

The Cane Store

207 Blackstock Rd, London N5 2LL. T/F:0171-354 4210. Restorers of canework. They can supply bamboo poles, cane poles, sheets of woven cane, chair cane, basket cane, seagrass, rush, raffia and willow.

HG Chard & Sons

Albert Rd, Bristol BS2 0X5. T:0117-977 7681. F:0117-971 9802. Materials for the restoration of ornamental plasterwork.

The Easy Chair Co

30 Lyndhurst Rd, Worthing, Sussex BN11 2DF. T:01903-201081. F:01903-237840. Complete range of DIY upholstery and curtain making products by mail order. Trade packs also available. There are adhesives, cane, castors, foam, hessians, piping cords, seagrass, staple guns, tacks, twines and a wide selection of upholstery nails in brass, steel and antique finishes.

Green and Stone

See entry under
**STENCILS/PIGMENTS
& SPECIALIST SUPPLIERS.**

Liberon Waxes

See entry under **WOOD FINISHES.**
Manufacturers and suppliers of restoration
products by mail order or through one of
their 2000 stockists. Furniture cleaning wax,
floor dyes, sealers and waxes, liming waxes,
marble reviver and all sorts of touch-up
pens to disguise scratches.

Picreator Enterprises

44 Park View Gardens, London NW4 2PN.
T:0181-202 8972. F:0181-202 3435.
Suppliers of professional conservation
materials. Their Renaissance furniture polish
can be used to take grime off wood, metal,
marble/onyx, shell, stone, ivory, plastics,
leather and even paper.

The Textile Restoration Studio

2 Talbot Rd, Bowdon,
Altrincham, Cheshire WA14 3JD.
T/F:0161-9280020. Specialist products for
the cleaning, repair, mounting, display and
storage of textiles. Plus Flameguard fire
retardant spray. All available by mail order.

Alec Tiranti

70 High St, Theale,
Reading, Berks RG7 5AR.
T:0118-9302775. F:0118-9323487
(Mail order). And at:
27 Warren St, London W1P 5DG.
T/F:0171-636 8565. Tools, materials and
equipment for carving, sculpture, modelling.
Also gold leaf, varnishes and gold paints for
picture framers.

SPECIALIST CLEANERS

See also **DYERS.**

Cadogan Company

95 Scrubs Lane, London NW10 6QU.
T:0181-960 8020. F:0181-960 4037.
Specialist cleaners and reglazers of chintz.
Will take down, clean and reline (or even
remake) curtains and then rehang them.

They offer a no-shrinkage guarantee. Can
clean carpets, rugs, tapestries, Aubussons
and even marble fireplaces.

Chem-Dry Acclaimed

Oakdene Cottage, 74 Portmore Park Rd,
Weybridge, Surrey KT13 8HH.
T/F:01932-859090. American franchise
operation. They clean carpets, upholstery
and blinds on site without soaps or oily
detergents. Good at stain-removal.

K's of Mill Hill

Unit 2A, Hurricane Trading Estate,
Avion Crescent, Grahame Park Way,
London NW9 5QW.
T:0181-200 9889. F:0181-200 3032.
This family firm has been going for 31 years
and can clean any type of blind. Work is
done on the premises, except on venetian
blinds which are sent away for a special
ultrasonic process.

KCP (Specialist Interior Cleaning & Scotchgarding Services)

Suite 5, Nightingale House,
1-7 Fulham High St, London SW6 3JH.
T:0171-823 3532. F:0171-736 0946.
And branch in Oxford. Full cleaning service
including carpets, Oriental rugs, fabric
walling and festoon blinds. They offer a
comprehensive 'after builders clean-up',
plus scotchgarding, either of full rolls of
fabric for the trade, or in-situ for furniture
and carpets.

Pilgrim Payne & Company

290-294 Latimer Rd, London W10 6QU.
T:0181-960 5656. F:0181-964 0598.
Established in 1859 and holders of a
royal warrant - very good for dhurries,
kelims, woollen pile rugs and valuable
rugs, including silk ones. They also clean
curtains, upholstery, loose covers, pelmets,
fabric wallcovering, tapestries and fitted
carpets. Plus re-upholstery and curtain
making service.

The Revival Company

The Old Stores, The Green,
Great Milton, Oxford OX44 7NT.
T:0800-393689. F:01844-279080.
Branches covering W/SW/NW London/

*** denotes
trade supplier.
Please phone
for retail outlets.** 197

SAFFRON

Middx/ West Surrey/Berkshire/Bucks/ Oxon. Upholstery and curtain cleaning; curtain-making service also available. They provide a fire and flood restoration service which includes specialist cleaning or water extraction, building restoration, re-upholstery and curtain and carpet supply.

Servicemaster in the Capital
Unit 12, The Hawthorn Centre,
Elm Grove Rd, Harrow, Middx HA1 2RF.
T:0181-427 5318. F:0181-427 5319.
For franchises in other part of the country phone 0116-2364646. Cleaning of domestic carpets using a rotary brush method, with hot-water extraction for very greasy jobs. After cleaning, the furniture is replaced on protective pads during the drying stage (4-6 hours). Estimates are free. Re-tufting repairs can also be carried out.

The Textile Conservation Studios
Apt 37, Lord Chamberlain's Court,
Hampton Court Palace, East Molesey,
Surrey KT8 9AU.
T:0181-781 9811. F:0181-781 9813.
Specialists in textile conservation, they undertake cleaning of tapestries and fragile textiles (up to 18ft by 28ft) using equipment developed for the conservation of the state furnishings at Hampton Court Palace.

DYERS

Harry Berger Cleaners & Dyers
25 Station Rd,
Cheadle Hulme, Cheadle, Cheshire SK8 5AF.
T:0161-485 7733. F:0161-485 6327.
Dyers of covers and curtains, especially velvets which can even be dyed lighter than the original colour (chart showing their 17 standard colours is £1.50).

Chalfont Cleaners & Dyers
222 Baker Street, London NW1 5RT.
T:0171-935 7316. F:0171-486 6375.
Dye small quantities: short rolls of fabric, curtains, upholstery, covers and clothes to 16 standard colours. Will colour match for special orders and also provide a flame-proofing service.

Goldsmith Dyers
1A Albert Ave, off Albert Square,
London SW8 1BX.
T:0171-735 9016.
Dyers of trimmings and small items.

Rainbow International
Spectrum House, Lower Oakham Way,
Oakham Business Park, Mansfield,
Nottingham NG18 5BY.
T:01623-422488. F:01623-422466.
Carpet dyers and cleaners with franchises all over the country. Plain wool, plain nylon or wool/nylon blend carpets can be dyed successfully (from £3 to £9 per square yard).

Renaissance Dying
Wallis Woollen Mill,
Ambleston, Haverfordwest,
Pembrokeshire, Dyfed SA62 5RA.
T:01437-731297. F:01437-731766.
Dyers of woollen yarns with natural dyes as used up to 1870. They have done commission work for the National Maritime Museum, Oxford City Church and private clients.

PAINT STRIPPING

*Langlow Products
PO Box 32, Asheridge Rd,
Chesham, Bucks HP5 2QF.
T:01494-784866. F:01494-791128.
Manufacturers of 'Peel Away Paint Removal System'. It is environmentally safe and can remove many layers of paint with one application. Particularly suitable for surfaces involving carvings or mouldings.

M & D
269 Putney Bridge Rd, London SW15 2PT.
T:0181-789 3022. They strip chairs, doors and sell old pine furniture and fireplaces.

The Specialist Paint Removal Service
50 Amersham Rd,
New Cross, London SE14 6QE.
T/F:0181-692 2016.
Removal of all types of paint from plaster, wood, metal, terracotta and stone using an electronic vapour machine.

Strippers Paint Removers
PO Box 6, Sudbury, Suffolk CO10 6TW.
T:01787-371524. F:01787-313944.
Claim to be able to remove paint, graffiti,
varnish and textured coatings from all
sorts of surfaces without damage.

METALWORK/IRONWORK

Adam Booth
Pipers Forge, 4 Victoria St, Kirkpatrick
Durham, Castle Douglas, DG7 3HQ.
T/F:01556-650513.
Metalworker specialising in one-off
commissions. Everything from a large
balustrade for a house in Antigua to gates
shaped like cathedral spires. Trellises,
railings, fireplaces and weathervanes -
anything in iron.

Capricorn Architectural Ironwork
Tasso Forge, Tasso Yard,
56 Tasso Rd, London W6 8LZ.
T:0171-381 4235. F:0171-603 1283.
All wrought iron commissions undertaken:
railings, gates, spiral staircases - from
reproduction to contemporary designs.

The Cast Iron Shop
394 Caledonian Rd, London N1 1DW.
T:0171-609 0934. F:0171-607 7565.
Victorian castings catalogue, with 1000s of
floor plates, treads, brackets, friezes, railing
heads, finials and railing panels in stock.

*Dorothea
Pearl House, Hardwick St,
Buxton, Derbys SK17 6DH.
T:01298-79121. F:01298-70866.
Manufacturers of railings, bollards, litter
bins, street lamps and seating, signs and
cast ironwork in both traditional and
contemporary styles.

Doverhay Forge Studios
Porlock, Minehead, Somerset TA24 8QB.
T/F:01643-862444. One of the country's
most established blacksmiths. Previous
large commissions include the screen and
railings for London's Savoy Theatre,
destroyed by fire in 1990, and the grille for
the dome of Sir John Soane's Museum.

House of Steel
400 Caledonian Rd, London N1 1DN.
T/F:0171-607 5889.
Treasure trove of antique ironwork. Will
tackle anything in metal, from restoration
to new designs: chairs and tables, lamps,
curtain poles, sundials, railings, gates
and spiral staircases.

James Hoyle & Son
The Beehive Foundry,
50 Andrews Rd, London E8 4RL.
T:0181-551-6764.
F:0181-550 9055.
Uses wooden moulds to make 350 types of
railing heads. Also giant lamps for bridges,
55 stock patterns of balcony
balustrades and special
commissions.

Malborough Forge
Newquay Workshop,
Embankment Rd,
Kingsbridge, Devon TQ7 1JZ.
T/F:01548-852390. Georgian
balconettes based on 18th and
19th century originals as well as
Victorian and simpler designs.
Prices from £150 to £400.
Also renovation of traditional
metalwork.

Richard Quinnell
Rowhurst Forge,
Oxshott Rd, Leatherhead, Surrey KT22 0EN.
T:01372-375148. F:01372-386516.
Received an MBE for his work in 1989.
Works in wrought and cast iron, steel,
copper, bronze, brass, aluminium and lead.
Founded the 'Fire and Iron Gallery', based at
his forge - an excellent place to look at his
own work and that of colleagues.

The Real Wrought Iron Company
Carlton Husthwaite,
Thirsk, N.Yorks YO7 2BJ.
T:01845-501415. F:01845-501072.
The only supplier in the United Kingdom
of real wrought iron (what most people call
wrought iron is actually steel). It hasn't been
manufactured by anyone else since the
1970s and they supply it worldwide.

* denotes
trade supplier.
Please phone
for retail outlets. 199

It comes in all sizes and shapes- round, flat or square. They also produce 'charcoal iron' which is what armour was made of.

Strawberry Steel
Broadway Studios,
28 Tooting High St, London SW17 0RG.
T:0181-672 4465. F:0181-767 3247.
From metal garden furniture to rose arches from this young team - chairs, dining tables, mirrors, fireguards, chandeliers, beds.

Chris Topp
Carlton Husthwaite, Thirsk, N.Yorks YO7 2BJ.
T: 01845-501415. F:01845-501072.
One of the North's most respected firms. Has done work at Downing Street, Chatsworth, The Guildhall, Waddesdon Manor and many other prestigious locations. Can be approached for even the smallest architectural ironwork. He also sells wrought iron in bar or sheet form.

Verdigris
Arch 290, Crown St, London SE5 0UR.
T:0171-703 8373. Manufacturers of pewter bars. They undertake metalwork restoration and colouring, bronzing, gilding, lacquering, plating and patination.

Villiers Brothers
Fyfield Hall, Fyfield, Essex CM5 0SA.
T:01277-899680. F:01277-899008.
One-off furniture and lighting in iron for interior designers, architects, films and theatre. Recent work includes an unusual chandelier for a church and fittings for the Ralph Lauren shop.

*DW Windsor
Marsh Lane, Ware, Herts SG12 9QL.
T:01920-466499. F:01920-460327.
Cast iron street furniture.

METAL SHEETING/ CHICKEN WIRE/ RADIATOR GRILLES

Antique Restorations
The Old Wheelwright's Shop,
Brasted Forge, Brasted, Kent TN16 1JL.
T:01959-563863. F:01959-561262.
Some 800 reproduction brass and foundry castings for furniture, doors and clocks reproduced (down to the blemishes) from 17th to 20th century fittings: chicken wire, capitals, keys, beading, backplates, finials, mounts, castors.

JD Beardmore
3-4 Percy St, London W1P 0EJ.
T:0171-637 7041. F:0171-436 9222.
Solid brass decorative grilles and frames.

The Brass Decorative Grille & Repolishing Company
Unit B7, Phoenix Ind. Estate, Rosslyn Crescent, Harrow, Middx HA1 2SP.
T:0181-863 8558. F:0181-863 5330.
Manufacturers of some 500 different decorative grilles, in brass, chrome, steel, aluminium, nickel or pewter finishes. Plus restoration of old grilles.

Builders, Iron & Zincworth
Millmarsh Lane, Brimsdown,
Enfield, Middx EN3 7QA.
T:0181-443 3300. F:0181-804 6672.
Aluminium, copper and zinc sheeting. Metal fabrication. They also supply rainwater products.

County and Capital Metals
Lockfield Ave, Brimsdown,
Enfield, Middx EN3 7PY.
T:0181-805 7277. F:0181-805 7308.
Fabricators and suppliers of stainless steel sheeting; brass, copper and aluminium to order.

DZ Designs
The Old Mill House, Stanwell Moor,
Staines, Middx TW19 6BJ.
T:01753-682266. F: 01753-685440.
Chicken wire in several finishes.

The Expanded Metal Company
PO Box 14, Longhill Ind Estate,
Hartlepool, N.Yorks TS25 1PR.
T:01429-867388. F:01429-866795.
Huge range of meshes in aluminium and plain, galvanised or stainless steel.

Gooding Aluminium
1 British Wharf, Landmann Way,
London SE14 5RS.
T:0181-692 2255. F:0181-469 0031.
Perforated and patterned aluminium sheets.

For more help: The British Artist Blacksmiths' Association (T/F:01845-501415) will send out a list of members in your area and information on how to commission work.

Metra Non-Ferrous Metals
Pindar Rd, Hoddesdon, Herts EN11 0DE.
T:01992-460455. F:01992-451207.
Supplier of zinc and copper sheet.

Smiths Metal Centres
42-56 Tottenham Rd, London N1 4BZ.
T:0171-241 2430. F:0171-254 9608.
Sheet aluminium and copper suitable
for wall cladding.

PLASTERWORK

Aristocast Originals
14A Orgreave Close, Dorehouse Ind.
Estate, Handsworth, Sheffield S13 9NP.
T:0114-2690900. F:0114-2690955.
An in-house sculptor can advise on
restoration work and the design,
manufacture and installation of decorative
mouldings in plaster, GRP and GRG.

Articole Studios
9 Alexander Rd, Stotfold,
Hitchin, Herts SG5 4NA.
T/F:01462-835640.
Specialist mould makers for building
restoration, architectural ornament, film
and advertising, etc. They take a mould
from the original object (or create a master
shape) in rubber or fibreglass; the final
object can then be produced in fibreglass,
reconstructed stone, plaster or resin marble.

H&F Badcock
Unit 9, 57 Sandgate Street,
Old Kent Road, London SE15 1LE.
T:0171-639 0304. F:0171-358 1239.
Well established manufacturer of high
quality fibrous plasterwork. Can match
existing mouldings or make them up to
the client's specifications.

Copley Decor
Leyburn, N.Yorks DL8 5QA.
T:01969-623410. F:01969-624398.
Cellular resin cornices, ceiling roses
and dados.

Designed Plastercraft Associates
35 Shore Road, London E9 7TA.
T:0181-985 8866. F:0181-986 3168.
Work includes the fibrous plaster vaulted

ceiling in the Tower of London,
commissioned by English Heritage.

Grandisson
The Mill, Alansway,
Ottery St Mary, Devon EX11 1NR.
T:01404-812876. Decorative plasterwork,
including columns, ceiling roses, panel
and dado mouldings, niches, cornices,
corbels, plaques.

L.Grandison
Innerleithen Road,
Peebles, Scotland EH45 8BA
T/F: 01721-720212.
Ornamental plasterwork and traditional line
plastering including stabilizing of ceilings.

Green & Veronese
Interiors House, Lynton Rd, London N8 8SL.
T:0181-348 9262. F:0181-341 9878.
Supply and installation of contemporary
fibrous plaster mouldings including cornices,
ceiling centres, wall and ceiling panels,
columns, capitals and niches.

EJ Harmer
19A Birkbeck Hill, London SE21 8JS.
T:0181-670 1017. F:0181-766 6026.
Plaster casts for restoration projects.

Hayles & Howe
25 Picton St, Montpelier, Bristol BS6 5PZ.
T:01179-246673/422863.
F:01179-243928. Cornices, wall friezes,
ceiling plates, panel mouldings, ceiling
roses, corbels, brackets, niches and wall
plaques. Jacobean strapwork ceilings,
columns and capitals, arches, urns and
statues all in ornamental plasterwork. They
made magnificent scagliola pedestals for the
Throne Room at Buckingham Palace.

Hodkin & Jones
Callywhite Lane,
Dronfield, Sheffield S18 6XP.
T: 01246-290890. F: 01246-290292.
Fibrous plaster cornices and centrepieces.

**For a list of
ornamental
plasterers contact
the National
Federation of
Plastering
Contractors, 18
Mansfield Street,
London W1M 9FG.
T:0171-580 5588.**

*** denotes
trade supplier.
Please phone
for retail outlets.** 201

G Jackson & Sons

Clark & Fenn, Unit 19, Mitcham Ind. Estate, Streatham Road, London CR4 2AJ. T:0181-648 4343. F:0181-640 1986. 200 year old plasterwork company. They restored the plaster mouldings for Uppark after the 1989 fire. Originally co-founded by Robert Adam.

Locker & Riley

23 Faraday Rd, Leigh-On-Sea, Essex SS9 5JU. T:01702-528803. F:01702-526125. Supply and install fibrous plaster cornices, panel moulds, plaques, dados, ceiling centrepieces, columns and arches. Period specialists. Will undertake commissions.

London Fine Art Plaster

8 Audrey Street, London E2 8QH. T:0171-739 3594. F:0171-729 5741. Plaster cornices and anything in ornamental fibrous plaster.

London Plastercraft

314 Wandsworth Bridge Road, London SW6 2UF. T:0171-736 5146. F:0171-736 7190. Interior and exterior moulded work. Production from stock moulds or tailor made service to architects' specifications: ceiling roses, fire surrounds, columns and pilasters.

Stevensons of Norwich

Roundtree Way, Norwich, Norfolk NR7 8SQ. T:01603-400824. F:01603-405113. Fibrous plaster and GRP cornices, mouldings, fireplaces, columns, arches, niches, panel moulds, corbels and ceiling roses. Matching service for existing ornamental plasterwork.

Troika Architectural Mouldings

Troika House, 41 Clun Street, Sheffield S4 7JS. T:0114-275 3222. F:0114-275 3781. Design, manufacture and installation of fibrous plasterwork: columns, domes, archways, fire surrounds, centrepieces, mouldings, friezes, niches and cornices. Will even design decorative ceilings (they did the Oriental ceilings in The Dorchester Hotel).

FRAMERS

Academy Framing

Off Burlington Gardens, London W1V 0DS. T:0171-494 5646. F:0171-434 0837. Affiliated with the Royal Academy, this framing shop offers high quality at reasonable prices and provides a restoration and conservation service.

*Art Contact

2 Rickett Street, London SW6 1RU. T:0171-381 8655. F:0171-386 9015. Trade only picture framing, art consultancy, gilding and installation. Sourcing of unusual prints and pictures for commercial or residential situations.

*Art Works

50 High Street, Walton-on-Thames, Surrey KT12 1BY. T/F:01932-226954. Call for retail outlets in Weybridge and Walton-on-Thames. Specialise in corporate framing and installation in pubs, hotels, restaurants or offices. Their retail shops offer a full framing service and a selection of limited edition prints.

Artefact

36 Windmill St, London W1P 1HF. T:0171-636 5244. F:0171-580 0987. Specialist framers who have a 48 page catalogue featuring their collection of frames and prints. Decorative accessories for the wall and mirrors ranging in style from the contemporary to the historical. Good selection of photo frames.

Blue Jay Frames

Possingworth Craft Workshops, Blackboys, E Sussex TN22 5HE. T:01435-866258. F:01435-868473. Will copy existing frames or frame to order from a large selection of mouldings and mounts. Free daily pick-up service in London and the South East.

Bourlet

32 Connaught Street, London W2 2AY. T/F:0171-724 4837. Hand-carved frames: in fruitwood, veneer, inlaid, with marquetry or gilded. Also one-off commissions.

Lucy B Campbell Gallery
123 Kensington Church St, London W8 7LP.
T:0171-727 2205. F:0171-229 4252.
Decorative and classical handmade frames
in all styles and finishes. Specialist framer
of antiquarian prints and naive paintings
(they have an excellent stock of both).

The Charles Daggett Gallery
153 Portobello Rd, London W11 2DY.
T:0171-229 2248. F:0171-229 0139.
Antique frame specialists who undertake
restoration, re-gilding, conservation work
and frame-making.

Sebastian D'Orsai
8 Kensington Mall, London W8 4EA.
T:0171-229 3888. F:0171-221 0746.
Specialist framers who can also clean prints
and watercolours and organise oil painting
restoration. Plus fan cases, limewash and
verre eglomisé mounts. They stock a large
selection of decorative paterae.

Euroframe
127 Munster Rd, London SW6 6DD.
T:0171-736 2167. F:0181-870 9234.
Bespoke framers. They also specialise
in box frames.

Fix-A-Frame
280 Old Brompton Rd, London SW5 9HR.
T:0171-370 4189. F:0171-244 7876.
Cost-effective DIY assembly rooms for
framing - the staff offer advice and do the
tricky bits. They will also do the whole job,
for a small premium.

Highgate Framers
26 Highgate High Street, London N6 5JG.
T:0181-348 7041. Framers of tapestries,
works of art, children's christening gowns.
They do box frames, dye mounts, stencilled
and découpage frames for mirrors, frames
in any other finish to order plus ready-made
photo frames.

John Jones Art Centre
Stroud Green Road, London N4 3JG.
T:0171-281 5439. F:0171-281 5956.
Framers and suppliers of art materials.
Conservation department with two full-time
gilders; perspex construction for displays.
Custom made and ready made frames.

Paul Mitchell
99 New Bond St,
London W1Y 9LF.
T:0171-493 8732.
F:0171-409 7136.
Long established family
firm specialising
in the framing and
conservation of old and
modern master
paintings and drawings.
They have an extensive
stock of period frames
over four floors of an
18th century town
house, but they can
also reproduce frames
of all styles and periods.

Pendragon Frames
5 Laburnum Street,
London E2 8BA. T/F:0171-729 0608.
Conservation framers; specialists in hand-
finished mouldings and gilding. Delivery
service in the West End of London.

Anthony Reed
94 Walcot Street, Bath BA1 5BG.
T/F:01225-461969. Picture frame
designers and makers.

The Rowley Gallery
115 Kensington Church St, London W8 7LN.
T:0171-727 6495. F:0171-229 5561.
Framing to order in a wide selection of
painted and gilded woods; fan cases,
black glass mounts, mirror frames made
and restored; gilding of small items like
candlesticks.

*D & J Simons
122-150 Hackney Rd, London E2 7QL.
T:0171-739 3744. F:0171-739 4452.
Wholesale framing suppliers - from frames
by the metre to small wooden balls to
embellish a frame.

Trowbridge Gallery
555 King's Rd, London SW6 2EB.
T:0171-371 8733. F:0171-371 8138.
Antique and reproduction print specialist
and custom framing from an extensive
selection of samples and styles.

* denotes
trade supplier.
Please phone
for retail outlets. 203

JOINERS

Richard Cullinan Joinery
8 Ferrier Street, London SW18 1SW.
T:0181-871 0029. F:0181-871 0020.
Custom-made cupboards, bookcases,
radiator covers: range of bespoke and
ready-made joinery.

Darwin Bespoke Furniture
38A Darwin Rd, London W5 4BD.
T/F:0181-560 0424. Top quality joinery
to order: cabinetry, hand-made doors,
panelling and furniture.

Hallidays
The Old College, Dorchester-on-Thames,
Wallingford, Oxon OX10 7HL.
T:01865-340028. F:01865-341149.
Bespoke furniture (mainly in pine) including
corner cupboards, bookcases, radiator
covers, TV cabinets.

Hayloft Woodwork
3 Bond St, London W4 1QZ.
T:0181-747 3510. F:0181-742 1860.
Complete service including radiator covers,
bathroom cabinetry, fitted kitchens and
unusual beds (including children's).

Charles Hurst
Unit 21, Bow Triangle Business Centre,
Eleanor St, Bow E3 4NP.
T:0181-981 8562.
Will design and build anything from
a complete kitchen to a bookshelf
to order in hardwood - either
varnished or in a paint finish,
typically with clean simple
lines. He also sells kiln dried
tongue and groove
panelling in pine, to four
designs (£2.85 metre
plus VAT).

Johnston & Pycraft
See entry under
OTHER SPECIALISTS.

Plain English
The Tannery, Combs,
Stowmarket, Suffolk IP14 2EN.
T:01449-774028. F:01449-613519.
Best known for their plain kitchen
cabinetry, Plain English can also provide
fitted bathrooms, simple staircases,
cupboards and wardrobes.

Raleigh Workshop
120 Hollydale Rd, London SE15 2TQ.
T:0171-733 8110. Team of three versatile
cabinet makers, each with his own style.
Good for innovative, modern designs -
kitchens, bathrooms, full range of cabinetry.

Templederry Design
Hornacott, South Petherwin,
Launceston, Cornwall PL15 7LH.
T/F:01566-782461.
As this husband and wife team work out of
their barn, overheads are low. They offer a
complete joinery service - bookcases, fitted
bathrooms, kitchens and hardwood doors.
Enquiries are welcome from London and the
South of England.

Trevor Toms Cabinetmakers
Fisherton Mill, 108 Fisherton Street,
Salisbury, Wilts SP2 7QY.
T:01722-331139. Bespoke cabinet makers
who can provide fitted and free-standing
bedroom and bathroom furniture including
alcove units, drawing room units and
bookcases.

Andrew Varah
Little Walton, Nr Pailton, Rugby,
Warwicks CV23 0QL.
T:01788-833000.
F:01788-832527.
Best known for bespoke
furniture, Andrew Varah
also provides a top-
quality joinery service.

WOOD CARVING

Bourlet
See entry under FRAMERS.
Supply, to order, architraves, cornices,
capitals, skirtings, balusters and
bolection mouldings.

Richard Burbidge
Whittington Rd, Oswestry,
Shropshire SY11 1HZ.
T:01691-655131. F:01691-657694.

Manufacturer of pine mouldings including cornices, wainscoting, dado rails, panel mouldings and ornaments.

A W Champion
Champion House, Burlington Road,
New Malden, Surrey KT3 4NB.
T:0181-949 1621. F:0181-949 0271.
And seven other branches. Timber merchants with a very large range of mouldings.

Denny and Fancourt
68-70 Choumert Road, London SE15 4AX.
T:0171-639 5719. F:0171-639 5664.
Joinery manufacturers and cabinet makers who can make fine wood mouldings.

Jali
Apsley House, Chartham,
Canterbury, Kent CT4 7HT.
T:01227-831710. F:01227-831950.
MDF decorative fretworks: there are shelf trims, pelmets, brackets and trellis, all designed for self assembly.

W H Newson & Sons
61 Pimlico Road, London SW1W 8NF.
T:0171-730 6262. F:0171-924 1682.
And branches.
Catalogue features over 200 items including mouldings, cornices, architraves, skirting and staircase parts in timber.

Oakleaf Reproductions
Ling Bob, Main Street,
Wilsden, Bradford BD15 0JP.
T:01535-272878. F:01535-275748.
High quality simulated wood mouldings in cellular resin. Rough-hewn oak beams, 'Jacobean' wall panelling, ornate cornice and frieze, carved panels, carved mirrors. Other mouldings to order.

Winther Browne
Nobel Road, Eley Estate, Edmonton,
London N18 3DX.
T:0181-803 3434. F:0181-807 0544.
Manufacturers of banisters and an extensive selection of wood carvings and mouldings - plus details to embellish plain doors, walls or bookcases. Screening panels and radiator cabinets; mouldings for picture framing; even replacement turned legs for furniture.

WALL PANELLING

Architectural Heritage
Taddington Manor, Taddington, Nr Cutsdean,
Cheltenham, Gloucs GL54 5RY.
T:01386-584414. F:01386-584236.
18th and 19th century panelling in oak, mahogany and pine.

Roy Blackman Associates
150 High Rd, Chadwell Heath,
Romford, Essex RM6 6NT.
T:0181-599 5247. F:0181-598 8725.
Tudor-style polyurethane 'wood' panelling - looks like the real thing.

Crowther of Syon Lodge
Busch Corner, London Road,
Isleworth, Middx. TW7 5BH.
T:0181-560 7978. F:0181-568 7572.
'Period' panelling from a team of expert joiners, polishers and woodcarvers. Tudor linenfold, Jacobean, Queen Anne, Georgian styles in oak or pine, antique or new.

Darwin Bespoke Furniture
38A Darwin Rd, London E5 4BD.
T:0181 560 0424.
High quality bespoke panelling.

Deacon & Sandys
Hillcrest Farm Oast, Hawkhurst Rd,
Cranbrook, Kent TN17 3QD.
T:01580-713775. F:01580-714056.

Oak-planked and panelled doors and all sorts of architectural woodwork from wall-panelling to balustraded stairways.

Bernard Dru Oak
Bickham Manor, Timberscombe, Minehead, Somerset TA24 7UA.
T:01643-841312. F:01643-841048.
Weathered oak panels supplied to architects, cabinet makers and institutions such as The National Trust.

Hallidays
The Old College, Dorchester-on-Thames, Wallingford, Oxon OX10 7HL.
T:01865-340028. F:01865-341139.
Panelling in 'antique' carved pine or limed oak.

CF Handerson
36 Graham St, London N1 8JX.
T:0171-226 1212. F:0171-490 4913.
Suppliers of beech, oak or cherry veneered boards for wall panelling.

Charles Hurst
Unit 21, Bow Triangle Business Centre, Eleanor St, Bow E3 4NP.
T:0181-981 8562.
Can supply four designs of kiln-dried pine tongue and groove panelling (£2.85 per metre plus VAT).

Oakleaf Reproductions
See entry under WOOD CARVING.
'Burnsall' panelling moulded from 17th century original designs but made in cellular resin. Carved 'oak' linenfold panels. Stiles are either grooved, floral or plain - finishes are limed oak, light oak, weathered oak, Jacobean oak or mahogany.

Stuart Interiors
Barrington Court, Barrington, Nr Ilminster, Somerset TA19 0NQ.
T:01460-240349. F:01460-242069.
16th and 17th century-style oak panelling, staircases, doors and interior joinery as well as restoration work.

Thornhill Galleries
Rear of 78 Deodar Rd, London SW15 2NJ.
T:0181-874 2101. F:0181-877 0313.
Top quality period panelling, mainly English and French; English and French chimney

pieces and architectural woodcarvings. Established in 1880.

Victorian Wood Works
Gliksten Trading Est, 118 Carpenter Rd, London E15 2DY.
T:0181-985 8280.
F:0181-986 3770.
3/4 million pounds worth of reclaimed timber in stock: oak, pine or jarrah (Australian wood), reclaimed beams, reclaimed flooring and traditional bead and buck pub panelling.

Woodstock Furniture
4 William St, London SW1X 9HL.
T:0171-245 9989. F:0171-245 9981.
Custom-made wood panelling in maple, limed oak or cherrywood. Full fitting service.

STAIRCASES & PARTS

Albion Design of Cambridge
Unit H3, Dales Manor Business Park, Sawston, Cambs CB2 4TJ.
T:01223-836128. F:01223-837117.
Manufacturer of spiral staircases and architectural metalwork.

Richard Burbidge
See entry under WOOD CARVING.
Manufacturer of stair balustrading in timber.

Bylaw (Ross)
The Old Mill, Brookend Street, Ross-On-Wye, Hereford HR9 7EG.
T:01989-562 356. F:01989-768145.
Solid oak staircases with traditional balustrading.

Capricorn Architectural Ironwork
See entry under
METALWORK/IRONWORK.

The Cast Iron Shop (R Bleasdale Spirals)
See entry under
METALWORK/IRONWORK Cast iron and steel specialist. Staircases designed with matching balconies. Large selection of spirals. Metal staircases for fire escapes.

Chilstone
Victoria Park, Fordcombe Rd, Langton Green, Tunbridge Wells, Kent TN3 0RE.
T:01892-740866. F:01892-740249.

See also
ARCHITECTURAL
SALVAGE

Reconstructed stone door surrounds, step treads and balustrades.

Gifford Mead
Cooper House, 2 Michael Road, London SW6 2AD.
T:0171-371 9444. F:0171-371 7880.
Wood turners who specialise in parts for traditional staircases: spindles, newel posts, hand and base rails. Styles include barley twist, fluting and reeding in any timber.

Haddonstone
The Forge House, East Haddon, Northants NW6 8DB.
T:01604-770711. F:01604-770027.
Large range of balustrading: ramped, curved, spiral - all made of reconstructed stone.

E A Higginson
Unit 1, Carlisle Road, London NW9 0HD.
T:0181-200 4848. F:0181-200 8249.
Italian timber and steel spirals and manufacturers of all types of timber stairs to order. Plus purpose made architectural joinery.

House of Steel
See entry under
METALWORK/IRONWORK.

Kensington Traders
Unit 27, Ribocon Way, Progress Park, Leagrave, Luton, Bedford LU4 9TR.
T:01582-491171. F:01582-491925.

Wooden and iron staircases and parts. Large selection of staircases in any design.

Anthony Lennon
9 Belmont Rd, Twickenham Middx TW2 5DA.
T:0181-894 4568. Specialist in antique spiral staircases, mainly in cast iron. Also reclaimed balustrading.

W H Newson & Sons
See entry under
WOOD CARVING. Staircase parts.

WR Outhwaite & Son
Town Foot, Hawes, N.Yorks DL8 3NT.
T:01969-667487. F:01969-667576.
Bannister ropes in 24mm and 30mm diametres and nine different colours.
Polished brass or chrome brackets.

Plain English
The Tannery, Combs, Stowmarket, Suffolk IP14 2EN.
T:01449-774028. F:01449-613519.
Simple staircases in wood. The original design was inspired by a Tudor pub dated circa 1558.

Safety Stairways
Unit 45, Owen Road Ind Estate, Owen Road, Willenhall, W.Midlands WV13 2PX.
T:0121-526 3133. F:0121-526 2833.
Reproduction and modern designs in cast iron and steel. Also fire escapes.

Stairways Products
102 Chingford Mount Road, London E4 9AA.
T:0181-527 6180. F:0181-529 0372.
Manufacturer of traditional stairways and component parts.

ARCHITECTURAL FEATURES

Alumasc Building Products
Apex Works, Llanbrynmair, Powys SY19 7DU. T:01650-521496. F:01650-521505.
Extensive stock and made to order range of ornamental rainwater heads, moulded gutters and fixings based on historic designs.

The Brick Centre
Brimington Rd North, Chesterfield S41 9BH.
T:01246-260001. F:01246-454597.
New and reclaimed brick suppliers. They can

*** denotes
trade supplier.
Please phone
for retail outlets.** 207

find bricks to match existing ones. They also sell 'Brickmatch' - a DIY paint which gives an instant weathered effect.

Broadmead Products

Broadmead Works, Hart St, Maidstone, Kent ME16 8RE.
T:01622-690960. F:01622-765484.
Manufacturer of reconstructed stone mouldings for renovation of traditional or modern buildings.

Delabole Slate

RTZ Mining and Exploration, Pengelly Road, Delabole, Cornwall PL33 9AZ.
T:01840-212242.
F:01840-212948.
This blue-grey roofing slate has been mined since the 11th century and is considered to be amongst the best in the country. It is popular for conservation projects - the most recent being The National Trust's Uppark.

Good Directions

Unit 15, Talisman Business Centre, Duncan Road, Park Gate, Southampton SO31 7GA.
T:01489-577828. F:01489-577858.
GRP cupolas and turrets with slate, lead or copper effect roofs in a choice of styles and sizes to fit any pitch of roof. GRP rainwater heads in Victorian, Edwardian, Georgian, Gothic, Rococo and Regency styles. Plus a range of classic clocks for outdoor use.

Keymer

Nye Rd, Burgess Hill, W Sussex RH15 0LZ.
T:01444-232931. F:01444-871852.
Handmade clay tiles, including peg tiles, finials and tiles to individual specifications.

Lambs Bricks & Arches

Nyewood Court, Brookers Road, Billingshurst, W.Sussex RH14 9RZ.
T:01403-785141. F:01403-784663.
Traditional methods are used to produce decorative bricks and gauged arches for restoration and architectural embellishment.

J & JW Longbottoms

Bridge Foundry, Bridge Lane, Holmfirth, Yorks HD7 1AW.
T:01484-682141. F:01484-681513.

Manufacturer of cast iron rainwater and soil products.

Norman & Underwood

11-27 Freeschool Lane, Leics LE1 4FX.
T:01162-515000. F:01162-532669.
One of the country's oldest and most respected makers of lead roofs and ornamental lead. Still use the original sand-casting method for restoration or new designs.

John Smith & Sons

Midland Clock Works, Derby Ltd, 27 Queen Street, Derby, DE1 3DU.
T:01332-345569. F:01332-290642.
Largest firm of tower clockmakers in the UK. They maintain over 4,500 public clocks throughout the British Isles.

Solopark

The Old Railway Station, Station Rd, Nr Pampisford, Cambs CB2 4HB.
T:01223-834663. F:01223-834780.
One of the largest salvage yards nationwide. They also supply an extensive range of bricks and paviours (at least 20 varieties), tiles and slates (pantiles, chimney pots, hips, ridges), doors, fire surrounds, grates and baskets, stained glass, ironmongery, plaster mouldings, pews, windows and features like weather vanes, porticos and garden seats. There's also a vast timber yard with everything from beams to dado rails.

Tetbury Stone Company

Veizey's Quarry, Avening Road, Tetbury, Gloucs GL8 8JT.
T:01666-503455. F:01454-228141.
These stone slates are made from blocks of stone which split naturally along fault lines. They are used extensively by English Heritage.

BUILDERS' MERCHANTS & TIMBER YARDS

Moss & Company

Dimes Place, 104 King St, London W6 0QW.
T:0181-748 8251. F:0181-741 2470.
High quality timber and board. Kitchen worktops.Selection includes mahogany, oak,

ash, teak, maple, lime Jelutong, sycamore, rosewood, ebony, Russian pine, red cedar, Quebec yellow pine and Douglas fir.

JR Nelson
The Sawmill, Newchurch, Romney Marsh, Kent TN29 0DT.
T:0123-373 3361. F:0123-373 3702.
Sawyers and fabricators of seasoned timber. Specialists in pitch pine in various grades and lengths. Stair products, architectural mouldings, worktops, structural timbers, flooring and panelling. Restoration specialists - everything from windmills to castles.

WH Newson & Sons
See entry under **WOOD CARVING.**
Call for branches. Primarily timber merchants supplying a range of mouldings, doors and windows, but they also stock security, decorating, some building materials, insulation and fencing. Tool hire service.

Nu-Line Builders' Merchants
305-317 Westbourne
Park Road, London W11 1EF.
T:0171-727 7748. F:0171-792 9451.
Several showrooms for paints, decorating and cleaning materials, timber, sheet metal, doors, glass, mirror, ironmongery, tools, boilers, security equipment - the list goes on and on. Free delivery within five miles.

Travis Perkins
727 South Lambeth Road, London SW8 1RJ.
T:0171-582 4255, F:0171-587 0453.
Call for branches nationwide. Vast timber yard supplying full range of flooring, wood carvings and everything from bricks, blocks, chimneys - just about anything to do with the building trade.

GYM & GAME ROOM EQUIPMENT

Bolton Shirland International
Boland House, Unit 1, Nottingham South Ind Estate, Ruddington Lane, Wilford, Nottingham NG11 7EP.
T:0115-982 2844. F:0115-981 7784.

Distributors for Tunturi, David, Fitness Quest, Hebb Industries multigyms, cycles, rowers, joggers and steppers. Agents for the 'Life Shaper' multi-exerciser. Installation for home or professional gyms.

Hamilton Billiards & Games
Park Lane, Knebworth Herts SG3 6PJ.
T:01438-811995. F:01438-814939.
Manufacturer and supplier of traditional games. Billiard and snooker table specialist, but also antique and new table tennis, chess, boules and croquet sets.

PJ Equipment
205 Leabridge Road, London E10 7PN.
T:0181-539 4689. F:0181-558 0377.
Suppliers and outfitters for home and commercial gymnasiums.

SECURITY

Alarm Detection Supplies
1 Cherington Rd,
Selly Park, Birmingham B29 7ST.
T:0121-4141226. F:0121-4154525.
Distributors of the full spectrum of security equipment, from burglar alarms and safes to close circuit TV and security lighting.

Architectural Components
8 Exhibition Road, London SW7 2HF.
T:0171-584 6800. F:0171-589 4928.
Supply a large selection of mortice, rim, barrier bolt locks, bolts, floor and wall safes and door viewers.

Banham Security
233-235 Kensington High Street, London W8 6SF.
T:0171-622 5151. F:0171-498 2461.
Supply and fit locks, grilles, gates, safes, burglar alarms and electronic security systems. Also a 'Patent Locks' division with a key security system where keys are numbered and registered.

*Guardall
Lochend Ind Estate,
Newbridge, Edinburgh EH28 8PL.
T:0131-333 2900. F:0131-333 4919.
Manufacturers of all types of electronic intruder detector equipment.

For more help: The British Security Industry Association has 300 specialist members, covering anything from safes to manguarding. T:01905-21464. F:01905-613625.

* denotes trade supplier. Please phone for retail outlets.

Guardian Security
131 Sidwell Street, Exeter, Devon EX4 6RY. T:01392-277467. F:01392-424817. Master key systems and door security furniture. Safes, fire equipment, roller shutters and grilles.

JHS (UK)
19 Raddlebarn Road, Selly Oak, Birmingham B29 6HJ. T:0121-471 1801. F:0121-414 1081. Safes, bars, grilles, locks, alarms: the full range of security equipment.

Nu-Line Builders Merchants
See entry under **BUILDERS' MERCHANTS & TIMBER YARDS**. Can supply all major brands of security equipment: Chubb, Yale, Ingersoll.

SBH-Fichet (UK)
3 Apex Point, Welham Green, Hatfield, Herts AL9 7HB. T:01707-271177. F:01707-260644. Manufacture and install security systems: safes, locks etc.

AUDIO-SYSTEMS

Gibson Music
Unit 7, The Broomhouse, 50 Sullivan Rd, London SW6 3DX. T:0171-384 2270. F:0171-731 1580. Residential installation of hi-fi, TV and video systems custom designed to make the best use of space. Multi-room systems with concealed loudspeakers. Satellite and telephone systems. Corporate and commercial video, slide projection, ceiling screens, integrated control systems, planning and installation of door entry and telephone exchanges.

Project Connection
26 Gowrie Rd, London SW11 5NR. T:0171-207 2727. F:0171-207 2828. Planning, design and co-ordination of hidden music systems. Telephones and unified television connections from room to room; stereo and big picture screens. Switching and control systems, including dimmers and light sensitive switches, timers and remote control. Full central systems can be programmed to control anything including lighting, audio and video equipment, plant watering, heating and air-conditioning.

OTHER SPECIALISTS

The Aquatic Design Centre
9 Little Portland Street, London W1N 5DF. T:0171-636 6388. F:0171-323 4305. Designs, manufactures, installs and maintains aquariums and ponds for domestic and commercial situations.

Robert Cresser
40 Victoria St, Edinburgh EH1 2JW. T:0131-225 2181. This company has been making and selling brushes near Edinburgh castle since 1873. There are brushes for almost any task: bannister and cobweb brushes, silver brushes, bagpipe-chanter brushes, teapot spout brushes, curved ones for the ins and outs of old-fashioned radiators, refills for fireplace brushes - and more.

*Dermide
Westfield Mill, Carr Rd, Barnoldswick, via Colne, Lancs BB8 5UU. T:01282-812581. F:01282-812366. White table felt with a brown top sold by the metre. Four different widths or circular.

FA Heffer & Co
24 The Pavement, London SW4 0JA. T:0171-622 6871. F:0171-498 3990. Very large range of painting/decorating and cleaning/industrial brushes. Plus ladders and steps, tarpaulins, dust sheets.

Johnston & Pycraft
453 Fulham Rd, London SW10 9UZ. T:0171-352 2888. F:0171-460 0958. 200 trained craftsmen on board: plumbers, heating and electrical engineers, roofing contractors, glaziers, builders, designers and decorators. They run a 24 hour helpline and can deal with anything from window and carpet cleaning to fridge and washing machine repair. Full property maintenance. Recommended by the Metropolitan Police.

* denotes trade supplier. Please phone for retail outlets.

Richard Kindersley

40 Cardigan St, London SE11 5PF.
T:0171-735 9374. F:0171-587 0546.
One of the country's leading letter-cutters.
He's as happy working on large scale
architectural commissions as on small
private jobs.

Scanachrome

49 Glebe Rd, East Gillibrands,
Skelmersdale, Lancs WN8 9JP.
T:01695-725486. F:01695-722695.
Amazing technique where images are
scanned onto large canvases or nylon for
exhibition, advertising or decorative display.

Screwdriver

15 Geraldine Rd, London W4 3PA.
T/F:0181-994 2920. Team of 120 men
nationwide (26 in London) who will assemble
flat-pack furniture for you at home or in
your office. Rates are £20 an hour. Time
necessary can be worked out in advance.

*Rachel Yallop

39 Straithblaine Rd, London SW11 1RG.
T/F:0171-585 3783. Specialist calligrapher
for corporate clients and design consultants.
She runs the 'Letter Exchange', and can
recommend professional letterers in all
disciplines (stone carvers, sign writers,
calligraphers) and all over the country.

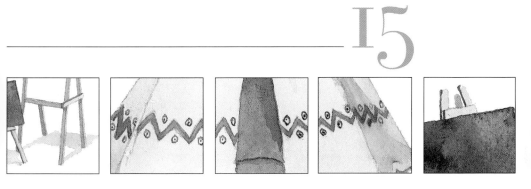

15

CHILDREN

CHILDREN'S FABRICS & WALLPAPERS

Celia Birtwell
71 Westbourne Park Rd, London W2 5QH.
T:0171-221 0877. F:0171-229 7673.
Sheer fabrics, cottons and linens handprinted with dots, stars and quirky animals.

*Brunschwig & Fils
10 The Chambers, Chelsea Harbour
Design Centre, London SW10 0XF.
T:0171-351 5797. F:0171-351 2280.
'Bunny Business' wallpaper and fabric.

Bundles Design
58 Church St, Twickenham,
London TW1 3NR.
T:0181-744 1440. F:0181-744 1442.
Large range of fabric and wallpaper designs:
ribbons and garlands, bunnies, soldiers and
drums, safari, owl and pussycat, plus
checks and spots with which they can be
matched. Also bedlinen, bedside lamps,
ceiling shades, accessories and a range of
painted and upholstered furniture.

*Chelsea of London
Springvale Terrace, London W14 0AE.
T:0171-602 7250. F:0171-602 9221.
'First Choice' range of fabrics with hippos,
lambs, fish, snakes, turtles and frogs;
'Beachcomber' range with fish.

*Chess Designs
Unit 10, Alma Rd,
Chesham, Bucks HP5 3HP.
T:01494-772074. F:01494-791575.
Fun prints on satin cotton in primary
or pastel colours. Designs include
Noah's ark and jungle patterns.

Designers Guild
267-271 & 277 King's Rd,
London SW3 5EN.
T:0171-351 5775. F:0171-243 7710.
Four collections of fabrics, wallpapers
and borders for children. 'Abracadabra',
'Toy Box Collection', 'Merry-go-round' and
'Hopscotch'. Plus old furniture painted in
wild colours, traditional toys and bedlinen,
with appliqué pillows and embroidered
sheets for cot and child's bed.

*** denotes
trade supplier.
Please phone
for retail outlets.** 213

Dragons
23 Walton St, London SW3 2HX.
T:0171-589 3795. F:0171-584 4570.
Hand-blocked wallpapers, borders and
fabrics in all sorts of designs including
Beatrix Potter characters, dragons, mice,
sailing boats. Plus large range of hand-
painted furniture and accessories.

*Doshi Wallcoverings
15 Whitburn Rd, London SE13 7UQ.
T:0181-690 9440. F:0181-690 4735.
Heavy vinyl wallcoverings, borders and
fabrics featuring Disney characters.

*Anna French
343 King's Rd, London SW3 5ES.
T:0171-351 1126. F:0171-351 0421.
'Ready Teddy Go' with teddy bears and safari
animals and 'Harum Scarum' with rag dolls
and rocking horses.

Nursery Window
83 Walton St, London SW3 2HP.
T:0171-581 3358. F:0171-823 8839.
Small-scale patterned wipeable wallpapers
and fabrics with trains, cars, fish, bunnies
and circus designs.

Osborne & Little
304 King's Rd, London SW3 5UH.
T:0171-352 1456. F:0171-351 7813.
Two children's collections: 'Scrapbook'
with Wind in the Willows characters and
'Charades' with moons and stars.

*Zoffany
Unit G12, Chelsea Harbour Design
Centre, London SW10 0XE.
T:0171-349 0043. F:0171-351 9677.
'Story Book' collection of co-ordinating
papers, borders and fabrics based on 19th
and 20th century documents. Designs
include alphabets, penny toys, soldiers,
butterflies, ships and Chinese music men.

CHILDREN'S FURNITURE

Bed Bazaar
The Old Station, Station Rd, Framlingham,
Suffolk IP13 9EE. T:01728-723756.
F:01728-724626. Victorian and Edwardian
iron cots and small single beds.

Bellpark
Unit A6, Brownlow Business Centre,
Darley St, Bolton BL1 3DX.
T/F:01204-387001. Reasonably priced
child's bed, wardrobe, chairs and other
items in white wood, a varnished finish
or hand-painted (including to order to
match wallpapers or fabrics).

Community Playthings
Darvell, Robertsbridge,
E. Sussex TN32 5DR.
Freephone: 0800-387457.
F:01580-882250. Suppliers of a wide range
(87 page catalogue) of very sturdy blocks,
toys, nursery gyms, rest and play mats,
playhouse furniture, rocking chairs, stools
etc. Most of it is in wood. They do a very
nice art centre (110cm high, £266) and
the 'Woodcrest' stacking chair, which is
lightweight and stable and has no joints
(from £42).

The Conran Shop
Michelin House, 81 Fulham Rd,
London SW3 6RD.
T:0171-589 7401. F:0171-823 7015.
Painted bed, wardrobe, dressing table
and cot; 'Cabina' striped fabric wardrobe
in red, blue, yellow or black.

Designers Guild
See entry under **CHILDREN'S FABRICS
& WALLPAPERS.**

Dragons
See entry under **CHILDREN'S FABRICS
& WALLPAPERS.**
Large range of furniture including
upholstered sofas and armchairs,
cupboards and wardrobes, chests of
drawers, tables and chairs, desks and
bureaus, cots and beds. They are available
with hand-painted designs from their own
repertoire or they can copy favourite toys,
pets and anything else. Mail order service.

Elephant Industries
Unit 14, Lansdowne Workshops,
London SE7 8AZ.
T/F:0181-850 6875. Handmade painted
wooden furniture to order. There's an
elephant step-stool, the 'Hangaroo' clothes'

horse, the 'Hopper' toy bin in the shape of a frog, and the snail-shaped 'Bookshell' which works as a reading seat and a double-sided bookshelf. Available by mail order.

*Farmer Foster
Tuff-Link House, Station Rd, Padiham, Lancs BB12 7AR. T:01282-779721. F:01282-777785. Wooden sand-pits and child-size picnic tables.

Habitat
196 Tottenham Court Rd, London W1P 9DL. T:0171-631 3880. F:0171-255 6043. For other branches call 0645-334433. Small range of simple painted items (fabric-lined wardrobe, four-poster bed, table and chairs), appliqué duvet covers and cushions in bold designs, wooden toys.

Harriet Ann Sleigh Beds
Standen Farm, Smarden Rd, Biddenden, Nr Ashford, Kent TN27 8JT. T/F:01580-291220. Restored wooden sleigh beds in all sizes (with the typical high sides) from Scandinavia and Eastern Europe. Mattresses made to order.

Harrods
Knightsbridge, London SW1X 7XL. T:0171-730 1234. Large range of baby to teenage furniture, including fire-engine beds and telephone box wardrobes.

Simon Horn
117-121 Wandsworth Bridge Rd, London SW6 2TP. T:0171-731 1279. F:0171-736 3522. Smart lit bateau that converts from a cot to a bed and then into a small two-seater sofa. The beds come in cherry, mahogany or oak and in Louis Philippe, Louis XV, Louis XVI and Empire styles. Prices from £1395.

IKEA
2 Drury Way, North Circular Rd, London NW10 0TH. T:0181-208 5600. And several other branches. Brightly coloured - and inexpensive - bunk beds, tables, desks, cots, even mini-armchairs. Plus toys and safety items like window catches and corner bumpers.

Joshua Jones
The Old Sawmill, Pamphill, Wimborne, Dorset BH21 4ED. T/F:01202-888821. Custom made painted furniture in pastel colours with contrasting lines, decorated to match fabrics or wallpapers, or available undecorated, ready to paint oneself. Plus Postman Pat and Racing Car beds.

Little Bridge
56 Battersea Bridge Rd, London SW11 3AG. T:0171-978 5522. F:0171-978 5533. Hand painted furniture painted with teddy bears, Noah's arks, soldiers, cars, dancers, children's names and any other motif to order.

Little Monsters
34 Geraldine Rd, London SW8 2NT. T:0181-874 6228. F:0181-870 4251. Painted round table and rush-seat chairs (£39). Bed linen and accessories.

Simon Maidment
Sam Design, 30 Underwood St, London N1 7JX. T/F:0171-251 5343. Designer of a smart and practical roll-top storage box/chair in solid beech and birch plywood with a red, yellow, green or blue plastic laminate finish. It's called a 'Baby Tambour' and costs £120.

*Purves & Purves
80-81 & 83 Tottenham Court Rd, London W1P 9HD. T:0171-580 8223. F:0171-580 8244. Danish 'Shack Engel' bed and living system in pine - from cots to triple bunks, desks and wardrobes. Also traditional wooden toys.

The Victorian Brass Bedstead Company
Hoe Copse, Cocking, Nr Midhurst, W.Sussex GU29 0HL. T:01730-812287. F:01730-815081. Metal cots which can be adapted for use as day beds later on. Fully restored metal cribs fitted with a custom-made mattress, lined and draped with muslin.

* denotes trade supplier. Please phone for retail outlets.

The Wadham Trading Company
Wadham, Southrop, Nr Lechlade,
Gloucs GL7 3PB.
T/F:01367-850499.
Smart set of child-size metal garden table,
bench and chairs in black lead-free paint.

Mark Wilkinson
Overton House, Bromham, Wilts SN15 2HA.
T:01380-850004. F:01380-850184.
Fairytale style furniture in ash, oak or pine
prepared for painting - all to order.

PLAYHOUSES & EQUIPMENT

Matthew Burt Splinter Group
Albany Workshops, Sherrington,
Warminster, Wilts BA12 0SP.
T:01985-850996. F:01985-850194.
Fantasy pavilions made from woodland
thinnings. There are four in the range, from
the small cabin-like 'Woodlander' (£2000)
to the 'Seven-Roomed Fantasy Pavilion'
with interconnecting rooms and a
verandah (£7000).

The Children's Cottage Company
The Sanctuary, Crediton, Devon EX17 1BG.
T:01363-772061. F:01363-777868.
Range of four handmade wooden
playhouses, available to order in any size.
Prices start at £1300.

The Children's Playhouse Company
11 Bowling Green Lane, London
EC1R 0BD. T:0171-336 8301.
F:0171-490 8641. Swedish-
style playhouse in painted
wood. It has a verandah, a
stable door and heart-
shaped windows and
costs £699. A
'Gingerbread
cottage' will be
available
next.

*Eibe-Play
Forest House, 8 Baxter Rd,
Sale, Cheshire M33 3AL.
T:0161-962 8295. F:0161-976 6295.
Playground and school furniture.
500 page catalogue.

*TP Activity Toys
Severn Rd, Stourport-on-Severn,
Worcs DY13 9EX.
T:01299-827728. F:01299-827163.
Suppliers of wood or galvanized steel
playground items: a pirates' deck tree
house, log cabins, rope ladders, climbing
ropes, firemen's poles.

Touch Design
51 High St, Sixpenny Handley,
Salisbury, Wilts SP5 5ND.
T:01725-552888. F:01725-552303.
Paint-your-own canvas teepee (£49.50)
and Plywood house (£109.75) with optional
extras like shutters, window boxes, shelves
and blackboard. Also available by mail order.

CHILDREN'S ACCESSORIES

The Blanket Box
Freepost LS6412, Garforth,
Leeds LS25 1YY. T:0113-287 6057.
F:0113-286 4438. Plain or cellular cot
blankets in white, bunk bed blankets in
22 colours.Mail order only.

The Conran Shop
See entry under **CHILDREN'S
FURNITURE.** Babar bedlinen; white
bedlinen with patchwork people or animals;
Tintin towels; soft and wooden toys.

Countrywide Workshops
47 Fisherton St, Salisbury, Wilts SP2 7SU.
T:01722-326886. F:01722-411092.
Traditional wooden toys, baby walkers,
rocking horses, croquet sets, hobby horses
and blackboards, all made by disabled
people and available by mail order.

Dragons
See entry under **CHILDREN'S
FURNITURE.** Painted clocks, shelves,
mirrors, lamps, book ends and pictures.

The Hill Toy Company
71 Abingdon Rd, London W8 6AW.
T:0171-937 8797. F:0171-937 0209.
And by mail order from:
PO Box 100, Ripon, N.Yorks HG4 4XZ.
T:01765-689955. F:01765-689111.
Traditional and soft toys, dressing up
clothes, dolls' houses. They can also turn
your children's drawings into melamine
plates, bowls, beakers and clocks.

IKEA
See entry under
CHILDREN'S FURNITURE.
Bed linen, cushions, bean bags, lamps.

Emma Jefferson
16 Cross Bank, Great Easton,
Market Harborough, Leics LE16 8SR.
T/F:01536-772074.
Wooden skittle-style lampstands, self-
assembly shelves and height-charts
painted as soldiers, dinosaurs, clowns, etc.
By mail order or through stockists.

Lion, Witch and Lampshade
89 Ebury St, London SW1W 9QU.
T:0171-730 1774.
And at:
Broxborne Barn, High St, Northleach,
Cheltenham, Gloucs G954 9EW.
T:01451-860855. F:01285-750430.
Dealers and restorers of antique rocking
horses.Will hunt for a particular type for you.

Little Monsters
See entry under CHILDREN'S
FURNITURE. Duvet covers and
pillowcases in gingham, denim, patchwork,
tartan or even cowboys. Children's dressing
gowns and pyjamas. Cot quilts and bumpers.
Laundry bags.

Melin Tregwynt
Tregwynt Mill, Castlemorris, Haverfordwest,
Pembrokeshire, Wales SA62 5UX.
T:01348-891225. F:01348-891694.
For mail order call: 01348-891644.
Pram, cot, baby and child size blankets in
up to twenty different designs, from plains
to bright checks.

Nursery Window
See entry under CHILDREN'S FABRICS

& WALLPAPERS. Cot bumpers, quilts,
duvets, headboards, lampshades, blankets,
Moses baskets, nursing chairs, laundry bags
and dressing gowns.

The Monogrammed Linen Shop
168 Walton St, London SW3 2JL.
T:0171-589 4033. F:0171-823 7745.
Can embroider a child's drawing on to a pure
cotton 12x16 pillowcase (from £36.50). Also
pram sets, cot sheets, towels, bath robes.

SKK
34 Lexington St, London W1R 3HR.
T:0171-434 4095. F:0171-287 0168.
Magic lanterns which project their pictures
on to the wall. Square and circular versions
with, amongst others, sheep jumping over
fences, spacemen, bubbles, teddies and an
aquatic world.

Stevenson Brothers
The Workshop, Ashford Rd,
Bethersden, Ashford, Kent TN26 3AP.
T:01233-820363. F:01233-820580.
New rocking horses to order (6-8 weeks)
in several sizes. Dapple-grey or in English
oak, mahogany or black American walnut.
Restoration service.

Stockwell Carpets
3rd Floor, 51-52 New Bond St,
London W1Y 0BY.
T:0171-629 0626. F:0171-409 2969.
Can weave your child's drawing into a
rug of any size.

The White Company
Unit 19c, The Coda Centre,
189 Munster Rd, London SW6 6AW.
T:0171-385 7988. F:0171-385 2685.
Mail order company. Their range includes
hemstitched white cotton sheets as well as
plaid and large check woollen blankets in
pram, cot and child sizes.

Windmill Antiques
4 Montpelier Mews,
Harrogate, N.Yorks HG1 2TJ.
T:01845-501330. F:01845-501700.
Antique and reproduction Victorian and
Edwardian rocking horses as well as a
restoration service. Antique children's
high-chairs and stick-back chairs.

*** denotes
trade supplier.
Please phone
for retail outlets.** 217

16

ARCHITECTURAL SALVAGE

LONDON

Architectural Antiques
66-68 Battersea High St,
London SW11 3HX.
T:0171-738 1690. Victorian bathroom
fittings, including roll top and unusual baths,
cast iron radiators, doors, fireplaces;
brass polishing.

Architectural Salvage Centre
30-32 Stamford Rd, London N1 4JL.
T:0171-923 0783. F:0171-923 9458.
All sorts of period fixtures and fittings: lots of
basins, cast iron baths, radiators, fireplaces,
garden benches and statues, a vast number
of doors and restored and unrestored
Victorian furniture.

Chancellors Church Furnishings
7 Homestead Rd, London SW6 7DB.
T:0171-385 7480. By appointment.
Clients are taken to their warehouse near
Hampton Court. Altar tables, bells, balcony
fronts, candlesticks, doors, fonts, lecterns,
paintings, organs and cases.

Fens Restoration & Sales
46 Lots Rd, London SW10 0QF.
T:0171-352 9883. Good for smaller items
like restored brass door furniture and
bathroom taps and mixers, but they also
have doors and furniture. Paint stripping,
caning, French polishing and general repair
work.Furniture made from old wood.

The House Hospital
68 Battersea High St, London SW11 3HX.
T:0171-223 3179. Big selection of cast iron
radiators, both plain and ornate, panelled
Victorian doors, baths and fireplaces.

London Architectural Salvage
& Supply Company (LASSCo)
St Michael's Church, Mark St, off Paul St,
London EC2A 4ER.
T:0171-739 0448. F:0171-729 6853.
Huge array of architectural salvage spread
over a Victorian church. From doorknobs to
complete panelled rooms. Architectural
stonework, garden ornament, ecclesiastical
pieces, chimney pieces and lighting. Table
tops made up from salvaged marble.

See also: Old
Doors, Reclaimed
Wood Flooring,
Antique & New
Fireplaces,
Reclaimed
Bathroom Fittings
& Taps, and
Antique Garden
Furniture &
Ornament in
other chapters. 219

SOUTHERN ENGLAND

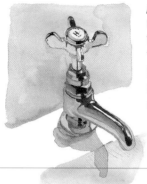

Ace Demolition and Salvage
Pine View, Barrack Rd, West Parley,
Wimborne, Dorset BH22 8UB.
T:01202-579222.
F:01202-582043.
Cast iron radiators, fireplaces,
doors, bathroom fittings, as well as
timber, slates, tiles and bricks.

Antique Buildings
Hunterswood Farm, Dunsfold,
Nr Godalming, Surrey GU8 4NP.
T:01483-200477.
F:01483-200752. Specialists in
timber buildings: they buy and sell complete
frames of barns, sheds and houses. Very
large stock of old oak beams, joists and
rafters, wide oak planks, doors and
handmade tiles and bricks.

Architectural Salvage
The Old Forestry Yard, Stanton Park, Nr
Kington St.Michael, Nr Chippenham,
Wiltshire SN14 6LA.
T:01666-837255. Mobile 0976-684896.
Period doors, fireplaces, pine, oak and elm
flooring, Cotswold and Pennant flagstones,
antique garden ornaments and reclaimed
building materials.

The Architectural Salvage Store
Unit 6, Darvell's Yard, Common Rd, Chorley
Wood, Herts WD3 5LP.
T:01923-284196. F:01923-284146.
Fire surrounds, doors, radiators,
garden statuary.

Au Temps Perdu
5 Stapleton Rd, Easton,
Bristol BS5 0QR.
T:01179-555223. General salvage,
from locks and hinges to re-usable
building materials.

Brighton Architectural Salvage
33-34 Gloucester Rd,
Brighton, E.Sussex BN1 4AQ.
T/F:01273-681656.
Fireplaces, new marble and slate hearths,
dressers and bookcases in reclaimed pine
and other salvage.

Chauncey's
16 Feeder Rd, Bristol B52 0SB.
T:0117-971 3131. F:0117-971 2224.
Mainly flooring, fireplaces and
some panelling.

Dorset Reclamation
Cow Drove, Bere Regis,
Wareham, Dorset BH20 7JZ.
T:01929-472200. F:01929-472292.
Reclaimed building materials, especially
bricks, tiles, wooden flooring. Bathrooms,
fireplaces, all sorts of architectural antiques,
matching and search service. Can arrange
delivery nationwide.

Drummond's of Bramley
Birtley Farm, Horsham Rd,
Bramley, Guildford, Surrey GU5 0LA.
T:01483-898766. F:01483-894393.
Large architectural salvage company set
in two and a half acres of grounds. It can
supply 'anything from the top of the chimney
to the garden gate'. Extensive range of
garden statuary, urns, benches, gazebos
and fountains. Specialists in restoring cast
iron baths with proper vitreous re-
enamelling. Also balustrades, gates,
radiators, doors, stained glass.

Frome Reclamation
Station Approach, Wallbridge,
Frome, Somerset BA11 1RE.
T:01373-463919. F:01373-453122.
Oak and pine floors, fireplaces and
beams, garden statuary, doors, slates,
bathroom fittings.

Robert Mills
Narroways Rd, Eastville, Bristol BS2 9XB.
T:0117-9556542. F:0117-9558146.
Ecclesiastical and other unusual
salvage - pews, stained glass,
even whole panelled rooms.

Marcus Olliff
26 Redland Court,
Redland, Bristol BS6 7EQ.
T:0117-942 2900. F:0117-944 2400.
Sourcing service for architectural salvage
and antique garden ornament. He also
carries quite a lot of stock (which is listed in
a brochure) : at the time of calling he had

three sets of room panelling, four or five marble fireplaces, several old stone windows and lots more.

Tower Materials
Tower Farm, Norwich Rd, Mendlesham, Suffolk IP14 5NE. T/F:01449-766095. Old oak and elm beams, pine flooring, complete oak framed barns, floor bricks and tiles, general salvage. They also stock new terracotta tiles and Mandarin slate tiles.

Walcot Reclamation
108 Walcot St, Bath BA1 5BG. T:01225-444404. F:01225-448163. Vast range of stock both for traditional building materials and architectural antiques.

Wells Reclamation
Coxley, Wells, Somerset BA5 1RQ. T:01749-677087. F:01749-671089. Four and a half acres of architectural salvage - reclaimed doors, fireplaces and especially what they call 'the heavy end of the market' i.e. building materials of all sorts.

The West Sussex Antique Timber Co
Reliance Works, Newpound, Wisborough Green, W.Sussex RH14 0AZ. T:01403-700139. F:01403-700936. Specialist joiners offering a full flooring service using reclaimed pine, pitch pine, old oak and new 'antiqued' oak. Plus panelling, kitchens, staircases, doors and furniture. Barn restoration service. Clients include The National Trust and Nicole Farhi's shop in Bond Street.

CENTRAL ENGLAND

Architectural Heritage
Taddington Manor, Taddington, Nr Cutsdean, Cheltenham, Gloucs GL54 5RY. T:01386-584414. F:01386-584236. Garden statuary, stone fire surrounds, fine antique panelled rooms and much more.

Architectural Heritage of Northants
Heart of the Shires, The Woodyard, A5 two miles north of Weedon, Northants NN7 49B. T:01327-349249. F:01327-349397.

Specialists in Victorian shop fittings, bathrooms and fire inserts.

Baileys
The Engine Shed, Ashburton Ind.Estate, Ross-on-Wye, Hereford HR9 7BW. T:01989-563015. F:01989-768172. Original and reproduction fireplaces, bathroom fittings, tiles, metalwork and garden ornaments.

Camtile - The Cambridgeshire Tile & Slate Company
35 Cheddars Lane, Cambridge CB5 8LD. T:01223-369666. F:01223-356466. Suppliers of reclaimed and new roofing materials.

Conservation Building Products
Forge Lane, Cradley Heath,Warley, West Midlands B64 5AL. T:01384-569551. F:01384-410625. The Midlands' largest stocks of reclaimed beams, slates, bricks, quarry tiles, plus exterior paviours, cobble setts and flagstones. They also sell doors, panelling, floor boards and interior staircases. Photo service available. Nationwide delivery.

Dickinson Architectural Antiques
140 Corve St, Ludlow, Shropshire SY8 2PG. T:01584-876207. Period bathrooms, doors, lighting, fireplaces and other fittings.

Reclamation Services
Catbrain Quarry, Painswick Beacon, Painswick, Gloucs GL6 6SU. T:01452-814064. F:01452-813634. Architectural antiques, garden statuary, traditional building materials.

Ronson's Reclamation
Norton Barn, Wainlodes Lane, Norton, Gloucs GL2 9LN. T:01452-731236. F:01452-731888. Stone and paving, roofing materials, timbers, ornamental stone, reclaimed bricks of all descriptions, garden furniture, brassware. Oak, elm and pine boards and block flooring.

Shiners Architectural Reclamation
123 Jesmond Rd, Jesmond,
Newcastle-upon-Tyne, Tyne & Wear NE2 1JY.
T:0191-281 6474. F:0191-281 9041.
Doors, fireplaces, taps, window catches,
door knobs and hinges.

Solopark
The Old Railway Station, Station Rd,
Nr Pampisford, Cambridge CB2 4HB.
T:01223-834663. F:01223-834780.
Six acre site with everything one might
need to reconstruct a building - from a claw-
foot bath to a cupola. Bricks and paviours
are sorted by size and shade. Slates can
be trimmed into required sizes. Period
and reproduction fireplaces, bathroom
fittings, door furniture, metal stairways,
radiators and endless other items.
Nationwide delivery.

Staffordshire Architectural Salvage
Stain House, Skidmore Rd, Coseley,
Bilston, W.Midlands WV14 8SE.
T:01902-401053. F:01902-405548.
Anything from cobblestones to statues.

NORTHERN ENGLAND

Bradford Slate & Salvage Co
Fred's Place, Sticker Lane,
Bradford BD4 8RL.
T/F:01274-680400. Slate, flags, crazy
paving, granite setts and bulding stone.

Cheshire Brick and Slate Company
Brook House Farm, Salters Bridge,
Tarvin Sands, Tarvin, Nr Chester,
Cheshire CH3 8HL.
T:01829-740883. F:01829-740481.
Large range of both constructional
and ornamental salvage: bricks,
roofing, stone paving, walling, gates
and railings, fireplaces, bathroom
fittings and garden statuary.

In-Situ Architectural Antiques
607 Stretford Rd, Old Trafford,
Manchester M16 0QJ.
T/F:0161-848 7454. Fireplaces,
doors, flooring, bathroom fittings
and garden ornaments.

Pine Supplies
Lower Tongs Farm,
Longshaw Ford Rd, Smithills,
Bolton, Greater Manchester BL1 7PP.
T:01204-841416. F:01942-840505.
Reclaimed pitch and yellow pine re-sawn
for flooring, skirtings, doors and windows.

Andy Thornton Architectural Antiques
Victoria Mills, Stainland Rd, Greetland,
Halifax, W.Yorks HX4 8AD.
T:01422-377314. F:01422-310372.
Vast warehouse for architectural antiques:
over 100 fireplaces always in stock, more
than 1000 doors, thousands of stained
glass windows, panelled rooms and even
complete chemist shops.

John Walsh & Sons
The Heritage Centre,
Lyntown Trading Estate, Old Wellington Rd,
Eccles, Manchester M30 9QG.
T:0161-789 8223. F:0161-787 7015.
Reclaimed bricks, roof slates, tiles, chimney
pots, Green Westmoreland and Yorkshire
grey slate. Nationwide delivery.

WALES

Cardiff Reclamation
Site 7, Tremorfa Ind.Estate, Martin Rd,
off Rover Way, Cardiff CF2 2SD.
T:01222-458995.
Traditional building materials, flagstones,
slates, good selection of fireplaces and
other architectural antiques.

Dyfed Antiques & Architectural Salvage
Wesleyan Chapel, Perrots Rd,
Haverfordwest SA61 2JD.
T:01437-760496.
Restored fireplaces, hob grates, stoves,
large stock of doors, windows, farmhouse
tables, garden statuary and roofing
materials. Handmade furniture to order.
National delivery service.

Gallop & Rivers
Tyr'a'sh, Brecon Rd,
Crickhowell, Powys NP8 1SF.
T/F:01873-811084.
Victorian fireplaces, tiles, sandstone paving,

stone finials, garden ornaments, stoves, doors, oak and pine flooring.

SCOTLAND

Easy Architectural Salvage
Unit 6, Couper St, Leith,Edinburgh EH6 6HH.
T:0131-554 7077. F:0131-554 3070.
And at:
85 Colvend St, Glasgow G40 4DU.
T:0141-556 7772. F:0141-556 5552.
Doors, shutters, Belfast sinks, stoves, radiators, fireplaces.

Tradstocks
Dunaverig, Thornhill, Stirling FK8 3QW.
T:01786-850400. F:01786-850404.
Traditional landscaping and building materials, with the largest selection of reclaimed natural stone in Scotland.

NORTHERN IRELAND

John Fyffe Architectural Salvage
Jennymount St, Belfast,
N.Ireland BT15 3HW.
T:01232-351475
Victorian fireplaces, quarry tiles, Belfast bricks, square setts; general architectural salvage including doors and fireplaces.

Wilsons Conservation Building Products
123 Hillsborough Rd, Dromore, Co Down,
N.Ireland BT25 1QW.T/F:01846-692304
Bangor blue slates, Rosemary roof tiles, quarry tiles, slate, sandstone and Yorkstone flags, reclaimed bricks (including Victorian and hand-made varieties); reclaimed and re-sawn timber flooring (maple, oak, teak, mahogany and pitch pine) and beams; cast iron and marble fireplaces, old street cobbles, church fittings, even ornate sandstone and granite archways.

REPUBLIC OF IRELAND

Architectural Salvage & Supply
19 South Gloucester St, Dublin 2, Eire
T:(00 353)88 551 299/87 551 299.
Huge range of brassware, lighting and timber

flooring. Specialists in joinery using old timber to make kitchens and bars. About 100 fully restored fireplaces on display. Good selection of stone porticos.

Belle Cheminée
106 Capel St, Dublin 1,Eire.
T:(00 353)872 4122.
F:(00 353)872 4528.
Antique and reproduction fireplaces including French and Adam style. Mainly Georgian, Victorian and Edwardian period examples in cast iron, slate, wood and marble. Cast iron insets made. Some colonial style furniture, also garden statuary and furniture.

Chirsty Bird
31-32 South Richmond St, Dublin 2, Eire.
T:(00 353 1)475 4049.
F:(00 353 1)475 8708.
Church seating, panelling, stained glass, brassware (including lamps), statues, doors, stoneware balustrading and metalwork. Also fireplaces, mouldings and old furniture (especially Victorian).

For more help:
The Architectural Salvage Index has a database of items wanted and for sale and tries to match them up. Cost £10 per entry. T:01483-203221. F:01483-202911.

Salvo
Ford Woodhouse,
Berwick-upon-Tweed,
Northumberland TD15 2QF.
T/F:01668-216494.
Established in 1992 to encourage the re-use of more building materials. It publishes a magazine which covers architectural auctions, dealers, items wanted and for sale (£20 for 10 issues). Also available: The Salvo Pack with a detailed list of dealers in your county and the four adjacent ones (£5.75); a French Listing; the trade Salvo News; architectural theft alerts on the Internet.

 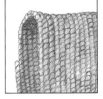   

17

ACCESSORIES

ONE-STOP

David Champion
199 Westbourne Grove,
London W11 2SB.
T:0171-727 6016. F:0171-792 2097.
This decorator's first retail shop. An eclectic
mix of ethnic accessories (Vietnamese
pottery, Indian carvings, cushions from
South Africa, brightly coloured 'Township'
frames, lacquered trays and boxes) and
artwork, cushions and throws by Royal
College of Art graduates.

The Conran Shop
Michelin House, 81 Fulham Rd,
London SW3 6RD.
T:0171-589 7401. F:0171-823 7015.
Best place to browse for all accessories
from bath sponges and toiletries to brightly
coloured decorative glass vases. Everything
for the kitchen plus elegant china, cutlery
and tablelinen. Storage items, photo
albums, briefcases, notebooks, clocks,
books and bedlinen .

Graham & Greene
4&7 Elgin Crescent,
London W11 2JA.
T:0171-727 4594. F:0171-229 9717.
One of Notting Hill Gate's landmarks from
before it became trendy. The two shops
are crammed with kitchen- and gardenware,
glass, pretty lighting, furniture and all sorts
of gifts. Another branch at:
164 Regents Park Rd, London NW1 8XN.
T:0171-586 2960. F:0171-483 0901.

Maison
Grand Illusions, 2-4 Crown Rd, St Margarets,
Twickenham, Middx TW1 3EE.
Orderline: 0181-892 2151.
F:0181-744 2017. Mail order company
inspired by French country style. The
accessories are in keeping with their painted
furniture: wire stands, enamel jugs and
gingham cutlery for the kitchen; a wire shelf
and a large metal trough for the garden;
starfish hooks and Marseilles soaps for the
bathroom. You can also visit their shop
at the above address.

Ocean
Freepost LON811, London SW15 1BR.
Orderline: 0800-132 985.
F:0181-780 5505. Mail order company
with over 500 items which can be delivered
the next day. Stylish furniture, lighting, linen
and all sorts of accessories, including for
kitchens and bathrooms - anything from
rattan furniture to pewter egg cups.

Roberto Pedrina
84 Fulham Rd, London SW3 6HR.
T:0171-584 0808. F:0171-823 9070.
Accessories and furniture designed or
sourced in Italy by designer Roberto Pedrina.
Papier maché, glass fom Murano, fabrics
from Como, candlesticks in copper wire
and Venetian beads, ceramics, lamps
and much more.

Purves & Purves
80-81 & 83 Tottenham Court Rd,
London W1P 9HD.
T:0171-580 8223. F:0171-580 8244.
Good one-stop accessory shop - mirrors,
clocks, vases, glassware, stationery, cards,
candles, kitchenware, bathroom items,
home-office accessories, wastebins,
baskets - even fire tools. All mainly by
contemporary British, European and
American designers and manufacturers.

Renwick & Clarke
190 Ebury St, London SW1W 8UP.
T:0171- 730 8913. F:0171-730 4508.
Suppliers of a vast selection of china,
glass, cutlery, silver, centre-pieces,
lighting, linen and even dried and
preserved flower arrangements to
interior decorators and private clients.

PRINTS / PAINTINGS & FRAMES

ARC
103 Wandsworth Bridge Rd,
London SW6 2TE.
T:0171-731 3933. F:0171-610 6591.
Reproduction classical and decorative prints
and a wide selection of mounts and frames.
Also print room fabrics and wallpaper.

Ariel Press at the Pigeonhole Gallery
13 Langton St, London SW10 0JL.
T:0171-352 2677/351 2470.
F:0171-376 8017. Fine art print
reproductions from 18th and 19th
century originals. Botanical and bird
themes in particular.Mounting and
framing service available.

Art Connoisseur
95/97 Crawford St, London W1H 1AN.
T:0171-258 3835. F:0171-258 3532.
Sell copies of paintings by past masters.
At least 50 paintings on show and many
more in stock. They can commission any
work from their stable of artists who are
specialists in different periods:
Impressionist, Renaissance etc.

*Art Contact
2 Rickett St. London SW6 1RU.
T:0171-381 8655. F:0171-386 9015.
Trade only supplier of prints, posters,
tapestries, mirrors, engravings, paintings -
from the antique to the contemporary.
Plus full framing and installation service.
Experts in commercial installations.

Art Works
50 High Street, Walton-on-Thames,
Surrey KT12 1BY.
T/F:01932-226954.
Supply art and artefacts from prints
to watercolours or oils - reproductions
and original works. Framing service.

Artefact
36 Windmill St, London W1P 1HF.
T:0171-636 5244. F:0171-580 0987.
Large selection of architectural, floral
and other prints and plaster intaglio seals.
Also faux-fresco panels, framed silhouettes,
facsimiles of 19th century tile friezes,
panel paintings of the Medici Villas, and
contemporary and period style mirrors.

Asprey Newton
16 The Terrace, London SW13 0NP.
T/F:0181-876 7178.
Classical and contemporary plaster
picture and mirror frames: fleur-de-lis,
tudor roses, stars and hemispheres
fixed to MDF frames: 30 designs in all.

Most companies
with a large range of
accessories also
stock frames.

For bespoke frames
see also SPECIALIST
SUPPLIERS &
SERVICES -
Framers.

226

Lucy B Campbell Gallery

123 Kensington Church St, London W8 7LP.
T:0171-727 2205. F:0171-229 4252.
Specialist in antiquarian prints and
showroom for contemporary naive paintings.
Extensive selection of decorative works
and hand-made frames and mounts.

Belinda Canosa

38 St Mary's Grove, London W4 3LN.
T:0181-747 0436. F:0181-995 1099.
They commission murals, trompe l'oeil,
frescoes and fine copies of paintings from
a wide range of artists on their books.

Christopher Dean

Fieldfare Barn, Wash Lane,
Banham, Norwich NR16 2HD.
T:01953-887480. F:01953-887389.
Unpainted picture frames.

*Dennison Drake

Broadrayne Farm, Grasmere,
Cumbria LA22 9RU.
T/F:015394-35733. Quality reproduction
framed period miniatures. Also decorative
accessories including mirrors, key
cupboards and letter racks.

English Portfolio Company

The Old Smithy, Burley,
Oakham, Rutland LE15 7TB.
T/F:01572-770729. Hand-finished
frames and mounts in a variety of
colours and finishes.

George D'Epinois

793 Fulham Rd, London SW6 5HD.
T:0171-736 2387. F:0171-736 0522.
Oleographs and fine art reproductions for
the stately home look. Also a range of silk
flowers in decorative pots.

Family Copies

19 Brechin Place, London SW7 4QB.
T:0171-373 5499. F:0171-835 0073.
Oleographs (oil painting facsimiles) to
order in any size (up to a maximum of
60 ft wide and 25 ft high). Copies are hand-
finished with brush strokes and cracking.
If you want a copy of a specific painting,
Family Copies can obtain a transparency
from the relevant museum.

Frame

137 Portobello Rd, London W11 2DY.
T:0171-792 1272. F:0171-586 7949.
Huge selection of reasonably-priced made
up frames, including unfinished, gilt and
leather examples.

Haute Deco

556 Kings Rd, London SW6 2DZ.
T:0171-736 7171. F:0171-736 8484.
Best known for resin knobs, they also
stock a collection of modern gilded frames.

Stephanie Hoppen

17 Walton St, London SW3 2HX.
T:0171-589 3678. F:0171-584 3731.
Watercolours and oils (from £125)
by modern living artists - the theme
changes monthly.

*Institute Of Fine Art

The basement, 5 Kirby St,
London EC1N 8TS.
T:0171-831 4048. F:0171-405 4448.
Oil paintings, drawings,watercolours, frames
and mirrors for the interior design trade and
restaurant/hotel industry. Keen pricing to
keep within clients' budgets.

Ochre

T/F:0171-244 7082.
By appointment. Customised frames in an
original selection of hand finishes - gesso,
bole, lacquer, gold and silver. Plus
lamps, clocks, mirrors and anything else
to commission.

*** denotes
trade supplier.
Please phone
for retail outlets.** 227

Porter Design
Trade: The Old Estate Yard, Newton St Loe, Bath, Somerset BA2 9BR.
T:01225-874250. F:01225-874251.
Retail: Shires Yard, Milsom St, Bath BA1 1BZ. T/F:01225-447261.
Reproductions of about 550 decorative images from the 16th to the 19th century - well known especially for their architectural prints. They also design frames for their own range.

The Quintessa Art Collection
T:0181-349 1505. F:0181-349 2416.
By appointment only. Fine art prints produced under licence from major museums. Also hand-painted frames and mounts.

*The Thomas Ross Collection
St. Mark's Rd, Binfield, Berks RG42 4TR.
T:01344-862686/303443.
F:01344-862575. The world's largest collection of reproduction etchings and engravings. There are 6500 plates available to interior designers and retail outlets - anything from botanicals to legal scenes.

Sudbury Picture Frames
Unit 9, Drury Lane, Woodhall Business Park, Sudbury, Suffolk CO10 6WA.
T/F:01787-376014. Frame makers.
Range includes modern, traditional, Louis XIV style and gilt frames.

Trowbridge Gallery
555 Kings Rd, London SW6 2EB.
T:0171-371 8733. F:0171-371 8138.
Hand-made custom frames and over 100 different techniques for their finishes.
Large range of antique and decorative prints. Animal, architectural and botanical themes included in their collection.

Wiseman Originals
34 West Square, London SE11 4SP.
T:0171-587 0747. F:0171-793 8817.
By appointment. Original modern prints by British and European artists, some signed, mainly small editions. Artists represented include Picasso, Matisse, Hockney, Frink, Moore and Hodgkin. Prices from £100 to £10,000. Good range under £1000.

CERAMICS

*Altfield
G4 and 2/22,
Chelsea Harbour Design Centre,
Chelsea Harbour, London SW10 0XE.
T:0171-376 5667. F:0171-351 5893.
Blue and White, Famille Rose, Famille Verte, Tobacco Leaf and monochrome porcelain from China.

Maryse Boxer at Chez Joseph
26 Sloane St, London SW1X 7LQ.
T/F:0171-245 9493. Gold and platinum-edged crackle-glaze porcelain; decorative glass.

Casa Catalan
15 Chalk Farm Rd, London NW1 8AG.
T:0171-485 3975. F:0171-485 7217.
Colourful Mediterranean-style ceramic pots from Spain and Thailand.

*The Classic Chair Company
Studio R, Old Imperial Laundry,
71 Warriner Gardens, London SW11 4XW.
T:0171-622 4274. F:0171-622 4275.
Chinese export and armorial porcelain.

CXV
376 King's Rd, London SW3 5UZ.
T/F:0171-351 5975. Chunky and pearly-white Italian glazed jugs, pots and planters.

Francis Ceramics
Llandre, Llanfyrnach, Crymych,
Pembrokeshire SA35 0DA.
T/F:01239-831657.
Reproduction hand-painted tulip vases, crocus pots and flower bricks based on 17th century English and Dutch designs.

Freud
198 Shaftesbury Ave, London WC2 3HB.
T:0171-831 1071. F:0171-831 3062.
Decorative ceramics and 'Alphabet' fine bone china.

Joss Graham Oriental Textiles
10 Eccleston St, London SW1W 9LT.
T/F:0171-730 4370. Celadon-ware made by three different master potters in Northern Vietnam. Some of the shapes are classical and could have been made 1000 years ago, others are surprisingly contemporary.

Green & Pleasant
129 Church Rd, London SW13 9HR.
T:0181-741 1539. F:0181-741 0816.
Tasteful selection of ceramic and glass
giftware including oversized hand-
thrown china plates and elegant,
simple glass vases.

Nicholas Haslam
12-14 Holbein Place, London SW1W 8NL.
T:0171-730 8623. F:0171-730 6679.
Ceramic and porcelain, suede and leather,
and silver gilt accessories in a clean and
elegant style inspired by Swedish and
classical designs. Creamy amphorae,
tureens and serving bowls.

Liberty
214-220 Regent Street, London W1R 6AH.
T:0171-734 1234. F:0171-573 9876.
Large section devoted to Chinese porcelain.

Onglaze
46 Harrington Rd, London SW7 3ND.
T:0171-823 8483. F:0171-589 0734.
Contemporary designs by Tim and Marissa
Wetherhead: teasets, vases, jugs and hand-
painted bone china.

Red Mud
Unit C & D, Linton House,
39-51 Highgate Rd, London NW5 1RS.
T:0171-267 1689. F:0171-267 9142.
Large range of ceramic pots in all sizes,
wonderful colours and shapes (from small
bowls and vases to large amphorae).
Regular stock and commissioned pieces.
They can convert all their pots to lamps on
request.

Renwick & Clarke
See entry under ONE-STOP. Victorian style
creamware: hand-crafted, press-moulded
vases, urns and centrepieces by Peter
Weldon. Also Chinoiserie Mandarin figures
by Charlotte Moss.

*Royal Creamware
6 Redworth Way, Newton Aycliffe,
County Durham DL5 6XF.
T:01405-817979. F:01405-815588.
Reproductions of 18th century British
creamware including plates, timepieces,
lamps, tea cups, candle-sticks etc.

Richard Taylor Designs
See entry under GLASS. Large collection of
cream-coloured pottery including lion head
vases, footed tureens and scallop-edged
bowls. Also high quality Renaissance-style
ceramic urns, lampbases and vases.

Van Posch
100 Jermyn St, London SW1Y 6EE.
T/F:0171-930 2211. High class porcelain
specialists: Herend, Ginori, Limoges -
tableware and giftware.

GLASS

Blue Crystal Glass
Unit 6/8, 21 Wren St, London WC1X OHF.
T:0171-278 0142. Stocks about 200 sizes
of salt cellar liners, including oval, round and
octagonal shapes. Special sizes to order.

Oliver Bonas
10 Kensington Church St, London W8 4EP.
T:0171-368 0035. F:0171-938 4312.
And branches in Fulham Rd and Battersea.
For mail order catalogue T:0171-627 4747.
Wide range of interior accessories, including
handmade Polish glass (vases, drinking
glasses, decanters, oil and vinegar bottles
etc), and Iranian and Mexican glass.

Bristol Blue Glass
Great Western Dock,
Gas Ferry Road, Bristol BS1 6TY.
T/F:0117-929 8900. 'Bristol Blue' hand-
blown glass made in the 17th century
manner including gilt-decorated decanters,
vases, bowls, jugs, glasses, scent bottles,
plates and desk accessories. Mail order
and worldwide export.

Ciel Decor
187 New Kings Rd, London SW6 4SW.
T:0171-731 0444. F:0171-731 0788.
Bubbly glassware from Biot in Provence.

Glass Heritage
Reynolds Warehouse,
The Docks, Gloucs GL1 2EN.
T:01452-503803. F:01452-504803.
Hand-blown decorative glass from this
company which specialises in glass
restoration, stained glass to design,

**See also
CRAFTSMEN &
RESTORERS - Glass
and DOORS &
WINDOWS - Glass
Manufacturers
& Suppliers.**

*** denotes
trade supplier.
Please phone
for retail outlets.** 229

blown or cast glass items
and hand-made window glass.

Joss Graham Oriental Textiles

See entry under **CERAMICS**.

Persian glass with a slightly frosted
finish in cobalt blue. There are vases,
glasses, jugs, fruit and salad bowls.

The Handmade Glass Company

Roxby Place, London SW6 1RS.
T:0171-610 3344. F:0171-610 3355.
Glassware ranging from small scent
bottles to large vases. Their own
collection is decorated with silver or
gold leaf, but they will make any design
to commission.

London Glassblowing Workshop

7 The Leather Market, Weston
Street, London SE1 3ER.
T:0171-403 2800.
F:0171-403 7778. Scent bottles,
glass sculptures and vases. Also limited
editions, corporate gifts, glass restoration
and workshops in glassblowing.

MAP

165A Junction Rd, London N19 5PZ.
T:0171-263 8529. F:0171-263 8523.
Hand decorated contemporary glass
products - everything from vases, bowls
and drinking glasses to picture frames
and toiletries in decorated glass bottles.
Also bone china.

*Mediterraneo

Studio C4, The Old Imperial Laundry,
71 Warriner Gardens, London SW11 4XW.
T:0171-720 6556. F:0171-720 6336.
Murano coloured glass, from a £3 hand-
blown ashtray to spectacular vases and
sculptures; hand-cut crystal by the Spanish
company Cristal de La Granja (established in
1727); reproductions of ancient glass;
moulded alabaster from Tuscany; china
designs by artists like Salvador Dali and
Javier Mariscal.

Merlin Glass

Barn St, Station Rd,
Liskard, Cornwall PL14 4BW.
T/F:01579-342399. Handmade jugs,
drinking goblets, and posy vases. Mail order.

*Porta Romana

Lower Froyle, Nr Alton,
Hampshire GU34 4LS.
T:01420-23005. F:01420-23008.
Iridescent cream-coloured glass
vases with a 'just excavated' look.

Renwick & Clarke

See entry under **ONE-STOP**. Hand-blown
gilded and silvered vases and tazzas in
three sizes and lots more decorative glass.

Richard Taylor Designs

91 Princedale Rd, London W11 4NS.
T:0171-792 1808. F:0171-792 0310.
Glass storm lanterns, bottles, decanters.
Decorative range including cut crystal and
plain crystal spheres on pedestals.

MIRRORS

Aspara Designs

17 Leamington Rd Villas, London W11 1HT.
T:0171-727 6935. F:0171-229 8017.
Specialists in 'verre eglomisé' (gilding
on glass) using silver, gold or copper.
They have a range of overmantle candlelit
mirrors and will produce decorative glass
panels to order.

Beaumont & Fletcher

261 Fulham Rd, London SW3 6HY. T:0171-
352 5553. F:0171-352 3545.Collection
of fine reproduction mirrors. Chinoiserie,
George I, Adam, Empire, Regency,
Chippendale and Georgian styles.
Also Chinese lacquer and japanned
frames, gilded jardinières, wall brackets
and torchères.

Oliver Bonas

See entry under **GLASS**.

Barbara Brownfield & Paul Verburg

Flat 2, Bellevue House, 39 Petersham Rd,
Richmond, Surrey TW10 6UH.
T:0181-948 0088. F:0181-891 3648.
Plaster mirrors with a 1940s look. Mainly
commissioned works - anything in plaster
can be made to order including furniture.

Chelsea Glass

650 Portslade Rd, London SW8 3HD.
T:0171-720 6905. F:0171-978 2827.

Very large range of antique, Art Nouveau and Art Deco, even tinted or convex mirrors. Restoration service. Also specialists in mirroring bathroom walls.

Peter Dudgeon
Brompton Place, London SW3 1QE.
T:0171-589 0322. F:0171-589 1910.
Agents for Desfosses French hand-carved mirrors and console tables. They're gilded with 22-carat gold or copper or left simply in plain oak.

Elizabeth Eaton
85 Bourne St, London SW1W 8HF.
T:0171-730 2262. F:0171-730 7294.
Triple dressing table mirrors.

Charles Edwards
582 Kings Rd, London SW6 2DY.
T:0171-736 8490. F:0171-371 5436.
Emma Foale's decorative mirrors in black and gold with faceted beads.

H & L Antiques
Unit 1J, Leroy House,
436 Essex Rd, London N1 3QP.
T:0171-359 2438. Fully-restored range of mainly French antique mirrors. Most are gilded and there is a good selection of overmantel styles.

*Just Mirrors
141 Greyhound Rd, London W6 8NJ.
T:0171-385 9613. F:0171-385 9604.
Period reproductions or modern styles, veneered, gilded, lacquered or hand painted.

The Looking Glass
96 Walcot St, Bath BA1 5BG.
T/F:01225-461969. Overmantel and wall mirrors, hand finished in Dutch gold metal leaf. Bare frames available for finishing at home. Range includes arched, balloon shapes, pier glasses with oakleaf friezes, tryptych and small convex mirrors. Also mirror restoration, antique re-silvering, bevelling and gilding.

Oakleaf Reproductions
Ling Bob Mill, Main Street,
Wilsden, Bradford BD15 0JP.
T:01535-272878. F:01535-275748.
Traditional range of fine 18th and 19th century reproductions cast from antique originals in either gilt or wood finishes, including a pickled pine garden mirror, a Regency overmantel, and a William & Mary antique gilt and ivory pier glass.

Ochre
T/F:0171-244 7082. By appointment.
Simple handmade mirrors in a wide range of finishes - they would look as good in classical or contemporary settings.

Ossowski
83 Pimlico Rd, London SW1W 8PH.
T:0171-730 3256. F:0171-823 4500.
Specialists in 18th century English giltwood mirrors.

Overmantels
66 Battersea Bridge Rd, London SW11 3AG.
T:0171-223 8151. F:0171-924 2283.
Victorian, Regency and French - style overmantels, pier glasses and oval mirrors made using 18th and 19th century moulds. Made to measure and specially designed frames. Plus a selection of antique mirrors.

John Tanous
115 Harwood Rd, London SW6 4QL.
T:0171-736 7999. F:0171-371 5237.
Reproduction mirrors in every style from an ornate Chinese Chippendale to a simple George I dressing table mirror.

Richard Taylor Designs
See entry under GLASS .
Decorative square, rectangular and circular mirrors surrounded by metal oak leaves which can be gilded. Also 'festoon' mirrors which are gilded metal and wooden frames which can be supplied lacquered or waxed.

Tempus Stet
Trinity Business Centre, 305-309 Rotherhithe Street, London SE16 1EY.
T:0171-231 0955. F:0171-252 3820.
Exact replicas of period mirrors using original moulds, including cherub winged dressing table mirrors, neo-classical designs with bevelled glass and rococo styles.

Through the Looking Glass
137 Kensington Church St, London W8 7LP.
T:0171-221 4026. F:0171-602 3678.
Also at:
563 King's Rd, London SW6 2EB.

For other mirror specialists contact: The Glass and Glazing Federation. T:0171-403 7177.

For antique mirrors see also under ANTIQUES - English & Continental Furniture & Decorative Arts.

* denotes trade supplier. Please phone for retail outlets.

T:0171-736 7799. Opulent 19th century
French, English, Italian, Austrian and a few
Scandinavian (mainly gilt) mirrors.

Tindle
162/168 Wandsworth Bridge Rd,
London SW6 2UQ.
T:0171-348 1485. F:0171-736 5630.
Range of reproduction and original period
decorative mirrors including Venetian styles.

Universal Providers
86 Golborne Rd, London W10 5PS.
T:0181-960 3736. Always an excellent
selection of restored French carved and
gilded period mirrors.

SW Wilcox
668 Fulham Rd, London SW6 5RX.
T/F:0171-736 2705. Antique shop with a
good selection of handmade reproduction
mirrors - mainly gilt, wood and overmantels
but also made to measure.

Tony Williams Fine Mirrors
White House Cottage, The Green,
Welbourn, Lincoln LN5 0NJ.
T:01254-878538. 19th century French
and English gilt mirrors.

WOODEN ACCESSORIES

Jali
Apsley House, Chartham,
Canterbury, Kent CT4 7HT.
T:01227-831710. F:01227-831950.
Unpainted fretwork shelf brackets
and edgings; also basic coat pegs
and book ends.

Charlie Roe
1 Firs Glen Rd, Talbot Park,
Bournemouth, Dorset BH9 2LW.
T/F:01202-546043. Painted shelves,
clocks, boxes, noticeboards, candlesticks
and furniture to order, mainly with Gothic or
folkloric themes.

Tempus Stet
See entry under MIRRORS.
Wall brackets and carvings.

Tindle
See entry under MIRRORS.
Carved wall brackets.

Woolpit Interiors
The Street, Woolpit,
Bury St Edmunds, Suffolk IP30 9SA.
T:01359-240895. F:01359-242282.
Dummy boards decorated with figures and
animals; small pieces of furniture such as
tables and tray stands. Good lighting
collection including painted tea canister
lamps and a new mahogany and tôleware
wall lantern after Thomas Chippendale.

Winston Yeatts of Warwickshire
14 Emscote Rd,
Warwick, Warwicks CV34 5QN.
T:01926-496761. F:01926-496720.
Decorative hand painted dummy boards, wall
shelves, folding screens, bookcases, boxes,
decanter stands, desk sets and painted
trunks, trays and other furniture.

Yellow House
Milepeal, Pyes Mill,
Station Rd, Bentham, Lancaster LA2 7LJ.
T:01524-262938. F:01524-261148.
Cabinets, trays, cutlery boxes, candle
cabinets, writing desks, cutlery trays,
sconces and peg rails in dark oak and
natural or antique pine.

SILVER

Renwick & Clarke
See entry under ONE-STOP.
Chinoiserie candlesticks and Neptune salts
which are reproductions from the collection
at Burghley House. Caviar dishes and
bejewelled cutlery by Duc de Guise.

David Richards and Sons
12 New Cavendish St, London W1H 7LJ.
T:0171-935 3206. F:0171-224 4423.
Large selection of photo frames,
candlesticks, cutlery, napkin rings, clocks,
teasets in silver and silver plate.

For silver see also
KITCHENS - Cutlery
and
ANTIQUE DEALERS -
Silver.

TÔLEWARE

Besselink & Jones
99 Walton St, London SW3 2HH.
T:0171-584 0343. F:0171-584 0284.
Tôle cachepots, urns, trays and bins.

*Golfar & Hughes
Unit C1, The Old Imperial Laundry,
71 Warriner Gardens, London SW11 4XW.
T:0171-498 0508. F:0171-622 4970.
Painted and gilded tôle wastebins, caddies,
trays, cachepots, coasters, wall clocks,
and reproduction Bouillotte lamps, painted
lampshades and candlesticks.

*Sarum Metalcraft
Rushmore Farm, Tollard Royal,
Nr Salisbury, Wilts SP5 5QA.
T:01725-516315. F:01725-516419.
Trade manufacturer of tôleware and furniture
- anything in decorative metal.

Tindle
See entry under **MIRRORS**. Cachepots,
urns and umbrella stands.

Winston Yeatts of Warwickshire
See entry under **WOODEN
ACCESSORIES**. Tôleware trays, planters,
cachepots and lamps.

BASKETS

Emma Bernhardt
T/F:0171-266 5522 for stockists.
Brightly coloured plastic baskets
hand-woven in Mexico.

Stanley Bird Basketware
1 Sutton Rd, Great Yarmouth,
Norfolk NR30 3NB.
T:01493-843392. F:01493-331813.
Balloon baskets, picnic hampers and
kitchen drawers in willow. Other baskets
in willow and cane.

*Chairworks
Unit 77, Chelsea Bridge Business Centre,
326-342 Queenstown Rd, London SW8 4NE.
T:0171-498 7611. F:0171-498 7613.
Trade suppliers of very competitively
priced baskets in a wide range of traditional
English designs. Harrods is a customer.

Jenny Crisp
The Old School House, Morton/Eye,
Nr Leominster, Hereford HR6 0DD.
T:01568-615772. By appointment. Turns
willow from her own home-grown beds into
trays, magazine racks, cradles and baskets
for fruit, logs and linen.

The Deben Craftsmen
The Old Horseshoes, Lower Tasburgh,
Norwich NR15 1AR.
T:01508-471656. Willow basketware made
by local craftsmen. There are log baskets,
linen and shopping baskets, hampers and
dog baskets as well as very strong display
and carrying baskets for bakers and
caterers. Plus a range of fine English
rush baskets.

English Hurdle
Curload, Stoke St Gregory,
Taunton, Somerset TA3 6JD.
T:01823-698418. F:01823-698859.
Fourth generation growers and weavers of
willow hurdles, garden gates, rose arches,
bower seats, arbours and baskets.

Waveney Apple Growers
Aldeby, Beccles, Suffolk NR34 0BL.
T:01502-677345. F:01502-678134.
Traditional rush baskets and matting.

M & J Wilson
146 Brighton Rd, Lansing,
W. Sussex BN15 8LN.
T:01903-752164.
Wicker baskets in all sizes and shapes -
all made out of willow from Somerset.
Anything can be made to order.

CUSHIONS

*Altfield
See entry under **CERAMICS**.
Large selection of hand embroidered
needlepoint cushions.

Chelsea Textiles
7 Walton Street, London SW3 2JD.
T:0171-584 0111. F:0171-584 7170.
Aubusson-style cushions in wool needlepoint
with tassel trim, handmade to 18th and 19th
century designs.

*** denotes
trade supplier.
Please phone
for retail outlets.** 233

Belinda Coote Tapestries
3/14 Chelsea Harbour Design Centre,
Chelsea Harbour, London SW10 0XE.
T:0171-351 0404. F:0171-352 9808.
Excellent range of woven cushions in all
sizes with animal and fruit motifs and
medieval themes. Paisley & tapestry throws
for tablecloths, curtains, bedspreads or
wallhangings. Showroom in Harvey Nichols.

Decorative Textiles of Cheltenham
7 Suffolk Parade, Cheltenham,
Gloucs GL50 2AB.
T:01242-574546. F:01242-578495.
Selection of cushions made from either
antique fabrics or from contemporary
designer silks and tapestries. Wide selection
of old and new trimmings, tassels, old
fabrics for upholstery and antique curtaining.

*The Felbrigg Design Company
Unit 1 Manor Stables, West Street, Great
Somerset, Wilts SN15 5EH.
T/F:01249-720076. Collection of cushions,
lampshades, footstools and occasional
chairs in velvet. Decoration includes 18th
designs like monkeys and garden bugs.

The Furniture Union
46 Beak Street, London W1R 3DA.
T:0171-287 3424 F:0171-498 1012.
Animal print cushions.

*Stothert Decorative Cushions
6.1.3. White Cross, Lancaster LA1 4XQ.
T:01524-844078. F:01524-849808.
Suppliers of tapestry, kelim, velvet and
printed fabric cushions to the trade.

Sussex House
92 Wandsworth Bridge Rd,
London SW6 2TF.
T:0171-371 5455. F:0171-371 7590.
Selection includes an animal collection
with a series of dogs, antique-style tapestry
cushions, leopard-print cushions and
throws and an exclusive range in jewel
tones which are hand-stitched with gold
silk ornamentation.

**For more statuary see
also GARDENS -
New & Reproduction
Statuary & Ornament.**

Tindle
See entry under **MIRRORS.**
Choice of fifteen needlepoint cushions
based on antique designs.

Georgina Von Etzdorf
50 Burlington Arcade, London W1V 9AE.
T:0171-409 7789. This designer's first
home collection includes luxurious velvet
cushions, bolsters and silky throws in
black, red and gold.

Wentworth Cushions
Unit 12, Britannia Ind. Park,
Dashewood Ave, High Wycombe,
Bucks HP12 3ES. T/F:01494-528697.
Suppliers of made to order cushion pads in
any size and with any filling: curled feather,
feather & down, hollow fibre, feather & foam
standard foam.

Alison White
Ground floor, Fitzpatrick Building,
York Way, London N7 9AS.
T:0171-609 6127. F:0171-609 6128.
Cushions in simple, modern designs in
basic white, black and tan cotton and linen.

PLASTER & RESIN CASTS

Artforum
Units 107-108 Coed Aben Rd, Wrexham Ind
Estate, Wrexham LL13 9UH.
T:01978-664949. F:01978-664747.
Reproduction Roman heads from the
Ashmolean, neo-classical lions, Egyptian
cats and more pieces in progress.

The British Museum Company
46 Bloomsbury Street, London WC1B 3QQ.
T:0171-323 1234. F:0171-436 7315.
Replica resin statues, reliefs, busts cast
from Charles Townley's 18th century
collection of ancient Greek and Roman
statuary. Catalogue and mail order.

Belinda Canosa
38 St. Mary's Grove, London W4 3LN.
T:0181-747 0436. F:0181-995 1099.
Marble resin casts of classical statues
and reliefs taken from the collection at the
Cambridge Museum of Archaeology. They
are resistant to frost and pollution and can
also be cast in any other material as well,
including stone and bronze.

Clifton Little Venice
3 Warwick Place, London W9 2PX.
T:0171-289 7894. F:0171-286 4215.
Replicas of antique statuary including
a 'Bust of Brutus', a Robert Adam frieze,
classical plinths, capitals, decorative
tiles, urns,masks, plaques and a plaster
cast of an antique foot and hand.

Belinda Coote Tapestries
See entry under CUSHIONS.
Plasterwork and resin cherubs, flowers
and fleur-de-lys. Also at Harvey Nichols.

Plasterworks
38 Cross Street, London N1 2BG.
T/F: 0171-226 5355.
Well-priced reproductions of ancient Greek
and Roman statuary as well as plaster
figures of old film stars and pharaoh's
heads. They stock a selection of
architectural features: corbels, capitals,
ceiling roses, plaques, masks and uplighters
mainly in plaster, some in resin. Also
restoration of old and fitting of new cornices.

Anthony Redmile
533 Kings Rd, London SW10 0TZ.
T:0171-351 3813. F:0171-352 8131.
Replicas and reductions of important
classical works of art from the Greek and
Roman era. They are made of faux-marbre
(resin and marble dust) which lends itself to
finely detailed busts, plinths and magnificent
vases and wall reliefs.

FAKE BOOKS

Brunschwig & Fils
10 The Chambers, Chelsea Harbour Drive,
London SW10 0XF.
T:0171-351 5797. F:0171-351 2280.
Famous for their book wallpaper, they
also have a cabinet
suitable for bedside
or drinks or simply
storage. It is fronted
with fake books and
comes in two sizes.

CVP Designs
27 Bruton Place,
London W1X 7AB.
T:0171-491 3724.
F:0171-355-4006.
Occasional table
fashioned as a pile of
'books'. Painted white
or in a customised finish.

Decora
51-53 Dollar Street,
Cirencester, Gloucs GL7 2AS.
T:01285-641919. False book giftware:
box files, paperweights, CD hide-aways,
video cases.

The Dummy Book Company
No 1 Cow Shed, Upton Grove,
Tetbury, Gloucs GL8 8LR.
T:01666-503376. F:01666-505205.
Full design, supply and fitting of book panels
for decorating. Also fake book ledgers, files,
bookends and paperweights.

The Manor Bindery
Fawley, Hants SO45 1BB.
T:01703-894488. F:01703-899418.
Supply and installation of replica book
panels, book boxes for video tapes,
CDs, desk accessories etc.

Oakleaf Reproductions
Ling Bob Mill, Main Street,
Wilsden, Bradford BD15 0JP.
T:01535-272878. F:01535-275748.
Simulated leather-bound book spines which
can be used to disguise doors, cupboards,
radiators etc.

* denotes
trade supplier.
Please phone
for retail outlets. 235

The Original Book Works
1 Wilkinson Rd,
Cirencester, Gloucs GL7 1YT.
T:01285-641664. F:01285-641705.
Manufacturers of storage items, furniture and panels made out of reproduction leather book bindings in a variety of colours. Advice on design and installation.

STORAGE

Cubbins & Co
Unit 1 Rampisham Manor,
Dorchester, Dorset DT2 OPT.
T:01935-83060. F:01935-83257.
Wastepaper baskets, tissue box covers, cotton wool boxes, linen bins, luggage racks and stools custom-covered in the customer's own fabric. They supply both the domestic and contract market where their painted range (the same items apart from the luggage rack and stools) is particularly popular for hotels. Minimum order (only for the painted range) of five items.

Cubestore Storage Systems
58 Pembroke Rd, London W8 6NX.
T:0171-602 2001. Modular storage systems. They have a bookcase sold in sections which can be built up, a wall-mounted shelving system made to the customer's measurements and trestles and worktops. Their versatile cubes can be used to make desks, beds and seating units. Also wardrobes.

The Empty Box Company
The Old Dairy, Coomb Farm Building,
Balchins Lane, Westcott, Nr Dorking,
Surrey RH4 3LE.
T:01306-740193. F:01306-875430.
Handmade boxes of all kinds covered in fabric or paper from their range. There are hat and wedding dress boxes, CD and toy boxes, and many more. Mail order.

*Hafele (UK)
Swift Valley Ind Estate,
Rugby,Warwicks CV21 1RD.
T:01788-542020. F:01788-544440.

Branches in London, Manchester and Ireland. Suppliers of a hydraulically operated 'wardrobe lift' which allows you to use the full height of a wardrobe. The unit costs £74 and is adjustable to fit widths 83-115 cm.

The Holding Company
243-245 Kings Road, London SW3 5EL.
T:0171-352 1600. F:0171-352 7495.
Everything to do with storage: boxes, chests, drawer organisers, home office units, chrome racking, systems for converting wardrobes to child height - the list goes on.

IKEA
2 Drury Way, North Circular Rd,
London NW10 0TH.
T:0181-208 5600. Call for other branches.
Racks, baskets and clothes' rails for the interiors of wardrobes, tables, bookshelves, cupboards with drawers, glass-fronted cabinets, storage combination units (including pull-out keyboard shelves) and inventive solutions including boxes which fit under beds and natural fabric wall pockets with 12 compartments. There's also a smart range of cardboard storage boxes, for everything from papers to toys and a variety of CD towers.

*Penny Kennedy Design
Unit 1, Jamestown Business Park,
Jamestown, Dunbartonshire G83 8BZ.
T:01389-755516. F:01389-721532.
Supplier of hat and storage boxes covered in plain, tartan, black and white or even leopard skin papers. Also bound notebooks, giftwrap, bags, ribbons, tissue and tags.

Muji
26 Great Marlborough Street,
London W1V 1HB.
T:0171-494 1197. F:0171-494 1193.
Call for mail order catalogue and other London branches. Large range of minimalist plastic storage boxes, fibreboard boxes and MDF and pulp furniture.

Newcome Marketing
Freepost, Dronfield, Sheffield S18 6QB.
T/F:01246-416306.
Plastic stacking boxes in a variety of sizes and colours for multiple home use.

*Noble Macmillan
9 Elvaston Mews,London SW7 5HY.
T:0171-581 4178. F:0171-581 4730.
Leather-bound files, photo albums,
wastepaper baskets and desk sets.

Paperchase
213 Tottenham Court Rd, London W1P 9AF.
T:0171-580 8496. F:0171-637 1225.
Call for branches and mail order. Plastic and
coloured cardboard storage boxes; coloured
sisal baskets in lots of sizes; three-drawer
file boxes.

FLORISTS & ARTIFICIAL FLOWERS

Chattels
53 Chalk Farm Rd, London NW1 8AN.
T:0171-267 0877. Dried flowers (lavender,
poppies, roses, sunflowers) in prepared
bouquets or any arrangement to order. Also
a large range of silk flowers and potpourri.

Caroline Dickenson Flowers
Hyde Park Hotel,
66 Knightsbridge, London SW1X 7LA.
T:0171-245 9599. F:0171-259 5014.
Daily deliveries in London and further afield
by arrangement. Specialist services include
the filling and maintaining of window boxes
and garden urns, seasonal decoration of
fireplaces, bridal and wedding flowers,
Christmas decorations and supply of
unusual and rare orchids, topiary trees,
dried displays, mossed animals and birds
and traditional posies, and baskets.

Faunus The Florist
69 Walmgate, York YO1 2TZ.
T:01904-613044. F:01904-621147.
Unusual selection of flowers, both dried
and fresh. Specialists in society weddings
and decorating hotels.

*Flowers by Charmian
Beckhaven House,
9 Gilbert Rd, London SE11 5AA.
T:0171-793 1797. F:0171-793 0537.
Dried and silk flowers - good range of
decorative containers. Contract work
for hotels.

Forever Flowering
Orchard House, Mortlake Rd,
Kew, Surrey TW9 4AS.
T:0181-392 9929. F:0181-876 6166.
Mail order gift company which supplies
beautifully wrapped living plants as well
as flowers and French lavender. Next day
delivery anywhere in the U.K.

Moyses Stevens
157-158 Sloane St, London SW1X 9BT.
T:0171-259 9303. F:0171-730 3002.
Established since 1876, Moyses Stevens
are expert in all aspects of floristry; they
decorate for all events and are wedding
specialists. Landscape gardening division.

Nimmo's
6 Horbury Crescent, London W11 3NF.
T:0171-792 0154. F:0171-221 7238.
By appointment. Original freeze-dried fruit
and flower arrangements including
strawberries or asparagus. Also silk flowers
and trees. A small table arrangement is £45-
£85, and one for a side table £85-£150.

Jane Packer
56 James St, London W1M 5HS.
T:0171-935 2673. F:0171-486 5097.
Individually made fresh or dried flower
arrangements including Christmas
decorations, ornamental trees and door
wreaths. Has her own range of vases and
candles. Her flowers adorn Terence
Conran's restaurants.

Paula Pryke Flowers
20 Penton St, London N1 9PS.
T:0171-837 7336. F:0171-837 6766.
Hand tied bouquets, daily deliveries,
Interflora, and complete service for
weddings and funerals and any large
function. Tropical, rare and cottage
garden flowers mixed to create heady
arrangements. The shop also stocks
vases, dried and freeze-dried flowers.

Pulbrook & Gould
127 Sloane St, London SW1X 9AS.
T:0171-730 0030. F:0171-730 0722.
Pioneers of the English country garden look
in London. Their pretty, loose arrangements
have been admired for 40 years.

*** denotes
trade supplier.
Please phone
for retail outlets.** 237

Anna Roberts Designs

Ripley House, Ripley, Surrey GU23 6BE.
T:01483-222998. F:01483-223020.
Mixed dried flower arrangements which
can be provided in a selection of antique
containers. Anything from wheat,
delphiniums and lavender to magnolia
leaves and rose trees. Plus swags,
firescreens and garlands in
imaginative designs.

Roots, Fruits and Flowers

451 Great Western Rd, Glasgow G12 8HH.
T:0141-339 5817. F:0141-334 3530.
Concentrate on the more unusual top-
quality fresh flowers from Holland with a
large selection always in stock (but no dried
flowers). Hand tied bouquets and country-
style specialists.

Semper Floreat

33 Larkhall Rise, London SW4 6HU.
T:0171-720 5780. F:0171-622 4594.
Silk and parchment flowers, either sold in
individual sprays or in country or formal
arrangements. Loan service for weddings
and other events.

Margaret Tregoning

8 The Priory, Queensway,
Birmingham B4 6BS.
T:0121-233 3314. F:0121-233 3315.
Established for 50 years, Margaret
Tregoning specialises in exotic Dutch
flowers and dried flower arrangements.

Kenneth Turner

125 Mount St, London W1Y 5HA.
T:0171-355 3880. F:0171-495 1607.
Fresh flowers, particularly orchids, and
unusual exotic stems; preserved roses and
leaves and customised floral decorations.
Also home fragrances and toiletries.

Wild At Heart

Turquoise Island, 222 Westbourne Grove,
London W11 2RJ.
T:0171-727 3095. F:0171-229 1174.
Famous as an architectural landmark, this
public toilet has become a shared site with
Wild At Heart who specialise in exotic
blooms including lilies, French tulips and
particularly cottage garden flowers.

Woodhams

60 Ledbury Rd, London W11 2AJ.
T:0171-243 3141.
Landscaping on:
T:0181-964 9818. F:0181-964 9848.
Everything from a tied bunch of flowers to a
full landscaping service, from window boxes
to complete garden design. Daily deliveries
in London and the home counties.
Containers, dried arrangements, smart
indoor plants, candles and accessories.

OTHER SUPPLIERS

Astral International

Astral House, Lonsdale St,
Stoke-on-Trent ST4 4DS.
T:01782-744044.
F:01782-744099.
Range of reproduction telephones which
includes the 1930s 'Whitehall' in black
or white.

The Clare Hall Company

The Barns, Clare Hall,
Clare, Suffolk CO10 8PJ.
T:01787-278445. F:01787-278803.
Replica 17th to 19th century terrestrial
globes. This company specialises in copying
antique furniture and decorative items.
They're consultants to the film industry and
their work has featured in many films
including 4 Weddings and a Funeral.

The Cross

141 Portland Rd, London W11 4LR.
T:0171-727 6760. F:0171-727 6745.
From appliqué blankets, antique ticking,
indigo cushions and original '60s glass to
recycled wood picture frames, baskets and
candles.

The Decorative Arts Company

5a Royal Crescent, London W11 4SL.
T:0171-371 4303. F:0171-602 9187.
Sells by mail order a large selection of MDF
accessories for painting, including clocks,
boxes, waste paper bins, hat-boxes, picture
frames. Also short courses on paint finishes
in London, Wiltshire, Yorkshire, Bristol,
Surrey, Essex and Lancashire.

Greaves & Thomas
PO Box 190, Richmond Surrey TW9 4ER.
T/F:0181-568 5885. 'Aged' decorative
globes and heraldic shields.

Gregory, Bottley & Lloyd
13 Seagrave Rd, London SW6 1RP.
T:0171-381 5522. F:0171-381 5512.
Specialists in fossils, minerals and
meteorites. They have been selling
rocks since 1858.

Get Stuffed
105 Essex Rd, London N1 2SL.
T:0171-226 1364. F:0171-359 8253.
Anything from framed insects (from £35) to a
kangaroo (£1250) to a tiger (£3,500). Exotic
animals like lions and tigers are bought from
zoos and safari parks after they die, and
British wildlife such as foxes and badgers
come from rescue centres or animal
hospitals if they don't survive their injuries.

Claire Guest
49 Chiltern St, London W1M 1HQ.
T:0171-224 2278. F:0171-224 2279.
Exclusive accessories including picture
frames, desk sets, bookends and
wastebaskets all decorated with découpage.
Faux-tortoiseshell, dogs, horses, wildlife,
flowers and anything else to order. Special
commissions undertaken.

Inflate
3rd floor, 5 Old Street, London EC1V 9HL.
T:0171-251 5453. F:0171-250 0311.
Inflatable plastic wine racks, egg cups,
fruit bowls, lights, mirrors etc.
Commissions undertaken.

*Thomas Messel
Bradley Court,
Wotton-under-Edge, Gloucs GL12 7PP.
T:01453-843220. F:01453-843719.
Lacquer trays and stands which can be
personalised with heraldic devices or
monograms: also wine coasters, drinks
coasters and tablemats. Plus black and
white lacquer clocks, tables and tulipières.

Otterswick Antique Telephones
6 Lady Lawson St, Edinburgh EH3 9DS.
T/F:0131-228 3690. Specialist in pre-
1960s telephones, particularly bakelite.

Candlestick and wooden wall varieties in
ivory, jade green and a 1930s style Chinese
red, and Fifties originals. Restoration and
conversion work undertaken.

Timothy Richards
59 West View Rd,
Keynsham, Bristol BS18 1BQ.
T:0117-986 2318. F:0117-986 1866.
By appointment. Book-ends which are
faithful plaster models of well known
buildings. Commissions undertaken.

Tapisserie
54 Walton St, London SW3 1RB.
T:0171-581 2715. F:0171-589 8609.
Hand painted canvases with matching
threads for needlepoint cushions.They also
run needlepoint classes.

Keith Tyssen
80 Gell St, Sheffield S3 7QW.
T/F:0114-273 0639. Modern pewterware
designs in limited editions: beakers, slim or
round vases, a flared pot which could be
used for serving ice-cream or soups
(because it insulates well), plates, dishes
and bowls. From £50 to £350.

GARDENS

ONE-STOP

Avant Garden
77 Ledbury Rd, London W11 2AG.
T:0171-229 4408. F:0171-229 4410.
Wrought-iron and wirework tables and chairs,
pots, architectural ironwork including topiary
frames and multi-plant racks.

The Chelsea Gardener
125 Sydney St, London SW3 6NR.
T:0171-352 5656. F:0171-352 3301.
Good selection of plants, including orchids
and cacti. Garden furniture, pots, books and
a 'Garden Treats' shop with gifts for
gardeners. Their 'Garden Provider' provides
and installs plants, window boxes, tubs,
troughs, trellis and artificial grass. They also
offer garden design and maintenance,
lighting and automatic watering systems.

Clifton Nurseries
5a Clifton Villas, London W9 2PH.
T:0171-289 6851. F:0171-286 4215.
Bedding and specimen plants, topiaries,
plus garden furniture and outdoor antiques

as well as a design, landscaping
and garden maintenance service.

The Conran Shop
Michelin House,
81 Fulham Rd, London SW3 6RD.
T:0171-589 7401. F:0171-823 7015.
Garden furniture, terracotta pots, galvanized
buckets, lanterns and stylish accessories.

The English Garden Collection
3 Langley Business Centre, Station Rd,
Langley, Berks SL3 8DS.
Catalogue request line:0800-103 000.
Order line:0800 203000.
Choose from 300 items for the garden
without leaving your deckchair. Well put
together selection of galvanised pots, long
Toms, urns, teak and metal furniture, a good
range of tools, and even tableware.

Judy Green's Garden Store
11 Flask Walk, London NW3 1HJ.
T:0171-435 3832. F:0181-201 8634.
Modern and antique gardening tools, pots
and window boxes, plus a team of designers
specialising in London gardens.

*** denotes
trade supplier.
Please phone
for retail outlets.**

The Traditional Garden Supply Company
Unit 12, Hewitts Ind Estate, Elmbridge Rd,
Cranleigh, Surrey GU6 8LW.
Orderline:01483-273366. F:01483-273388.
Gardening catalogue with all sorts of
equipment. Particularly strong on cedar
cold frames, boot benches, tool stores
and mini greenhouses.

ANTIQUE GARDEN
FURNITURE & ORNAMENT

Architectural Heritage
Taddington Manor, Cutsdean, Cheltenham,
Gloucs GL54 5RY.
T:01386-584414. F:01386-584236.
Selection includes stone sundials, cast iron
fountains, lead cherubs, Portland stone
urns, pergolas, and cast iron or limestone
garden seating.

Baileys
The Engine Shed, Ashburton Ind Estate,
Ross-on-Wye, Hereford HR9 7BW.
T:01989-563015. F:01989-768172.
Lead planters, lion's head fountains, stone
troughs, garden benches, old French
watering cans and gardening implements.

Crowther of Syon Lodge
Busch Corner, London Rd,
Isleworth, Middx TW7 5BH.
T:0181-560 7978. F:0181-568 7572.
Dealers in architectural antiques for 120
years. Stock includes antique garden
ornaments, mantelpieces and panelling
dating from the 17th to the 19th century.

Drummond's of Bramley
Birtley Farm, Horsham Rd,
Bramley, Guildford, Surrey GU5 OLA.
T:01483-898766. F:01483-894393.
Large architectural salvage company set in
two and a half acres of grounds. It can
supply 'everything from the top of the
chimney to the garden gate'.

Nicholas Gifford-Mead
68 Pimlico Rd, London SW1W 8LS.
T:0171-730 6233. F:0171-730 6239.
18th and 19th century English sculptural
and architectural pieces.

**For more
suppliers see also
ARCHITECTURAL
SALVAGE.**

Holloways
Lower Court, Suckley, Worcs WR6 5DE.
T:01886-884665. F:01886-884796.
Statues, bird baths, sundials and other
antique garden ornaments, plus
reproduction conservatory furniture.

Jardinique
Kemps Place, Selborne Rd, Greatham,
Liss, Hampshire GU33 6HG.
T:01420-538000. F:01420-538700.
Antique decorative garden items.

Seago
22 Pimlico Rd, London SW1W 8LJ.
T:0171-730 7502. F:0171-730 9179.
17th, 18th and 19th century garden
ornament and statuary.

Sweerts de Landas
Dunsborough Park, Ripley, Surrey GU23 6AL.
T:01483-225366. F:01483-224525.
Large range of 18th and 19th century
garden ornaments, statuary and fountains
displayed in two walled gardens, a water
garden, a sunken garden and a formal
Victorian winter garden. Viewing by
appointment only.

Talisman
The Old Brewery, Wyke,
Gillingham, Dorset SP8 4NW.
T:01747-824423. F:01747-823544.
Fountains, statuary, well-heads, pond
surrounds, as well as a vast stock of
interesting furniture and decorative items.

NEW & REPRODUCTION
STATUARY & ORNAMENT

The British Museum Company
46 Bloomsbury St, London WC1B 3QQ.
T:0171-323 1234. F:0171-436 7315.
Replica statues, reliefs and busts cast from
Charles Townley's 18th century collection of
ancient Greek and Roman pieces.Mail order.

The Bronze Collection
The Dovecote, Bourne Lane, Much Hadham,
Herts SG10 6ER.
T:01279-842685. F:01279-843646.
Large range of bronze statuary and animals,
plus carved Japanese stone lanterns.

The Bulbeck Foundry
Reach Rd, Burwell, Cambs CB5 0AH.
T:01638-743153. F:01638-743374.
Reproduction antique designs in lead: shell-shaped bird baths, wall masks, copies of old water tanks, custom-made plant containers with heraldic motifs. Repairs undertaken. Mail order.

Belinda Canosa
38 St.Mary's Grove, London W4 3LN.
T:0181-747 0436. F:0181-995 1099.
Marble resin casts of classical statues and reliefs taken from the collections at the Cambridge Museum of Archaeology. They are resistant to frost and pollution and can be cast in any other material as well, including stone and bronze.

George Carter
See entry under
WOODEN FURNITURE.
'Baroque' (and other) concrete urns on plinths which are cast to look like stone.

Chilstone
Victoria Park, Fordcombe Rd,
Langton Green, Kent TN3 0RE.
T:01892-740866. F:01892-740867.
Reconstituted stone statues, fountains, sundials, troughs and architectural elements (columns, temples, ball finials, mullions, sills and copings).

Clifton Little Venice
See entry under
WOODEN FURNITURE.
Huge range of high quality replicas in plaster or jesmonite available in many finishes. There are plaques, urns and vases, plinths and planters, fountain masks, sphinxes, lions, griffins, hands, feet, capitals. Also fancy wirework jardinières, baskets and topiary balls.

H Crowther
5 High Rd, London W4 2ND.
T/F:0181-994 2326.
This company has been producing hand-made lead garden ornaments since 1908. You can order planters, plaques, statues, fountains and jardinières from hundreds of master patterns.

Forest Stonecraft
Yew Tree Cottage, Bradley Hill,
Soudley, Gloucs GL14 2UQ.
T:01594-824823. F:01594-824317.
200 different concrete ornaments priced from £4.95 to £400.

Haddonstone
The Forge House, East Haddon,
Northants NN6 8DB.
T:01604-770711. F:01604-770027.
Large range of architectural features and statuary in reconstituted stone. More than 500 statues, urns, troughs, sundials, fountains and columns available in four finishes: Portland, Bath and Cotswold stone and terracotta. The company can also produce custom-made items and replications for restoration projects.

Herons Bonsai
Wire Mill Lane, Newchapel,
Nr Lingfield, Surrey RH7 6HJ.
T:01342-832657. F:01342-832025.
Designers of Japanese gardens and suppliers of all the related accessories - lanterns, bamboo, screens, bonsai and beautifully-shaped maples and pines.

*Marble-Arte
Dragons Lane, Cowfold, Sussex RH13 8DX.
T:01403-864814. F:01403-864597.
Reconstituted marble fountains, urns, furniture and statuary imported from Italy - anything from the Madonna of Lourdes to useful columns and bases.

Pyramidion
PO Box 3, Hay-on-Wye, Hereford HR3 5YA.
T:01497-847171. F:01497-847063.
Detailed copies of antique garden statuary cast in limestone and marble. There are about 50 different pieces, from 18" Jekyll griffins to 6' classical statues. Also sundials, armillary spheres, columns and obelisks.

Rattee & Kett
Purbeck Rd, Cambridge CB2 2PG.
T:01223-248061. F:01223-410284.
Reconstituted stone, bronze and marble statuary and features.
Restoration department.

* denotes trade supplier. Please phone for retail outlets. 243

Redwood Stone
46 North Rd, Wells, Somerset BA5 2TL.
T:01749-673601. F:01749-675701.
Classical English and oriental-style
ornaments in reconstituted stone
and granite.

Renaissance Casting
Manor Farm, Hunningham Rd, Offchurch
Nr Leamington Spa, Warwicks CV33 9AG.
T/F:01926-885567.
Lead statuary, fountains, vases, rainwater
heads and anything else to commission.

The David Sharp Studio
201a Nottingham Rd,
Somercotes, Derbys DE55 4JG.
T:01773-606066. F:01773-540737.
Over 1000 ornamental stonework designs
for architectural and garden ornament,
including lions, busts, urns and plinths, balls
and finials, benches, sundials, obelisks,
temples and colonnades.

Thomason Cudworth
The Old Vicarage, Cudworth,
Nr Ilminster, Somerset TA19 OPR.
T:01460-57322. F:01460-53737.
Maker and restorer of decorative
architectural terracotta using a recipe
based on 18th century Coade Stone.
Vases, statues, columns, finials and
anything made to commission.

Whittaker's Sculpture Craft Workshop
11 Queen Anne's Grove, London W4 1HW.
T:0181-995 9255. F:0181-743 3003.
By appointment. Elizabeth Whittaker casts
from originals or accepts commissions in
bronze, reconstituted stone or marble, lead
or bronze-finished resin. She will also
restore stone or terracotta statuary.

WOODEN FURNITURE

Barlow Tyrie
Springwood Ind Estate,
Braintree, Essex CM7 2RN.
T:01376-322505. F:01376-347052.
Manufacturers of teak steamers, dining and
director's chairs, tables, corner seats,
benches and circular tree seats.

Barnsley House
Barnsley House,
Nr Cirencester, Gloucs GL7 5EE.
T:01285-740561. F:01285-740628.
Wide range of traditional teak benches,
seats, steamers and loungers designed
by Charles Verey.

Benchmark
128 Church Rd, Wheatley, Oxford OX33 1LU.
T:01865-873868. F:01865-875353.
Verandah and garden furniture inspired by
traditional swing beds and colonial designs
from India. Hand-crafted in iroko hardwood,
the 'Maharaja's swing bed' has decorative
side panels and a canopied frame.

Brookgate Designs
Brookgate Farm Oast,
Hurst Green, E.Sussex TN19 7QY.
T:01580-860627. F:01580-861316.
Small range of iroko New England style
furniture, including a traditional Adirondack
chair with matching footstool.

Sarah Burgoyne Revivals
Old Whyly, East Hoathly, E.Sussex BN8 6EL.
T:01825-840738. Handmade beech and
canvas steamer and terrace chairs
reproduced from Edwardian originals. Also
hammocks large enough to lie in diagonally !

George Carter
Silverstone Farm,
North Elmham, Norfolk NR20 5EX.
T/F:01362-668130. Inspired variations on
classical themes. George Carter designs
and makes chairs, tables, benches, urns
and garden buildings, aviaries and even the
smartest 'Dutch mannerist' kennels.

Chatsworth Carpenters
Edensor, Bakewell, Derbys DE45 1RJ.
T:01246-582394. F:01246-583464.
Traditional hardwood benches, chairs,
tables and trellis made to order.

Julian Chichester Designs
Unit 12, 33 Parsons Green Lane,
London SW6 4HH.
T:0171-371 9055. F:0171-371 9066.
Craftsman-made teak benches with
designs inspired by Chippendale, Sheraton
and Hepplewhite.

Clifton Little Venice
3 Warwick Place, London W9 2PX.
T:0171-289 7894. F:0171-286 4215.
Elegant wooden garden chairs and benches
based on antiques. There is an unusual
double-backed bench based on an 18th
century French one at the Palace of
Versailles, one with small folding tables at
the sides, and another small semi-circular
bench ideal for a small garden.

Andrew Crace Designs
Bourne Lane,
Much Hadham, Herts SG10 6ER.
T:01279-842685. F:01279-843646.
Wide selection of garden seating, from a
Chinoiserie bench to a Lutyens seat.

Frolics of Winchester
82 Canon St, Winchester SO23 9JQ.
T:01962-856384. F:01962-844896.
Wide range of painted garden benches,
including some with ornate back panel
designs. Also tree seats and tables
made to order.

Gaze Burvill
Plain Farm Old Dairy,
East Tisted, Hants GU34 3RT.
T:01420-587467. F:01420-587354.
Oak seats, benches, and tables in
slightly curved designs.

Greene's Garden Furniture
Lower Farm House, Preston Crowmarsh,
Wallingford, Oxon OX10 6SL.
T:01491-825519. Chunky wooden
chairs, benches, tables in simple designs.
Plus trolleys on wheels, trellis, pyramids,
arches, pergolas.

Michael Hughes
Kingstone Cottages, Weston-under-Penyard,
Ross-on-Wye HR9 7NX.
T:01989-565267. Custom made benches,
seats round trees, arches, plus restoration
of old garden furniture.

Indian Ocean Trading Company
155-163 Balham Hill, London SW12 9DJ.
T:0181-675 4808. F:0181-675 4652.
Claims to be the UK's largest teak garden
furniture showroom. Chairs, tables,
benches and parasols.

Iain McGregor Designs
Greenbank, West End, Gordon,
Berwickshire TD3 6JP.
T/F:01573-410277. Oak and ash chairs
and benches in four styles: Edinburgh,
Aberdeen, Kelso and Glasgow (which is
Mackintosh-inspired). They can all be
ordered with a high back or in any length.

*Rusco Marketing
See entry under **METAL GARDEN
FURNITURE.** Folding hardwood tables,
benches, chairs, butlers' trays and a
swing seat for three with a canvas shade.
Plus American rope hammocks and
hammock stands.

Stuart Garden Architecture
Burrow Hill Farm, Wiveliscombe,
Somerset TA4 2RN.
T:01984-667458. F: 01984-667455.
Iroko tables, dining chairs and carvers,
some of them folding. Plus benches made
to order in styles ranging from the simple
slatted 'Barrington' to the ornate 'Dragon'.

Summit Furniture
198 Ebury St, London SW1W 8UN.
T:0171-259 9244. F:0171-259 9246.
Sturdy American furniture in eco-sound
hardwoods.

The Teak Tiger Trading Co
Freepost, Sudbury, Suffolk CO10 8YZ.
T:01787-880900. F:01787-880906.
Deckchairs, stools, recliners by mail order.
Items are delivered fully assembled.

METAL GARDEN
FURNITURE

Calmels
3/7 Southville, Wandsworth Rd,
London SW8 2PR.
T:0171-622 6181. F:0171-498 2889.
Scrollwork metal chairs, wrought-iron tables
with glass, metal, wood or marble tops, and
any other furniture to order in all sorts of
metals and finishes. The company has done
a lot of theatrical work, including the sets for
Sunset Boulevard and the chandeliers for
Phantom of the Opera.

*** denotes
trade supplier.
Please phone
for retail outlets.** 245

The Cast Iron Shop
394 Caledonian Rd, London N1 1DW.
T:0171-609 0934. F:0171-607 7565.
Ornate benches and chairs, brackets for
hanging baskets and thousands of castings
for balusters, gates, staircases and railings.

Graham & Greene
4,7 &10 Elgin Crescent, London W11 2JA.
T:0171-727 4594. F: 0171-229 9717.
Café chairs and tables; teak furniture.
Lots of accessories.

Christopher Hartnoll
Little Bray House, Brayford, Nr Barnstaple,
N.Devon EX32 7QG. T:01598-710295. Iron
seats and benches including Gothic and
Regency styles.

The Heveningham Collection
Weston Down, Weston Colley, Micheldever,
Winchester, Hampshire SO21 3AQ.
T:01962-774990. F:01962-774790.
Wrought-iron furniture in simple lines for
both interior and exterior use. It is supplied
painted black or green with canvas cushions.

Michael Hill
Cressy Hall, Gosberton,
Spalding, Lincs PE11 4JD.
T:01775-840925. F:01775-840008.
Cast iron copies of classic 19th century
benches, chairs, tables and fountains.

House of Steel
400 Caledonian Rd, London N1 1DN.
T/F: 0171-607 5889. Reclaimed, restored
and reproduction furniture and accessories.

The Iron Design Company
Summer Carr Farm, Thornton-Le-Moor,
Northallerton, N.Yorks DL6 3SG.
T:01609-778143. F:01609-778846.
Large range of metal chairs, tables, screens,
shelves in scroll or simple designs and a
variety of paint finishes.

Oxley's Furniture
Lapstone Barn, Westington Hill, Chipping
Camden, Gloucs GL55 6UR.
T:01386-840466. F:01386-840455.
Cast aluminium chairs, tables and recliners
in a variety of verdigris finishes. Can also
recondition any metal item and repaint it in
one of their specialist finishes.

For stone furniture see New & Reproduction Statuary & Ornament

*Rusco Marketing
Little Farringdon Mill,
Lechlade, Gloucs GL7 3QQ.
T:01367-252754. F:01367-253406.
French folding bistro tables and chairs and
stackable American wrought iron range.

WICKER/RATTAN/LLOYD LOOM FURNITURE

Albrissi
1 Sloane Square, London SW1W 8EE.
T:0171-730 6119. F:0171-259 9113.
Smart teak and rattan daybed with a cream
cushion; dining chairs in a Louis XVI style
with a rush seat and cane back - they look as
though they are made out of rope. Plus
eclectic selection of accessories from all
over the world.

Besselink & Jones
99 Walton St, London SW3 2HH.
T:0171-584 0343. F:0171-584 0284.
Smart range of rattan furniture.

Peter Dudgeon
Brompton Place, London SW3 1QE.
T:0171-589 0322. F:0171-589 1910.
Agents for McGuire International's rawhide
and rattan furniture. Also tables made of
bamboo hand-fitted over a welded metal
frame for strength, and several designs
in teak.

English Hurdle
Curload, Stoke St.Gregory,
Taunton, Somerset TA3 6JD.
T:01823-698418. F:01823-698859.
Reproduction bentwood willow Canadian
Adirondack chairs and basketwork
'Bower' seats.

*Grange
4 St.Paul's St, Stamford, Lincs PE9 2FY.
T:01780-54721. F:01780-54718.
Woven rattan furniture in lots of colours.

Habitat
196 Tottenham Court Rd, London W1P 9LD.
T:0171-631 3880. F:0171-255 6043.
For other branches call: 0645-334433.
Affordable range of rattan furniture, including
a sectional sofa, armchairs, coffee tables.

Holloways
See entry under **ANTIQUE GARDEN FURNITURE & ORNAMENT.**
Stockists of over 40 styles of English willow, rattan and cane furniture. Mail order.

Interdesign
Unit G30, Chelsea Harbour Design Centre, Chelsea Harbour, London SW10 0XE.
T:0171-376 5272. F:0171-376 3020.
Suppliers (to order) of fine wicker furniture by the Italian company Pierantonio Bonacina, who have been manufacturing it since the turn of the century. The range comprises many chairs, sofas, beds and night tables.

Lloyd Loom Furniture
Wardentree Lane, Pinchbeck, Spalding, Lincs PE11 3SY.
T:01775-712111. F:01775-761255.
Traditional loom chairs and tables plus the 'Trader' range of hotel bedroom furniture which includes everything from headboards to mirrors.

W Lusty & Sons
Hoo Lane, Chipping Camden, Gloucs GL55 6AU.
T:01386-841333. F:01386-841322.
Manufacturers since 1922 of Lloyd Loom furniture which is woven from Kraft paper wrapped around a steel wire. They can also strip pieces using a special technique which avoids wetting (from £30 a chair) and have a repainting service.

Marston & Langinger
192 Ebury St, London SW1W 8UP.
T:0171-824 8818. F:0171-824 8757.
Classic wicker sofas and chairs in buff, bleached or painted English willow with feather-filled cushions. There are four styles of chairs and three sizes of sofa.

*Pavilion Rattan
Unit 4, Mill 2, Pleasley Vale Business Park, off Outgang Lane, Pleasley, Derbys NG19 8RL. T:01623-811343. F:01623-810123.
Handmade furniture in rattan, seagrass, steel and wood. The range includes sofas, dining chairs and tables as well as outdoor pieces.

WIREWORK FURNITURE

Matthew Eden
Pickwick End, Corsham, Wilts SN13 0JB.
T:01249-713335. F:01249-713644.
Wirework table and tub chairs inspired by Regency originals. Also domes, arches and obelisks. Oak seats in Lutyens designs.

Marston & Langinger
See entry under **WICKER/RATTAN/ LLOYD LOOM FURNITURE.**
Wirework chairs in three styles: Regency, 1920s, and Gothick.

Rayment Wirework
The Forge, Durlock, Minster,Thanet, Kent CT12 4HE.
T:01843-821628. F:01843-821635.
Specialists in wirework chairs, tables, arbour and canopy seats, chaises longues, planters, hanging baskets and chandeliers. The galvanised iron is intricately woven and hand-painted in black, white, antique, eau de nil or forest green.

CONSERVATORIES

Alitex
Station Rd, Alton, Hants GU34 2PZ.
T:01420-82860. F:01420-541097.
Victorian-style greenhouses in durable cast aluminium. Reconstruction of decaying conservatories.

* denotes trade supplier. Please phone for retail outlets.

Amdega/Machin
Faverdale, Darlington, Co.Durham DL3 OPW.
T:0800-591523. F:01325-489209.
One of the longest established conservatory companies. Wide range of stock styles in cedar wood or aluminium as well as a bespoke service.

Bartholomew Conservatories
Unit 5, Haslemere Ind.Estate, Weydown Rd, Haslemere, Surrey GU27 1DW.
T:01428-658771.
F:01428-656370.
Hardwood double-glazed conservatories, glazed links, swimming pool covers. The company has its own joinery and glassworks and can tackle particularly difficult sites.

Glass Houses
63 Islington Park St, London N1 1QB.
T:0171-607 6071. F:0171-609 6050.
Classically-inspired conservatories, orangeries and lanterns as well as gazebos and summerhouses.

Lloyd Christie Garden Architecture
1 New King's Rd, London SW6 4SB.
T:0171-731 3484. F:0171-371 9952.
Conservatories, gazebos, pergolas, trellis and decking, available in an attractive range of stains and paints.

Marston & Langinger
See entry under WICKER/RATTAN/ LLOYD LOOM FURNITURE.
Will tackle jobs all over the world. They are currently working on a new conservatory at Kew. Huge choice of furniture, flooring, underfloor heating and blinds.

Oak Leaf Conservatories of York
Clifton Common Ind. Park, Kettlestring Lane,York YO3 4XF.
T:01904-690401. F:01904-690945.
Hardwood conservatories, custom-designed for each property.
The company has a 'library' of moulds for cast iron brackets and finials.

The Conservatory Association
T:01480-458278.
Brochure answer-phone:
T:01480-411326.
F:01480-411326.
Leaflets on choosing a conservatory and free advice service. All their members offer an insurance-backed guarantee scheme.

Further help:
The Glass and Glazing Federation,
44-48 Borough High St, London SE1 1XB.
T:0171-403 7177.
F:0171-357 7458.
Advice and leaflets on glass, windows, conservatories. Can send you a list of members divided by region.

Town & Country Conservatories
Thumb Lane, Horningtoft, Dereham, Norfolk NR20 5DY.
T:01328-700565. F:01328-700015.
Individually designed timber conservatories.

Vale Garden Houses
Melton Rd, Harlaxton, Nr Grantham, Lincs NG32 1HQ. T:01476-564433. F:01476-578555. Conservatories, orangeries and pavilions. Recent commissions include a big open pavilion in the South of France inspired by the aviary at Waddesdon Manor.

GARDEN HOUSES/ GAZEBOS/PAVILIONS

Artech Garden Architecture
146-148 Church Walk, London N16 8QP.
T:0171-241 6251. F:0181-340 2856.
Garden pavilions with trellised back panels made in western red cedar for a natural look or in treated Douglas fir to be painted.

Carpenter Oak & Woodland Company
Hall Farm, Thickwood Lane, Colerne, Chippenham, Wilts SN14 8BE.
T:01225-743089. F:01225-744100.
Specialists in repairing old oak buildings and designing and erecting green oak frames for barns, barnhouses, stables, bridges, boathouses, roofs and conservatories.

George Carter
See entry under
WOODEN FURNITURE.
Designer and maker of fanciful garden structures, including a 'Baroque' alcove and a sentry box topped with a giant acorn finial. His wooden obelisks add instant architectural interest to a garden.

Chilstone
See entry under
NEW & REPRODUCTION
STATUARY & ORNAMENT.
Architectural features in handmade reconstituted stone: temples, columns, pavilions. Plus fountains, statues, urns and balustrading.

Country Garden Retreats

Talk's Farm, East Martin,
Fordingbridge, Hampshire SP6 3LJ.
T/F:01725-519202. Individually designed
oak-framed garden buildings, summer
houses, gazebos and Wendy houses.

Courtyard Designs

Suckley, Worcester WR6 5EH.
T:01886-884640. F:01886-884444.
New 'Office in the Garden' range - 4 sizes of
timber offices fitted with power, lighting and
communication cabling, from around
£10,000. They take about 3 days to erect,
normally without needing planning
permission. Plus garages, summerhouses,
garden stores and annexes.

Andrew Crace Designs

See entry under
WOODEN FURNITURE. Hexagonal,
New Jersey and Chinoiserie pavilions,
all in hardwood with moulded GRP roofs.
They can be left open like a bandstand or
half-enclosed with trellis or walls, or fully
enclosed with doors and windows.

English Hurdle

Curload, Stoke St.Gregory,
Taunton, Somerset TA3 6JD.
T:01823-698418. F:01823-698859.
Woven willow summer houses, as well
as panels, gates, garden furniture and
plant climbers.

Haddonstone

See entry under
NEW & REPRODUCTION STATUARY
& ORNAMENT. Vast range of architectural
stonework, including grand pavilions,
classical temples, pergolas, ruins, follies
and grottoes.

Harvey's Garden & Leisure Buildings

Woodside Garden Centre, Arterial Rd,
Rayleigh, Essex SS6 7TZ.
T/F:01268-775770. Garden rooms,
summer houses, cabins, gazebos.

Little Thatch Company

Box Cottage, 11 Upper Neatham, Mill Lane,
Holybourne, Hampshire GU34 4EP.
T:01420-84165. You can pretend you live in
a thatched cottage in their 'Tudorbethan'

thatched
summerhouse.
It is part of a range
of garden houses,
all of which can be
modified to suit
customers'
requirements. They
also do restoration.

Robus Ceramics

Evington Park, Hastingleigh,
Ashford, Kent TN2 55JH.
T/F:01233-750330. Columned terracotta
gazebo with a Kent-peg tiled roof. It is
supplied in kit form with detailed
instructions.

Scotts of Thrapston

Bridge St, Thrapston, Northants NN14 4LR.
T:01832-732366. F:01832-733703.
Timber gazebos, lawn houses, pavilions in
several styles and sizes. Plus garden seats,
period-style windows and other custom-
made joinery.

The Secret Garden Company of Ware

Ware, Herts SG12 0YJ. T/F:01920-462081.
Iroko and cedar summerhouses and
gazebos. Prices for a gazebo start at about
£3600, summerhouses at £6000-£10,000.

The David Sharp Studio

See entry under NEW &
REPRODUCTION GARDEN
STATUARY & ORNAMENT.
Reconstituted stone temples and a
vast range (over 1000 designs) of other
architectural and decorative ornaments,
from finials to lions.

Stuart Garden Architecture

See entry under
WOODEN FURNITURE. Hexagonal
gazebos with simulated lead or open trellis
roof - some with Gothic arches, others with
tongue-and-groove dado panels.

T&C Designs

260 Boldmere Rd, Sutton
Coldfield, W.Midlands B73 5LW.
T:0121-373 8586. F:0121-382 1216.
Summerhouses and garden seats in
Gothic designs.

*** denotes
trade supplier.
Please phone
for retail outlets.** 249

Terrace and Garden
Orchard House, Patmore End, Ugley,
Bishop's Stortford, Herts CM22 6JA.
T:01799-543289. F:01799-543586.
Charming twiggy look-out, which would also
make a lovely support for climbing roses.
Plus gazebos, twig baskets and trellis.

GREENHOUSES/SHEDS

*Hartley Botanic
Greenfield, Oldham, Lancs OL3 7AG.
T:01457-873244. F:01457-870151.
Large range of domestic and commercial
size greenhouses, vine houses and plant
houses in aluminium.

Lawson Fencing
1208 High Rd, London N20 0LL.
T:0181-446 1321. F:0181-446 2509.
And at:
19 Pinner Rd, Harrow, Middx HA1 4ES.
T:0181-427 6903.
And: 308 Burnt Oak Broadway, Edgware,
Middx HA8 5ED. T:0181-952 0111.
Range of sheds and specials to order.

*Supersheds
Coppice Rd, Willaston,
Nantwich, Cheshire CW5 6QH.
T:01270-68121. F:01270-669280.
Range of timber sheds.

Two Wests & Elliott
Unit 4, Carrwood Rd, Sheepbridge
Ind.Estate, Chesterfield, Derbys S41 9RH.
T:01246-451077. F:01246-260115.
Nationwide mail order service for a wide
range of greenhouse equipment.

White Cottage Leisure Buildings
White Cottage, Grange Lane,
Winsford, Cheshire CW7 2PR.
T:01606-594751. F:01606-557433.
Traditional Victorian-style greenhouses in
timber or aluminium. Can also repair or
rebuild existing structures. Local site work,
but nationwide supply.

CH Whitehouse
Buckhurst Works, Bells Yew Green,
Frant, Tunbridge Wells TN3 9BN.
T/F:01892-750247.

Traditional high-sided sectional or brick-
based greenhouses in western red cedar, as
well as specialist orchid or alpine versions,
summer houses and garden frames.

FENCING & WOODEN GATES

Architectural Fencing
Mayside House, Hawks Hill, Bourne End,
Bucks SL8 5JQ. T/F:01628-522541.
Pressure-impregnated finials to add to the
top of your fence. Choose from acorns, balls,
square-turned bishops and pyramids.

British Gates & Timber
Biddenden, Nr Ashford, Kent TN27 8DD.
T:01580-291555. F:01580-292011.
Wide range of timber garden, field and
entrance gates plus specials to order.

English Hurdle
See entry under WICKER/RATTAN/
LLOYD LOOM FURNITURE.
Traditional willow hurdles.

Forest Fencing
Stanford Court, Stanford Bridge,
Nr Worcester, Worcs WR6 6SR.
T:01886-812451. F:01886-812343.
Wide range of wooden fencing.

HS Jackson & Son
Stowting Common, Ashford, Kent TN25 6BN.
T:01233-750393. F:01233-750403.
Full range of security, agricultural, domestic
and equestrian fences in metal or timber
(including automated). Their 'Jakcured'
timber gates are guaranteed for 25 years.
Nationwide fence erection service.

Lawson Fencing
See entry under GREENHOUSES/
SHEDS. Large range of lap fencing and
trellis panels, gates (and specials to order).
Erection service for fencing in London and
Home Counties.

NDS Manufacturing
Rose Tree Farm,
29 Nine Mile Ride, Finchampstead,
Wokingham, Berks RG40 4QD.
T:01734-734203. F:01734-328054.
Panels made up from imported French

heather in 3m rolls and three heights (1m,1.5m and 5m). They are erected between bamboo posts with straining wires. Also reed panels, wattle hurdles, split cane, peeled reed, bamboo fencing and even a thatched sun-shade kit for picnic tables.

Sandhill (Bullion)
Merchant Trading Dept, PO Box 11, Wetherby, W.Yorks LS22 6GL. T:01423-358440. F:01423-358434. Big section bamboo poles in a variety of diametres to use for garden structures and fences. Poles are supplied in 20ft lengths or cut to measure. Also rot-proof Hempex rope for the bindings.

Stuart Garden Architecture
See entry under **WOODEN FURNITURE**. Gates in timber, ironwork or both : plain picket gates, solid boarded entrance gates, iron 'estate' gates, Victorian lodge gates.

Summers & Co
Firs Farm, Winston, Stowmarket, Suffolk IP14 6LQ. T:01728-860012. Handsome gates made from straight-grained English oak in several styles. They all have pinned mortise-and-tenon joints and bolts in either galvanised metal or black enamelled steel. One-off designs as well.

METAL GATES & RAILINGS

Architectural Heritage
See entry under **ANTIQUE GARDEN FURNITURE & ORNAMENT**. Entryway and drive gates in cast or wrought iron.

The Great Victorian Railing Company
Runnymede Malthouse, Runnymede Rd, Egham, Surrey TW20 9BD. T:01784-250500. F:01784-242534. Wide spectrum of gates, railings and balustrades using steel and aluminium. Mainly bespoke commissions.

House of Steel
See entry under **METAL GARDEN FURNITURE**. Stocks lots of reclaimed gates as well as old grilles

and wrought iron panels which can be made up into gates of any dimension.

Renzland Forge
83a London Rd, Copford, Colchester, Essex CO6 1LG. T:01206-210212. F:01206-211290. Gates, railings, rose arches, weathervanes and other cast iron features. Will also make up any design to order.

Chris Topp
Carlton Husthwaite, Thirsk, N.Yorks YO7 2BJ. T:01845-501415. F:01845-501072. Restores and copies wrought-iron gates, balustrades and railings for The National Trust and English Heritage.

Tudor Wrought Ironwork
11 Westmoor St, London SE7 8NR. T:0181-853 1438. F:0181-858 7414. Wrought-iron gates and railings to commission.

CANOPIES & PARASOLS

Andrew Crace Designs
See entry under **WOODEN FURNITURE**. Oriental umbrellas handmade in bamboo and oil-based proofing cotton available in 13 colours.

Greenham Trading
671 London Rd, Isleworth, Middx TW7 4EX. T:0181-560 1244. F:0181-568 8423. Supply Terram industrial fabric (spun polyester, white) which can be stretched and used as a wind break.

Jopasco
Unit 1, Trident Ind. Estate, Blackthorne Rd, Colnbrook, Berks SL3 0AX. T:01753-680858. F:01753-680223. Hardwood frame and canvas shade parasols. Round, square and rectangular versions. Hardwood furniture.

Proctor Masts
Duncan Rd, Swanwick, Southampton SO31 1ZQ. T:01489-583111. F:01489-577889. Manufacturers of masts and fittings for sailing boats. Their skills are also used by

For more blacksmiths and metalworkers see also SPECIALIST SUPPLIERS - Metalwork/Ironwork, and ARCHITECTURAL SALVAGE or contact The British Artist Blacksmiths' Association on 01845-501415 which will send a list of members in your area and give information on how to commission work.

* denotes trade supplier. Please phone for retail outlets. 251

architects who want their high-tensile yachting equipment, flagpoles and canopies for building projects. They have supplied an atrium roof-structure for a Kingston shopping precinct and suspended balconies for a London Docklands development.

*Paul Reef Parasols
Merchant Trading Dept, PO Box 11, Wetherby, W.Yorks LS22 6GL.
T:01423-358440. F:01423-358434.
Canvas parasols in various colours (natural, burgundy, navy blue, green and terracotta) and in diametres from 2.1m to 5m.

*Rusco Marketing
See entry under METAL GARDEN FURNITURE. 'Piazza' canvas parasols in ten sizes, American rope (traditional or acrylic) hammocks and stands.

WOODEN TRELLIS & OBELISKS / WILLOW SUPPORTS

Anthony de Grey Trellises
Broadhinton Yard, 77a North St, London SW4 OHQ.
T:0171-738 8866. F:0171-498 9075.
Architectural trellis in 68 different colours and any number of different designs and lattice patterns. Plus gazebos, rose walks, arches, pavilions, seats, planters and decking.

English Hurdle
See entry under WICKER/RATTAN/ LLOYD LOOM FURNITURE.
Wattle hurdles and willow supports.

Frolics of Winchester
See entry under WOODEN FURNITURE.
Painted trellis panels in many designs and sizes. Also trompe l'oeil columns, arches, trees and silhouettes.

Greene's Garden Furniture
See entry under WOODEN FURNITURE. Trellis, arches and pyramids in many styles in untreated iroko, which weathers to a silvery grey. Commissions undertaken.

Jason Griffiths Underwoodsman
Higher Tideford Farm, Cornworthy, Totnes, Devon TQ9 7HL.
T:01803-712387. F:01803-712388.
Uses coppice wood materials for trellis, benches, tables and chairs - all made to order. Sells raw materials and runs courses.

Lloyd Christie Garden Architecture
See entry under CONSERVATORIES. Finest hardwood trellis: 130 frames to choose from. Free design and site visit service. Colours available: deep green, grey blue or brown Sadolin stain and other finishes for a small charge.

Stuart Garden Architecture
See entry under WOODEN FURNITURE. Wide range of iroko wood modular trellis components which can be used in all sorts of combinations, plus posts, finials and accessories all available from stock. Their integral planting boxes allow the trellis to be self-supporting and used as a screen.

Terrace and Garden
See entry under GARDEN HOUSES/ GAZEBOS/PAVILIONS. Topiary frames made in the Philippines from black hardwood twigs. Lots of other accessories by mail order: wind chimes, sundials, armillaries, wooden garden stakes, brass door bells.

Trelliscope
Units 4&5, Second Avenue, Millwey Rise, Axminster, Devon EX13 5HH.
T:01297-35735. F:01297-33550.
Range of standard hardwood modular panels and custom-built service as well. Plus garden furniture, especially tree seats.

Trellysian
Trellysian House, 31 Collwood Close, Poole, Dorset BH15 3HG.
T:01202-385181. F:01202-385203.
Range of architectural trellis panels in square or diagonal grid patterns with posts and columns in various designs.

Tim Wade
The Woodland Skills Centre, The Church Hall, Llanafan Fawr, Builth-Wells, Powys LD2 3PN.
T/F:01597-860469. Commissions

undertaken for supports, hurdles and wooden rustic furniture. Also runs courses and sells the raw materials from his own 175 acres of woodland.

Christopher Winder Master Carpenters
See entry under OUTDOOR PAVING & SURFACES. Trellis panels in a wide range of standard designs or made to suit the client's requirements.

IRON & WIRE PLANT SUPPORTS

Agriframes
Charlwoods Rd,
East Grinstead, W.Sussex RH19 2HG.
T:01342-328644. F:01342-327233.
Mail order only. Large range of floral arches, screens, supports, bowers and pergolas.

Burgon & Ball
La Plata Works,
Holme Lane, Sheffield S6 4JY.
T:0114-233 8262. F:0114-285 2518.
Hand-forged 'creeping sticks' for vines or pear trees, 'wiggly sticks' for growing tomatoes, topiary frames and plant elevators. Hanging herb drier, hose-pipe support for aiming at a particular plant and lots of other garden products and tools. Mail order.

Clifton Little Venice
See entry under NEW & REPRODUCTION STATUARY & ORNAMENT. Fancy wirework baskets, topiary balls and night light holders plus spiral wirework 'wobblers' in five sizes from 30cm to 81cm.

Matthew Eden
See entry under WIREWORK FURNITURE. Wirework rose arches, obelisks and pleasure domes based on 19th century designs.

James Gilbert & Sons
129 The Vale, London W3 7RQ.
T:0181-743 1566. F:0181-746 1393.
Traditional woven and plaited wirework to order. Arched structures are £5 to £15 per metre depending on height (plus p&p), but they also do radiator grilles, security bars, church window guards and hand-lace work.

Marston & Langinger
See entry under WICKER/RATTAN/LLOYD LOOM FURNITURE. Elaborate wire jardinières and wire trellis in round and gothic styles.

Newton Forge
Stalbridge Lane, Sturminster Newton, Dorset DT10 2JQ. T:01258-472407. F:01258-471111. Galvanized steel frames for fan-training plants, obelisks, garden hoops, all made to order.

*Pavilion Rattan
See entry under WICKER/RATTAN/LLOYD LOOM FURNITURE.
Good range of painted (green or black) wire accessories, including hanging baskets, jardinières and corner units.

Rayment Wirework
See entry under WIREWORK FURNITURE. Topiary frames, from £16 to £90, hanging baskets, and anything in wire to order.

Celestino Valenti Wireworks
The Wire Workshop, Brewery Arts, Brewery Court, Cirencester, Gloucs GL7 1JH. T:01285-642583. F:01285-652554. Hand-made wirework - anything from small baskets to chandeliers (they recently made one with a 6ft drop). Also urns, sconces and all sorts of large display pieces.

The Wadham Trading Company
Wadham House, Southrop,
Nr Lechlade, Gloucs GL7 3PB.
T/F:01367-850499. Ironwork topiary urns and a rose/climber support; big range of galvanized steel wire topiary animals.

FOUNTAINS/WATER PUMPS/TAPS

Architectural Heritage
See entry under ANTIQUE GARDEN FURNITURE & ORNAMENT.
Antique and reproduction fountains and wall fountains in stone, bronze, lead, cast iron and frost-resistant terracotta.

For a list of blacksmiths who could make up frames for training plants etc see SPECIALIST SUPPLIERS - Metalwork.

* denotes trade supplier. Please phone for retail outlets. 253

Aston Matthews
141-147a Essex Rd, London N1 2SN.
T:0171-226 3657. F:0171-354 5951.
Selection of garden taps in various finishes
and with or without hose attachments (from
£17 a pair).

Bel Mondo Garden Features
11 Tatnell Rd, London SE23 1JX.
T:0181-291 1920.
Cast iron wall and free-standing fountains
in traditional designs, plus stone backing
pieces if required and a good range of brass
taps and spouts.

Brookbrae
53 St.Leonard's Rd, London SW14 7NQ.
T:0181-876 9238. F:0181-878 9415.
A group of artists who design and make to
order fountains, roof decorations (pinnacles
& weather vanes), sculpture (low and high
relief work), special clocks.

The Bulbeck Foundry
See entry under NEW &
REPRODUCTION STATUARY &
ORNAMENT. Lead fountains.

Capital Garden Products
Gibbs Reed Barn, Pashley Rd,
Ticehurst, E.Sussex TN5 7HE.
T:01580-201092. F:01580-201093.
Wall fountains, rainwater tanks, tubs, urns,
planters in Verine faux-lead or Bronzage
(both made of fibreglass) or real lead .

Chilstone
See entry under
NEW & REPRODUCTION
STATUARY & ORNAMENT. Hand-made
reconstituted stone fountains and other
garden ornaments.

Drummond's of Bramley
See entry under
ANTIQUE GARDEN FURNITURE
& ORNAMENT. Antique hand-pumps.

*Erin-Gardena
Dunhams Lane, Letchworth,
Herts SG6 1BD.T:01462-475005.
F:01462-686789. Drip-feed or sprinkler
irrigation systems, hoses and accessories.

Fountains Direct
The Office, 41 Dartnell Park, West Byfleet,

Surrey KT14 6PR.
T:01932-336338. F:01932-353223.
Grand water features designed for parks
and public areas combining water and light.
Also garden pools, fountain pumps and
underwater lights.

Good Directions
Unit 15, Talisman Business Centre, Duncan
Rd, Park Gate, Southampton SO31 7GA.
T:01489-577828. F:01489-577858.
Pre-aged brass taps with animal figure
handles and lawn sprinklers in duck,frog
and snail designs.

Haddonstone
See entry under
NEW & REPRODUCTION STATUARY
& ORNAMENT. Range in reconstituted
stone includes a simple Roman pool
surround, a very ornate 'Raphael' surround,
a shell wall fountain, dolphin fountains and
wall masks.

Marston & Langinger
See entry under
WICKER/RATTAN/LLOYD LOOM
FURNITURE.
Cast iron lion's head water tap reproduced
from a 19th century design.

The Oak Barrel Company
Pipers Lane, Ansley Common,
Nr Nuneaton, Warwicks CV10 0RH.
T:01203-392700. F:01203-395992.
Cast iron pumps, Tasmanian oak barrels and
water features which combine them both.

*Pumps & Tubs
Unit H1, Holly Farm Business Park,
Honiley, Kenilworth, Warwicks CV8 1NP.
T:01926-484244. F:01926-484194.
Cast-iron pumps, water butts and barrels.

Seago
See entry under
ANTIQUE GARDEN STATUARY &
ORNAMENT. Antique stone fountains.

Thru the Looking Glass
Priory Lanes, Northgate,
Chichester, Sussex PO19 1AR.
T:01243-538133. Reinforced bronze and
fibreglass fountains with a verdigris finish.
No pump required. Mail order.

OUTDOOR PAVING & SURFACES

Blanc de Bierges
Eastray Rd, Whittlesey,
Peterborough, Cambridge PE7 2AG.
T:01733-202566. F:01733-205405.
Hand-crafted alternative to natural stone,
suitable for patios, conservatories and
swimming pool surrounds.

Civil Engineering Developments
728 London Rd, West Thurrock,
Grays, Essex RM20 3LU.
T:01708-867237. F:01708-867230.
Specialists in natural stones for restoration
work from over 800 quarries all over Britain.
Many are suitable for landscape gardening:
boulders, walling stone, rockery stone,
all sorts of flagstones, even ten types
of cobbles.

Tim Coppard
72 Bruce Rd, London E3 3HL.
T:0181-980 8773. Mosaic surfaces made
of beach stones and rolled-marble pebbles
to order. Anything from plain squares to very
intricate designs with lettering. From about
£250 per sq m.

Forest Fencing
See entry under
FENCING & WOODEN GATES.
Sell timber squares to lay down on the roof.
They are 20" square and have been
pressure-impregnated with preservative and
algaecide and are guaranteed for 15 years.

Greensward Co
The Old Hall, Langham,
Oakham, Leics LE15 7JE.
T:01572-722923. F:01572-724386.
'Lazylawn' artificial turf in 2m and 4m
widths. It lasts about 5 years, does not fade
and can be hosed down to keep it clean.

Slot Kerr-Wilson
Flat 3, 1-3 William St House,
William St, London SW1X 9HH.
T:0171-235 4093. F:0171-371 8174.
Pebble mosaic floors and walls to
commission (from about £75 a sq m).
She uses both marble and beach pebbles to
create symmetrical patterns, which are hard-
wearing and maintenance-free.

Lloyd Christie Garden Architecture
See entry under
CONSERVATORIES.
Western red cedar decking pallets or
bespoke decking designs - also
available stained in an attractive range
of colours.

London Decking Company
1 Dockhead Wharf,
4 Shad Thames, London SE1 2YT.
T:0171-378 1061. F:0171-357 9592.
Their treated softwood decking is
guaranteed for 30 years. Full
installation service.

Michelmersh Brick & Tile Company
Hillview Rd, Michelmersh, Hants SO51
ONN. T:01794-368506.
F:01794-368845. Hand-made and machine-
made clay pavers in all shades. Matching
facing bricks and specials to order.

Redwood Decking & Landscaping
Bridge Inn Nurseries,
Moss Side, Formby, Merseyside L37 0AF.
T:01704-832355. F:01704-832354.
Bespoke design, manufacture and
installation service for structures in timber
including decks, boardwalks, bridges,
pergolas and gazebos.

Silverlands Stone
Holloway Hill, Chertsey, Surrey KT16 0AE.
T:01932-569277. F:01932-563558.
Wide range of natural stone products:
paving, walling, rockery, boulders, pebbles.
Also man-made products and reclaimed
granite, setts and paving.

Christopher Winder Master Carpenters
Court Lodge Farm,
Hinxhill, Ashford, Kent TN25 5NR
T:01233-625204. :01233-621155.
Specialists in garden structures and
fittings, including decking, trelliswork,
gazebos, bridges, fencing, seating and
planters. Decks and boardwalks are
contructed in tanalised softwoods and
hardwoods and can incorporate steps
to accommodate changes in level.

*** denotes
trade supplier.
Please phone
for retail outlets.** 255

SWIMMING POOLS

GW Green Swimming Pools
Regency House, 88a Great Brick Kiln St,
Graisley, Wolverhampton WV3 0PU.
T:01902-27709. F:01902-22632.
Construction, equipment and service of
domestic and commercial pools plus
accessories, saunas, spas.

Rainbow Leisure
3 Albion Wharf,
Hester Rd, London SW11 4AN.
T:0171-720 7181. F:0171-622 9080.
Designers and installers of luxury pools -
from a back garden pool to the new
'Roman bath' they built in the basement
of a house in Mayfair.

Rutherford - The Pool People
The Swimshop, Rutherford Business Park,
Marley Lane, Battle, Sussex TN33 0RD.
T:01424-775060. F:01424-772249.
Suppliers for 70 years of all swimming pool
equipment, covers, water filtration and
chemicals, spas, saunas.

For more
information and a
copy of 'The
Swimming Pool
Guide' (£4.95)
contact The
Swimming Pool &
Allied Trades
Association on
T:01264-350565.

POTS/PLANTERS/ WINDOW BOXES

Les Amis du Jardin
87 Sussex Gardens, London W2 2RH.
T/F:0171-262 9141. Self-watering classical
wooden plant containers.

Barbary Pots
45 Fernshaw Rd, London SW10
0TN. T:0171-352 1053.
F:0171-351 5504.(Office only).
Hand-thrown pots from Morocco
including huge Ali Baba versions.
The larger ones come in made-
to-measure cane baskets to
protect them whilst in transit.

Black Lane Pots
Hempworth, Salisbury, Wilts SP5 2DS.
T/F:01794-390796.
Handmade traditional Long Toms, in 2",4"
and 6" sizes, with matching saucers and
trays. They are also made in white clay and
all sorts of other colours. Mail order.

See also
GARDENS -
One Stop .

256

The Bulbeck Foundry
See entry under
NEW & REPRODUCTION
STATUARY & ORNAMENT.
Quality lead garden ornaments reproduced
from antique designs. Custom-made plant
containers in any size and with heraldic
motifs, initials, dates etc.

*Capital Garden Products
See entry under FOUNTAINS/WATER
PUMPS/TAPS. Fibre-glass urns, container
and planters in faux lead or faux bronze
finishes - they are indistinguishable from the
real thing, light to lift, and rot/frost-proof.
The company also makes real lead and
mahogany planters. Stockists include The
Chelsea Gardener and Clifton Nurseries.

Andrew Crace Designs
See entry under WOODEN FURNITURE.
Versailles boxes ranging in size from 18" to
36" with GRP liners.

Jacqueline Edge
1 Courtnell St, London W2 5BU.
T:0171-229 1172. F:0171-727 4651.
Importer of colonial antiques and new
products from Burma, including ceramic
pots, planters and urns.

S&B Evans & Sons
7a Ezra St, London E2 7RH.
T:0171-729 6635. F:0171-613 3558.
Wide range of glazed and unglazed terracott
pots made in an on-site workshop in
Columbia Rd Market. Open only Fri 9-5 and
Sun 9-1.30. Seconds sale on first Sunday of
the month.

Frolics of Winchester
See entry under WOODEN TRELLIS &
OBELISKS. Wooden window boxes with
decorative cut-out facades.

Joss Graham Oriental Textiles
10 Eccleston St, London SW1W 9LT.
T/F:0171-730 4370. Very wide range of
Vietnamese stoneware pots in beautifully-
coloured glazes. They are frost-proof, and
priced from £20 to £195 (for a 30" size).

Patio
155 Battersea Park Rd, London SW8 4BU.
T:0171-622 8262. F:0171-978 1557.

Provencal jars in 11 sizes. Italian frost-proof terracotta pots.

Pots & Pithoi
The Barns, East Street, Turners Hill,
W.Sussex RH10 4QQ.
T:01342-714793. F:01342-717090.
Hand-made frost-resistant Cretan pots in 85
styles and 190 sizes. There are 12,000 pots
in stock. Plus recycled Cretan glassware and
painted china.

Red Mud
Unit C&D, Linton House,
39-51 Highgate Rd, London NW5 1RS.
T:0171-267 1689. F:0171-267 9142.
Large range of ceramic pots from small
bowls to huge amphorae. The selection
includes glazed pots from Anduze in the
Gard region of France where they have been
made for hundreds of years. They come in
five sizes and five colours.

Robus Ceramics
See entry under **GARDEN HOUSES/
GAZEBOS/PAVILIONS.** Large range of
English terracotta pots.

Valis
43 St.Andrews Rd,
Henley-on Thames, Oxon RG9 1HZ.
T/F:01491-578910. Unusual 'Gargoyle'
window boxes decorated with a mythical
Green Man, a Dragon or a Vampire.

Whichford Pottery
Whichford, Shipton-on-Stour,
Warwicks CV36 5PG.
T:01608-684416. F:01608-684833.
English terracotta hand-made and frost-proof
pots ranging in price from £3 to £1500.

ACCESSORIES/TOOLS

Alitags
Bourne Lane, Much Hadham,
Herts SG10 6ER. T:01279-842685.
F:01279-843646. Aluminium, copper and
teak plant labels in many sizes.

*Bulldog
Record Bulldog Tools, Parkway Works,
Sheffield, York S9 3BL.
T:01142-449066. F:01142-434302.

Mail order & retail:
Tabwell Tools, Rutland Sq, Bakewell, Derbys
DE45 1BZ. T:01629-814416. F:01629-
814993. Traditional quality tools.

Burgon & Ball
See entry under
IRON & WIRE PLANT SUPPORTS.
Established in 1730, this is Britain's only, as
well as the world's largest, sheep shear
manufacturer. It is also Britain's oldest
garden tool manufacturer, still producing
tools such as scythes and grass hooks,
manure forks and hay knives, billhooks and
rosewood handled pocket knives.

The Garden Gate
Sholebroke, Whittlebury,
Towcester, Northants NN12 8TF.
T:01327-857414. F:01327-857178.
Decorative garden ornaments including
rustic willow 'wigwams', wire frames,
reproduction Dutch pea sticks, baskets,
edging bricks, more unusual terracotta pots.

*Haemmerlin
The Washington Centre,
Halesouen Rd, Netherton,
W.Midlands DY2 9RE.
T:01384-243243. F:01384-243242.
Traditional galvanised wheelbarrows
in 50 different designs.

Hortus Ornamenti
23 Cleveland Rd, Chichester,
W.Sussex PO19 2HF.
T/F:01243-782467.
Traditional handmade garden tools,
accessories, plant frames and
obelisks in wood, stone and metal.
Mail order.

Touch Design
51 High St, Sixpenny,
Handley, Salisbury, Wilts SP5 5ND.
T:01725-552888. Lead and glass
handmade cloches and glass bell jars
by mail order.

Wells & Winter
Mere House Barn, Mereworth,
Maidstone, Kent ME18 5NB.
T:01622-813627. Garden labels in copper,
zinc, aluminium, coloured plastic and wood.

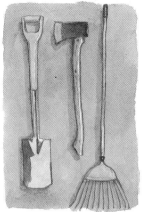

*** denotes
trade supplier.
Please phone
for retail outlets.** 257

Their mail order catalogue includes an apron with legs so one can kneel and a 'List of Plants that rabbits don't generally eat' (40p).

Yew Tree
Yew Tree Cottage,
Whipsnade, Beds LU6 2LG.
T:01582-872514. F:01582-873816.
By appt. and at antique fairs. 18th and 19th century farming and agricultural tools.

SPECIALIST NURSERIES

Jacques Amand
The Nurseries, Clamp Hill,
Stanmore, Middx HA7 3JS.
T:0181-954 8138. F:0181-954 6784.
Unusual bulbs.

Architectural Plants
Cooks Farm, Nuthurst,
Horsham, W.Sussex RH13 6LH.
T:01403-891772. F:01403-891056.
Exotic and hardy architectural plants.
There are 35,000 varieties on the premises.

David Austin Roses
Bowling Green Lane, Albrighton,
Wolverhampton WV7 3HB.
T:01902-373931. F:01902-372142.
English roses.

Peter Beales Roses
London Rd, Attleborough, Norfolk NR17 1AY.
T:01953-454707. F:01953-456845.
Old-fashioned roses.

Citrus Centre
Mare Hill Nursery, West Mare Lane, Mare Hill, Pulborough, W.Sussex RH20 2EA.
T/F:01798-872786.
Over 90 varieties of citrus plants. Mail order.

Countryside Wildflowers
Chatteris Rd, Somersham,
Cambridge PE17 3DN.
T:01487-841322. F:01487-740206.
Lady's mantle, goatsbeard, cranesbill, loosestrife, cowslips and all those other wild flowers from your grandma's garden.

Fisk's Clematis Nursery
Westleton, Nr Saxmundham, Suffolk IP17 3AJ. T:01728-648263.
Up to 200 varieties of clematis.

Catalogues are available from most of the nurseries listed. Some are only open on certain days or by appointment. Please phone them for details. Most also do mail order.

Hardy's Cottage Garden Plants
The Field, Priory Lane, Freefolk Priors, Whitchurch, Hants RG28 7NL.
T:01256-896533. F:01256-896572.
Specialists in old-fashioned perennials and lavatera.

Herons Bonsai
See entry under
NEW & REPRODUCTION STATUARY & ORNAMENT. Japanese garden specialists. Bonsai and beautifully shaped maples and pines plus accessories like bamboo, screens and lanterns.

*Hillier Nurseries
Ampfield House, Ampfield, Romsey,
Hampshire SO51 9PA.
T:01794-368733. F:01794-368813.
Call for their 90 nationwide stockists of over 2000 plants, including many suitable for conservatories.

Landford Trees
Landford Lodge, Nr Salisbury,
Wilts SP5 2EH.
T:01794-390808. F:01794-390037.
Deciduous and ornamental trees in girths up to 16-18cm.

Langley Boxwood Nursery
Rake, Nr Liss, Hants GU33 7JL.
T:01730-894467. F:01730-894703.
Open by appointment. Wide range of topiary and box hedging.

Reads Nursery
Hales Hill, Loddon, Norfolk NR14 6QW.
T:01508-548395. F:01508-548040.
Widest range of vines in the country, plus figs and conservatory plants.

The Romantic Garden Nursery
The Street, Swannington, Norwich NR9 5NW
T:01603-261488. F:01603-871668.
Specialise in clipped topiary evergreens - box, bay, laurel, holly and privet are trained into balls and all kinds of creatures.

Tendercare Nurseries
Southlands Rd, Denham,
Uxbridge, Middx UB9 4HD.
T:01895-835544. F:01895-835036.
By appointment. Specialists in mature and formal garden plants and trees.

MISCELLANEOUS

*American Appliance Centre
Larkshall Business Park, 52 Larkshall Rd,
Chingford, London E4 6PD.
T:0181-529 9665. F:0181-505 8700.
Suppliers of the hat-shaped 'Phoenix Patio
Heater'. It is free-standing, requires no
electricity and provides up to 20ft circle
of heat.

Architectura in Horto
68 Stanford Ave, Brighton,
E.Sussex BN1 6FD.
T:01273-558654. F:01273-388931.
Dovecotes inspired by 18th century follies -
Palladian, Gothic and Chinoiserie. Traditional
wooden wheelbarrows.

Brookbrae
See entry under **FOUNTAINS/WATER
PUMPS/TAPS.** Made to order sundials,
weathervanes, plaques, armillary spheres
(including one at the Royal Botanic Gardens,
Kew), special clocks, wall reliefs and roof
decorations (they recently completed a
gold leaf pinnacle for the Standard Life
building in Edinburgh).

Chalwyn
Chalwyn Ind.Estate,
Poole, Dorset BH12 4PF.
T:01202-715400. F:01202-715600.
Traditional paraffin hurricane lanterns
with a burning time of 20 hours.

Dorset Weathervanes
284 Bournemouth Rd, Charlton Marshall,
Blandford Forum, Dorset DT11 9NG.
T/F:01258-453374. Forty standard designs
plus special commissions.

Belinda Eade
Great Western Studios, Lost Goods Building,
Great Western Rd, London W9 3NY.
T/F:0171-229 5911. Makes grottoes and
produces shellwork and carvings for indoors
and out (including fountains). Has worked on
the restoration of grottoes at Hampton Court
and Leeds Castle.

Eaton's Shell Shop
30 Neal St, London WC2H 9UE.
T/F:0171-379 6254.

Shells of all types for sale and by mail order
(no catalogue). Plus bamboo poles,
raffia, caning materials.

Forsham Cottage Arks
Goreside Farm, Great Chart,
Ashford, Kent TN26 1JU.
T:01233-820229. F:01233-820157.
Wooden dovecotes, duckcotes, poultry
houses and kennels.

Glowcroft
Unit K2, Innsworth Technology Park,
Innsworth Lane, Gloucs GL3 1DL.
T:01452-731300. F:01452-731301.
Suppliers of 'Swellgel' water-releasing
granules to mix with compost to improve
water-retention.

Good Directions
See entry under
FOUNTAINS/WATER PUMPS/TAPS.
'Aged' copper weathervanes. Sundials.

Blot Kerr-Wilson
See entry under
OUTDOOR PAVING & SURFACES.
Makes shell houses to commission.

Richard La Trobe-Bateman
Elm House, Batcombe,
Shepton Mallett, Somerset BA4 6AB.
T/F:01749-850442. Elegant oak and
stainless steel bridges to order. Designer of
garden structures and furniture; recent
commissions include a look-out above
Tintern Abbey.

New England Gardens
22 Middle St, Ashcott, Somerset TA7 9QB.
T/F:01458-210821. Selection of bird
houses and feeders based on traditional
New England designs.

Whitchester Wood Design
P&A Group, Mold Ind.Estate, Wrexham Rd,
Mold, Clwyd CH7 4HE.
T:01352-752555. F:01352-755200.
Self-assembly flat-pack bridge, suitable for a
5ft to 12ft crossing.

**The Society of Garden
Designers can give
you advice on
comissioning a
professional designer
and suggest one
of their 65 members
nationwide.
They are at:
6 Borough Rd,
Kingston upon Thames,
Surrey KT2 6BD.
T/F:0181-974 9483.**

*** denotes
trade supplier.
Please phone
for retail outlets.** 259

ochre, Burnt um
um, scarlet.

WOODWORK

COURSES & INFORMATION

HISTORY OF ART COURSES

Christie's Education

63 Old Brompton Rd, London SW7 3JS.
T:0171-581 3933. Christie's has been
running its Fine Arts Course since 1978.
There are two full-time (1 year) Diploma
courses in Fine & Decorative Arts from
Antiquity to the Renaissance or from the
Renaissance to the present day. Fees are
£6200 + VAT. There is also a part-time
'London Art Course' which covers similar
ground, and 'Modern Art Studies' on
contemporary art from 1850 to today.

Sotheby's Institute

30 Oxford St, London W1N 9FL.
T:0171-323 5775.
Undergraduate and postgraduate courses in
fine and decorative arts. Two year Diploma
'Works of Art' Course. There are separate
15-week courses including 'Styles in Art',
'17th & 18th century Fine and Decorative
Arts', '19th & 20th century Fine
and Decorative Arts'.

The Study Centre for the History of the Fine & Decorative Arts

21 Palace Gardens Terrace, London W8 4SA.
T:0171-229 3393. F:0171-229 4220.
The longest established private art history
course in London. Ten week course on the
decorative arts from the 16th to the 20th
century. Short courses include 'The English
Country House', 'English Interiors and
Furniture', 'French Interiors & Furniture',
'European Ceramics'. They also run
evening courses.

INTERIOR DESIGN COURSES

Chelsea College of Art & Design

Manresa Rd, London SW3 6LS.
T:0171-514 7889. F:0171-514 7884.
One year, full time 'College Certificate in
Interior Design and Decoration'. Intensive
course covering all aspects of design
including art and architectural history, model
making, building construction, technical

drawing, lighting, rendering, paint effects and an introduction to computer aided design. Also 3 year full-time BA (Hons) Interior Design.

Glasgow School of Art
167 Renfrew St, Glasgow, Scotland G3 6RQ. T:0141-353 4500. F:0141-353 4528. Four year BA (Hons) in Interior Design.

Inchbald School of Design
7 Eaton Gate, London SW1W 9BA. T:0171-730 5508. F:0171-730 4937 And at: 32 Eccleston Square, London SW1V 1PB. T:0171-630 9011/2/3. F:0171-976 5979. One year diploma course in interior design; two year higher diploma courses combining interior design with either garden design or design history; three year master diploma course in 'Design History', 'Interior Design' and 'Garden Design'. Also a variety of ten week courses in the history of interior decoration, furniture or design and decoration. Short courses on everything from 'Computer Aided Design' to 'Business Management for Interior Designers'.

KLC School of Interior Design
Springvale Terrace, London W14 0AE. T:0171-602 8592. F:0171-602 1964. One year (30 week) diploma course, centering around projects to design a variety of interior spaces. Also a ten week certificate course. There's a 'Home Study' diploma or certificate program which students can complete in their own time. Plus many short courses including on 'Computer Aided Design'.

Kingston University
Knights Park, Kingston-upon-Thames, KT1 2QJ. T:0181-547 2000 ext 4165. F:0181-547 7365. Three year BA (Hons) interior design course concentrating on architectural design.

London College of Printing & Distributive Trades
Elephant and Castle, London SE1 6SB. T:0171-514 6500. F:0171-514 6535. One year full time 'College Certificate in Interior Design and Ornamental Textiles'.

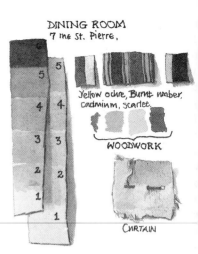

DINING ROOM
7 rue St. Pierre,

Yellow ochre, Burnt umber, cadmium, scarlet.

WOODWORK

CURTAIN

Rhodec International
35 East St, Brighton BN1 1HL. T:01273-327476. F:01273-821668. Two to three year correspondence diploma course or a one year associate diploma course leading to a certificate in interior design.

Royal College of Art
Kensington Gore, London SW7 2EU. T:0171-584 5020. F:0171-584 8217. Two year course in 'Architecture and Interior Design'. Also furniture courses.

Westminster Adult Education Service
See entry under OTHER COURSES. 10 week beginners or intermediate courses in interior decoration and design.

PAINT FINISHES & STENCILLING COURSES

Belinda Ballantine
The Old Dairy, Pinkney Park, Malmesbury, Wilts SN1B 0NX. T:01666-841144. F:01666-841155. One, two, three and five day courses on furniture painting, gilding and découpage. Prices start at £65 per day.

Angela Beaumont
12-14 Hainworth Village, Nr Keighley, W.Yorks BD21 5QH. T:01535-604381. One or two day courses in stencilling (and advanced stencilling), paint effects, metallic finishes, special effects for period homes

nd workshops where students can dictate
hatever they want to learn about paint
nishes. Small groups (between 2-6).
vernight accommodation provided. Annual
ourse on 'Stencilling for Christmas'.

riend or Faux
8 Earsham St, Bungay, Suffolk NR35 1AG.
:01986-896170. F:01502-714246.
ne day or weekend residential courses on
asic paint effects, from how to hold a brush
simple finishes. Also master classes on
ore sophisticated techniques like faux-
ood graining, marbling, lapis, malachite
nd gilding.

ampstead Decorative Arts
/20 Highgate High St, London N6 5JG.
:0181-348 2811. School of decorative
ainting - all finishes including gilding,
raining, stippling and antique finishes.
ve part-time courses leading to a
ertificate in Decorative Painting'.

troductory course in trompe l'oeil
ecoration. Full time courses also available.

ampstead School of Art
ing's College Campus,
9-21 Kidderpore Avenue, London NW3 7ST.
:0171-431 1292. F:0171-794 1439.
termediate and advanced courses on
ainted furniture.

LC School of Interior Design
ee entry under **INTERIOR DESIGN
OURSES**. Short courses offered on
Decorative Paint Finishes'.

**Roger Newton School of Decorative
inishes**
tudio 52,
Varriner House, The Business Centre,
40 Battersea Park Rd, London SW11 4NB.
:0171-498 1798. F:0171-207 2992.
ive day courses on furniture painting, gilding
nd lacquering are held every month (except
ug and Dec). There are also three month
pprenticeship courses.

Paint Magic
79 Shepperton Rd, London N1 3DF.
T:0171-354 9696. F:0171-226 7760.
Jocasta Innes runs five day courses on
'Becoming a Decorator' and one or two day
courses at all the branches of her shop on
basic paint effects, furniture painting and a
variety of finishes (gilding, découpage,
trompe l'oeil, Scandinavian look).

Angela Shaw
Flexford House, Hogs Back,
Guildford, Surrey GU3 2JP.
T/F:01483-810223.
One day courses with a maximum of seven
students in a group. Stencilling, paint
finishes, découpage, and gilding. Cost £50-
£55, depending on materials needed.

GARDEN DESIGN COURSES

College of Garden Design
(Administrative Office), Cothelstone,
Taunton, Somerset TA4 3DP.
T:01823-433215. F:01823-433811.
This college (established for 10 years) offers
a 'Diploma in Garden Design' course (over
16 months - one day per week). Courses are
held at Pershore College, Pershore, Worcs.

The English Gardening School
At the Chelsea Physic Garden,
66 Royal Hospital Rd, London SW3 4HS.
T:0171-352 4347. F:0171-376 3936.
Professional part-time one year diploma
courses in garden design, practical
horticulture or plants and plantsmanship as
well as correspondence courses and a
variety of short courses and workshops.

The Gardeners' Academy
PO Box 262, Guilsborough,
Northants NN6 8RS.
T/F:01234-826077. Numerous single day
courses, mostly aimed at the interested
amateur. Also 15 week (1 day a week)
courses on anything from how to survey a
garden to pruning or preparing plans.

The Inchbald School of Design
See entry under **INTERIOR DESIGN
COURSES**. Various short courses like

'Business Support for Garden Designers' (a five day course concentrating on computer skills and business management) and 'Inspirational Gardens' (a five day course on contemporary approaches to garden design). Also one year diploma courses in garden design; two year higher diploma courses in garden design and a related subject plus other short courses.

KLC School of Interior Design

See entry under **INTERIOR DESIGN COURSES.** Short 'Garden Summer School', to include garden design, planting, conservatories, furniture, urns and finishing touches.

Plumpton College

Ditchling Rd, Plumpton,
Nr Lewes, E. Sussex BN7 3AE.
T:1273-890454. F:01273-890071.
One year certificate course in 'Garden Design' plus ten week courses in 'Garden Design' and 'Garden Design & Construction'.

Royal Botanic Gardens (Adult Education Section)

Kew, Richmond, Surrey TW9 3AB.
T:0181-332 5623/6. F:0181-332 5610.
Three year diploma course in horticulture; 'Kew International Diplomas' in specialist subjects lasting up to two months; short courses and one day courses in: hellibores, bulbs, pruning and propagating, painting flowers, basketry, botanical illustration, plant photography.

OTHER COURSES

Anne Adams

Stanton Soft Furnishings, Barn Close, 12 Lambridge, Bath BA1 6BJ.
T:01225-336698. Courses in basic or advanced curtain, blind, headboard, pelmet, swag & tail, cushion, and kelim stool making. Maximum of 4 students for a one day class.

For a comprehensive listing of part-time and evening classes in the Greater London area, there are two useful publications available from newsagents and bookshops: Floodlight, £3.50 and On Course, £2.95.

City & Guilds of London Art School

124 Kennington Park Rd, London SE11 4D.
T:0171-735 2306. F:0171-582 5361.
Courses in ornamental wood carving & gilding and architectural stone carving.

The City Lit

16 Stukeley St, off Drury Lane,
London WC2B 5LJ.
T:0171-242 9872. F:0171-405 3347.
Large range of courses, including gilding, bookbinding, mosaics, picture framing, stained glass, basketry and history of art.

KLC School of Interior Design

See entry under **INTERIOR DESIGN COURSES.** Short courses on 'Window Treatments' and 'Curtain Making'.

London College of Fashion

20 John Princes St, London W1M 0BJ.
T:0171-514 7400. F:0171-514 7530. Sho
'Introduction to Textiles for Interiors' and 'Interior Furnishing Workshops'.

London College of Printing & Distributive Trades

See entry under
INTERIOR DESIGN COURSES.
Bookbinding courses, at various levels.

Guy Mallinson Furniture

7 The Coachworks, 80 Parson's Green Lane
London SW6 4HU.
T:0171-371 9190. F:0171-371 5099.
Ten week cabinet making course held six times a year on Tuesday evenings. The cost is £325 plus VAT.

Richmond Adult and Community College

Clifden Centre, Clifden Rd,
Twickenham TW1 4LT.
T:0181-891 5907.
F:0181-892 6354. Courses in furniture restoration, French polishing, indigo dying, soft furnishings and much more.

West Dean College

West Dean, Chichester,
W. Sussex PO18 0QZ.
T:01243-811301. F:01243-811343.
One, two or three year courses in Antique Furniture Restoration; Porcelain & Ceramic

Conservation; Bookbinding and the Care of Books; Antique Clock Restoration; Metal Restoration; Tapestry Weaving.

Westminster Adult Education Service
Amberley Road Centre,
Amberley Rd, London W9 2JJ.
T:0171-289 2183. F:0171-286 1838.
10 week courses in interior decoration, furniture restoration, gilding and framing, and flower arranging, plus short courses on découpage, marbling etc.

UK DESIGN & GARDEN EXHIBITIONS 1997/1998

4-9 March '97
Country Living Show
Business Design Centre, Islington, London N1. Organisers: Business Design Centre.
T:0171-359 3535. F:0171-288 6446.

13 March - 6 April '97
Ideal Home Exhibition,
Earl's Court Exhibition Centre, London SW5.
Organisers: DMG Exhibition Group.
T:01895-677677. F:01895-676027.

16-19 March '97
Interior Design Week includes:
Living Design London
Battersea Park.
Organisers: Art & Design Promotions.
T:0171-833 3373. F:0171-833 3379.

Chelsea Design Week.
Some 15 showrooms in Chelsea will be showing their new fabrics, wallpapers, lights, floorcoverings and furniture.
Contact: Pelicans PR
T:0171-937 3585. F:0171-937 7373.

Chelsea Harbour Spring Week
Chelsea Harbour Design Centre, London SW10. Some 50 showrooms will exhibit the latest fabrics, wallpapers, floorcoverings, furniture and accessories. There will also be lectures and demonstrations. The 16th,17th and 18th are trade days, the 19th is public day. Contact: Alison Shields
T:0171-351 4433. F:0171-352 7868.

17-20 March '97
Spectrum '97

Royal College of Art, London W8
(Contemporary contract products showcase).
Organisers: The Design Exhibition Club.
T:01727-854304. F:01727-846873.

20-23 March '97
The Individual Homes, Home Building & Renovating Show,
NEC, Birmingham.
Organisers: Centaur Communications.
T:0171-287 5000. F:0171-287 0710.

11-13 May '97
Top Drawer,
Earl's Court Two, London
Organisers: P&O Events.
T:0171-244 6433. F:0171-370 8142.

20-23 May '97
Chelsea Flower Show
Royal Hospital, Chelsea, London SW3
Organisers: Royal Horticultural Society.
For information T:0171-344 4444.
For tickets T:0171-344 4343.

20-22 May '97
Hilight and Lightex
(Commercial Lighting Show)
NEC, Birmingham. Organisers:
Institution of Lighting Engineers.
T:01788-576492. F:01788-540145.

10-13 and 17-20 June '97
New Designers
Business Design Centre, Islington, London N1. Organisers: Business Design Centre.
T:0171-359 3535. F:0171-288 6446.

26-29 June '97
The Daily Telegraph / House & Garden Fair
Olympia, London W14.
Organisers: National Events.
T:0171-571 6603. F:0171-571 6601.

8-13 July '97
Hampton Court Palace Flower Show
Hampton Court Palace, East Molesey, Surrey. Organisers:
Royal Horticultural Society. For information T:0171-649 1885. F:0171-344 4444.

14-18 July '97
Harrogate Gift Fair
Harrogate, Yorkshire.
Organisers: P&O Events.
T:0171-244 6433. F:0171-370 8142.

Also this year:
4-22 June '97
The British Interior Design Exhibition 1997,
1 Cambridge Gate, Regent's Park, London NW1.
A magnificent forty room Victorian house will be the showcase for the work of thirty leading designers.
For tickets and information
T:0171-731-6327.
F:0171-736-3573

17-20 August '97
BFM Summer Furniture Show
NEC, Birmingham. Organisers: BFM.
T:0171-724 0851. F:0171-706 1924.

31 August-2 September'97
Top Drawer
Earl's Court Two, London
Organisers: P&O Events.
T:0171-244 6433. F:0171-370 8142.

27 September -1 October '97
Decorex International
Syon Park, Isleworth, Middx. Organisers:
Decorex International. T:0171-833 3373.
F:0171-833 3379.

28 September - 1 October '97
100% Design
Duke of York's Headquarters, Chelsea,
London SW3. Organisers: 100% Design.
T:0181-849 6211. F:0181-849 6214.

28 September - 1 October '97
Home Interiors
Olympia, London.
Organisers: P&O Events.
T:0171-370 8216/8210.F:0171-370 8235.

14-19 & 21-26 October '97
Chelsea Crafts Fair
Chelsea Old Town Hall, King's Rd, London
SW3. Organisers: Crafts Council.
T:0171-278 7700. F:0171-837 6891.

7-10 November '97
The Country Living Christmas Fair
Business Design Centre, Islington, London
N1. Organisers: Business Design Centre.
T:0171-359 3535. F:0171-288 6446.

23-28 November '97
Interbuild / Restorex
NEC, Birmingham.
Organisers: Montgomery Exhibitions.
T:0171-486 1951. F:0171-487 3260.

January '98
Art '98 - The London Contemporary Art Fair
Business Design Centre, Islington, London
N1. Organisers: Business Design Centre.
T:0171-359 3535. F:0171-288 6446.

18-21 January '98
The Furniture Show / Decorative Interiors /
KBB97 (Kitchens, Bedrooms, Bathrooms),
NEC, Birmingham.

Organisers:
Blenheim Exhibitions & Conferences.
T:0181-742 2828. F:0181-742 3608.

1-5 Feb '98
International Spring Fair
NEC, Birmingham
Organisers: Trade Promotion Services.
T:0181-855 9201. F:0181-316 5719.

MAJOR ANTIQUES FAIRS
1997/1998

25 February- 2 March '97
The Fine Art & Antiques Fair
Olympia, London W14. Organisers:
P&O Events. T:0171-370 8211/8234.

12-18 March '97
British Antique Dealers' Association Fair
Duke of York's Headquarters, King's Rd,
London SW3. Organisers: BADA.
T:0171-589 4128. F:0171-581 9083.

18-23 March '97
The Decorative Antiques & Textiles Fair
Riverside Terrace, Battersea, London SW11.
Organisers: Harvey Management Services.
T:0171-624 5173. F:0171-625 8326.

3-6 April'97
NEC Easter Antiques Fair
NEC, Birmingham.
Organisers: Centre Exhibitions.
T:0121-780 4141. F:0121- 767 3540.

5-15 June '97
The Fine Art & Antiques Fair
Olympia, London W14. Organisers:
P & O Events. T:0171-370 8211/8234.

12-21 June '97
Grosvenor House Art & Antiques Fair
Park Lane, London W1.
Organiser: Alison Vassière .
T:0171-495 8743. F:0171-495 8747.

13-16 June '97
International Ceramics Fair & Seminar,
Park Lane Hotel, London W1.
T:0171-734 5491.

7-10 August '97
NEC Summer Antiques Fair
NEC, Birmingham.
Organisers: Centre Exhibitions.

14-17 August '97
West London Antiques & Fine Art Fair
Kensington Town Hall, London W8.
Organisers: Penman Fairs.
T:01444-482514. F:01444-483412.

24-28 September '97
The 20th Century British Art Fair
Royal College of Art, London SW7.
Organiser: Gay Hutson. T:0181-742 1611.

23-28 September '97
The Decorative Antiques & Textiles Fair
Riverside Terrace, Battersea Park,
London SW11.
Organisers: Harvey Management Services.
T:0171- 624 5173. F:0171-625 8326.

14-19 October '97
LAPADA Antiques Fair
Royal College of Art, London SW7.
Organisers: LAPADA.
T:0171-823 3511. F:0171-823 3522.

30 October-2 November '97
Kensington Antiques & Fine Art Fair,
Kensington Town Hall, London W8.
Organiser: Penman Fairs.
T:01444-482514. F:01444-483412.

18-23 November '97
The Fine Art & Antiques Fair
Olympia, London W14. Organisers:
P&O Events. T:0171-370 8211/8234.

11-14 December '97
NEC Christmas Antiques Fair
NEC, Birmingham.
Organisers: Centre Exhibitions.
T:0121-780 4141. F: 0121-767 3540.

14-18 January '98
The LAPADA Antiques & Fine Art Fair,
NEC, Birmingham.
T:0121-780 4141. F:0121-767 3540.

21-25 January '98
The Decorative Antiques & Textiles Fair
Riverside Terrace, Battersea Park,
London SW11.
Organisers: Harvey Management Services.
T:0171-624 5173. F:0171-625 8326.

Jan/Feb
World of Drawings & Watercolours Fair
Dorchester Hotel, London W1.
Contact: Ivan Winstone. T:0171-411 3166.

ORGANISATIONS & SOURCES OF INFORMATION

The Architectural Salvage Index
c/o Hutton & Rostron, Netley House,
Gomshall, Guildford, Surrey GU5 9QA.
T:01483-203221. F:01483-202911.
Can help you find a buyer for any materials
you wish to sell.

**Association of British
Picture Restorers (ABPR)**
Station Avenue, Kew, Surrey TW9 3QA.
T/F:0181-948 5644. There are some 360
members: mainly oil painting restorers,
but some wall painting restorers as well.
For restoration projects they recommend
one of their 80 fellows (members for at
least seven years whose work has been
carefully assessed).

**Association of Master Upholsterers
& Soft Furnishers**
Frances Vaughan House, 102 Commercial
St, Newport, Gwent NP9 1LU.
T:01633-215454. F:01633-244488.

The Bath Restoration Council
c/o The Bath Doctor, Prospect House,
Canterbury Rd, Challock, Ashford, Kent
TN25 4BB. T/F:01233-740532.
Provides a fact sheet and has nine
members nationwide.

Bathroom Showroom Association
Federation House, Station Rd,

Stoke-on-Trent ST4 2RT.
T:01782-844006. F:01782-844614.
Can help with any queries related to
bathroom design or products. Free
'Essential Bathroom Guide' leaflet.

The Brick Development Association
Woodside House, Winkfield,
Windsor, Berks SL4 2DX.
T:01344-885651. F:01344-890129.
Technical advice given on the application
and specification of brick and brickwork
and the mortars that go with them. Technical
advisory line on: 0891-6152290.

BFM
30 Harcourt St, London W1H 2AA.
T:0171-724 0851. F:0171-706 1924.
The association for British furniture
manufacturers.

British Antique Dealers' Association
20 Rutland Gate, London SW7 1BD.
T:0171-589 4128. F:0171-581 9083.
Founded in 1918. Their list of 400 members
is free of charge. Also advice on buying
antiques and general information leaflets.
They can certify antiques for shipment
abroad. Friends of the BADA Trust gain free
entry to fairs, galleries and master classes.
Membership costs £20.

British Antique Furniture Restorers' Association (BAFRA)
The Old Rectory, Warmwell,
Dorchester, Dorset DT2 8HQ.
T:01305-854822. F:01305-852104.
Over 100 members who specialise mainly
in English furniture, but there are also
experts on marble, carving & gilding,
lacquerwork, tortoiseshell, ivory and
traditional upholstery. Their ' Directory of
BAFRA Members & Guide to Antique
Furniture Restoration' costs £6.25 inc p&p.

British Artist Blacksmiths' Association
c/o Chris Topp, Carlton Husthwaite,
Thirsk, N.Yorks YO7 2BJ.
T/F:01845501415. Will send out a list of
members in your area and information on
how to commission work.

The British Bathroom Council
Federation House, Station Rd,

Stoke-on-Trent, Staffs ST4 2RT.
T:01782-747074. F:01782-747161.
Trade association for the major UK
manufacturers of bathroom products.

British Blind and Shutter Association
42 Heath St, Tamworth, Staffs B79 7JH.
T:01827-52337. F:01827-310827.
There are 250 blind and shutter
manufacturers on their books nationwide.

British Carpet Manufacturers' Association
5 Portland Place, London W1N 3AA.
T:0171-580 7155. F:0171-580 4854.

British Decorators' Association
32 Coton Rd, Nuneaton,
Warwicks CV11 5TW.
T:01203-353776. F:01203-354513.
There are 1800 firms nationwide who
abide by a code of practice.

British Horological Institute
Upton Hall, Upton, Newark, Notts NG23 5TE.
T:01636-813795. Has a list of 3500
restorers of clocks, watches, barometers,
chronographs, musical boxes and sundials.
Their museum is open Easter to September.

The British Oriental Rug Dealers' Association (BORDA)
c/o Oriental Rugs Gallery,
115-116 High St, Eton, Berks SL4 6AN.
T:01753-623000. Advice on oriental rug
dealers across the country, and on cleaning,
repairs and valuations.

The British Security Industry Association
Federation House, Station Rd,
Stoke-on-Trent, Staffs ST4 2RT.
T:01905-21464. F:01905-613625.
300 specialist members, covering anything
from safes to manguarding.

The Building Centre
26 Store St, London WC1E 7BT.
T:0171-637 1022. F:0171-580 9641.
Good bookshop covering all aspects of
building work. Standing exhibition of nearly
200 manufacturers. There's a library of
product literature covering 3000 products
and a reference library covering an additional
100,000. Free access to the public.
Brochures available.
Helpline on: 0897-161136.

The Conservation Unit
16 Queen Anne's Gate, London SW1H 9AA.
T:0171-233 4200. Has a database of
restorers and specialist conservators.
Charges £5 per five local names.

The Contract Flooring Association
4C St Mary's Place, The Lace Market,
Nottingham NG1 1PH.
T:0115-9411126. F:0115-9412238.

**Council for Registered Gas Installers
(CORGI)**
1 Elmwood, Chineham Business Park,
Crockford Lane, Basingstoke, Hants RG24
8WG. T:01256-372200. F:01256-372310.
Can recommend a registered gas installer
in your area.

The Crafts Council
44a Pentonville Rd, London N1 9BY.
T:0171-278 7700. You can use their
Photostore computer information service to
see over 30,000 pieces by the craftspeople
on the Council's 'Index of Selected Makers'.
The service is free. Also information on fairs
and courses.

Disabled Living Foundation
380-384 Harrow Rd, London W9 2HU.
T:0171-289 6111. F:0171-266 2922.
This charity has a showroom with room
settings displaying appliances and
equipment for the disabled.
Free 'With A Little Help' brochure.

English Heritage
23 Savile Row, London W1X 1AB.
T:0171-973 3000. F:0171-973 3001.
English Heritage can offer information
about the 400 historic properties including
landmarks, romantic ruins, castles and
abbeys they care for. They can also answer
questions about obtaining grants or caring
for listed buildings and can recommend
experts to help. Membership scheme.

Federation of Master Builders
14-15 Great James St, London WC1N 3DP.
T:0171-242 7583. F:0171-404 0296.
Can suggest members from the 'National
Register of Warrantied Builders': contractors
who can give an insurance-backed guarantee
for their work.

The Georgian Group
6 Fitzroy Square, London W1P 6DX.
T:0171-387 1720. F:0171-387 1721.
Offer a series of 15 leaflets (£2.75 each)
on windows, brickwork, doors and other
subjects relevant to the restoration of period
properties. They also hold lectures and
symposiums and organize daily and
weekend visits for members.

The Glass and Glazing Federation
44-48 Borough High St, London SE1 1XB.
T:0171-403 7177. F:0171-357 7458.
Gives advice on glass, choosing windows
or conservatories, and can send a list of
members in your area.

**Guild of Antique Dealers
and Restorers (GADR)**
23 Belle Vue Rd,
Shrewsbury, Shropshire SY3 7LN.
T:01743-271852. Has between 300-400
members nationwide. They are mainly
restorers, covering everything from china
restoration to re-silvering.

**Interior Decorators & Designers
Association (IDDA)**
1/4 Chelsea Harbour Design Centre,
Lots Rd, London SW10 0XE.
T:0171-349 0800. F:0171-349 0500.
The IDDA has some 450 members so they
can put you in touch with the right specialist
for the job.

The Kitchen Specialists Association
Riverbank House, Putney Bridge Approach,
London SW6 3JD. Consumer helpline on
01905-726066. Can help you locate
specific kitchen manufacturers.

The Landmark Trust
Shottesbrooke, Maidenhead,
Berks SL6 3SW.
T:01628-825920. F:01628-825417.
Charity that rescues remarkable historical
buildings and lets them afterwards. There
are 160 properties, including follies, forts,
manor houses, a number of towers, a railway
station, even an arsenic mine. Plus four
buildings in Italy and one in Vermont. Their
handbook is £8.50.
Booking office: 01628-825925.

LAPADA (London and Provincial Antique Dealers' Association)
535 King's Rd, London SW10 0SZ.
T:0171-823 3511. F:0171-823 3522.
Their free membership directory lists 700 members who are governed by a code of practice. Export service includes providing a 'Certificate of Age'.

The Lighting Association
Stafford Park 7, Telford, Shropshire TF3 3BQ.
T:01952-290905. F:01952-290906.
Decorative lighting suppliers - some 300 members nationwide.

The Lighting Industry Federation
207 Balham High Rd, London SW17 7BQ.
T:0181-675 5432. F:0181-673 5880.
Trade association for commercial and industrial lighting manufacturers, with about 92 members.

National Association of Chimney Sweeps & Chimney Lining Engineers
St Mary's Chambers, 19 Station Rd, Stone, Staffs ST15 8JP.
T:0800-833464. F:01785-811732.
Will give information about chimney sweeps in your area.

The National Association of Plumbing, Heating & Mechanical Services Contractors
14-15 Ensign Business Centre, Westwood Way Business Park, Coventry.
T:01203-470626. F:01203-470942.

National Federation of Plastering Contractors
18 Mansfield St, London W1M 9FG.
T:0171-580 5588. Contact them for a list of ornamental plasterers.

National Federation of Terrazzo, Marble and Mosaic Specialists
PO Box 50, Banstead, Surrey SM7 2RD.
T:01737-360673.

National Institute of Carpet and Floor Layers
4d St.Mary's Place, The Lace Market, Nottingham NG1 1PH.
T:0115-958 3077. F:0115-941 2238.
Will send a list of carpet fitters in your area.

They have 400 members nationwide, and guarantee the work of their 'master fitters'.

The National Trust
36 Queen Anne's Gate, London SW1H 9AS.
T:0171-222 9251.
Provides general information on and opening times of their properties.
They also have holiday cottages to let.
Membership scheme.

The National Trust for Scotland
5 Charlotte Square, Edinburgh EH2 4DU.
T:0131-226 5922. F:0131-243 9501.
Information on the opening hours of the over 100 properties open to the public which are managed by the Trust.

Royal Incorporation of Architects in Scotland
15 Rutland Square, Edinburgh EH1 2BE.
T:0131-229 7545. F:0131-228 2188.
Clients advisory service. For smaller projects (under £100,00) the local chapter president will compile a short list of suitable architects. For major projects the president of the the society selects qualified members.

Royal Institute of British Architects
66 Portland Place, London W1N 4AD.
T:0171-580 5533. F:0171-255 1541.
Can give you a shortlist of experts from their database of architects.

Royal Institute of Chartered Surveyors
12 Great George St, London SW1P 3AD.
T:0171-222 7000. F:0171-222 9430.
Can suggest three local surveyors, for anything from the survey of a home and a boundary or party wall dispute,to queries regarding standards of builders. Free brochures: 'Letting Your Home - A Guide For Would-Be Landlords' and 'Renting Your Home - A Guide For Would-Be Tenants'.

Rug Restorers' Association
c/o Orientis, Digby Rd, Sherborne, Dorset DT9 3NL.
T:01935-816479. Information about rug restorers and advice on whether restoration or conservation is required.

Salvo
Ford Woodhouse, Berwick-upon-Tweed,

Northumberland TD15 2QF.
T/F:01668-216494. Established in 1992
to encourage the re-use of more building
materials. It publishes a magazine which
covers architectural auctions, dealers, items
wanted and for sale (£20 for 10 issues).
Also available: The Salvo Pack with a
detailed list of dealers in your county and the
four adjacent ones (£5.75); a French Listing;
the trade Salvo News; architectural theft
alerts on the Internet.

Historic Scotland Conservation Bureau
Longmore House, Salisbury Place,
Edinburgh EH9 1SH. T:0131-668 8668.
F:0131-668 8669.

The Sleep Council
High Corn Mill, Chapel Hill,
Skipton, N.Yorks BD23 1NL.
Helpline :01756-792327. For advice on
buying a bed and for bed manufacturers.

**Society for the Protection
of Ancient Buildings**
37 Spital Square, London E1 6DY.
T:0171-377 1644. F:0171-247 5296.
Publish leaflets giving technical advice on
the repair of old buildings. They offer a two
day course for amateurs called 'Introduction
To The Repair Of Old Buildings'. Also a six
day 'Repair Of Old Buildings' course for
professionals.

Society of Garden Designers
6 Borough Rd, Kingston-upon-Thames,
Surrey KT2 6BD. T/F:0181-974 9483.
Advice on commissioning a professional
designer. They can suggest one of their
65 members nationwide.

The Solar Trade Association
Pengillan, Lerryn,
Lostwithiel, Cornwall PL22 0QE.
T/F:01208-873518. Help and information
on solar heating suppliers and installers.

**The Swimming Pool
& Allied Trades Association**
T:01264-350565. For information on
swimming pools and a copy of 'The
Swimming Pool Guide' (£4.95).

The Victorian Society
1 Priory Gardens, London W4 1TT.

T:0181-994 1019. F:0181-995 4895.
Can provide leaflets (£3 each) on period
doors, tiles, fireplaces, interior mouldings,
cast ironwork, wallcoverings.

Wallcovering Manufacturers' Association
James House, Bridge St,
Leatherhead, Surrey KT22 7EP.
T:01372-360660. F:01372-376069.

Wallpaper History Society
c/o The Victoria & Albert Museum,
Exhibition Rd, London SW7 2RL.
T:0171-938 8626. Can identify and date
wallpapers and advise on treatments and
conservation or decoration for period rooms.

20th Century Renaissance *178*
AA Coal & Log Fires *156*
AEG (UK) *20*
AEL (Acoustics & Environmetrics) *159*
ARC *90,226*
A-Z Studios *105*
Robert Aagaard *153*
Abacus *29*
The Abbey Bookbindery 170
Abbey Heritage 163
Abbott & Boyd *78,88*
Abbott Upholstery *149*
Academy Framing *202*
Ace Demolition and Salvage *220*
Acorn Ceramic Tiles *114*
Acova Radiators *37*
Acres Farm *121,157*
Actel Sunblinds *147*
James Adam *65*
Anne Adams *264*
Adams & Co *143,150*
Adcopa *87*
Peter Adler *187*
Aero *14,38,51,61,124,161*
Afia Carpets *102,115*
After Noah *14,67*
Aga/Rayburn *18,157*
Agnew's *183*
Agora London *106*
Agriframes *253*
The Air Improvement Centre *161*
Aktiva Systems *124*
Akzo-Nobel *95*
Alarm Detection Supplies *209*
Albion Design of Cambridge *206*
Albrissi *52,246*
Alfie's Antique Market *173*
Alitags *257*
Alitex *247*
Allemuir Contract Furniture *62*
Nick Allen Studios *54*
Allibert Bathrooms *36*
Allmilmö *13*
Alscot Bathrooms *35*
The Alternative Flooring Company *101*
Alternative Plans *29*
Altfield *45,60,95,96,97,104,228,233*
Alton-Brooke/Brooke London *78*
Altro Floors *107*
Alumasc Building Products *207*
Amana *20*
Jacques Amand *258*
Amari Plastics *37*
Amazing Grates *153*
Bill Amberg *115*
Amdega/Machin *248*

American Appliance Centre *18,259*
American Shutters *137*
Majid Amini, Persian Carpet Gallery *180*
Les Amis du Jardin *256*
Amtico *107*
Anchor Food Service Equipment *17*
And So To Bed *65*
Andersen Window & Patio Doors *136*
GEC Anderson *15,17,20,22,34,37*
Andersons Blinds *147*
Maria Andipa *187*
Angelic *122*
Anglepoise *124*
Mark Angus *140*
Anita Marquetry *167*
Ann's *117,121*
Anta Scotland *23,73,85,102*
Antaeus *54*
Anthemion *164,165*
Antiquarius *173*
The Antique Bath and Tap Studio *35,41*
Antique Baths of Ivybridge *35,41*
Antique Beds *67*
Antique Buildings *220*
Antique Designs *70*
Antique Desks *57*
The Antique Fireplace Warehouse *153*
Antique Leathers *149,167*
The Antique Lighting Company *182*
Antique Restorations *133,149,165,167,200*
Antique Terracotta *114*
Antique West *184*
The Antiques Market *173*
Antiques Pavilion *173*
Antiquus *175*
Apenn Fabrics *90*
Appalachia *106*
Appeal Blinds *147*
Aqualisa Products *31*
The Aquatic Design Centre *210*
Aram Designs *52,124*
Ruth Aram Shop *52,124*
Arbon Interiors *153*
Arboretum Bespoke *74,143*
Arc Linea *13,20*
Architectura in Horto *259*
Architectural Antiques *153,219*
Architectural Antiques *153*
Architectural Components *38,128,133,157,209*
Architectural Fencing *250*
Architectural Heritage
    153,205,221,242,251,253
Architectural Heritage of Northants *221*
Architectural Plants *258*
Architectural Salvage *220*
Architectural Salvage Centre *219*

INDEX

The Architectural Salvage Store *220*
Architectural Salvage & Supply *223*
Aria *14,36,38*
Ariel Press at the Pigeonhole Gallery *226*
Aristocast Originals *201*
Ariston *20*
Armitage Shanks *15,31*
Armstrong World Industries *108*
Arrow Fires *157*
Art Connoisseur *226*
Art Contact *202,226*
Art on Tiles *115*
Art Works *202,226*
Artech Garden Architecture *248*
Artefact *202,226*
Artemide GB *124*
Artforum *234*
Artichoke Interiors *58*
Articole Studios *201*
Artisan *145*
Artisans of Devizes *112*
Ashburton Marbles *154*
Ashfield Traditional *133*
Laura Ashley *78*
Morse Ashworth *143*
Aspara Designs *230*
Asprey *23,26*
Asprey Newton *226*
Aston Matthews *15,29,254*
Astral International *238*
At the Sign of the Chest of Drawers *49*
Atag (UK) *20*
John Atkinson & Sons *73*
Atlantic Bay Carpets *181*
Atrium *52,87,124*
Attica *113,114*
Au Temps Perdu *35,220*
Auro Organic Paint Supplies *191*
David Austin Roses *258*
Austrian Bedding Company *74*
Authentics *14,36*
Avant Garden *241*
Avenue Technology *148*
Jonathan Avery *49,51*
Aylsham Bath & Door *29*
BCG Shades *121*
BHS *117*
Babylon Design *124*
The Bacchus Gallery *187*
H &F Badcock *201*
Baer & Ingram *93,94*
Baileys *35,221,242*
G P & J Baker *78,86,88*
Baldwin Plastic Laminates *17*
David Ball Restoration *163*
Belinda Ballantine *262*

Ballantyne Booth *167*
David Bamford Marketing *166*
Banhams Security *209*
Sebastiano Barbagallo Antiques *58*
Barbary Pots *256*
Barber Wilsons & Co *15,32*
Robert Barley Antiques *176*
Barlow Tyrie *244*
A Barn Full of Sofas and Chairs *43,70*
Barnsley House *244*
Barrett Gray *18*
Bartholomew Conservatories *248*
Nigel Bartlett *154*
The Bath Doctor *35,41*
Bath Knob Shop *133*
Bathroom City *29*
Bathroom Discount Centre *29*
The Bathroom Store *29*
The Bathroom Studio *30*
The Bathroom Warehouse Group *30*
Bathrooms International *32*
Bathshield *35,41*
Bauknecht *20*
Baumatic *20*
Bazar *178*
Beagle Gallery *184*
Peter Beales Roses *258*
JD Beardmore & Co *128,133,200*
Alexander Beauchamp *94*
Beaudesert *65*
Angela Beaumont *262*
Beaumont & Fletcher *43,78,117,230*
Bed Bazaar *67,214*
Bedfordshire Bathroom Distributors *32*
Bedstock *70,75*
Beechams Furniture *48,167*
Beedham Antiques *175*
Behar Profex *166*
Bel Mondo Garden Features *254*
Alexander Beleschenko *140*
Jeff Bell *35*
Bella Figura *117*
Belle Cheminée *223*
Belle du Jour *25,124*
Belling Appliances *20*
Bellpark *214*
Below Stairs *25*
Benardout & Benardout *181*
Benchmark *244*
Bennett Silks *84*
Bennison Fabrics *78*
Benson Environmental *159*
Vanessa Benson *54,114*
Bentley & Spens *82,84*
Harry Berger Cleaners & Dyers *198*
Berkshire China Co. *26*

Bermondsey (New Caledonian) Market *174*
Emma Bernhardt *233*
Berrycraft *196*
Henry Bertrand *84*
The Berwick Street Cloth Shop *81*
Bery Designs *60,84,101,106*
Besselink & Jones *117,121,233,246*
Best & Lloyd *117,120,124*
Big Table Furniture Co-operative *65*
Christy Bird *223*
John Bird Antiques *176*
Stanley Bird Basketware *233*
The Birmingham Guild *138*
Celia Birtwell *82,213*
Bisca Design *38,55,145*
Bisque *159*
Black Country Heritage *38,39*
Black Lane Pots *256*
David Black Oriental Carpets *105,181*
Norman Blackburn *183*
Roy Blackman Associates *205*
Thomas Blakemore *118*
Blanc de Bierges *255*
Blanco *15,20*
The Blanket Box *73,216*
Blenheim Carpets *102*
Blind Fashion by Sander-Shade *148*
The Blinds Company *148*
Blue Crystal Glass *229*
The Blue Door *25,49,178*
Blue Jay Frames *202*
Blunderbuss Antiques *187*
JW Bollom *81,191*
Bolton Shirland International *209*
Bonar & Flotex *108*
Oliver Bonas *56,229,230*
Bond Street Silver Galleries *186*
Bonhams *174*
Adam Booth *199*
Joanna Booth *179*
Bopsom & Son *74*
Borgia Interiors *86*
Bosanquet Ives *102*
Bosch Domestic Appliances *20*
Julia Boston *183*
Boulet Frères *145*
Bourlet *170,202,204*
Bourne Street Linen *25,81*
Bower & Child *156*
Box Products *124*
Maryse Boxer at Chez Joseph *23,26,39,228*
John Boyd Textiles *90*
Philip Bradbury Glass *138*
Bradford Slate & Salvage Co *222*
Ray Bradley *138*
Bragman Flett *17*
Braquenié *102*
The Brass Decorative Grille
    & Repolishing Company *200*
Brass Knight *67*
Brass Tacks Hardware *133*

Brass & Traditional Sinks *16,26*
Brats *191*
Adam Bray *187*
Breezeway *148*
Arthur Brett & Sons *45,57*
C.Brewer & Sons *96,191*
The Brick Centre *207*
Christine Bridge Antiques *186*
Bridge of Weir Leather Company *87*
Lawrence T. Bridgeman *191*
Emma Bridgewater *23*
Brighton Architectural Salvage *220*
Brighton Regency Leathers *167*
Brights of Nettlebed *45*
Brintons *103*
Bristol Blue Glass *229*
Britannia Catering *22*
British Gates & Timber *132,250*
The British Museum Company *235,242*
British Trimmings *89*
Broadmead Products *208*
Brodie & Middleton *194*
The Bronze Collection *242*
Brookbrae *254,259*
Brooke London *105*
Brookgate Designs *244*
G W Brooks *108*
Brora *85,103*
Alasdair Brown *176*
B. Brown *81*
I & JL Brown *175*
J. Brown & Son *108*
Barbara Brownfield & Paul Verburg *230*
Brunschwig & Fils
    43,49,78,82,84,86,88,96,118,213,235
Buck & Ryan *170*
Budget Furniture *57*
Stuart Buglass *122*
Builders, Iron & Zincwork *17,200*
The Bulbeck Foundry *243,254,256*
Bulldog *257*
Bullers *135*
Bulthaup *13,14,18*
Bundles Design *213*
Peter Bunting *175*
Richard Burbidge *204,206*
Burge & Gunson *30*
Burgon & Ball *253,257*
Sarah Burgoyne Revivals *244*
Jean Burhouse Furniture *167*
Peter Burian Associates *129*
Burlington Slate *113*
WGT Burne *186*
Matthew Burt Splinter Group *216*
Gaze Burvill *244*
Buyers & Sellers *18*
By Design *134*
Bylaw (Ross) *45,136,206*
Byron & Byron *145*
CVP Designs *235*
CXV *228*

Caddum Designs *48*
Cadogan Company *151,161,197*
Adam Calkin *195*
Calmels *56,245*
Calor Gas *20*
Camden Passage *174*
Lucy B. Campbell Gallery *184,203,227*
Campbell, Marson & Company *106*
Campbell & Young *106*
Camtile -The Cambridgeshire
   Tile & Slate Company *221*
Candell Lighting *124*
Candy *20*
Candy Tiles *111*
The Cane Store *167,196*
Canework and Rush Restoration *167*
Belinda Canosa *195,227,235,243*
Manuel Canovas *78,82,84,86,88,94,97*
Capital Fireplaces *111,154*
Capital Garden Products *254,256*
Capricorn Architectural Ironwork *199,206*
Caradon Bathrooms *32*
Caradon Stelrad *159*
Carden Cunietti *23*
Cardiff Reclamation *107,222*
Carew Jones *52,58*
Carpenter Oak & Woodland Company *248*
Carpenters *21*
The Carpet Library *103*
Carpets International *103*
John Carr *132*
Carron Phoenix *16*
David Carter *50,195*
George Carter *243,244,248*
Carvers & Gilders *167*
Casa Catalan *228*
Casbah Tiles *111*
Jack Casimir *187*
The Cast Iron Shop *199,206,246*
Manuel Castilho *175*
Casting Repairs *165*
Catalytico *125*
Rupert Cavendish *178*
The Ceramic Stove Company *157*
Ceramica Blue *111*
Certikin International *114*
Chad Lighting *125*
Chairs *48*
Chairworks *233*
Chalfont Cleaners & Dyers *198*
Chalon *15,50*
Chalwyn *259*
A W Champion *205*
David Champion *225*
Chancellors Church Furnishings *219*
Chandelier Cleaning
   & Restoration Services *120,165*
Chandni Chowk *104*
Nicholas Chandor & Andrew Hirst *178,182*
Chanée Ducrocq *86*
Chanteau *45*

Albert E Chapman *149,150*
HG Chard & Sons *196*
Charlotte's Living Room *75*
Chase Erwin *84,87*
Chatsworth *103*
Chatsworth Carpenters *244*
Chattels *237*
Chauncey's *107,220*
Chelsea Antiques Market *173*
Chelsea College of Art & Design *2 261*
The Chelsea Gardener *241*
Chelsea Glass *138,230*
Chelsea Harbour Design Centre *77*
Chelsea Lighting Design *128,129*
Chelsea of London *78,213*
Chelsea Plumbing & Heating
   Centre Suppliers & Installers *34*
Chelsea Textiles *73,83,88,233*
Chelsom *118,127*
Chem-Dry Acclaimed *197*
Antoine Chenevière Fine Arts *176*
Chenil Galleries *173*
Cheshire Brick and Slate Company *222*
Chess Designs *213*
The Chester Cooker Co *18*
Julian Chichester Designs *39,46,245*
The Children's Cottage Company *216*
The Children's Playhouse Company *216*
Chilstone *206,243,248,254*
China Matching Service *26*
China Repairers *164*
Chinasearch *26*
Christie's *174*
Christie's Education *261*
Christofle *23*
Jane Churchill *78,83,84,191*
John Churchill *133,157*
Ciel Decor *90,97,229*
Citrus Centre *258*
City & Guilds of London Art School *264*
The City Lit *264*
Civil Engineering Developments *255*
The Clare Hall Company *238*
Claremont Furnishing Fabrics *78*
Kenneth Clark Ceramics *111*
Clarke's of Buckfastleigh *154*
The Classic American Fridge Company *18*
The Classic Chair Company *46,48,228*
Classic Upholstery *149*
Classical Flagstones *113*
Suzie Clayton *121*
Jane Clayton & Co *70,149*
Clayton Munroe *133,145*
Clearview Showroom *157*
Clement Brothers *136*
Clifton Little Venice *235,243,245,253*
Clifton Nurseries *241*
The Clock Clinic *170,187*
Clock House Furniture *48*
The Cloth Shop *81*
Clyde Combustions *159*

Fergus Cochrane and Leigh Warren *182*
Coexistence *52,62*
Cole & Son *94,96,192*
Colefax & Fowler *78,83,88,88,94,176*
John Coleman *54*
College of Garden Design *263*
Charles Collinge Architectural
    Ironmongery *39,134*
Colnaghi *183*
Cologne & Cotton *71*
Colour Blue *57,67,124*
Colourman Paints *192*
Colourwash Bathrooms *30*
Community Playthings *214*
The Complete Bathroom *30*
Concord Bega *127*
Concord Sylvania *125*
Connaught Flameproofing Services *90*
Connection Seating *57*
Connolly *87*
The Conran Shop
    21,39,52,65,81,83,214,216,225,241
The Conran Shop Contracts *62*
Conservation Building Products *221*
Contemporary Applied Arts *55*
Continental Awnings *148*
Contravent Regal *148*
Richard Cook *27*
Cooper Dryad *134*
HW Cooper & Co *138*
Belinda Coote Tapestries *90,234,235*
Lucy Cope Designs *121*
Cope & Timmins *145*
Copley Decor *201*
Tim Coppard *255*
Corcoran & May *90*
L.Cornelissen & Son *194*
Corres Tiles *114*
Cotswood Doors *132*
Country Cookers *15,18*
Country Desks *57*
Country & Eastern *59*
Country Garden Retreats *249*
Country Stoves *157*
Country Weavers *101*
Countryside Wildflowers *258*
Countrywide Workshops *27,216*
County and Capital Metals *200*
County Hardwoods *132*
Courtaulds Textiles (Ashton) *71*
Courtyard Designs *249*
Cover Up Designs
    50,51,70,75,81,83.89,143,149
Crabtree Kitchens *11*
Andrew Crace Designs *245,249,251,256*
Craig & Rose *192*
Crangrove *20,32*
Creda *20*
Robert Cresser *210*
Mrs ME Crick Chandeliers *182*
Jenny Crisp *233*

Crispin & Son *170*
Criterion Tiles *110*
Crittall Windows *136*
The Cross *238*
Crown *192*
H.Crowther *243*
Crowther of Syon Lodge *154,205,242*
Crucial Trading *81,101*
Cubbins & Co *39,236*
Cubestore Storage Systems *236*
John Cullen *125,127,129*
Richard Cullinan Joinery *204*
Curragh Tintawn *103*
The Curtain Agency *147*
The Curtain Exchange *147*
The Curtain Rack *147*
The Curtain Ring *147*
The Curtain Shop *147*
The Curtain Trading Centre *147*
Curtains Complete *143,147*
Wendy Cushing Trimmings *89*
Custom Carpet Company *103*
Cwt-y-Bugail Slate Quarries *113,154*
Czech & Speake *30,39*
DLW Flooring *108*
DZ Designs *123,200*
Daedalian Glass *138*
The Charles Daggett Gallery *203*
Amanda Dakin *105*
Dalsouple Direct *108*
Kathy Dalwood *55*
Damask *73*
Andrew Dando *185*
Danico Brass *32,145*
Thomas Dare *89,90*
Darwin Bespoke Furniture *132,204,205*
Daryl Industries *32*
Daubneys *55*
Dauphin Display Oxford *58*
Elizabeth David Cookshop *22*
J & N Davidson *71*
R & D Davidson *46,55*
Barry Davies Oriental Art *184*
Davies, Keeling Trowbridge *195*
Davis Electrics *18*
Ben Dawson Furniture *61*
Tulissio de Beaumont *182*
J. De Bruyn Flooring Services *108*
De Dietrich *20*
de Gournay *94*
Anthony de Grey Trellises *252*
De La Torre Tiles *111*
De Le Cuona Designs *90*
Louis de Poortere *103*
Deacon & Sandys *15,46,132,205*
Christopher Dean *227*
The Deben Craftsmen *101,233*
Deck 2 Lighting *125*
Decor Shades *97,148*
Decora *235*
The Decorative Arts Co *238*

Decorative Fabrics Gallery 77
Decorative Living 178
Decorative Textiles of Cheltenham 179,234
Delabole Slate 16,113,208
Jacob Delafon 32
Delblanco Meyer 71
Delomosne & Son 182,186
Paul Dennis & Sons 165
Dennison Drake 227
Denny and Fancourt 205
R Denny 37
George D'Epinois 227
Deptich Designs 65
Dermide 210
Descamps 26,71
Design American 52
Design Archives 78
Design Fireplaces 154
Designed Plastercraft Associates 201
Designer Bathrooms 30
Designer Light Shop 125
Designers Guild 23,52,71,78,98,213,214
The Francesca Di Blasi Company 196
Caroline Dickenson Flowers 237
Dickinson Architectural Antiques 21
Dickson of Ipswich 46
Dimplex (UK) 38
Dinan & Chighine 184
The Dining Chair Company 48
The Dining Room Shop 23,26,27,46,187
Directive Office 61
The Display Stand Company 58
Divertimenti 22
Martin J.Dodge 46
Domain 52,61,62
The Domestic Paraphernalia Company 27
Domus Tiles 111
Donghia 52,78,86,96,97
Dorma 71
The Dormy House 51,60,70
Dornbracht 32,39
Dor-O-Matic 132
Dorothea 127
Dorothea Restorations 199
Sebastian D'Orsai 170,203
Dorset Reclamation 220
Dorset Weathervanes 259
Doshi Wallcoverings 214
Richard Doughty Bathrooms 30
Doverhay Forge Studios 199
Dovre Castings 157
Brian & Angela Downes 185
Dragons 214,216
Geoffrey Drayton 66
Dreams 71
Bernard Dru Oak 106,206
Drummond's of Bramley 35,41,220,242,254
A F Drysdale 77
Peter Dudgeon 43,57,231,246
Dulux 192,193
The Dummy Book Company 235

Dunlopillo (UK) 68
A. Dunn 168
DuPont Corian® 17,37
Duresta Upholstery 43
Duro Lino 108
Dyfed Antiques
    and Architectural Salvage 154,222
EFR 19
Belinda Eade 259
Early's of Witney 74
Easy Architectural Salvage 223
The Easy Chair Co 149,196
Elizabeth Eaton
    46,70,81,96,118,120,121,134,231
Eaton's Shell Shop 259
Matthew Eden 247,253
Jacqueline Edge 59,256
Andrew Edmunds 184
Charles Edwards 118,176,182,231
Edwins Plumbing & Heating Supplies 34,159
Egyptian Touch 123
Eibe-Play 216
Eiderdown Studio 75
Eighty-Eight Antiques 49
Electrolux 20
Elephant Industries 214
Elgin and Hall 154
Elon Tiles 30,111
The Empty Box Company 236
The English Garden Collection 241
The English Gardening School 263
English Hurdle 233,246,249,250,252
English Portfolio Company 227
The English Stamp Company 194
Erco Lighting 125
Ergonom 61
Erin-Gardena 127,254
Eskenazi 184
Essential Items 43
Ethos Candles 122
Euroframe 203
Euromarble 37
European Heritage 110
G D Evans 19
Guy Evans 79,94
S&B Evans & Sons 256
Ever Trading 74,88
Exclusive Furnishings 59
The Expanded Metal Company 200
FSB Design Hardware 134
Faber Blinds 148
Nicole Fabre 178,179
The Facade 179
The Fairchild Company 69
Jack Fairman Carpets 105,181
Falcon Catering Equipment 19
Family Copies 227
Fans and Spares Group 161
Fantasia 161
Faraday Trading 59
Faral Radiators 159

Peter Farlow 176
Farmer Foster 215
Farmington Fireplaces 154
Farmington Stone 113
Christopher Farr 53,105,125
Farrow & Ball 94,192
Tom Faulkner Designs 56
Faunus The Florist 237
The Feather Bed Company 69
The Felbrigg Design Company 234
Fens Restoration & Sales 49,219
Thomas Ferguson & Co 26,71
Stephanie Fernald Ceramic Designs 23
Harvey Ferry & William Clegg 176
Fesco Tiles 113
Fibre Naturelle 81
Fiesta Blinds 148
The Final Curtain Company 26,81,143
Hector Finch Lighting 182
The Fine Art Society 183
Finewood Floors 17,106
The Fire Place 154
Firecraft 154
Fired Earth 83,101,105,110,191
The Fireplace 154
First Floor 108
Fisk's Clematis Nursery 258
Fitzroy Fabrics 86
Fix-A-Frame 203
Flaminia Murals 195
Flo-Rad Heating Systems 160
Flos 125
Flowers by Charmian 237
Flying Duck 19
Foamplan Rubber & Plastics 69
Focal Point Original Fires 155
Focus 156
Fogarty 71
Forbes & Lomax 128
Don Forbes Sash Fittings 136
Forbo CP 18
Forbo-Nairn 108
Forest Fencing 250,255
Forest Stonecraft 243
Forever Flowering 237
Forgeries 134
Formica 17
Forsham Cottage Arks 259
Fountains Direct 254
Fourneaux de France 19
Ann Fowler 50
Mark Fox 27
Mary Fox Linton 79,86
Foxell & James 192
Frame 227
Francis Ceramics 228
The Mark Francis Collection 56
Franco-file 140
Franke 14,16
Anna French 79,83,89,214
The French Linen Company 71

Frette 71
Freud 46,161,228
Pierre Frey 79,88
Friend or Faux 196,263
Frolics of Winchester 245,252,256
From The Top 144
Frome Reclamation 220
Froyle Tiles 111
Fritz Fryer Antique Lighting 165,182
Fuelmizas A.T 157
Cliff Fuller 168
The Furnishing Workshop 149
The Furniture Cave 174
The Furniture Union 44,53,56,125,234
The Futon Company 68
Futon Express 68
John Fyffe Architectural Salvage 223
GLPC International 46
GMW 81
GP Contracts 68
GWB Products 69
Mark Gabbertas 55
Robin Gage 157
Gaggenau (UK) 20
Gainsborough Silk Weaving Company 84
Gallery 19 60
The Gallery of Antique
    Costume & Textiles 89,144,180
Gallery Yacou 181
Gallery Zadah 181
Gallop & Rivers 222
The Garden Gate 257
Garden & Security Lighting/
    Lightscape Projects 127
The Gardeners' Academy 263
Garin 84
Garland Catering 19
Garrard & Co 25,27,186
Garrods of Barking 27
Marilyn Garrow 67,178,180
William Garvey 35
Gazco 157
General Plumbing Supplies 34
General Trading Company 24,26
Gentle & Boon 50
Gerflor 108
Gerrietts GB 81
Get Stuffed 238
Christopher Gibbs 187
Gibson Music 210
Gifford Mead 207
Nicholas Gifford-Mead 242
James Gilbert & Sons 253
Joan Gilbert Cane & Rush Seating 168
David Gill 179
Glasgow School of Art 262
Glass Heritage 140,229
Glass Houses 248
Glazebrook & Co 25,27
Glover & Smith 135
Glowcroft 259

Goddard & Gibbs Studios 140
Michael Goedhuis 184
Goldsmith Dyers 198
Golfar & Hughes 122,233
Good Directions 208,254,259
The Good Flooring Company 114
Thomas Goode 24,26,27
Gooding Aluminium 200
Gove Marble 112
Graham & Green 24,39,83,105,225,246
Joss Graham Oriental Textiles
     74,180,181,228,230,256
L.Grandison 201
Grandisson 132,201
Grange 46,246
Denzil Grant 175
Grays Antique Market 174
Great Brampton House Antiques 176
The Great Victorian Railing Company 251
Greaves & Thomas 238
Green & Pleasant 229
Richard Green 183
Green and Stone 194,197
GW Green Swimming Pools 256
Green & Veronese 201
Greene's Garden Furniture 245,252
Greenham Trading 251
Judy Green's Garden Store 241
Greensward Co 255
J F Greenwood 90
Judy Greenwood Antiques 67,178,180
Gregory, Bottley & Lloyd 239
Grey & Company 13
Jason Griffiths Underwoodsman 252
Grohe 32
Guardall 209
Guardian Security 210
Claire Guest 239
Guinevere 176,186,187
Linda Gumb 180
A & J Gummers 32
Gunning Engineering 159
H & D Fireplace Company 155
HDB 148
H & L Antiques 231
Habitat 15,22,39,105,215,246
Haddonstone 63,207,243,249,254
Haemmerlin 257
Hafele (UK) 14,236
Halcyon Days 188
Hallidays 155,176,204,206
Hallis Hudson 145
James Halstead 108
Rosemary Hamilton 164
R.Hamilton & Co 128
Hamilton & Tucker Billiard Company 209
Hamilton-Weston Wallpapers 93,94
Hammerite Products 192
Hampstead Decorative Arts 196,263
Hampstead School of Art 263
C F Handerson 206

Handles & Fittings 135
The Handmade Door Company 132
The Handmade Glass Company 230
The Handmade Wooden Tea Tray Company 63
Hannings Furniture Company 17
Hansen's Kitchen & Bakery Equipment 19,23
Hansgrohe 32
Charles Harden 135
John Hardman's Studios 140
Sidney Hardwick 41
The Hardwood Flooring Co 17,106
Joyce Hardy Pine and Country Furniture 49
Hardy's Cottage Garden Plants 258
E J Harmer 201
J A Harnett Antique Restoration 168
Edward Harpley 145
Harriet Ann Sleigh Beds 67,215
Harris Fabrics 86,90
Jonathan Harris 177
L G Harris & Co 194
Rupert Harris 166
Harrison Drape 145
Harrods 24,215
C P Hart 14,16,30,36
Hartley Botanic 250
Christopher Hartnoll 246
Harvey Maria 108
Harvey's Garden & Leisure Buildings 249
Nicholas Haslam 50,79,88,229
Haslam and Whiteway 179
H J Hatfield & Son 168
Brian Haughton Antiques 185
Haute Deco 125,135,146,227
Havenplan 131
Haworth (UK) 61
Jeanette Hayhurst 186
Hayles & Howe 155,201
Hayloft Woodwork 11,36,204
Heal's 22,69,86
Heart of the Country 192
Heart of the Home 11
The Heated Mirror Company 39
Samuel Heath & Sons 39
Heating World Group 38
FA Heffer & Co 210
Heirloom and Howard 185
Heirlooms 71
Hemisphere 179
Heraz 180
Nicholas Herbert 56,91,98
ADC Heritage 186
Heritage Antiques 175
Heritage Bathrooms 33
Hermitage Antiques 178
Herons Bonsai 243,258
James Hetley & Co 138
The Heveningham Collection 56,123,246
Hewi (UK) 40,135
Allegra Hicks 83
E A Higginson 207
Highgate Framers 203

Highly Sprung 44
Michael Hill 246
Hill & Knowles 79
The Hill Toy Company 217
Hillier Nurseries 258
Hitch/Milius 53
Carlton Hobbs 177
Hodkin & Jones 201
Hodsoll McKenzie 44,46,79,94
Hogarth & Dwyer 22
The Holbein Collection at Titley & Marr 146
The Holding Company 236
Holloways 242,247
Holman Specialist Paint 192
Hoover 20
Stephanie Hoppen 46,227
Simon Horn 66,68,215
Jonathan Horne 185
Hortus Ornamenti 257
Hot & Cold 19
Hotpoint 20
The House Hospital 35,219
House of Steel 68,199,207,246,251
House of Stone 158
How of Edinburgh 186
Howard Chairs 44,98,150,151
Christopher Howe 87,150,177,182
Howe's Design 47,58,118,122
James Hoyle & Son 199
Hozelock 127
Hudevad 159
Michael Hughes 245
Alastair Hull 181
Humpherson's 13
The Humphries Weaving Co 84
Hunter Douglas 148
Hunter Hyland 146
Charles Hurst 11,37,204,206
Christopher Hyde 118
Hymas Refrigeration 19
ICC (Internal Climate Control) 159
ICI Acrylics 37
TW Ide 138
Ideal Standard 33
iGuzzini 125
IKEA 13,22,57,215,217,236
Image Line 82
The Imperial Bathroom Company 33
Imperial Towel Rails 38
In Doors 131
In n Out Trading 59
In Situ 111,
In-Situ Architectural Antiques 131,222
Inchbald School of Design 262,263
Indesit 20
The Indian Collection 74
Indian Ocean Trading Company 245
Inflate 127,239
Inglenook Canopy Company 155
Inhouse 53,125
Institute of Fine Art 227

Intec 115
Interdesign 247
Interior Art Metalworks 123,146
Interiors Bis 60
International Matting Company 102
Into Lighting Design 129
Invisible Heating Systems 160
Iona Antiques 183
The Irish Linen Company 72
The Iron Bed Company 66
The Iron Design Company 56,66,146,246
Isis Ceramics 24,118
The Isle Mill 85
Isometrix 129
JAB Anstoetz 79,84,85,86
JCA (UK) 19
JHS (UK) 210
J & R Marble Company 161
HS Jackson & Son 250
G Jackson & Sons 202
Jacuzzi 33
Leon Jaeggi & Sons 23
Jali 205,232
Japanese Gallery 185
Jardinique 242
Java Cotton Company 91
Jaymart Rubber & Plastics 109
Emma Jefferson 217
Jendico 40
John Jenkins & Sons 24
Jerry's Home Store 22,40
John Jesse 179
Jetmaster Fires 155
Jinan Furniture Gallery 53,105
C.John 181
H & R Johnson Tiles 111,115,170
Johnston & Pycraft 204,210
Jones 182
Harvey Jones 11
Jen Jones 166,180
John Jones Art Centre 203
Joshua Jones 215
Peter Jones 22,77
Jones Tiles 111
Jopasco 251
Jorgen Antiques 178
Junckers 17,106
Just Bathrooms 30
Just Desks 57
Just Kitchens 13
Just Mirrors 231
K. Restorations 167,168
KCP (Specialist Cleaning
   & Scotchgarding Services) 197
KLC School of Interior Design 262,263,264,
K's of Mill Hill 197
Ka International 91
Kampmann 160
Kappa Lambda 106
The Kasbah 59,111,192
Kedddy-Poujoulat 158

REH Kennedy 47
Kennedy Carpets 104
Penny Kennedy Design 236
Kensington Lighting Company 120,123
Kensington Traders 207
Thomas Kerr at #12 175
Blot Kerr-Wilson 255,259
Kersaint Cobb 109,115
Ketcher & Moore 144
The Keyhole 140
Keymer 208
Cath Kidston 15,40,96,98
The Kilim Warehouse 105,181
JB Kind 132
Richard Kindersley 211
Kingcome 44
Kings of Sheffield 25
Kingston University 262
Kirkstone Quarries 16,37,113
Knobs & Knockers 134
Knoll International 61
Marjorie Knowles 114
Koralle 33
Kyte Marketing 158
LASSCo (London Architectural
    Salvage & Supply Company) 63,219
LASSCo Flooring 107
LEC Refrigeration 20
LHA-SCAN 158
La Conch Lighting 125
La Cuisinière 21
La Maison 155,178
Stephan La Grange and Justin Manley 151
Richard La Trobe-Bateman 259
The Lab 41
The Lacquer Chest 188
The Lacy Gallery 188
NT Laidlaw 40,135
Lakeland Plastics 27
Lambs Bricks & Arches 208
Landford Trees 258
Prue Lane 49
Langfords 25,166,186
Langfords Marine Antiques 188
Langley Boxwood Nursery 258
Langlow Products 198
Lattice Windows 136
Laufen/Bellgrove 33
Ralph Lauren Home Collection 72,85
Lawson Fencing 250
Lawson Wood 44
Richard Lawton 27
Maurice Lay Distribution 19
Lyn le Grice 194
The Leather Conservation Centre 167
Lefroy Brooks 33
Christopher Legge Oriental Carpets 181
Leisure 16
Lelièvre 79,85,86,87,88
L'Encoignure 175
Anthony Lennon 207

Let It Loose 144
Geneviève Lethu 24,26
The Letterbox Company 140
MP Levene 186
Guy Lewis 49,55
John Lewis 77
Liberon Waxes 193,197
Liberty 22,40,53,77,88,123,179,229
Libra Antiques 185
Liebherr 20
Lienzo De Los Gazules 91
The Life Enhancing Tile Company 112
Light Projects 126,128,129
The Light Store 126,127
Limestone Gallery 113
Lindman 137
The Linen Cupboard 26,72
Linen and Lace Company 72
Ann Lingard 25
David Linley Furniture 55
Lion, Witch and Lampshade 120,121,217
Ann Lister Historic Furnishings 144
Litchfield Clare 87
Little Bridge 215
Little Monsters 215,217
Little Thatch Company 249
Litvinoff & Fawcett 66
Living Art 169
Lloyd Christie Garden Architecture 248,252,255
Lloyd Loom Furniture 247
Lloyd of Bedwyn 16
Locker & Reilly 202
London Architectural Salvage
    & Supply Company (LASSCo) 219
London Brick Cleaning Service 163
London College of Fashion 264
London College of Printing
    & Distributive Trades 264
The London Crown Glass Company 138
The London Curtain Shop 147
London Decking Company 255
London Door Company 132
London Fine Art Plaster 202
London Glassblowing Workshop
    (Peter Layton Associates) 165,169,230
London Lighting 126,128
London Plastercraft 202
London School of Printing
    & Distributive Trades 262
London Shutter Company 138
The London Silver Vaults 186
The London Wall Bed Company 68
The London Waterbed Company 68
London West Ten Glass 139
London's Georgian Houses 138
J & JW Longbottoms 208
Longpre Cabinet Makers 55
The Looking Glass 231
The Loose Cover Company 144
Clive Loveless 181
Lullaby Handmade Mattresses 69

Lumley's 31
Lunn Antiques 72,180
W. Lusty & Sons 168,247
Luxcrete 139
MAP 230
MAS Furniture Contracts 62
M & D 198
M & F Caners 168
MHS Radiators 38,160
Maaz 18
MacCulloch & Wallis 82
Andrew Macintosh Furniture 11
Hugh Mackay Carpets 103
Mackinnon & Bailey 134
John Maclean 166
Mad Hatters 194
Made of Waste 17,53
Maecenas Decoration 98
Maggs Bros 188
Magpie's 25
Simon Maidment 215
Maison 51,225
Maison d'Art International 40
The Majestic Shower Company 33
John Makepeace 55
Malabar 79,83,85
Malborough Forge 199
Mallett & Son 177
Mallett at Bourdon House 177
The Mallett Gallery 183
Guy Mallinson Furniture 13,15,55,265
Malthouse Fabrics 83
Ian Mankin 82
Daniel Mankowitz 175
Brett Manley and Ann Sams 164
The Manor Bindery 235
Manorhouse Stone 113,155
Mansour Carpets 181
The Map House 184
Marabout 115
Marble Arch 37
Marble-Arte 243
Marble Hill Fireplaces 155
Marcatre 61
Marlborough Tiles 114
Marley Floors 109
Marston & Langinger
    123,160,247,248,253,254
Andrew Martin 44,47,79,86,87,96
Martin & Company 134
Martin & Frost 109
Marvic Textiles 79,84
Material World 83,91
Mathmos 127
Matki 33
Ann May 49
Mark Maynard 178
McCEd 177
McClenaghan 177
McCloud & Co 56,118
Ian McGregor Designs 245

McKinney & Co 135,146
Cynthia McNair China Restoration 165
McVeigh and Charpentier 177
Mediterraneo 230
William Mehornay Porcelain 118
Melin Tregwynt 74,217
David Mellor 22
Merchants 146
Mercury Antiques 185
Merlin Glass 136,230
Thomas Messel 50,239
David Messum 183
The Metal Window Company 136
Metra Non-Ferrous Metals 17,201
Michelmersh Brick & Tile Company 255
Microlights 126
Arthur Middleton 188
Miele 21
Millenium Design International 15
Herman Miller 62
Millers Specialist Floorcoverings 109
Robert Mills 220
E. Mills & Son 103
Mira Showers 33
Miscellanea of Churt 31
Paul Mitchell 170,188,203
Mobili 53
Modus Design 158
Moffat 21
Molesey Refrigeration 19
Jennie Moncur 109
Monkwell 79,97
Monogrammed Linen Shop 72,217
Mrs Monro 79
Alison Moore Ceramics 24
Christopher Moore Textiles 91,94
Moriarti's Workshop 66
Morley Marketing 158
Katherine Morris 98
Morso 158
Mosaic Arts 115
Mosaic Workshop 115
Mosaik 115
Clare Mosley 169
Moss & Company 208
Moyses Stevens 237
Mr Light 118
Andrew Muirhead & Son 87
Muji 14,236
Mulberry Home Collection 79,86,89
Multibeton 160
Mumford & Wood 137
Muraspec 96
S & M Myers 103
Myson 38
NCR 19
NDS Manufacturing 250
Sylvia Napier 177
National Trust Enterprises 97
The Natural Fabric Company 82,89
Natural Flooring Direct 102

The Natural Furniture Company *69*
Natural Stone Products *113*
The Natural Wood Floor Co *106,107*
Naturestone *16,113*
Neff (UK) *21*
J R Nelson *209*
Nelson Catering Equipment *19*
Nero Signs (Glass/Designs) *139,140*
New Century *179*
New England Gardens *259*
New World Domestic Appliances *21*
Henry Newbery & Co *89*
Newcastle Furniture Company *11*
Newcome Marketing *236*
Daniel Newlyn *150*
W H Newson & Sons *37,132,205,207,209*
Newton Forge *253*
Roger Newton & Company *168*
Roger Newton School of Decorative Finishes *263*
Nice Irma's *84,105*
Nicholls & Clarke *109*
Nimmo's *237*
Nobilis-Fontan *79,86,89,96*
Noble Macmillan *237*
Nomad *75*
Nordic Style at Moussie *26,50,82*
Norfolk Stove Co *158*
Norman & Underwood *208*
RJ Norris *69*
Northmace *14*
Nu-Life Upholstery Repairs *75*
Nu-Line Builders' Merchants *209,210*
Nursery Window *214,217*
Nutshell Natural Paints *193*
The Oak Barrel Company *254*
Oak Leaf Conservatories of York *248*
DJ Oakes *49*
Oakleaf Reproductions *205,206,231,235*
Roger Oates Design *102,103*
Ocean *161,226*
Ochre *123,227,231*
The Odiham Gallery *181*
Oggetti *14*
Christina Ojo *89*
Old Door & Fireplace Company *131,155,160*
Old Fashioned Bathrooms *36*
Old Town Bedlinen *72*
Old World Trading Company *155*
Olicana Textiles *82*
John Oliver *93,95,96,97,98,193*
Olivers Lighting Company *128*
Marcus Olliff *220*
Onglaze *229*
Jacqueline Oosthuizen *185*
Optelma Lighting *126,128*
Optime Lighting *126*
The Oriental Gallery *184*
Oriental Rug Gallery *105*
Orientalist *104*
Orientique *59*
Original Bathrooms *31*

The Original Book Works *123,236*
The Original Box Sash Window Company *137*
Original Door Specialists *12,131*
The Original Silver Lining *72,82,144*
Original Style *112*
The Original Tile Company *110*
Ornamenta *91,96,97,98*
Ornamental Arts Trading *135*
Osborne & Little *79,83,85,86,95,96,98,214*
The O'Shea Gallery *184*
Ossowski *168,231*
Ostermann & Scheiwe (UK) *194*
Otterswick Antique Telephones *239*
Out of Time *161*
Out of the Wood *50*
Outdoor Lighting (OLS) *128*
WR Outhwaite & Son *207*
Ouzledale Foundry Company *158*
Overmantels *231*
Oxford Sash Window Company *137*
Oxley's Furniture *168,246*
PGI *70*
P J Equipment *209*
PMP *38,160*
Jane Packer *237*
Angela Page Antiques *175*
Charles Page Furniture *53,66*
Kevin Page Oriental Art *185*
Pages *23*
Paine & Company *150*
Paint Library *193*
Paint Magic *194,263*
Paint Service Company *193*
The Painted Loo Seat Company *40*
Pairs *188*
Pallam Precast *16,112*
Paper Moon *84,97*
Paperchase *237*
Paper and Paint Effects *193*
Papers and Paints *193*
Paris Ceramics *110,115*
Parker & Farr Furniture *44*
Parker Knoll *80*
Parsons Table Company *47*
Charles Pateman and Company *150,151*
Patio *256*
M Pauw Antiques *58*
Pavilion Antiques *180*
Pavilion Originals *195*
Pavilion Rattan *61,247,253*
Peacock Blue *72*
Roger Pearson *155*
Roberto Pedrina *226*
Pegler *33*
Pella at WHN Distributors *132*
Pembroke Squares *74*
Pendragon Frames *203*
Penrose & Rietberg *44*
Pentonville Rubber Company *109*
Percheron *80,85,86,88,89*
Perez *104*

Period Brass Lights *120,165*
The Period House Group *133,134*
Charles Perry Restorations *169*
John Perry Wallpapers *95*
The Persian Carpet Studio *105*
Peter Place at I&JL Brown *119*
Petit Roque *156*
Peter Petrou *188*
Pew Corner *188*
Phillips *174*
ES Phillips *140*
SJ Phillips *187*
D M Philp *144*
Richard Philp Gallery *183*
Picreator Enterprises *197*
The Pier *40*
Mikhail Pietranek *85*
Geoffrey Pike *112,113*
Max Pike Bathrooms *31*
Pilgrim Payne & Co *151,197*
Pilkington Glass Products *139*
Pine Grove *49*
Pine Supplies *222*
Pine Warehouse *49*
Pipe Dreams *31*
Pisani *112*
Plain English *12,36,204,207*
Charles Plante *183*
Plasterworks *235*
Plasticotter (UK) *91*
The Platonic Fireplace Company *156*
Simon Playle *83*
E Ploton *195*
Plowden & Smith *164,166,170*
Plumbcraft *34*
Plumpton College *264*
Poggenpohl *13*
Pongees *85*
FW Poole *113*
Porta Romana *50,119,123,230*
Porter Design *228*
John Porter *133*
Porter Nicholson *82*
Portobello Road Market *174*
Posh Tubs *36,41*
Pot Luck *24*
Potmolen Paint *193*
Pots & Pithoi *257*
Jonathan Potter *184*
Potterson Myson *160*
HW Poulter & Son *155,161,164*
Simon Poyntz *66*
Preedy Glass *139*
Preferred Electrical *128*
Premdor Crosby *133*
Price's Patent Candle Co *122*
Primo Furniture *62*
Proctor Masts *251*
Project Connection *210*
Prolumena *126*
Pruskin Gallery *179*

Paula Pryke Flowers *237*
Pukka Palace *59,60,81,101*
Pulbrook & Gould *237*
Pumps & Tubs *254*
Purves & Purves *54,66,126,106,215,226*
Pyramidion *243*
Quadrant 4 *58*
Qualitas Bathrooms *33*
Quality Lock Co *141*
Carolyn Quartermaine *85*
Quebec St George *47*
Patrick Quigly *121,127*
A Quiligotti & Co *112*
Richard Quinnell *141,166,199*
The Quintessa Art Collection *228*
RBI International *80*
Radford & Ball *139*
Radiant Distribution *126*
Radiating Style *38,160*
Rainbow International *198*
Rainbow Leisure *256*
Raleigh Workshop *204*
Ramm, Son & Crocker *80,86*
Rankins *139*
Rapid Racking *61*
Rattee & Kett *163,243*
Derek and Tina Rayment Antiques *170,187*
Rayment Wirework *247,253*
Reads Nursery *258*
Real Flame *155,156*
The Real Wrought Iron Company *199*
Realstone *114*
Reclamation Services *221*
Recline & Sprawl *44*
Red Mud *119,229,257*
Camilla Redfern *169*
Anthony Redmile *123,235*
Redwood Decking & Landscaping *255*
Redwood Stone *244*
Gordon Reece Gallery *181,185*
Anthony Reed *203,*
Reed Harris *112,114*
Peter Reed Group *72*
Paul Reef Parasols *252*
Reeves Dryad Craft Centre *195*
Refurb-a-Sash *137*
Reject China Shop *24*
Reject Pot Shop *24*
The Reject Tile Shop *110*
Relics of Witney *195*
Relyon *69*
Carlos Remes Lighting Company *119*
Renaissance Casting *244*
Renaissance Dying *198*
Renaissance Partnership *163*
Renubath *41*
Renwick & Clarke *25,50,66,72,87,119,120,*
122,226,229,230,232
Renzland Forge *251*
The Repro Shop *15,47,134*
Resina Designs *146*

Rest Assured 69
Restall Brown & Clennell 47
The Revival Company 150,197
Revival Upholstery 150
Rezai Persian Carpets 105
Rhode Design Furniture 12
Rhodec International 262
Jon Rhodes 144,151
David Richards and Sons 232
Timothy Richards 239
David Richardson Oriental Carpets 150
Richmond Adult and Community College 264
Adam Richwood 47
Mark Ripley Antiques and Forge 155
Ripples 31
Risky Business 188
Anna Roberts Designs 238
R & S Robertson 119
Robinson and Cornish 12,36
Robus Ceramics 114,249,257
Roca 33
Roche-Bobois 54,58
Rockingham 146
Charlie Roe 232
Rogier Antiques 119,178
Deborah Rolt 104
The Romantic Garden Nursery 258
Romany's Architectural Ironmongers 134
Romo 80
Ronson's Reclamation 221
Rooksmoor Mills 102
Roomservice Furnishing Group 63
Roots, Fruits and Flowers 238
Rose Hill Restorations of Chobham
    165,166,169
Rose of Jericho 193
Rose's Mill 83
Roset (UK) 54,67
The Thomas Ross Collection 228
VV Rouleaux 89
Alain Rouveure Galleries 106
Row & Sons 15
The Rowley Gallery 170,203
Royal Auping 68
Royal Botanic Gardens
    (Adult Education Section) 264
Royal College of Art 262
Royal Creamware 229
The Royal Doulton Company 27
The Royal School of Needlework 166
Ruffle & Hook 144
Suzanne Ruggles 56
Rusco Marketing 245,246,252
Russell & Chapple 82
Rustica 112,114
Rutherford - The Pool People 256
SBH-Fichet (UK) 210
SCP 36,54,62
SKK 40,126,127,128,128,129,217
SW82 Glass & Design 139
Sadolin (UK) 194

Safety Stairways 207
Sahco Hesslein (UK) 80,83,86
Dyala Salam 188
David Salmon 47
Don Sambrook 137
Alistair Sampson 175,185
Sanderson 77,80,87,93,95,193
Ian Sanderson 80,87
Sandhill (Bullion) 251
Sandiford & Mapes 98
B C Sanitan 33
Sanitary Appliances 19,34
Sans Frontières 102
Santric 35
Sarum Metalcraft 233
The Sash Window Workshop 137
Sashy & Sashy 137
Satana (UK) 40
Satelliet (UK) 62
Jill Saunders 150,169
Savoy Bedworks 69
Sayers & Bays 144
The Scagliola Company 164
Scanachrome 211
W Schneider & Co (UK) 36
Scholtes 21
Manfred Schotten 188
The Schuster Gallery 184
Scotts of Thrapston 249
Screwdriver 63,211
Sculptures-Jeux 127
Scumble Goosie 51
Seago 242,254
Sealy (UK) 70
The Secret Garden Company of Ware 249
M&D Seligmann 175
Semper Floreat 238
Servicemaster in the Capital 198
Seventh Heaven 68,72
Jean Sewell Antiques 185
David Seyfried 44
Shades 149
Shades (Screenprint) 139
Shaker 15,47,67,73,193
The David Sharp Studio 244,249
Angela Shaw 263
William Sheppee 59,122,123,128
Margaret Sheridan 144
George Sherlock 44,177
Shiners 134
Shiners Architectural Reclamation 222
Shires Bathrooms 33
Shiuli Johanna 74,85
Shiver Me Timbers 107
Showeristic 33
The Shutter Shop 138
Sibley & Son 137
Sibona 74
SieMatic 13
Siemens Domestic Appliances 21
Siesta Cork Tiles 109

Silent Gliss 146,149
Silentnight Beds 70
The Silk Gallery 85
Silks of Copenhagen 73
Silvan 83
Silvergate Papers 95
Silverlands Stone 255
Simon & Simon 122
Simoniz International 193
D & J Simons 203
Simply Bathrooms 31
Sinclair Melson 45,60
Sinclair Till Flooring Company 102,109
W & G Sissons 35
W Sitch & Co 165,182
Sitting Pretty 31
Keith Skeel 177,189
Sleepeezee 70
Sleeping Partners 70
Slingsby Commercial
    and Industrial Equipment 61
Slumberland 70
Smallbone Of Devizes 12,36
Smeg (UK) 20
George Smith 45
John Smith & Sons 208
Smiths Metal Centres 201
Peta Smyth Antique Textiles 180
Soho Silks 82,88
Solaglas 139
Solnhofen Natural Stone 16
Solopark 107,208,222
Somerset House of Iron 51,57,67
Sommer (UK) 109
Sommer Allibert (UK) 62
Sotheby's 174
Sotheby's Institute 261
Sottini 33
Frances Soubeyron 89
Souleiado 91
The Source 22,40,73
Southern Stone Restorations 164
Space 54
The Specialist Chimney People 161
Specialist Needlework 89
The Specialist Paint Removal Service 198
George Spencer Decorations 80
Simon Spero 185
Spink Leger Galleries 183
Spink & Son 185,189
St. Blaise 163,170
Staffordshire Architectural Salvage 222
Staines Catering Equipment 23
Stair & Company 177
Stairrods (UK) 103
Stairways Products 207
The Stamping Ground 195
Starlite (Chandeliers) 120
Steelcase Stratfor PLC 62
Steeles Carpets 103
The Stencil Library 195

The Stencil Store 195
Stovax 158
Stevenson Brothers 217
Stuart Stevenson 195
Stevensons of Norwich 202
Ghislaine Stewart Designs 124,135
Stiffkey Antiques 131
Stiffkey Bathrooms 36,41
Stiffkey Lamp Shop 182
Stockspring Antiques 186
Stockwell Carpets 103,217
Stoddard Templeton 104
Edward Stoddart 119
Carolyn Stoddart-Scott 186
Stone Age 114
Stonehealth 163
Stonell 114
Stonewest 164
Stothert Decorative Cushions 234
Stovax 156
Stoves 21
John Strand 14
Strawberry Steel 57,200
Strebel 160
F R Street 82
Strike One (Islington) 187
Strippers Paint Removers 199
DC Stuart 47
Stuart Garden Architecture 245,249,251,252
Stuart Interiors 47,67,123,133,206
Stuart Renaissance Textiles 91
The Studio 179
The Study 54,126,135
The Study Centre for the History
    of the Fine & Decorative Arts 261
Succession 45,58
Sudbury Picture Frames 228
Summerill & Bishop 22
Summers & Co 251
Summit Furniture 245
Sundown Quilts 75
Supersheds 250
NT Sussex Brassware 129
Sussex House 74,234
John Sutcliffe 97,122
Oliver Sutton 186
Sweerts de Landas 242
Sylmar Technology 37
Robin Symes 189
T&C Designs 249
TP Activity Toys 216
Tableware? 27
Take 60
Talisman 177,242
John Tanous 45,48,231
Tansu 59
Tantofex 34
Tapisserie 239
Target Furniture 62
Targetti 126
Tarkett 109

Tatra Glass (UK) *139*
Dr Brian J Taylor *89*
Richard Taylor Designs *57,119,120, 229,230,231*
The Teak Tiger Trading Co *245*
Technical Exponents *34*
Techniform Graphics *141*
Templederry Design *12,204*
Temptation Alley *82,89*
Tempus Stet *119,146,231,232*
Tendercare Nurseries *258*
The Tenterden Collection *27*
Terrace and Garden *250,252*
Terranova *110*
Tessier *187*
Tetbury Stone Company *208*
The Textile Conservation Studios *198*
Textile Management Services *75*
The Textile Restoration Studio *166,197*
Themes & Variations *161,179*
ThermoFloor (GB) *160*
Thomason Cudworth *244*
Bryony Thomasson *180*
Jim Thompson *85,88*
Thornhill Galleries *156,206*
Andy Thornton *62*
Andy Thornton Architectural Antiques *222*
Bernard Thorp & Co *80*
Through the Looking Glass *231*
Thru the Looking Glass *254*
Tidmarsh & Sons *149*
W Tierney *158*
The Tile Gallery *110*
The Tile Shop *110*
Timney Fowler *91,98*
Tindle *48,104,119,120,122,232,233,234*
Chris Tipping *109*
Alex Tiranti *197*
Titchmarsh and Goodwin *48*
Titian Studio *169*
Titley & Marr *80,85*
Tobias And The Angel *25,26,180*
Today Interiors *97*
The Tôle Candle Company *122*
Tomkinson Stained Glass Windows *140*
Tomkinsons *104*
Trevor Toms Cabinetmakers *12,204*
Tomtom *179*
Tones Specialist Decoration *98*
Top Knobs *136*
Chris Topp *200,251*
Kenneth Topp *87*
Tor Coatings Group *193*
Totem Design *18*
Touch Design *216,257*
Touch of Brass *129*
Touchstone Design *196*
Tower Materials *221*
Town & Country Conservatories *248*
Town & Country Fires (Pikering) *156,158*
Townsends *156*

Tracking and Hanging *151*
Clifford J Tracy *169*
Trade Eighty *85*
The Traditional Garden Supply Company *242*
Tradstocks *223*
Travis Perkins *209*
Margaret Tregoning *238*
Trelliscope *252*
Trellysian *252*
Trevi Showers *34*
Tribal Traders *60,123*
Tricity Bendix *21*
Trident Systems (UK) *156*
Bruno Triplet *98,102*
Triton *34*
Troika Architectural Mouldings *156,202*
Trowbridge Gallery *184,203,228*
Gabriela Trzebinski *40*
Tudor Wrought Ironwork *251*
Turnell & Gigon *80,87,88,90*
G & J Turner & Co *90*
Kenneth Turner *238*
Simon Turner *55*
Turnstyle Designs *41,135*
Turquaz *26,73*
Twentieth Century Design *179*
Two Wests & Elliott *250*
Twyfords *34*
Tyrone Textiles *83*
Keith Tyssen *239*
Edgar Udny *115*
United Cutlers of Sheffield *25*
Universal Providers *61,178,232*
Upholstery Express *150*
Vale Garden Houses *248*
Celestino Valenti Wireworks *253*
Valis *257*
Rafael Valls *183*
Valtti Specialist Coatings *194*
Jo van Gerbig & Co *169*
Katrien Van Liefferinge *127*
Van Posch *229*
van Schelle & Gurland *96*
Andrew Varah *55,204*
Vaughan *119*
Venetian Blind Manufacturing Co *149*
Ventrolla *137*
Verdigris *166,200*
Vermont Castings *158*
Vernon Tutbury *34*
Viaduct *13,54,60,61,67,126*
Warris Vianni *85*
The Victorian Brass Bedstead Company *68,215*
Victorian Wood Works *107,206*
Viking *21*
Villa Garnelo *48*
Villeroy & Boch (UK) *34*
Villeroy & Boch Factory Shop *24*
Villiers Brothers *57,127,146,200*
Vi-Spring *70*
Vitra *54*

INDEX

Vitruvius *16,37,112*
Vitsoe (UK) *61*
Vogue *38*
Vola *34*
Georgina Von Etzdorf *234*
V'soske Joyce (UK) *104*
Pierre Vuillemenot *151*
Sasha Waddell at Kingshill Designs *51*
Tim Wade *252*
Valerie Wade *84,104*
The Wadham Trading Company *216,253*
David Wainwright *60,136*
Sebastian Wakefield *196*
Walcot Reclamation *107,221*
Walley *23*
John Walsh & Sons *222*
Walton & Company *26*
Wandsworth Electrical *129*
Sasha Ward *140*
Warner Fabrics *80,95*
Water Front *41*
The Water Monopoly *36,41*
Waterford Wedgwood *24*
Waterhouse & Dodd *183*
E & A Wates *169*
Gordon Watson *179*
Watts of Westminster *91,95*
Waveney Apple Growers *102,233*
Wax Lyrical *122*
Webster Weave *73,91*
Welcome Fireplace Company *156*
Well Hung *147*
Wells Reclamation *221*
Wells & Winter *257*
Wemyss Houles *90*
Wemyss Weavecraft *80*
Wenderton Antiques *25*
Wentworth Ceramics *112*
Wentworth Cushions *234*
Wesley-Barrell *45*
West Dean College *264*
West London Bedding *70*
West London Tiles *110*
Mark J West (Cobb Antiques) *186*
West One Bathrooms *31*
The West Sussex Antique Timber Co *221*
Westminster Adult Education Service *262,265*
Wey Plastics *17*
Whaley *82, 87*
Whichford Pottery *257*
Whirlpool *21*
Whistler Brush Co. *195*
Whitchester Wood Design *259*
Alison White *60,149,234*
The White Company *73,74,217*
White Cottage Leisure Buildings *250*
White Dog Reproductions *49*
The White House *26,73*
Whitehall Worksurfaces *18*
S & J Whitehead *164*
CH Whitehouse *250*

Whiteway & Waldron *140,189*
Whittaker's Sculpture Craft Workshop *244*
Whittle Brothers *88*
Wicanders *109*
Wilchester County *121*
SW Wilcox *232*
Wild At Heart *238*
David J.Wilkins *181*
Wilkinson *121,165,169*
Mark Wilkinson *12,216*
Tony Williams Fine Mirrors *232*
M & J Wilson *233*
OF Wilson *177*
Wilsons Conservation Building Products *223*
GR Wiltshire *37*
Christopher Winder Master Carpenters *253,255*
Windmill Antiques *217*
DW Windsor *128,200*
Nicola Wingate-Saul Print Rooms *97*
Winther Browne *156,205*
Wiseman Originals *228*
Tim Wood *12,36*
Wood & Mott *48*
Wooden Tops and Tin Men *67,123*
Woodhams *238*
Woodstock *12,206*
Woodward Grosvenor *104*
Wool Classics *104*
Woolpit Interiors *120,121,232*
The Workroom *145*
World's End Tiles *110,115*
AJ Worthington *90*
Christopher Wray Lighting *120,121,129*
Robert Wyatt *122,124*
Wychwood Design *63*
Wye Valley Stoves and Fireplaces *159*
B & P Wynn & Co *16,31,41*
Xpelair *161*
Yakamoto Futons *68*
Rachel Yallop *211*
NT Yannedis *134*
Brian Yates *81,97*
Winston Yeatts of Warwickshire *51,60,232,233*
Yellow House *232*
Yeoman Stoves *159*
William Yeoward *24,45,51,120*
Yew Tree *258*
The Yorkshire Pine Company *133*
Young & D *25,57,67,122,124*
Robert Young Antiques *175*
Zanussi *21*
Zarka Marble *16,37,112*
Zehnder *38,160*
Zimmer & Rohde (UK) *81*
Zodiac International Company *41*
Zodiac Upholstery *150*
Zoffany *81,84,87,95,97,214*
Zora *74*
Zuber & Cie *95*